CW00554662

OSCAR HAMMERSTEIN II AND THE INVENTION OF THE MUSICAL

LAURIE WINER

Oscar Hammerstein II and the Invention of the Musical

Yale UNIVERSITY PRESS NEW HAVEN AND LONDON

Published with assistance from the foundation established in memory of James Wesley Cooper of the Class of 1865, Yale College.

Yale University Press books may be purchased in quantity for educational, business, or promotional use. For information, please e-mail sales.press@yale.edu (U.S. office) or sales@yaleup.co.uk (U.K. office).

Set in Scala type by Integrated Publishing Solutions.
Printed in the United States of America.

Library of Congress Control Number: 2022937033
ISBN 978-0-300-22379-8 (hardcover : alk. paper)

A catalogue record for this book is available from the British Library.

This paper meets the requirements of ANSI/NISO Z39.48-1992 (Permanence of Paper).

10 9 8 7 6 5 4 3 2 1

For Sam and Sylvia, who loved musicals
And for Tom, who does not, but who makes the world sing

CONTENTS

ACKNOWLEDGMENTS

Steve Wasserman, Sarah Miller, Adina Berk, and Ash Lago shepherded this manuscript through its long gestation. The meticulous Nicholas Taylor was an always-entertaining sounding board for how and when to employ twenty-first-century language in a book about the twentieth. Thanks to Ted Chapin for being the dapper and patient gentleman he is. Eternal thanks to Mark Horowitz for his deep knowledge and sound counsel. Thanks, too, to the dedicated staff at the Library of Congress and the Lincoln Center Library for the Performing Arts.

My gratitude to the world's most fascinating interview subjects: Stephen Sondheim, Nicholas Hytner, Bartlett Sher, and André Bishop.

Thanks also to: Sandy Dijkstra and Elise Capron, for your unflagging enthusiasm and support. Karen Shatzkin, who can only be described as a force for good. Relatives and friends who put me up and put up with me while I dug into archives: Richard Kilberg and Barbara Margolis, Randi and Steve Adelberg, Susan Gordon and Chuck Freed, Sara and Jon Rund, Susan Chumsky, Bobbie Bristol, Cameron Diaz, Margo Baender (we'll always have Wisconsin). Tom and Bonnie Winer and Darcy and James Gregory Gordon, for helpful sibling rivalry. Children (and their peerless mates) who welcomed my idiosyncrasies: Jesse Lutz and Guillermo Lozana, Yarrow Lutz and Ken Swift, Cody Lutz and April Prosser. Mayela Lozana, for being a delightful theater pal. Soul companions: Dorothy and Leo Braudy. Friends over the years who delved into musicals with me: Amy Fribush, Cindy Gold, Adam Heller, Liz Larsen, Bill Finn, Pam Galvin, Kimberly Gordon, Steve Lichtman, Mark Schwartz (aka Max), and Maria Schlatter and her writing partner Glen Roven, gone too soon. Poker buddies and good listeners: Margot Frankel, Joel Goldberg, Mark Hattenbach, Victor Talmadge, Russell McClain, Norman Chad, Paul Mandelbaum, Elena Song, Colin Campbell, and Pavel Wonsowicz. Sustaining friends: Albert Litewka and Erika Rothenberg, Nancy and John Romano, Jon Wiener and Judy Fiskin, Janet Fitch and Andrew Nicholls, Jenny Williams and Joan Henehan, Gary Murphy and Jason La Padura, Susan Kaiser Greenland and Seth Greenland. Accomplices: Judith Freeman, Michelle Huneven, Rebecca Kennerly, Gail Lerner, Louise Steinman. Hair and makeup (and advice): Susan Brodsky Thalken.

I would also like to thank Graham Coleman, Andrew Boose, and Rick Pappas, and acknowledge the kind permission courtesy of Harrigan Logan and the Joshua Logan Estate, Anne Fadiman and the Estate of Clifton Fadiman, the Estates of Richard Rodgers and Mary Rodgers Guettel, as well as the Estate of John O'Hara. Also with gratitude to Waverly Scott Kaffaga, Executor for the Estate of Elaine A. Steinbeck.

Max Wilk interviews used by permission of David Wilk for the Estate of Max Wilk. Permission for excerpt of letter by Sister Gregory granted by Sinsinawa Dominican Archives, Sinsinawa, Wisconsin. Excerpt from letters of Stephen Sondheim used by permission of Stephen Sondheim. All rights reserved.

All materials herein created by Oscar Hammerstein II are used in this work by permission of the Trust and under the Will of Oscar Hammerstein II and Hammerstein Properties LLC.

I could not have written this book without the insight machine that is Tom Lutz. He is a superb editor, a steady presence, and the best company.

OSCAR HAMMERSTEIN II AND THE INVENTION OF THE MUSICAL

Introduction

AN UNFASHIONABLE TAKE ON AN UNFASHIONABLE MAN

LIKE SO MANY AMERICAN CHILDREN of the 1960s and '70s, I filled the unnerving void after lights-out and before sleep by listening to records on the stereo by my bed. My parents had collected about thirty Broadway cast albums, and I went through them one by one in what we now recognize as a ritual for those who would become my theater-loving tribe. In the stillness of night, these songs unveiled the secrets of the adult universe, the reasons things were the way they were and turned out the way they turned out. I barely moved as I listened. With closed eyes I left the constraints of childhood and leapt into the lives emanating from the vinyl—vivid lives filled with obstacles and heartbreak, but also with wit and optimism, unexpected generosity, sudden adventure, friendship, and love.

If a song made me weep or contained a clever joke or some wisdom that seemed worth remembering, I sat up and ever so gently opened the dresser drawer so as not to disturb the spinning turntable on top, retrieved my notebook and pen, and, by the glow of a nightlight, transcribed the lyrics. This was a painstaking process. Bent over my work, I leaned in every ten seconds or so to pick up the needle and gently move it back, ensuring I got each word exactly right. I didn't know why I was compelled to perform this task, but watching the ink seep into the paper seemed to confirm that the lyrics were imprinting on my consciousness. I sensed that these songs conveyed, with an economy unavailable to the authors I read and the movies

I watched, the profound and thrilling emotions I would soon be feeling—indeed, was already feeling, alone in the dark.

And so, late at night, I diligently transcribed something I didn't know was called the American Songbook and, it turns out, began my thinking on this project, this appreciation of Oscar Hammerstein II.

Musicals are elemental, which is why children adore them. As they careen between their two natural states—being overwhelmed by the world and achieving some small mastery over it—children feel grounded and clever when singing a witty couplet, and sophisticated when its meaning is just out of reach. Frank Loesser's "Guys and Dolls," for instance, is a tonic for the child who understands maybe half the words:

When you meet a mug lately out of the jug
And he's still lifting platinum folderol
Call it hell, call it heaven
It's a probably twelve to seven
That the guy's only doing it for some doll.

As a child, I intuited—and I now know—that the American musical, in its collection of such moments of quotidian wisdom, proffers a coherent philosophy about how to live, how to deal with reality. The world in which I came of age, middle-class America in the second half of the American century, held the musical in a place of honor among the popular arts. My parents and their friends, almost all born, raised, and working in Baltimore and its suburbs, were salespeople, homemakers, shop owners, lawyers, dentists, and accountants; they were the dedicated audience for these shows and found their values both reflected in and shaped by them.

And as we endured the civil strife and cataclysmic assassinations of the 1960s, these shows helped ground us; they offered an ethic of caring closely related to what used to be called liberalism—a belief in the improvability of the human condition. They were written for a burgeoning middle class, audiences who, if they did not attend the shows on Broadway, saw them performed by touring companies, and they bought original cast albums by the millions. Some of these shows sailed past cultural and political boundaries and were embraced by people around the globe. Taken together, they defined a progressive American ethos, one that says if we are not all interconnected in some fundamental way, we are lost.

■ ■ ■

My first idea for this book was to curate ten great American musicals and then examine the personalities and beliefs of the artists (mostly white men) who wrote them: a kind of cultural biography of the twentieth century through musical theater. My working title was *Mame and the Meaning of Life,* after Jerry Herman's (and Patrick Dennis's) effervescent heroine, a Manhattanite who raises her orphaned nephew to seek joy and fight the powerful need for conformity—a need that the musical both represented and rebelled against. It seemed right to single out *Mame,* which, like *The Sound of Music,* was a gateway drug for the genre. The unconditional love that Mame bestows on the nine-year-old Patrick shook the foundations of many an American childhood, I'm sure. No one's mother was that good while simultaneously being chic and funny. Mame loves Patrick and pushes him out of the nest with grace, moving on to her next adventure when he enters school—no blame, no guilt. Her recipe for living life to the fullest (you can celebrate Christmas any day of the year, anytime you feel like it) is a primer in being responsible for your own happiness. As a bonus the show also fosters an appreciation for modern art, female friendship, and vaudeville timing.

But as I worked on the outline, I kept fiddling with my list of musicals. Picking ten posed all sorts of problems. For one, I had nothing at all by Cole Porter or Irving Berlin, whose storytelling in their shows seemed left over from a laxer era, but still. Was there a way to work in Jule Styne and Bob Merrill's *Funny Girl,* or were its concerns too limited? Should I include William Finn and James Lapine's *Falsettos,* a rollercoaster of wit and trauma that beguiled a new generation processing narrative faster than the one before? Then I saw two great twenty-first-century musicals—*Fun Home* and *Hamilton*—and realized my list would be reductive and arbitrary or else would need to include fifty works. I lost heart.

As I pored over the list for the eighty-ninth time, seeing if there was a way to work in *South Pacific* after *Show Boat* and *Carousel,* the solution dawned on me. The musicals at the core of the list, the ones that remained however many times I revised it, were all written by one man. This man created the first fully realized American musical play in 1927, with composer Jerome Kern. An epic tapestry of racism and ill-fated romance and a meta-analysis of theater itself, *Show Boat* laid the groundwork in tone and content for everything significant that followed.

Then, a decade and a half later, that same man fundamentally transformed the musical again when he teamed up with Richard Rodgers on *Oklahoma!,* a celebration of country with none of the crude jingoism common in wartime musicals; its definition of America was distilled in generous possibility. *Oklahoma!* prefigured *Hamilton* as surely as Woody Guthrie prefigured Bob Dylan. And of course Hammerstein mentored Stephen Sondheim, an artist who himself re-created the musical for his own era and in turn was an inspiration to *Hamilton*'s author Lin-Manuel Miranda. As in a family in which a child is more spiritually connected to the grandfather than the father, it was Miranda who replicated Hammerstein's method—utilizing theater's communal nature to invite a collective reimagining of America in a bountiful and hopeful way.

Like *Hamilton, Oklahoma!*—with its young and largely unknown cast—seemed to come out of nowhere. Word spread so fast that snagging a ticket felt like winning the lottery. Everyone wanted to have the ecstatic experience they were sure the show provided. That said, both Hammerstein and Miranda obscured or ignored certain inconvenient facts in order to achieve the overwhelming emotions their shows wrung from audiences. Complexity is a hindrance in a peak emotional experience, during which all counter facts are rendered irrelevant. In *Hamilton,* Miranda eschews his hero's real-life elitism and exaggerates his abolitionist impulses, and he makes no mention of Alexander Hamilton's belief that a president should be a kind of monarch. Also like *Oklahoma!, Hamilton* is silent on the fate of Native Americans, though Miranda would not appear wrapped in a Navajo blanket and wearing an "Indian headdress" for the fourth anniversary of his show, as Rodgers and Hammerstein did in in 1947. Times had at least changed that much.

Although I had listened to the musicals of Oscar Hammerstein II countless times over the decades, I found they continued to reveal layers of complexity, which surprised and soothed me as I aged. Some songs I had ignored as a young person—for instance, "Something Wonderful," a woman's paean to lifelong devotion, I rejected as housewifery nonsense. But almost all the songs came alive as I studied Hammerstein's biography. "Some Enchanted Evening," once likewise overlooked as a vaguely operatic cliché, now conjures for me a long-ago scene on a transcontinental ocean liner, the sea breeze blowing, and a young man's overwhelming sense of destiny as he exchanges glances with a woman on the arm of her husband. Songs that demonstrate the gift of being thrilled by ordinary things, like "When the Children Are Asleep" or "Edelweiss," became unbearably moving as I matured. I came to hear many of the songs I loved as a child as if from another plane—like I had polished a jewel and found the reflection of a much younger self who was somehow exactly the same.

The more time I spent on Hammerstein—the more I read about his life, imagined his childhood, his youth, his early success, his decade-long struggle with irrelevance, and his eventual triumph in the 1940s when he returned to Broadway as an artist reborn with a new writing partner—the more I knew I didn't want to write about the ten greatest musicals, but about the musicals created by Hammerstein. I wanted to focus on the most important progenitor of the form.

I proceeded to read everything that had been published on him. I then went to the Library of Congress, where I introduced myself to music specialist and author Mark Horowitz (if you look, you will find him sincerely thanked in virtually every book about the American musical written in the past two decades). With his help, I combed through thirty-plus boxes of Hammerstein's papers, some so big it took two people to safely transfer them from a cart to the table. There I took notes and pictures and left tiny piles of brown particles in my wake. I went through folders that held notes, manuscripts, worksheets with drafts of lyrics, and letters that Hammerstein wrote and received between the 1920s and August 1960. Like his protégé Sondheim would be, Hammerstein was diligent in answering letters and produced a prodigious correspondence file. I then repeated this process in other libraries and archives. I immersed myself, trying to draw as much as possible from original letters and papers rather than the stack of scholarly and popular books that tended to recycle the same stories.

Collecting biographical details, I worked against idealizing the man until I acquired a real sense of his limitations, aesthetic as well as personal. I began to see where his ego, complacency, or privilege got the better of him, and where he condescended toward those who crossed him, or exhibited cruelty to his own brood. For instance, he could be patronizing to his wife or casually mean to his children, and he learned to be cold-blooded in business. Like all of us, he had his blind spots.

At times, his insistence on optimism and hope—cloying to some but spiritually fortifying to many—carried a personal cost, especially in his continued inability to read the tea leaves when he went to work in Hollywood in the 1930s. As for his tussle with the House Un-American Activities Committee in 1953, he emerged with his passport intact but a fissure in his reputation for courage and integrity.

But he never stopped pushing himself to be better, as a human and as a craftsman. Near the end, his idea of the musical, though still immensely popular, was no longer the glass of fashion and the mold of form. A critical backlash that started building in the early 1950s acquired velocity when his last show, *The Sound of Music,* debuted the year before his death.

I've heard it said that one needs to fall *out* of love with one's subject in order to write a biography. That isn't what happened, exactly, but I got to know Hammerstein well enough to be at times embarrassed for him, to recognize the mortal who made the immortal work, and to see a man of his time, if not entirely for ours.

Hammerstein's genius is inseparable from his embrace of simplicity and unadorned essentiality. Through decades of success and years of hard failure, he strove to write without pretension or cliché, though many of his phrases grew so famous they became cliché. His lyrics, naked and direct, might appear artless until the moment they overcome the listener with emotion. In one of his most well-known songs, for example, two young lovers imagine riding to and from a party. On their pretend journey, they travel in a horse-drawn carriage tricked out with the latest luxuries. Rodgers's melody, which repeats one note five times, followed by a progression that reaches higher in three successive jumps, mimics the rhythm of the horse's hoofs. In the carriage, the couple feels and hears nature all around them—amphibians, animals, birds, the breeze—everything is alive and present, even the surrey's "two bright side lights winkin' and blinkin'." For this couple the river will "ripple out a whispered song," one that mirrors what vibrates inside of them, and "whispers it over and over":

> Don't you wisht y'd go on ferever?
> Don't you wisht y'd go on ferever?
> Don't you wisht y'd go on ferever and ud never stop?

These lines ingeniously represent the experience of the sublime. Hammerstein switches the colloquial spelling of "you'd" from "y'd" to "ud" at the end of the last line, employing the informality of what he would consider Oklahoman dialect to represent the intimacy of the two characters singing. Was the spelling change an oversight or did he mean to further condense an already condensed word, to move from conversation to monologue, the "ud" (still pronounced as "you'd") signaling a person in communion with the eternal life force? This may seem like an overreading, but it's exactly such infinitesimal touches that add to the profundity of these simple lines. Was this change meant only as a hint to the singer about what is happening in the song? What we are left with, finally, is the precision of an artisan concerned with even the smallest orthographic decisions.

"The Surrey with the Fringe on Top" from *Oklahoma!* was one of the first songs Hammerstein wrote with Rodgers. Sixteen years later they completed their last, "Edelweiss," a deceptively spare composition filled with the melancholy of leave-taking. The song has the bittersweet clarity of a Henri Matisse cutout from the artist's final year. Hammerstein knew he was dying when he wrote the lyric for the Austrian captain in *The Sound of Music*. For both the character and the writer, "Edelweiss" is a benediction for those they leave behind. Hammerstein's final lyrical thought was "bless my homeland forever."

Of course, one woman's profundity is another's useless sentimentality, and this dialectic informs much of the aesthetic debate about the musical—and popular song—since before the dawn of cultural studies. Hammerstein, especially, has come under fire for dwelling too much on the sunny side of the street. In his 2006 book *Jerome Kern,* musicologist Stephen Banfield sums up an objection that became widely shared by scholars: "One cannot imagine Hammerstein as the librettist for *Tosca* because his overwhelming sympathy for human beings seems to have prevented him from wanting to take their actions to logical and heartless conclusions." In other words, Hammerstein was too softhearted, too idealistic, to be a true artist.

As Sondheim told me, Hammerstein "loved the world and loved people, but he was not a naïf. So many anti-Hammerstein people say he was a hayseed; he was not." Nor was he a hayseed dramatist. The suggestion that Hammerstein protected his characters from what was inevitable would come as a surprise to *Show Boat*'s Julie LaVerne, who, after a humiliating exile from her community, becomes an alcoholic with no money or friends. Banfield also claims that Hammerstein sensed this dramaturgical insufficiency and "tackled *Carmen Jones* . . . by way of redress." And by this I think he means that *Carmen Jones*, like *Tosca*, ends with the heroine's death and therefore is a classic tragedy, in which actions have been taken to their logical and heartless conclusions, something Hammerstein otherwise seemed uninterested in doing.

While I don't want to get sidetracked by discussions of genre, it matters very much where a writer chooses to end a tale. Because Hammerstein was interested in redemption, restoration, and renewal—in how one goes on *after* a tragedy—none of his works outside of *Carmen Jones* concludes with an emphasis on death (even as the King expires during *The King and I* finale, Hammerstein shifts the audience's focus to Siam's better future). On why this makes him a lesser artist Banfield does not elaborate, but he is correct in saying that Hammerstein possesses an overwhelming sympathy for human beings, as do most great narrative artists. Like Giacomo Puccini, who was dedicated to verismo in storytelling—an operatic version of literary naturalism—Hammerstein enlarged the musical's capacity so that in the future it could take on any subject under the sun.

Born fifty-three years before Hammerstein, William James said that his generation's great discovery was that individuals could alter their lives by altering their attitudes. In the opening to *The King and I*, Anna imparts this Jamesian wisdom to her ten-year-old son when they arrive in the strange kingdom of Siam:

> Make believe you're brave
> And the trick will take you far.
> You may be as brave
> As you make believe you are.

As I went deeper into my research, I found many similarities between William James's search for meaning and Hammerstein's, though one wrote thick books in complex sentences and the other usually concise songs in mostly short syllables. They both represent what seems to me a uniquely American way of seeking—one tied to the mystical but at the same time the practical, and one that leaves lots of room for individual interpretation. For instance James, in *The Varieties of Religious Experience*, wrote that "the visible world is part of a more spiritual universe from which it draws its chief significance," "that union or harmonious relation with that higher universe is our true end," and that "prayer or inner communion with the spirit thereof—be that spirit 'God' or 'law'—is a process wherein work is really done, and spiritual energy flows in and produces effects, psychological or material, within the phenomenal world." For his part, here's how Hammerstein put it to an interviewer: "I don't know why I was born, beyond the fact that I know why everybody was born. Everybody was born to advance the life in this universe, the life that we all live." What a biographer wrote of William James applies just as well to Hammerstein: "He was too sensitive to ignore evil, too moral to tolerate it, and too ardent to accept it as inevitable."

In his final show Hammerstein's lyrics venture stealthily into the philosophical realm, where they engage James's theory of pragmatism:

> A bell is no bell till you ring it.
> A song is no song till you sing it.

James's theory says that the nature of knowledge, meaning, and belief are best understood in terms of their practical uses: "The truth of an idea is not a stagnant property inherent in it. Truth *happens* to an idea. It *becomes* true, is *made* true by events. Its verity *is* in fact an event, a process, the process namely of verifying itself, its verification. Its validity is the process of its *validation*." Hammerstein wrote:

> And love in your heart
> Wasn't put there to stay—
> Love isn't love
> Till you give it away.

And, just as James had shown little interest in politics before America's military adventures in the Caribbean and the Philippines, Hammerstein was largely apolitical prior to the rise of Adolf Hitler. In the 1890s James got involved in the Anti-Imperialist League, and in 1936 Hammerstein became an early and active member of the Hollywood Anti-Nazi League. When Hammerstein grew rich in the 1940s and '50s, his progressivism and sense of responsibility blossomed. The list of causes he funded and supported is extensive. The development of the hydrogen bomb turned him into an adherent for one-world government, which he saw as the only way to preserve humanity in the nuclear age. Later he focused on more achievable goals, and in April 1960, a few months before he died, he reached out, as a board member for the National Committee Against Discrimination in Housing, to the thirty-one-year-old Martin Luther King Jr. to help in this cause.

But his story wasn't all pragmatism, hopefulness, and action. During the 1930s, a decade of professional irrelevance for him when he should have been at the height of his powers, Hammerstein worked every day to reject bitterness, self-pity, and blame. Despite countless slights to his pride, he kept his sense of wonder alive. When he finally starting writing with Rodgers in 1942, his debut lyric was a paean to gratitude—"Oh, what a beautiful mornin'!"—which leapt from his pen into the bank of unforgettable phrases.

That song introduces us to Curly, a cowboy hero who is utterly engaged with the world around him. To Curly, all the sounds of the earth are like music. He can hear this music because he sees himself as part of the world, not master of it. As he rides along the prairie, he is ignored by cows and laughed at by a tree, "an ol' weepin' willer," the irony of which pleases him. Hammerstein was aware of the privilege of being Curly, a man to whom the river delivers messages about the ecstasies of existence. Sixteen years earlier, he wrote an African American character, Joe in *Show Boat,* who implores the river to share its knowledge with him. Joe would like to converse with the river, which "must know sumpin' / but don't say nothin'." Receiving no message at all, Joe, like the river, must keep rolling along.

What scholars call "the great man theory of history" has fallen out of favor, which is largely for the good. A new generation interprets history and biography with a new set of eyes; we now see more clearly how one "great man," enjoying wealth and leisure made possible on the backs of others, takes credit for the innovations of many who remain in shadow. Cultures roil forward as artists of all kinds respond not just to the world but to each other, borrowing from what came before, benefiting from forces much larger than themselves. And because we understand that art depends on evolution, on restatement, on remixing all the bits and pieces of the past, we no longer credit anyone with being the inventor of anything.

And yet, any critique of the great man theory of history cannot in good faith ignore the existence of remarkable people. There are innovators in every field whose impact is so significant that it must be recognized, individuals whose work is so influential it becomes iconic. No one begrudges Thomas Edison the title of inventor of the light bulb, except possibly the relatives of Humphrey Davy, who seventy years earlier connected two wires to a battery and produced a glow. Forty years after that, Heinrich Göbel encased a carbonized bamboo filament in a pear-shaped glass, creating an incandescent lamp. But it was Edison who made a bulb that remained lit and would transform lives. *Show Boat* and *Oklahoma!* should be seen, I argue, in a similar light.

When Hammerstein wrote propaganda like *The Myth That Threatens the World,* a disarmament playlet created for the World Federalists in the late 1940s, he was no more convincing than any adequate proselytizer. Some of the Broadway shows he wrote in every decade of his professional life are disturbingly flat. But in the end, the ineffaceable stamp he left on the musical play is his, not his zeitgeist's. To this day the form bears the imprint not only of his methods for integrating song into story but also of his worldview, his sense of humor, his ethical and generous nature. No one person has a better claim to the musical's "invention," a word I know will annoy historians and for which I ask the readers' forbearance. Scholars will quarrel with this categorization and rightly list other artists whose ideas gave shape to the musical play. But those same scholars also consistently divide the development of the musical into one of two categories—everything that came before and after *Show Boat,* or everything that came before and after *Oklahoma!* That is no coincidence.

In the hands of great theater artists, Hammerstein's work still reaches a spiritual plane, carrying audiences to blissful absolution before sending them back out into the night feeling reconnected to their own imperfect world. His work appeals to the best in human nature with an astonishing force that can still be accessed today.

While he shied from making pronouncements about his work, Hammerstein did say that, when the curtain goes down, the "God in man must be present." This is a rare mention of a deity for Hammerstein, as he and most of his cohort were deeply secular, art being their one true religion. (Richard Rodgers, for instance, wrote that he "insist[ed] on acting and thinking like an American primarily, and a Jew if I want to.") Hammerstein argued that, in art, "the goodness of the human spirit must be fighting for its life whether or not it wins the round that is depicted in one play. People must leave the theater, the church or the lecture hall with a deeper faith and a higher interest in mankind than they brought in with them. This must be accomplished if the institutions are to survive." A manifesto from a man not comfortable with making them, this is one of the few explicit links Hammerstein draws between his work and the character of the nation.

Hammerstein was a classic fortunate son. Born to a well-off, culturally connected family, he was petted and loved almost from the cradle to the grave, though he weathered a challenging decade, as I said, and a few dark nights of the soul. He tried hard to live a private life he could be proud of, or at least not be ashamed of, and his public life was rigorous, particularly once he awoke politically during the 1940s. He devoted a fair amount of time to petitioning for civil rights and humanitarian causes through organizational work (not to mention the more subtle form of proselytizing he practiced in his art—if you can call genuinely moving masses of people proselytizing). From boyhood, he was conscious of the outsider's travails; he somehow grasped the arbitrary gift of being born an insider.

Of course he had faults. Sometimes he did not treat those closest to him with the respect they craved. When he won a "Father of the Year" award in 1958, Hammerstein remarked that it would come as a "big surprise" to his children. But his letters, especially to first wife, Myra Finn, show him to be a more involved parent than has been previously understood. Others found Rodgers and Hammerstein to be needlessly greedy—Agnes de Mille and Josh Logan had legitimate complaints about compensation which they both spoke about until the end of their lives. On the other hand, Hammerstein lent and gave money generously. He supported, mostly without complaint, his brother Reggie, Myra Finn, and assorted relatives on and off for most of his adult years.

His approval was coveted. Colleagues desired to be closer to a spirit so invariably dependable, wise, and, starting in the 1940s, rich. Once he teamed up with Rodgers, everyone wanted to work with the pair, and no one wanted to *stop* working with them. Mary Martin, the original Nellie Forbush in *South Pacific,* went on to play the role for years in London, longer than she would have liked; all the while, she and her husband, Richard Halliday, aggressively cajoled Hammerstein to find and write her a new role. A few years later when Martin and Halliday (along with producer Leland Hayward) acquired the rights to a film based on the life of Maria von Trapp, they took the project to Rodgers and Hammerstein and once again struck gold together. After Hammerstein's death and as she was nearing her own, Martin had a series of dreams in which Hammerstein approached her excitedly, saying,

Old friends Mary Martin and Oscar Hammerstein II.
Courtesy of Photofest

"Mary, you've got to see the theater up here. You've never seen a theater this gorgeous." Spending eternity with Oscar was probably the dream of many in the theater.

To tell his story it is necessary to tell stories of those around him, particularly the artists closest to him: Richard Rodgers and Stephen Sondheim. (After Hammerstein died, the two acceded to his suggestion that they collaborate, although they could offer each other none of the magnanimity they encountered in Hammerstein.) Biographers have not dwelled on the material differences in the way Rodgers and Hammerstein treated their wives and others in their business and personal orbits. Most draw a moral equivalency between Rodgers's compulsive womanizing ("He used women . . . like a piece of toilet paper," Agnes de Mille told author Max Wilk) and Hammerstein's intermittent parenting, the latter a deficit the two men shared.

In fact, they lived different sorts of lives; to help illustrate this point I pay more attention than is customary to their wives, the two Dorothys, as well as to Hammerstein's first wife. Another tale I tell more fully here is Rodgers and Hammerstein's questionable treatment of Josh Logan, a creative partner closer to each of them than they were to each other. Around the time of *South Pacific* the duo, caught up in the excitement of being on a seemingly unstoppable roll, shut Logan out of a financial windfall he had earned. This incident, more than any other, contributed to their reputation for greed. It demonstrates that at the moment they became the kings of Broadway, their impulse was to build a moat and seal off the castle.

At the Library of Congress I read the last letters he wrote to his children, his friends, and his lawyer, and those he received from the few friends close enough to know the end was near. It did not surprise me to learn that he approached death with the same grace with which he had lived.

On August 3, 1960, Oscar and Dorothy packed and left their Manhattan townhouse at 10 East Sixty-Third Street for the last time. Before the month was out he would die at his farm in Pennsylvania, the country retreat the couple bought in 1940, where, poised at his standing desk, he'd written "Oh, what a beautiful mornin'!" and so many other indelible lyrics. He implored Dorothy not to fall apart when he died, saying that it would be "like having everything in the world and then crying for more." He died just after midnight on August 23 and was cremated the next day at Ferncliff Cemetery in Westchester County, New York.

Manhattan offered a unique tribute to this native son, the second Oscar Hammerstein to transform the cultural life of both the city and the country. On the day Oscar II was born, July 12, 1895, his grandfather Oscar I was building the first theater in "Thieves Lair"—so nicknamed because the city's electric lights stopped at Forty-Second Street. This unlit neighborhood, running from the Forty-Second Street intersection of Broadway and Seventh Avenue up to Forty-Seventh Street, was officially named Longacre Square, though that changed in 1904 when the *New York Times* opened its headquarters on Forty-Third Street and rechristened the area Times Square. This soon became known as the Great White Way and has remained the heart of American commercial theater to the present day.

On September 1, 1960, to honor all the light Oscar II had contributed, one of the most trafficked areas in the world turned entirely dark for the first time since World War II. At 8:57 p.m. a red flare pierced the air over Duffy Square, near where the TKTS booth now stands. Then, at 9:00 p.m. sharp, out went the glow from miles of streetlamps, billboards, hotels, restaurants, movie and theater marquees, engulfing theatergoers and bystanders together in a dark quiet. As reported in the *New York Times,* "Penny arcades and hot dog stands and juke boxes became silent. Sidewalk preachers paused. Traffic was halted and automobiles, buses, and taxis stopped and turned off their headlights. Light was reduced to traffic signals and some luminous patches in tall buildings. At 9 o'clock, Broadway stood still. Many in the crowd of 5,000 at Duffy Square bowed their heads." Then two musicians blew taps. The country had lost a man who, despite his privileged upbringing, spoke to all.

That night Mary Martin's Maria won the hearts of seven children onstage at the Lunt-Fontanne Theater on West Forty-Sixth Street. Her costar Theodore Bikel remembered that every time she turned her back to the audience, her face emptied of its put-on joy and became a mask of pain and grief. Richard Rodgers sent a note to *The Sound of Music* cast asking that there be no mention of Hammerstein's death during the performance or curtain call, a tribute to the lyricist's humility and insistence that the show always go on.

I left the library feeling the loss of his light, a diminishment of the cumulative decency on earth. Then, dining at a small Indian restaurant in DC, I experienced an uncontrollable crying jag, causing many of the female patrons to glare severely at my husband, who was nothing but supportive. It was just that Oscar Hammerstein II had died again that day.

If it isn't clear already, I'll just say it: theater is my religion. In the presence of others, the social animal finds the fortitude to contemplate its own impermanence. Friedrich Nietzsche would disagree; for him, "No one brings along the finest senses of his art in the theater, least of all the artist who works for the theater—solitude is lacking; whatever is perfect suffers no witnesses." But for many since the sixth century BCE, the meaning of life may be accessed during a performance and recede as soon as it is over. Marcel Proust's Charles Swann discovers this at a concert, where he hears, in a sonata, a series of notes, a "little phrase," which lingers in the air "like an iridescent bubble that floats for a while unbroken." Swann "dared not move and would have liked to compel all the other people in the room to remain still also, as if the slightest movement might imperil the magic presence, supernatural, delicious, frail, that was so soon to vanish."

Every great play exploits this parallel between the temporal nature of theater, meaning, and life itself, ushering us to a shared psychic space where we can fathom what we would normally avoid. This is of course what Shakespeare is up to in the culmination of his final play, *The Tempest,* when Prospero invites us to mourn ourselves and all that we love:

> Our revels now are ended.
> These our actors, as I foretold you, were all spirits and
> Are melted into air, into thin air:
> And, like the baseless fabric of this vision,
> The cloud-capp'd towers, the gorgeous palaces,
> The solemn temples, the great globe itself,
> Yea, all which it inherit, shall dissolve
> And, like this insubstantial pageant faded,
> Leave not a rack behind.
> We are such stuff
> As dreams are made on, and our little life
> Is rounded with a sleep.

Because going to the theater can be an exercise in existential wonder and sorrow, when it fails, it often does so spectacularly. And of all theatrical experiences, none is as ambitious or abundant as the musical: leash the inevitable progress of story to that of music, add the quicksilver eroticism of the human body and voice, and you cut a path to the sublime.

Richard Wagner believed he had achieved *Gesamtkunstwerk*—the total work of art—in his masterwork *Der Ring des Nibelungen* (*The Ring* cycle). After he died it was generally agreed that the composer and librettist who chiseled his stories from the stone of Norse and Teutonic myth had in fact reached the holy grail of musical storytelling—that he was in fact the greatest of all time. However, despite the immensity of his influence and his own estimation of his gifts, Wagner's storytelling is no match for the power of his melody, unless you happen to love German nationalism, overstatement, and magical thinking (and what could go wrong there?). His stories rely on forces beyond human control, and his events are determined by foreordained phenomena. If Wagner's music is able to take us to the far reaches of the human mind and spirit, we get there *despite* and not because of the story—tales in which a helmet makes you invisible, a potion wipes clear your memory, and a taste of blood enables you to understand the language of birds. "Opera is like an oyster; it must be swallowed whole, or not at all," wrote Spike Hughes and Barbara McFadyean in their 1948 book *Nights at the Opera*. "It is probably the most ludicrous way of filling a theater that ever existed."

But what Wagner achieved—the rendering of perception in the form of what he called endless or infinite melody—became the sine qua non of storytelling, a place where lyrics and music, thought and feeling, slide imperceptibly into each other. In the words of the critic Alex Ross, Wagner's music suggests a "continuous, formless flow of consciousness." That combination of ecstasy and tranquility, of being and oblivion, is what the musical reaches for and occasionally achieves.

Oscar Hammerstein I was so obsessed with opera he referred to it as "a disease." A German-born impresario, he built nine theaters in New York and two more in London and Philadelphia. His need to produce opera and theater was as outsized as Wagner's, though the Sorcerer of Bayreuth was not one of his favorites.

Famous for his stubbornness, his audacity, and his determination to prevail at any cost, Oscar I seemed fundamentally incapable of managing money. His fanaticism for opera disrupted the lives of all his family members, causing most of them, including his famous grandson, to dislike the form's overstatement and caprice. "Have you got a load of *The Magic Flute?*," Oscar II wrote in a draft of an essay that I found at the Library of Congress. "It's got a beautiful, beautiful score and a completely incomprehensible book. You can't understand it." In a rare snarky mood, he told an Australian newspaper in 1930, "Grand opera is always capitalized by the music and neglects the dramatic side entirely. I have seen two small men in *Pagliacci* in a fight to the death over a two-ton prima donna who, when she walked on the stage, made the boards creak. No one believed it at all, and if they are merely going to appear for songs the artists may as well come in evening dress and be done with it." It became his mission in life to hold the storytelling in "musical plays," as he called them, to the same standard as the songs and the acting. "Oscar was trying to do something based on reality instead of some kind of fairy tale," said Stephen Sondheim. If Hammerstein didn't *invent* the musical as we know it today, he certainly perfected the form and built a model that all who came after would follow, try to re-create, or even demolish.

Although his work continues to find large audiences all over the world, Hammerstein does not make the lists of twentieth-century American artists who changed the genres in which they worked, like, say, Ernest Hemingway, Martha Graham, Jackson Pollock, Andy Warhol, or Philip Glass. The critical turn against him at the end of his career coincided with the birth of the cool, an aesthetic opposed to sincerity and sentiment—in other words, to everything embodied by his last musical, *The Sound of Music*. At the time of his death, the showbiz bible *Variety* suggested that his personality and manner might overshadow the importance of his work: "To those who knew him, Hammerstein's professional successes were largely incidental to his qualities as a person. His quiet strength, unaffected modesty, equanimity, friendliness, honesty, tolerant good nature, gentleness and humor were a legend." It was a backhanded compliment, at best.

To the hip critics of the 1960s and '70s like Kenneth Tynan and Pauline Kael, Hammerstein was the poet of the unexciting, a spokesperson for married people stranded on the wrong side of the sexual revolution. He deserved his place in the remainder bin of culture. His innate humility prevented him from making large claims for himself, as did the correspondingly modest nature of the lyrics themselves. Phrases like "Oh, what a beautiful mornin'!" and "These are a few of my favorite things" require no exegesis and therefore don't give a critic much to work with.

A bit later, Rodgers and Hammerstein were panned by academics for perpetuating paternalism, whiteness, and other crimes. They even got blamed for America's involvement in Vietnam. Bruce A. McConachie, editor of the scholarly journal *Theatre Annual*, published a 1994 article arguing that "the popularity of Rodgers and Hammerstein's 'oriental' musicals . . . helped to establish a legitimate basis for the American war against the people of Southeast Asia in the 1960s." The shows achieved this by "reinforcing the dominant culture of the era" and by justifying "the American empire in the East on humanitarian as well as political grounds." The three musicals in question—*Flower Drum Song, The King and I,* and *South Pacific*—all demonstrate humanitarian concerns, yes, and without question helped to shape mainstream American culture. But it would be more defensible to say that Hammerstein contributed to the anti-war and civil rights movements than that he helped justify the Vietnam War. The "dominant culture of the era" was anti-war as well as pro-war, anti-racist as well as racist, and Hammerstein was clearly on the anti-war and anti-racist side of the arguments that defined American culture in his time and beyond.

In 2007 novelist and essayist Wilfred Sheed published his final book, *The House That George Built,* a meditation on the American Songbook that cast George Gershwin as its patron saint and celebrated the contributions of Irving Berlin, Cole Porter, and "a crew of about fifty" (as the subtitle put it). There was but one dud in the mix, according to Sheed: Oscar Hammerstein II, who was a "pantywaist" and a drag on the whole enterprise. That Hammerstein structured and wrote the lyrics and dialogue for the two most influential musicals in history is an annoyance that Sheed explains away.

"There have been three generally acknowledged (though seldom by the same people at the same time) revolutions in the American musical theater," writes Sheed, "but since two of these involved Oscar Hammerstein, one might expect those ones anyway to have rolled backward. Oscar loved the past like a trendy taxidermist who is happy to use the latest techniques to bring it back to life."

I will not pause here to enjoy how badly Sheed writes in this section. He continues: "Hammerstein's role in two of these so-called revolutions was never more than what the AA people would call an enabler. In the case of the great *Show Boat,* it was Kern who first read the book and insisted on its musical possibilities. And with the groundbreaking *Oklahoma!* the equally strong-willed Richard Rodgers not only found it but had also tried the story on his old partner, Larry Hart, before springing it on Hammerstein. So it looks as if both men chose Oscar Hammerstein partly because he was so obliging and adaptable."

True, the musicalization of Edna Ferber's novel *Show Boat* was Kern's idea, but Kern chose Hammerstein for the project over much more experienced writers. Further, the idea to adapt the plays that launched *Oklahoma!* and *Carousel*—Lynn Riggs's *Green Grow the Lilacs* and Ferenc Molnár's *Liliom,* respectively—came from producer Theresa Helburn, not Rodgers. No matter. Sheed continues, recounting his own experience of seeing *Oklahoma!* as a child:

> As a youngster myself, perched in the back of the theater, watching *Oklahoma!,* I can still feel the surge and glow that rose

> through the house with the title song. Yessir! If we could tame this great crazy bronco of a country, I reckon we can patch up this funny old world any time we put our minds to it. And the simple fact that I was there should have told me something too, namely, that all the grown-ups were missing, all of the male persuasion that is, except for the very occasional serviceman and for the odd businessman, who really did look tired by now and didn't care if the showgirls wore bloomers and didn't kick, anyway. However, all over the place were the ladies from Scarsdale, probably calling the new tunes as much as anyone.

Ladies, *you* ruined the American Songbook with all your emotion!

It is worth noting that Sheed was interested less in embedded showtunes than in popular song. Such a distinction was often invisible in the twentieth century, when songs frequently fell into both categories. Hammerstein's innovations made it more problematic to perform show songs out of context, eventually helping to ghettoize the musical in a certain sense. "Hammerstein taught us that the story came before the songs" is how Sondheim put it.

Sheed prefers the work of Rodgers and lyricist Lorenz Hart. Indeed, the songs by that team possess a sublimity for which I find no equivalent in the music of my own time. Hart was a poet of tenderness, and he brought out Rodgers's supplest melodies:

> Isn't it romantic?
> Merely to be young on such a night as this?

In his 1972 book *American Popular Song,* Alec Wilder acknowledged that Rodgers wrote "great songs" with Hammerstein. But Wilder, a great songwriter himself, detected "an almost feverish demand in Hart's writing which reflected itself in Rodgers' melodies, as opposed to the almost too comfortable armchair philosophy in Hammerstein's lyrics." You could say that Hart evoked more feeling in Rodgers, or that he took him to a darker emotional level. And given Hart's unique brilliance and his frequently distressed state of mind, it makes sense that he engaged more of Rodgers's heart in the latter's younger years.

Hart could also write a deliciously acerbic lyric, but the genius of Rodgers and Hart reached its apex in songs of sweet heartbreak. "Glad to Be

Unhappy," Hart's song from *On Your Toes* (1936), could just have well as been the title of his autobiography. For Hart it really was a pleasure to be sad, which is how he instilled so much rue in his ballads. The courting of heartbreak and self-pity is a dangerous game, and we might even say it ruined Hart, a closeted gay man whose alcoholism and self-disgust accelerated his end. "I probably could have been a genius," he told lyricist Alan Jay Lerner a few years before his death at age forty-eight, "but I just don't care."

One *could* argue—and many have—that, with Hammerstein, Rodgers did not write a song as bittersweet as "My Funny Valentine," as aching as "This Funny World," or as bereft as "It Never Entered My Mind." These melodies convey the shelter Rodgers wanted to provide his partner as well as the knowledge that nothing could save Hart from himself. As enduring as their songs are, the shows of Rodgers and Hart are flimsy and rarely performed today, unless a writer steps in to "fix the book," which usually means updating the story. With Hammerstein, Rodgers would write not only sturdy shows but also openhearted songs of love freely exchanged, songs that look forward to and celebrate lasting contentment. The latter was not a state Hart could access.

Rodgers described the differences between his writing partners in a 1961 interview with Arnold Michaelis: "Oscar was interested in the 'what.' And I think Larry was interested even more in the 'how.' 'How do you say it?' Oscar was interested in 'What do you say?' Larry had a peculiar, exciting way of saying things. Oscar said them with a great deal more purity." Another way to look at the difference is that Hart wrote about sex and Hammerstein wrote about love. And love is the deeper, if less sexy, subject.

In his introduction to Hugh Fordin's biography of Hammerstein, Sondheim wrote that his mentor was a "giant" who had "changed the texture of the American musical theater forever, first with Kern, then with Rodgers." "And to change that," he added, "means not only to change musical theater all over the world, but to change all American theater as well, because musical theater has affected playwriting profoundly and permanently. There may be librettists and lyricists (very few) whose work is admired more, but there are none greater."

When I spoke to him, Sondheim added, "People forget what an experimental playwright Oscar is; he is not adequately represented as a maker of theater. Cole Porter was a songwriter. Oscar was a playwright. He was an inventor. In *Carousel,* he invented the musical soliloquy. In *Oklahoma!* he invented the ending as a hymn to the vitality of life."

Others, like writer Howard Lindsay, believed Hammerstein's greatness came from who he was more than what he did, though the two necessarily intertwine: "No man can work as long as Oscar did in a public medium without making a complete disclosure of himself. So he is there, undisguised, in the lyrics he wrote. There you find his basic qualities: simplicity, integrity and compassion. . . . I do not know of any voice that sang affirmation as strongly since the days of Walt Whitman. As certain as one can be about a contemporary, I am certain that Oscar Hammerstein had greatness. It is my conviction that he has left his mark upon this century."

He also, I hope to show, played a crucial role in defining the meaning of America in what was called the American Century, charting a progressive vision of not only civil rights but also the relation of the country and the city, the rich and the poor, America and the rest of the world. I write what follows in the belief that his vision can be a touchstone for us today, just as it was for his enormous mid-century audience.

CHAPTER ONE

A Good Boy

OSCAR HAMMERSTEIN II seems to have been born with a healthy sense of self-worth, which he maintained for most of his sixty-five years. But he never developed excessive self-regard; the megalomania of his grandfather, the impresario Oscar Hammerstein I, produced in him a distrust and dislike of bragging. The boy rarely saw his famous namesake, but his grandfather's presence loomed. Oscar II's father, Willie, and his Uncle Arthur spoke constantly of "the old man," usually joking about how crazy he was, but Oscar II "could discern quite easily the awe and fear" he engendered. Much later Oscar II figured out that his Uncle Arthur did not like his own father, Oscar I, and "now, at the age of eighty, still has a frightened look in his eye when he speaks of him."

Strangers often inquired about the impresario, causing the grandson to wonder what was so great about him. "My other grandfather was so much nicer. . . . He bought me hard candy and took me for walks in the park."

Much of what we know about Hammerstein's youth comes from a series of letters he sent to his son Billy in late 1952 and 1953. These missives are the closest he came to writing an autobiography. They are notable for everyday details about New York at the start of the twentieth century (like the horse-drawn cart that sold Moxie, a syrupy sweet drink for children that Oscar was not allowed to have) and for young Oscar's flashes of insight about the workings of the world and of his own humming consciousness.

They suggest that, had Hammerstein ever published a memoir, it would *not* have been a best seller. He portrays himself as an observant child who kept himself on a consistently even keel, even after the sudden death of his adored mother.

Of course, these missives were written in tranquility by a celebrated artist in his fifties, someone who felt that life had worked out rather as it should have. Some passages are the literary equivalent of portrait sitting and are at best candid-adjacent: "If peace means peace of mind, I have this to an amazing degree compared to all the other people I know. I have always had this somehow. I have never been harried or extremely worried except for temporary specific causes. In a confused world I am confused, but I am not thrown into a panic by confusion. I am not unduly distressed by it."

And yet there was tumult. The history of the Hammersteins taught me that two activities were more common among urbanites in the aughts than I assumed: fisticuffs and the packing of belongings. Apartment- and tenement-dwelling New Yorkers changed residences often in the early twentieth century—the less-well-off Gershwin family, for instance, moved more than twenty times when Ira and George were boys. In Oscar's first nine years, the Hammersteins occupied at least six homes, all in Harlem or the Upper West Side. Oscar was largely unaware of how much all this moving had to do with the family's financial fluctuations, all tied to the unpredictable decisions of Oscar I, for whom Oscar's father worked.

Of his mother Oscar II wrote, "I don't know which she enjoyed most—dismantling a house preparatory to moving or setting up in a new house." But really, how fun could that have been?

"We never had poverty, and yet we never had luxury" was how Oscar described their economic situation. Until his grandmother Janet Nimmo died in 1902, Oscar lived with his parents, maternal grandparents, and younger brother Reggie. They all shared one bathroom, which was "luxury enough in those days," wrote Oscar. "I was made to know that one had to do without things, and this never bothered me very much. I just did without them. It always seemed to me that I had a great deal anyway, and as a matter of fact I had. I had the security of a family of adults who were at my beck and call and seemed to be doing everything for me always, and always with the attitude that I was worth doing it for. I was brought up like a crown prince, not materially, but spiritually."

As his grandmother tucked him in at night, she reminded him to keep his legs straight so he would grow tall. When he had a cold, she rubbed goose fat on his chest. She made sure he knew the alphabet and rudimentary math before he started school. "I quickly amassed a large vocabulary for my age," Oscar wrote, adding, "Now I have a very small vocabulary for my age." His mother, Allie, was equally protective. She promptly returned the red wagon she got him for his fourth birthday after the boy fell off it.

Oscar knew enough to sense that the outside world might not think as highly of him as did his mother and her parents. He wrote that as a boy he was never certain if his confidence was real: "I somehow always sensed that things were too good at home, and that things would be tougher outside, and I was always steeled to meet more resistance outside. I knew I would have to work harder among strangers, and happily I worked harder. I might have run from the task. I didn't and I can't tell you why."

This work ethic, combined with a belief in his innate worth, stayed with him until the end.

The Hammerstein clan was secular. A Scottish-born Presbyterian, Janet Nimmo went to church periodically, and the family fasted on Good Friday. On most other Fridays they ate fish, though they were not strict about it. Though Oscar I had been raised as a Jew, his grandsons received no Jewish education whatever—the first Seder Hammerstein attended was in Hollywood in the 1930s. Describing his informal belief system, Oscar II wrote that he struck "a fine balance between a kind of half skepticism and a half faith" and that "this seems to have been a pattern which has followed me through life, or perhaps which I have followed through life." "I am not a cynic at all," he added, "but I do not expect too much of human nature."

A fair-haired boy, Oscar had a disarming confidence, his blue eyes conveying a sweet directness. He and his mother were so close that he felt a telepathic connection. "I adored her. She was my friend, my confidante, obviously my worshipful admirer, and also the firmest and strongest person I knew," Hammerstein wrote to Billy. "Without ever punishing me, and without ever seeming stern, she had a way of letting me know when she meant a thing to be done or not to be done. I did not fear her but somehow I couldn't have borne the thought of displeasing her."

Alice Vivian Nimmo, called Allie, was a pretty woman, also with fair hair and blue eyes, "too stout according to modern ideals," wrote her son, but sporting a lovely, voluptuous figure. Willie was jealous and protective of her. He didn't want her to be friends with his half sister Stella, an actor Willie considered "fast." Willie also disapproved of Allie's sister Annie, known as Mousie, who was tattooed and wore suits that tapered "very tight at the waist." She also smoked, though not in public. "Mousie was always in and out," wrote Hammerstein. "She lived somewhere else. I think she lived with another young woman. She was not married, and professed an elaborate disdain for men."

After the death of Janet Nimmo, the Hammersteins relocated to 145th Street. Oscar was sent to a new school but quickly removed because "it was full of toughs." The Hammersteins then moved to the Endicott on Eighty-First Street and the boys were entered into PS 9. After that they lived in the Aylsmere at 60 West Seventy-Sixth Street for almost two years—"a long time for us," he wrote.

Oscar described his parents' marriage as a "big love affair." They didn't go out often, but when they did there was usually drama. One night the Hammersteins were enjoying some alfresco theater at the Victoria Roof Garden, which Willie managed, when they noticed a man in a nearby box who seemed interested in Allie. He was wearing a Panama hat turned up in the front. "He looked at my mother one time too often and my father went into his box and punched him in the nose," recalled Oscar. "He was insanely jealous of my mother and so was she of him. Her social life was very confined. They would go to the opening of the roof garden each summer, but most of the time my mother was kept cooped up, and seemed happy enough with that life."

At home, it wasn't uncommon for Oscar to witness either his parents, or Allie and her sister Mousie, physically assault each other when fighting, "trying to beat each other's brains out," he wrote. He found he could usually end the melees by crying.

The rare times Oscar got in trouble he was with his little brother Reggie. One day the boys chased their schoolmates Bobby and Junie Goldman to their front door and threw tar pitch on the white marble stoop. Mrs. Goldman came out and "drew her two big sissies to her hips and yelled out to us that we should go back to Amsterdam Ave. and not be on a nice street like 76th Street," wrote Oscar. "Reggie and I didn't often go in for this kind of thing, and I don't know what started it that day," adding, "The only other thing I can say is that they became Goldman Sachs later on."

Another time the brothers were playing when their ball rolled off the pavement and Reggie ran into the street to retrieve it. This was not allowed. Oscar told Allie and was at once rebuked for it. "My mother let me know that she did not admire me for having informed on my brother, especially since it was my ball he had rescued," he wrote. "I was ashamed of myself then and I am still ashamed. I wonder what made me do it?"

As a boy Oscar "never had any urge to break a rule. This desire to show independence and to be as unshackled as possible, which almost all human beings have, is something which I never had. Maybe there's some old Teutonic streak in me which respects rules and even enjoys them," he wrote. This law-abiding impulse served Hammerstein well once he dedicated his life to the discipline of rhyme and meter. Moreover, for him, it rarely conflicted too much with his impulse to stand up for people who he felt needed and deserved help. When he found himself caught in Joseph McCarthy's crosshairs, however, with the rest of his career at stake, he retreated to safety as quickly as possible.

Wanting to show off his fine mind, his mother sometimes invited Oscar to recite songs and poems for guests. The one he remembered best, not destined for immortality, was "Black Boy" by John Ernest McCann, a purveyor of popular verse who seems to have been influenced by William Blake's "The Little Black Boy." As Oscar remembered it, McCann's poem started:

> Little Boy Black was five years old
> His father and mother were dead
> Day after day he would sit on the step
> Of his old red house
> Watching the little white boys at play
> Like a poor little frightened mouse.

Oscar loved bringing tears to ladies' eyes with "the crusher at the finish"—the reveal that, after his death, "Little Boy Black is white." However racist and condescending McCann's poem seems to us, it was an attempt to say that we are all the same underneath our skin, and Oscar was drawn to the message. "I could render this recitation with heartbreaking effect because in some way I could break my own heart while I was doing it, and the ladies just loved me for it," he wrote. He could recall "the mysterious looks" the women exchanged with one another. "They thought they were fooling me, but I knew very well that those looks were saying, 'this boy is a genius,' and I would skip from the room very happily."

He fantasized about what those flattering glances meant for his future: "I think I believed that I would become a great actor, and that I would hold much larger audiences in the palm of my hand, and the prospect was very pleasant indeed." That dream of going onstage may have been crushed a little later when a teacher told him that he sang like an otter.

Still, he liked nothing better than to overhear adults discuss his intellectual precociousness: "I used to sit and listen to the grownups talk a great deal, and I listened very carefully and sometimes they would catch me with this thoughtful expression on my face and Grandma would say: 'Yon boy's been here before.' She meant that I was reincarnated. Obviously I couldn't have all this wisdom at my age if I hadn't been here before."

The first time he tried out his bodhisattva role for his peers, it seemed to work. He was playing with friends at the house of Leroy Harding, who had gotten a toy wigwam for Christmas. The boys pretended to be Native American chiefs having a powwow, and "we slipped into more or less permanent characters," Oscar wrote. He took the part of the witch doctor, "the sort of wise man, aloof from the battles that the warriors engaged in. I remember how I would squat in a corner with a long pipe or something that pretended to be a pipe, and I would squint my eyes and look very wise and somehow felt that the other kids were being awed." Oscar liked this part so much he worked to actualize it as a grown man.

Allie indeed believed that Oscar was a genius, and she considered her younger son a clown. Reggie was famous in the family for the day he went into a neighbor's kitchen to fetch a light for Mousie's cigarette. When he returned with a whole box of matches, Mousie said, "How did you get these?" He answered, "I just went up to the cook and said, 'Nigger, give me a match.'" "He pronounced it 'Nidder,'" Oscar wrote, and "this was considered a terribly funny story in those days and was told again and again."

Reggie became the eternal ne'er do well, and Oscar was generous toward him even into adulthood, when the younger Hammerstein had trouble keeping jobs, wives, and appointments. "Everyone thought it was kind of cute that Reggie didn't like school, and in front of him they told stories about how he fell asleep in class," wrote Oscar. "If he couldn't distinguish himself as a scholar, I imagine he found it attractive to distinguish himself

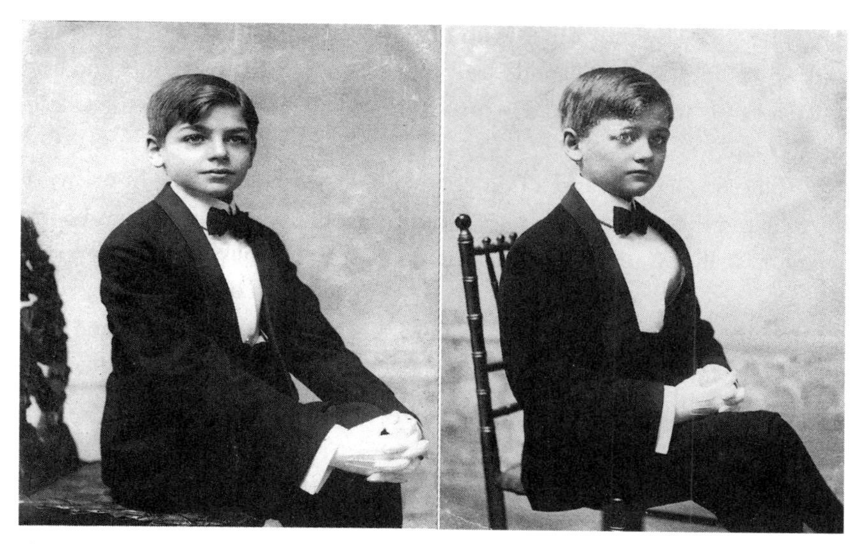

The Hammerstein brothers, Oscar (*left*) and Reggie (*right*).
Courtesy of the Hammerstein family

as a comedian—an unfortunate compensation to have chosen, but a very forgivable one."

The boys started school in 1902, when Oscar was seven and Reggie six. Oscar skipped ahead two classes in three years while Reggie was left back, adding to the gulf between them. "Reggie was given the short end of everything," Oscar wrote. "I don't know why this was." In the boys' childhood portraits, Oscar's white-gloved hands are folded assertively over one knee as he confidently looks ahead as if to his own future. The diffident Reggie seems in need of a hug. (Much later, Arthur confessed to Oscar that "when you were six your father said to me that you would do big things in your life but Reggie would always suck his thumb. How right he was.")

Family life was regular and pleasant, especially after Willie was installed as the manager of the Victoria Theatre in 1904 and found the stability he'd always wanted. The Hammersteins rose at six thirty, breakfasted, and saw Willie off to work. "Kissing him goodbye in the morning and hello in the evening was nearly the whole story of my experience with my father during my early youth," wrote Oscar. Watching for Willie's return, the boy would lean out of an upper-story window until his father emerged from a streetcar and crossed the street, looking up to see if "any of us were there" and waving as he walked. Willie dined with the family at six o'clock and then went back down to the Forty-Second Street theater until the show started and box office receipts were counted. He came home again at nine, when the whole family went to bed.

Willie was a loner and a homebody. "My father liked to be home with his coat and his collar off," wrote Oscar. If he entered the house and heard a visitor, Willie would sneak into the bedroom and call for his wife from there.

Improbably, Willie bloomed in the wilds of vaudeville. As Oscar II recalled, "My father didn't go to the theater much. He didn't like the theater. He only liked his own theater. Plays bored him. Operas bored him even more and even got him angry because it always meant ruin to his father. He didn't even go to other vaudeville shows. If he heard about an act being good, he would book it. When people suggested that he go over to Union Hill, New Jersey, to see an act, he would say, 'If it's any good, it'll come to me. People will talk about it.'"

Willie priced tickets starting at twenty-five cents so that almost anyone could afford the shows at the Victoria. He booked carnival "freak acts" like "The Only Legless Lady Ever Born, Discovered Last Summer by Mr. Hammerstein at a Remote Five-Cent Side Show" (which he most assuredly never did). He pioneered the art of booking fallen celebrities, like Evelyn Nesbit on her red velvet swing. When Nesbit's ex-husband escaped from the asylum to which he'd been committed after killing her lover Stanford White, Willie supplied his star with an armed guard; the publicity brought in hordes of theatergoers. He also booked big stars like Will Rogers, W. C Fields, Charlie Chaplin, Al Jolson, Eddie Cantor, Harry Houdini, and the Three Keatons (Buster, age ten, was the straight man). The nineteen-year-old Mae West debuted at the Victoria as a comedian. Willie made the Victoria into *the* venue for all things vaudeville. The phrase "Direct from Hammerstein's New York" became a golden endorsement, hung on banners outside hundreds of theaters across the country.

Willie was acknowledged as the cleverest vaudeville manager of his day. "He did it all from the lobby of the theater" wrote Oscar. "He had no office and he had no talent scouts."

Within his small circle of friends, Willie was known as a practical joker with a bit of a mean streak. Willie once told his friend Alexander "Doc" Steiner he had wagered Harry Houdini that the magician could not free a man from handcuffs if he, Willie, chose the man and the handcuffs. Steiner agreed to be handcuffed to a radiator in a building lobby, but as soon as the cuffs were snapped Willie and the group of onlookers vanished. Willie's proclivity for tricks would be picked up by his famous son. During his first marriage, Oscar II liked to place a phonebook on top of a partially closed door so that when his wife, Myra, opened it, the tome fell on her head. Billy recalled that Myra did not find this funny. Later, when he was living in Hollywood, Oscar sometimes asked Billy to phone the friends he was about to visit for dinner and inform them he would have to cancel. They timed the prank so that the call came just a minute before Oscar and Dorothy arrived at the door. If Oscar's pranks got more sophisticated as he grew older, they kept some meanness, though friends say the mischievous glint in his eyes always made things OK.

In July 1910, Allie Hammerstein died from a surgery-related infection after lying unconscious for five days in the family's apartment on Ninety-Second Street and Central Park West. Oscar had just turned fifteen. When recalling the trauma Hammerstein never acknowledged any messy despair. In 1958 he described to interviewer Arnold Michaelis how he coped:

> I felt the necessity to steel myself and not to give way and I—it's a strange thing for a boy of fifteen to have as much common sense as I think I had—but I walked down to the corner store and bought an empty book and pasted a lot of athletic pictures that I had been saving and cutting out for a long time, and occupied myself during the day pasting these pictures in. And then I went for long walks and thought it all over, and began to adjust myself all by myself. I never felt like going to anybody for help. And while I don't quite understand this, I know this is what happened. And I also know that it has crystallized an attitude I have toward death ever since. I never feel shaken by death, as I would have been if this had not happened to me when I was fifteen. I received the shock and took it, and sort of resisted as an enemy the grief that comes after death, rather than giving way to it. I get stubborn about it and say this is not going to lick me, because it didn't then.

From then on Hammerstein opposed grief as a matter of principle and always tried to get through mourning as quickly as possible. He ruminated on this idea in the many eulogies for theater folk he was called on to deliver. Speaking at the funeral for Gertrude Lawrence, who died only months after winning the Tony award for her performance in *The King and I,* he said, "Today let us accept our gratitude for her and not our mourning. Mourning is surrender to an illusion—the illusion that death is complete and final. Mourning is a distortion that exaggerates death." He went on to quote the Bengali writer Rabindranath Tagore: "If we kept the searchlight of our observation turned on the fact of death, the world would appear to us like a huge charnel house; but in the world of life the thought of death has, we find, the least possible hold on our minds."

Hammerstein's reading of Tagore, who received the Nobel Prize in Literature in 1913, may have influenced his political ideas as well. Tagore traveled widely, and everything he saw reinforced his belief that the best hope for humankind lay in us realizing our commonalities. Tagore saw nationalism as madness, "a disease to be cured only by a universal ideal of humanity." Hammerstein came to be devoted to this philosophy after World War II, as evidenced in the many causes he championed and supported, and it informed his passionate advocacy for the World Federalists, who called for an enforceable international rule of law in order to prevent future wars.

One year after Allie's death, Willie married Mousie, the tattooed, tight-suited sister-in-law of whom he had previously so disapproved. Pragmatic marriages were common in 1911; they kept households running smoothly amid higher death rates. A popular vaudeville joke of the time was "I married my wife's sister. Didn't want to break in a new mother-in-law." Mousie apparently stepped easily into her role of mother to the nephews she loved and who loved her.

Summing up his childhood for Billy, Oscar wrote that he was treated like "a little atom swirling around among millions of atoms very much like himself [who] must be given the illusion that they are not so like himself, that he is something very special, worth promoting, worth perfecting, worth building up to that position of prominence and achievement where he can lie down in his bed or stand on a hill or walk down a street and say to himself with conviction 'What a good boy am I.'"

The designation stuck to him. Agnes de Mille told author Max Wilk that when Hammerstein and Rodgers began collaborating, Dorothy Hammerstein confided her worries to the choreographer, saying she felt her husband was "like a very good little boy who's gotten involved with a nasty little boy who knows nasty tricks."

Hammerstein never outgrew or became embarrassed about the virtues of being a good boy. In 1956, at age sixty-one, he penned a letter of tribute to his onetime collaborator Otto Harbach upon the older man's eighty-third birthday, writing, "You radiate good things, and all your friends have to do is catch them and hold them up for you to see, so that like Jack Horner you can say, 'What a good boy am I!' Since you are too modest to ever say this, I will say it for you. 'What a good boy are you!'"

Oscar tried to remain a good boy and a good citizen throughout his life, a quality that informed his successes as much as his shortcomings. He saw safety and sanity in numbers, in consensus with "millions of atoms very much like himself": Americans who lived through the Second World War and basked in their part as heroic victors in an epic world struggle.

Hammerstein's most troubled characters, Jud in *Oklahoma!* and Billy Bigelow in *Carousel,* are doomed by their inability to find a place within their communities. Jud lives in a shed where he broods over his resentments and ogles his prized collection of dirty postcards; he sits by himself "like a cobweb on a shelf / All alone in a lonely room," while Billy, the bad-boy carnival barker, has at least the presence of mind to gaze up at the night sky and wonder "what life is all about." The only conclusion Billy can draw, however, is the hopeless nature of his own insignificance, that "two little people, you and I, we don't count at all."

Billy has a broader perspective than does Jud; he can see the web of life but is lost because he does not discern that he is part of it. For Hammerstein, a loner or an outsider cannot achieve anything significant. "What one group considers a good thing to do may be thought the worst thing in the world by another group, but if you don't belong to a group that is doing something or thinks it is doing something, you haven't a chance," wrote Oscar to Billy at the end of 1951. As a lyricist, he'd been brewing this community-centric view of life at least since he married Dorothy Blanchard in 1929. That year he wrote, moonily, "What is the good of me by myself?" in a song with existential leanings titled "Why Was I Born?" (Interestingly, the song has virtually nothing to do with the plot of its show, *Sweet Adeline.* It seems Hammerstein simply had to write it whether he had a reason or not.)

Connection is the essence of life, and it alone supplies a road back in the face of devastating loss. Hammerstein returns to this idea repeatedly but never as powerfully as in "You'll Never Walk Alone" from *Carousel.* When Billy lies dying after a failed robbery attempt, his pregnant wife, Julie, finds him in his final moments. Not able to tear herself from the body, Julie is gently pulled away by her Aunt Nettie, who urges her to sing the song, which begins in dirge mode. Julie tries to sing but is overcome, and the tune is continued by Nettie. Having one character drop a lyric that is then picked up by another is a technique Hammerstein used to remarkable effect (see, for one instance, the final scene in *South Pacific*). In this case it demonstrates with extreme economy the fact that Julie, despite Billy's isolationism, has someone to bring her back from the brink we are all pushed to from time to time. Hammerstein believed that humans, like nations, are doomed if they forget that all our fates are tied together.

Hammerstein's belief in the need for community as a universal ideal was of its time. He died in the first year of a ragged decade marked by assassinations and bloody skirmishes for civil rights. The Vietnam War sliced a bitter divide between the left and the right, and for each side the other represented the death of reason. With Americans being killed in jungles overseas and on city streets at home, with faith in government eroded, young people began to turn inward in search of answers. "Finding oneself" became a primary goal. A new generation of lyricists, including Hammerstein's protégé Stephen Sondheim, began to sound that bell. In this new age, one needed to stand apart from the crowd to understand one's true nature.

When a musical called *Golden Rainbow* opened on Broadway in 1968, *New York Times* critic Clive Barnes predicted "instant oblivion" for the songs by Walter Marks. But one song, "I Gotta Be Me," enjoyed an extraordinary life, kicked off that same year when Sammy Davis Jr. recorded it as a single (the B side featured a similarly messaged tune called "Bein' Natural Bein' Me"). For better or worse, it became an anthem of its time. Whether he is right or wrong, whether he finds his rightful place in the world or does not, the singer repeats over and over, "I gotta be me." What else, after all, can any of us be?

With its tautological wisdom, the song treats the act of self-discovery as life's greatest adventure, as the one true path to a state beyond self-doubt. This lonely but stirring message of empowerment was recorded by dozens of artists in the late 1960s and '70s, including Frank Sinatra, Tony Bennett, Ella Fitzgerald, Stevie Wonder, and even a young Michael Jackson. For a dozen years it seemed impossible to turn on the radio and not hear this song, the story of someone who would forgo finding their place in the human community, would forgo love, in order to better understand their individual consciousness. In this era, Hammerstein's ethos did not provide the same sort of cohesion for audiences. It began to seem dated, and the musicals of Rodgers and Hammerstein slid toward irrelevance.

In came the pill and the sexual revolution. Promiscuity suddenly carried less of a cost, especially for women, and Americans saw their new freedoms as brave rather than selfish. Writers of rueful ballads readjusted. A new genre, the magnanimous break-up song, was born. Burt Bacharach and Hal David were pioneers in the field, writing "Make It Easy on Yourself" in 1962, and Sondheim himself supplied a wonderfully touching example, "With So Little to Be Sure Of," from his 1964 show *Anyone Can Whistle*.

By 1968, the American Songbook's golden age was over. Two years later Sondheim, working for the first time with director Hal Prince, premiered *Company*, his breakout work as a lyricist and composer, with a book by George Furth. The protagonist Bobby is the lone singleton in a group of married friends. The characters spend a lot of time analyzing what is gained and lost by merging identities in marriage. Sondheim, by his own account, did not fall in love until he turned sixty. Only forty when *Company* opened, Sondheim's first impulse for the song that would represent Bobby's epiphany was called "Happily Ever After," a biting renunciation of the comforts of marriage that, according to Sondheim, Bobby knows is a lie. That idea proved far too subtle and left audiences unsatisfied, so Sondheim delivered a new song. "Being Alive" provided the more straightforward realization that "alone is alone, not alive." But while a musical might well begin with that position, as a conclusion the insight requires some emotional reinforcement, which Sondheim's melody corroborates, particularly in its overheated climax. The song protests too much, and it ends the musical with an exclamation mark.

It is worth noting that the most famous and lucrative song in Sondheim's catalogue tells a story of missed connections. Written in 1973, "Send in the Clowns" focused on the lonely part of the new sexual freedoms and was the closest the composer came to reflecting the current moment in pop music. Like Leonard Cohen's "Bird on a Wire" (1968) and Jerry Leiber and Mike Stoller's "Is That All There Is?" (a Top 40 hit in 1969), these songs captured the era's particular ennui and melancholy.

The '70s gave way to the '80s. Ronald Reagan was president, greed was good, government was bad, and the introspection of the Me Decade waned. In the 1980s Sondheim shed his partnership with Hal Prince to collaborate with an artist two decades younger, the playwright and director James Lapine. Their work together revealed that age had brought Sondheim much closer to Hammerstein's understanding of connection. In 1984 Lapine and Sondheim debuted *Sunday in the Park with George,* in which an artist who has lost his way comes up with a mantra to help him out of the darkness—"Connect, George, connect." Two years later came *Into the Woods,* in which Sondheim shows a hard-won generosity of spirit. I think Hammerstein would have liked "No One Is Alone," the song in the show's penultimate or epiphany position. Here Sondheim acknowledges his own understanding of our essential aloneness while also allowing for the profound comfort that company brings.

"No One Is Alone" is a spiritual companion to "You'll Never Walk Alone" from *Carousel.* In it, a lyricist known for wit and wordplay embraces the directness that was Hammerstein's hallmark, a trait Sondheim had always appreciated but not always emulated (though "Send in the Clowns" achieves its complexity through a sparse lyric). "One reason I admire Oscar is that he's the least verbose, if sometimes plain to the point of being uninteresting," said the composer. "'Less is more' is a lesson learned with difficulty."

Into the Woods ends in a shattered world; a devastating attack has left only four characters standing with almost no foundations on which to build. It's interesting to contrast this battered group with the assemblage onstage during *Carousel's* finale, set at a high school graduation. In that 1945 show, the speaker is a pediatrician, the "most popular, best-loved man in our town." The community is healthy and thriving, eager to welcome any stragglers ready to take their place within it. The physician is a clear stand-in for Hammerstein, who saw America as a meritocracy. "You don't lean on the success of your parents," he tells the class. "That's their success. And don't be held back by their failures! Makes no difference what they did or didn't do. You jest stand on your own two feet." The doctor then reveals what Hammerstein believed was the secret of belonging, tossing off the advice casually: "Try not to be skeered o' people not likin' you—jest you try likin' them."

For Hammerstein this healthy-minded friendliness was an essential tool for living, one he practiced with ease. Before joining forces with Richard Rodgers, he'd successfully collaborated with many different kinds of composers and writers, even those whose bad judgement harmed him. Producer Max Gordon, for instance, forced Hammerstein into a disastrous rewrite of his 1939 musical *Very Warm for May* at a particularly vulnerable time for the lyricist, and the show's failure almost torpedoed what little confidence Hammerstein had left. Yet, the following year, when Gordon was suffering from depression, Hammerstein walked with him every day in Central Park and reminded him that all the producer's accomplishments could not be ascribed to luck and that many triumphs awaited him.

Hammerstein's humanism naturally informed his political activism. He could not be silent in the face of overt wrong, and to that end he joined committees, raised money, wrote articles, and, more subtly, strived to change hearts and minds through his art. While Sondheim commented with notable brilliance on his culture, Hammerstein actively urged *his* to evolve. "The essence of democratic life," he wrote in a 1952 letter, "is the chance for people to better themselves as individuals and as a group." However, his progressivism could only be extended so far. Hammerstein never conceived of or condoned a life lived outside the system, for he was too much a beneficiary of it. In that way, he was a man of his time and social class. It is equally true, though, that his vision of community reminds us that democracy is a great social experiment that lives or dies based on our ability to grasp the idea of a common good.

CHAPTER TWO

Free for All

THE TERM "MELTING POT" comes from the theater—it was popularized by a 1908 drama with that title about a Russian composer who loses his family in the 1903 Bessarabia pogroms, emigrates to America, and falls in love with the daughter of the officer responsible for his family's murder. Such was the compression of migrants in the first decades of the new century. In fact, about fifteen million eastern and southern Europeans arrived in the United States between 1900 and 1915. In 1907 Ellis Island received its highest number of immigrants in a single year, processing more than one million arrivals. In the public sphere, all these cultures introduced themselves on the stages and in the audiences of vaudeville, the American equivalent of the British music hall.

Willie Hammerstein managed the country's premiere vaudeville house from 1904 until 1913, so his son Oscar II grew up at the epicenter of a cultural mashup unlike anything that had come before. In an oral history he recorded for Columbia University, Oscar remembered going to his father's theater, the Victoria, every Sunday, where the performers taught him everything he needed to know about comedy and pacing.

Ticket prices were low and audiences comprised many nationalities. Since a good number of performers and spectators alike had escaped famine or pogroms or the social rigidity of the Old World, their evenings together at the theater were fueled by a giddy sense of possibility, both for themselves and for their new country. For instance, "It Isn't What You Used to Be, It's What You Are Today" was a staple song for comedian Al Shean, born Abraham Adolph Schönberg in Germany in 1868.

From the 1880s to the early 1930s, peaking from 1905 to 1915, vaudeville presented a unique parade of cultures. Here is where theater became integral to constructing a multihued American identity, a space to figure out who we were and who we wanted to become. A dictionary defines vaudeville as "a comedy without psychological or moral intentions," and it was this very insignificance that lent the form its power.

With political correctness a concept far in the future, ethnic stereotyping was the entire point of acts like "Harry Harvey, the Quaint Hebrew Comedian," "The Original Wop," "The Wop and the Cop," "9 Orientals 9," "Two Funny Sauerkrauts," and "The Sport and the Jew." Al Shean's sister Minnie managed and sometimes acted with her five sons, later known as the Marx Brothers, who presented several nationalities in one family. Their first stab at ethnic comedy was an act from 1911 or 1912 called "Fun in Hi Skule": Groucho, playing a thickly accented German teacher, tried, and failed, to control his students, including Harpo (representing the Irish in a bright red wig), Gummo (with a Yiddish accent), and Paul Yale, who played a gay man with a limp wrist. (Chico, who would play the Italian, had not yet joined the act.) Groucho remembered the skit as a big hit, evoking lots of laughter.

In 1905, journalist Hartley Davis wrote an appreciation of vaudeville in *Everybody's Magazine,* declaring it to be the "most significant development in American amusements of the last decade":

> There is a cheerful frivolity in vaudeville which makes it appeal to more people of widely divergent interests than does any other form of entertainment. It represents the almost universal longing for laughter, for melody, for color, for action, for wonder-provoking things. It exacts no intellectual activity on the part of those who gather to enjoy it; in its essence it is an enemy to responsibility, to worries, to all the little ills of life. It is joyously, frankly absurd. . . . Vaudeville brings home to us the fact that we are children of a larger growth. It supports the sour Schopenhauer theory—one of those misleading part truths—that life consists in trying to step aside to escape the immediate trouble that menaces us.

Later, when the musical evolved to embrace virtually any subject that could be broached by a play or novel, it kept something of this cheerful frivolity. Even tragic and historically illuminating musicals, like *The Scottsboro Boys* (2010) or *Shuffle Along* (2016), employ the percussive delights of tap or the offhand elegance of a hat-and-cane number, if only to emphasize the cruel distance between representation and reality. That these songs are performed on the very stages that hosted legends like George M. Cohan and the Nicholas Brothers adds a visceral link between the past and present.

An era's popular culture can tell us more than its high art, though critics at the time often have trouble seeing it. About vaudeville, most contemporary commentators sniffed. For instance, critic and playwright Channing Pollock wrote in 1911 that vaudeville "addresses itself to amusement seekers incapable of giving, or unwilling to give, concentrated or continuous attention." For his part, J. Brooks Atkinson of the *New York Times* enjoyed the Yiddish-accented vaudevillians Potash and Perlmutter's 1926 play *Abe and Mawruss (God Forbid!)*, but allowed that the act "makes no pretense to mental clarity." Audiences, less exacting, showed up to absorb the jabs and jokes, and the country expanded itself nightly in their laughter. In this way vaudeville provided context and backstory to the progressive nature of American theater and its playwrights, from Eugene O'Neill to August Wilson, Tony Kushner, Anna Deavere Smith, and Lin-Manuel Miranda.

In Willie's day, a typical vaudeville bill consisted of nine acts, the order of which spilled over into the Broadway musical of the 1920s. First up was a "dumb act," mimes or dancers or animals, so that latecomers would not annoy fellow audience members too much, just as, on Broadway, the introductory song was a throwaway having little to do with story, such as it was. The biggest names—acts like Will Rogers, the Three Keatons, or Mrs. Patrick Campbell—took either the third slot or the penultimate place, just as, on Broadway, songwriters reserved their most rousing treat, known as "the eleven o'clock number," for second to last. And the evening ended with something graceful or otherworldly, like an equestrian or trapeze artist, an act that sent the audience out into the night feeling buoyant or revived.

Vaudeville bookers liked to mix high and low culture, and an evening out might feature an opera singer or actor from the "legitimate" theater along with acrobats, animals, and mimes. But the beating heart of vaudeville was its comedy routines, derived directly from the travelling minstrel show. These often impeccably timed sketches ran from six to fifteen minutes and prodded every manner of human foible, cleverly or not. And since humor often involves misdirection, stereotypes, with one notable exception, were constantly mixed up and subverted. Fanny Brice, for example, convulsed audiences by bestowing a Yiddish accent on an "Indian squaw" named Rosie Rosenstein. Other Jewish comedians, like the Ross Brothers and Levi and Cohen, performed as Italians. Some comedians switched ethnicities in the middle of an evening or even a sketch. Buried not very deeply beneath the chaos and the audience's raucous laughter was a connection and the possibility of a dizzyingly inclusive definition of Americanness.

Theater uses artifice to examine what is real and what is possible. Since the time of ancient Greece, when men played the parts of women, theater has also been a testing ground for cross-dressing and gender boundaries, and vaudeville was no exception. The British music hall star Vesta Tilley first performed in boy's clothes at age six, became one of the highest-paid acts in the world for almost forty years, and toured the United States six times. Slight in stature, her many roles included the foppish Burlington Bertie ("I rise at ten thirty") as well as a cop, a soldier, and a clergyman. She brought something "curiously gentle" that "allowed you to laugh" at a character "without bringing him into the zone of the ridiculous," according to one critic. She paid meticulous attention to posture and costume and billed herself as "the most perfectly dressed young man in the house."

Using gruff voices, slapping each other, and showing their underwear while winking at men in the audience, the Russell Brothers had enormous success with an act called "The Irish Serving Girls" until a contingent of angry Irish pelted them with lemons and eggs (the Russells subsequently modified and denationalized their act). But the men who performed as women with the greatest artistry were Julian Eltinge, who designed his own gowns, and British-born Bert Errol, who changed from man to elegant woman before the audience's eyes, inspiring one critic to say he "has carried female impersonation beyond mimicry and placed it upon a plane of genuine art." And so vaudeville was a laboratory for identity and serves as a reminder of how mutable gender divisions have always been (though Eltinge cultivated a virile image offstage, and Errol made sure audiences knew he was married to a woman, whom he brought onstage at the end of the act).

The twentieth century also saw a mellowing of some of the stage's most grotesque caricatures. In Groucho Marx's hands, the "stage Jew"—

Vesta Tilley (*left*) and Bert Errol (*right*) are part of the theater's great tradition of gender fluidity.
Left: Courtesy of the New York Public Library; *right:* Courtesy of the Wellcome Collection

recognized by his long black coat, beard, slouched posture, exaggerated putty nose, and obsession with money—threw off most of his customary garb along with his menace. The Marx Brothers mocked their own masquerade, and their assault on propriety and high culture delighted audiences, who ipso facto agreed that the upper classes were innately snobbish and out of touch. Theirs was an omnidirectional, uplifting set of insults—a kind of inclusiveness through leveling. Onstage and later in film, the Marxes helped to allay a widespread cultural fear of immigrants as unassimilated and unassimilable.

Outside the theater, then as now, many Americans feared being overrun by migrant caravans. Nationalists scored a legislative victory with the Immigration Act of 1917, the most restrictive bill the federal government had yet devised, which imposed literacy tests on immigrants from Europe and barred new arrivals from the "Asia Pacific Zone." But inside auditoriums, immigration was addressed in a more sociable and openhearted way. Entertainers like the husky-voiced singer Belle Baker (a good friend of Irving

Berlin), portrayed a variety of ethnicities as a way of showing solidarity. Baker had worked in a shirtwaist factory where she studied the characteristics of her fellow immigrants. "When I sing an Italian or Irish or Yiddish song," she said, "I have a definite character in mind that I've known for years. I present the character from that point of view—not the outsider's."

As ever, popular entertainment was ahead of politics, and more democratic. Prices were reasonable and the family was welcome, thanks largely to producer Tony Pastor's campaign to welcome ladies by clamping down on profanity. At the height of vaudeville, around 1915, at least two thousand theaters throughout the country devoted themselves to the format.

Still, the atmosphere was wholesome in only the most superficial ways. Most routines were, in the fashion of the time, appallingly racist and sexist. Whether Black or white, women were portrayed as nagging, avaricious, frigid, and stupid, and it was not unusual for a sketch to end with a husband shooting his wife. Fair targets also included the mentally ill, gay people, little people, and the obese. But the artists that we still discuss today—whether Bert Williams, Fanny Brice, or the Marx Brothers—stretched the status quo by challenging the stereotypes they traded in.

For African Americans, who sat only in the balcony if they were admitted at all, pretending to be someone else was not an option. Minstrelsy and its attendant reality were inescapable. Black actors on the vaudeville stage almost exclusively portrayed characters who were dumb, lazy, or dishonest. Even the most successful Black performers, like the Bahama-born Williams, could not playfully switch identities like European artists; they were forced to double down on their Blackness by a bizarre expectation that they, like Caucasian actors playing Black people, cover their skin with a sticky mixture of burned cork and oil or water. The "more serious" of the white impersonators called themselves *Ethiopian delineators* or *dialecticians* and considered themselves above the fray (it was in reaction to these designations that comedians Bert Williams and George Walker billed themselves as "Two Real Coons").

Anyone who doubts the primacy of popular culture in shaping the life of a nation need only recall that the term "Jim Crow"—which came to mean any kind of discrimination against African Americans, physical or psychic—is the name of the character that launched blackface and minstrelsy. Crow was invented by Thomas Dartmouth Rice, a traveling white actor who, probably in 1828, spotted an elderly Black man singing and dancing a jig of his own design in a Louisville stable owned by someone named Crow. The enslaved man, whose back was hunched and whose left leg was crooked, ended each of his stanzas with a little jump. When he landed on his lame side, it "set his heel a-rockin'." This anonymous dance became one of the most influential performances in history.

Wearing the man's rags and applying burned cork to his face, Rice incorporated the routine, which he called "Jump Jim Crow," into his traveling show. Word spread as he continued to perform the act in Baltimore and Philadelphia before bringing it to New York's Bowery Theatre on November 12, 1832, an event that contemporary critic Wesley Morris refers to as "the night that American popular culture was born." On the centenary of that performance the *New York Times* published a tribute to it by Frederic Sanborn. After Rice introduced "Jump Jim Crow," reports Sanborn, "the orchestra pit and the four circling balconies rocked and cheered," and patrons "forgot even to munch peanuts and throw the shells about." They brought Rice back for six encores. In closing, Sanborn calls Rice, who died in 1860, "almost the dean of American theatre" and a man who "never forfeited the respect of the public or the goodwill of his fellow men."

How to explain the hideous encumbrance of blackface, employed by both white and African American actors for more than a hundred years? First and foremost, it iterated the reality that "the black was the truly inassimilable individual in society," as Camille Forbes writes in her biography of Bert Williams. The expectation was that white audiences simply would not accept Black actors onstage outside the stock roles they were expected to play, which were further exaggerated by the cork. Seeing Black artists unadorned, playing characters endowed with full human dignity, would obliterate any argument for the historical necessity of slavery, thereby exposing Caucasians as perpetrators of a horrific crime. White America was not willing to contemplate that truth in the first decades of the new century.

By 1910, audiences recognized Bert Williams as the funniest performer on earth. For his part Williams explained, with terrible understatement, that it was "not a disgrace to be black. Just inconvenient." As a young man he teamed up with George Walker and together they worked the national minstrel circuit. While acutely aware that Black roles should be better than they were, Williams and Walker could not afford to ignore the reality "that white people are always interested in what they call 'darky' singing and dancing," reports Forbes. The taller and lighter-skinned of the two, Williams felt

Bert Williams explained, with terrible understatement, that it was "not a disgrace to be black. Just inconvenient."
Courtesy of the New York Public Library

it necessary to significantly "black up," making his lips so white and huge they took up the bottom part of his face. He played a version of the shuffling "plantation darkie," who was lazy and sly but also loveable. The actor radiated a conspicuous intelligence and often slipped out of dialect, making it clear that his "real" voice was the straightforward, educated-sounding one that emerged between characters. Williams humanized whatever stereotype he played; he was such an original that theatergoers could still see his humanity under all the cork.

And so Black artists challenged and reshaped stereotypes from undercover, as it were. And it was during vaudeville's roiling conversation about race and ethnicity that young Oscar came of age. Soon enough he would contribute significantly to the nation's discourse on social justice, though how much he moved the needle is debated to this day.

■ ■ ■

In June 1914 at age thirty-eight, Willie died suddenly of undetected kidney disease. Literally from his deathbed he asked his brother Arthur to make sure his shining son, the one named for his father, did not follow him into the theater. Arthur, also a producer, complied only briefly and, even then, half-heartedly. Three and a half decades later, on the opening of *South Pacific,* Arthur recalled, "After the curtain dropped . . . all I could hear was his father's last words to me—don't let Oscar ever get into the show business. If only he would have looked down that night. It was the night of my life for here now lives the greatest Hammerstein. I am not taken much to sentiment, but that night I was born over."

Oscar II entered Columbia Law School in 1916, as he promised his father he would. That year he performed a number in blackface and wrote a scene for the school varsity musical, *The Peace Pirates,* which featured a book by Herman Mankiewicz and the twenty-year-old Lorenz Hart as Mary Pickford. Interestingly Hammerstein's first lyric, a song called "Shakespeare Up-to-Date," imagines what might happen if George M. Cohan made musicals from Shakespeare's plays:

Henry VIII would wave a flag and sing "Hooray for the U.S.A."
Shylock would seek his pound of flesh in a patriotic way
Then Cleopatra might be seen in tights
Or dancing with Romeo

At age twenty Hammerstein was already envisioning a new kind of musical play. The following year he cowrote, with Herman Axelrod, the college show *Home, James* and played the role of an inept French waiter named Dubonnet. Hart, serving now as the college newspaper's drama critic, wrote that Hammerstein was "thoroughly original and distinctly funny." After one matinee, Mortimer Rodgers, a classmate of Oscar's, brought his fourteen-year-old brother Richard backstage to meet the cast. According to Richard Rodgers, "meeting this worldly college junior was pretty heady stuff for a stage-struck kid." Hammerstein, he recalled, "accepted my awkward praise with unaffected graciousness and made me feel my approval was the greatest compliment he could receive." A connection between Rodgers and Hammerstein was established that night, and they retained cordial feelings for each other as they crossed paths while working with other collaborators over the next twenty-five years. Later Hammerstein said he could still see "behind the sometimes too serious face . . . a dark-eyed little boy."

Hammerstein knew what he wanted but was looking for a green light from the universe. He met with his adviser at Columbia, Carl Van Doren, a scholar who helped secure the reputation of an underappreciated novelist named Herman Melville and would later join Hammerstein as a World Federalist. When Hammerstein told Van Doren that he planned to be a lawyer, Van Doren seemed to wince. Hammerstein asked, "What's the matter with that?" "Nothing," Van Doren said. "Only I had an idea that you were going to be a writer." This struck Hammerstein as a "kind of endorsement of a wild dream." He remembers "floating down Morningside Drive" afterward, "filled with an ambition which now seemed more possible than I had ever believed it to be."

That spring Oscar flirted with the petite, vivacious Myra Finn at a party at Deal Beach, New Jersey, kissed her in a game of spin the bottle, and married her in August at her parents' apartment on West End Avenue. While honeymooning he wrote to his stepmother, Mousie, saying, "As for married life, I am sure that I was cut out for it." He was, but not with Myra.

By September, Hammerstein had left the law firm Blumenstiel and Blumenstiel and was working in the theatrical offices of his Uncle Arthur, who agreed to hire him as long as his nephew did not attempt playwriting for a full year. Oscar happily complied. During the day he ran errands and read plays; at night he worked backstage on a show appropriately called *You're in Love*. One year later, Myra and Oscar welcomed their first child, William, called Bill or Billy throughout his life.

In those days, Hammerstein recalled, the putting on of musicals was "more of a free-for-all, slapdash kind of thing." A theater might book a show based on only a title or a star, and the writers would scramble to "whip up" a book and music and lyrics. The second act was usually written during rehearsals. "We knew, you see, that the book didn't matter in a musical comedy," wrote Hammerstein. "What counted was the music and the jokes and the talents of the cast. We knew this because everybody said so, and because we could see it for ourselves in the Broadway shows we went to. We accepted the book as a device for leading into songs."

Neither was the business of producing fully professionalized. When Oscar worked as an assistant stage manager, "the girls and boys in the cho-

"As for married life, I am sure that I was cut out for it," wrote Oscar. He was, but not with his first wife, Myra Finn.
Courtesy of the Library of Congress

rus were getting $18 a week, and the girls had to supply their own shoes and stockings after they wore out the first set," he recalled. Managers and producers were "usually gambling with their own money," and "they didn't always pay the actors and the authors because sometimes they didn't have it."

Even then, in "those careless times," Hammerstein noticed anything that seemed like innovation. *The Merry Widow,* a Viennese operetta that became an international hit, featured a daring plot element—"the heroine was not a virgin, and the hero was trying to get her money," recalled Hammerstein. Such small changes in acceptable topics made a difference, and literary realism and naturalism were on the rise.

Subject matter alone can't advance a form, but it's a component of broader change. While the libretti for most musical comedies consisted of unrelated diversions strung together between songs, writers of operetta overcompensated by injecting their plots with as many complications as possible, thereby arriving at roughly the same level of inconsequentiality. These entertainments, a chief export of the Habsburg Empire, were originally fashioned for Vienna's upper crust. They followed the exploits of sheiks and dukes disguised as peasants who did things for reasons that simply did not add up. In America the middle class, undoubtedly harboring aristocratic fantasies, embraced operetta, which offered more lavish stagecraft than the comparatively shabby acts of vaudeville.

To say the world was shifting in August of 1914 would be the understatement of the century. As war erupted across Europe, Jerome Kern composed a last-minute addition to *The Girl from Utah,* a show written by others that was in the middle of a transfer from London to Broadway. Reviewing the August 24 opening, the *New York Times* called the show "just a nondescript jumble" and did not mention a song called "They Didn't Believe Me." But that number, with Kern's melody which Alec Wilder described "as natural as walking," captivated most listeners, including the fifteen-year-old George Gershwin, the twelve-year-old Richard Rodgers, and probably the nineteen-year-old Hammerstein as well. The lyric, by a press agent who had just changed his name from M. E. Rourke to Herbert Reynolds, is strikingly free of the floral verbiage that defined love songs of the era. It begins in an offhand manner (and, if you skip the verse, which most singers do, in the middle of a conversation): "And when I told them / How beautiful you are." Then, a chronological shuffling lands us in a moment that predates the song's opening: "And when I tell them / And I'm certainly going to tell them / That I'm the man whose wife someday you'll be . . ." Was it an oversight or did Reynolds mean to approximate the tangle of swirling emotions in which the singer finds himself? The song turns the almanac inside out and upside down; the singer exists in a state beyond time.

Most love songs from the period came wrapped in waltz time; Kern instead chose a 4/4 signature, giving the tune a fresh sound, which Wilder said was "unlike any of [Kern's] predecessors or contemporaries." When sung at a leisurely pace, the song expresses an unhurried thoughtfulness—the stillness of a person on the precipice of great change. A bittersweet quality tells us the singer is simultaneously experiencing the joy *and* the sorrow

In 1914 Jerome Kern, pictured here, wrote "They Didn't Believe Me," with lyrics by Herbert Reynolds. With this one tune the popular love song grew up, becoming something richer and more complex than it was before.
Courtesy of the Hammerstein family

that accompanies any major transformation. Of course the young Rodgers and Gershwin noticed it because, with this one composition, the popular love song grew up, becoming something richer and more complex than it was before.

The tiny Princess Theatre on Thirty-Ninth Street and Sixth Avenue, which had opened the year before, was struggling to make a profit with its menu of short plays by young dramatists. For help, theater manager F. Ray Comstock turned to an agent named Elisabeth Marbury known for her business savvy. Given that the theater had only 299 seats, Marbury needed to produce something on the cheap, and she already knew that one-acts by unknown playwrights were not the answer. Her first thought was to contact the thirty-year-old who had just become the toast of the town for composing "They Didn't Believe Me," Jerome Kern.

Kern's mother, Fannie, a second-generation American, was an amateur pianist, a great reader, and a theatergoer. His father, Henry, immigrated from Baden-Baden to New York where he owned or managed stables and eventually invested in real estate. Jerome was raised in Newark, attended Newark High School, and at sixteen wrote the score to an *Uncle Tom's Cabin* spoof performed at the Newark Yacht Club. By the time he was twenty he had a hit song—"How'd You Like to Spoon with Me?"—in a Broadway show. When Marbury contacted him, Kern suggested bringing in Guy Bolton, a thirty-year-old British-born American librettist with whom he'd just written a musical, *Ninety in the Shade.*

For their first Princess Theatre show, *Nobody Home,* Kern and Bolton decided to write what they called situation songs, numbers that grew out of what was happening in the scene. As commonsensical as that sounds, in 1915 it was an original concept; within fifteen years critics would be using the term "integrated" to describe what the musical was trying to become. A simple way to describe an integrated musical is that every song in it is necessary to the literal and emotional coherence of the whole. But integration also meant that each element of the written show—the music, story, dialogue, and lyrics—was held to the same standard and contributed equally to the show's power, unlike in opera, where the music was king, or in the Gilbert and Sullivan operettas, where wordplay, satire, and ideas were the main attraction. While the Princess musicals would not be considered integrated today, they began the process of balancing the scales.

Later that year Kern and Bolton were joined by British humorist and lyricist P. G. Wodehouse for *Very Good Eddie,* and it was in this second Princess musical that certain New Yorkers noticed a new esprit on the horizon. Richard Rodgers, now thirteen, saw the show "at least a half dozen times" and found in Kern's sound something "new and clear." This music, which did not have "any of the Middle European inflections of Victor Herbert," was for Rodgers "truly American." In the *New York Tribune* Heywood Broun wrote that the show's "charm lies in the possession of more or less artless high spirits. Of course they are not really artless but merely seem so."

By the third Princess musical audiences were hooked—*Oh, Boy!* ran for

463 performances and produced three road companies. To the good people of Manhattan these shows were as fresh and renewing as spring air, drawing to the theater young sophisticates like Lorenz Hart and George S. Kaufman. Dorothy Parker wrote in *Vanity Fair,* "Bolton and Wodehouse and Kern are my favorite indoor sport. I like the way they go about a musical comedy. . . . I like the way the action slides casually into the songs." Robert Russell Bennett, who went on to orchestrate *Show Boat, Carmen Jones,* and seven Rodgers and Hammerstein musicals, said the names Bolton, Wodehouse, and Kern "stood for pure nonsense, really, but it was nonsense you wanted to throw your arms around and hug. All three of them devoted their lives to making life a little less serious."

Despite charming the cognoscenti of the day, the musicals' appeal proved ephemeral. Eighty-some years later, Stephen Sondheim weighed in on them in a conversation with Frank Rich for the *New York Times:* "Ninety percent of [the Princess musicals were] pitta, pitti, pitti—vamps—and those very wordy Wodehouse lyrics. A lot of that stuff is no good at all. On the other hand, you listen to 'They Didn't Believe Me' and you never want to write a song again."

By 1919 the experiment was over. Kern and Bolton argued about payments and percentages, and Wodehouse decided to focus more on his fiction, having introduced the duo that would define his adult career: the deadpan valet Jeeves, who regularly rescues his boss, Bertie Wooster, from his own idiocy. At this point, Kern had many options—his biographer Gerald Bordman wrote that the composer was "undoubtedly the glittering hope of the American musical theater."

Ironically the most lasting song to come out of the Princess musicals would be "Along Came Bill," which never even made it to the stage. Cut from the show *Oh, Lady! Lady!!,* the song would find its audience nine years later titled simply "Bill."

True to his word, Uncle Arthur absolved Oscar after a year, and in 1919 he produced his nephew's first play, *The Light,* which out-of-town critics characterized with adjectives like "deadly dull" and "absurd." After seven performances it went—as a critic in Springfield, Massachusetts, predicted it would—"back to the darkness from which it emerged." Oscar left a New Haven, Connecticut, performance midway through, went into a nearby park, and started working on a new show.

Arthur soon paired his nephew with a librettist he had been cultivating named Otto Harbach, twenty-two years Oscar's senior. The move would launch Oscar on his one true path.

Born to Danish immigrants who had adopted the German name Hauerbach when they landed in Salt Lake City, the twenty-eight-year-old writer made his way to New York in 1901 and settled in the largely undeveloped Longacre Square three years before it became Times Square—"it was like the country up there," he recalled. He loved the stage, and once it was built he often spent evenings at Willie's Victoria Theatre.

Hauerbach's first writing partner was a composer from Bohemia named Karl Hoschna, and together they wrote several musicals from 1908 until Hoschna's death in 1911 (the year that saw the Broadway opening of Hauerbach's *The Fascinating Widow,* a great hit for female impersonator Julian Eltinge, with music by Kerry Mills). In 1912 Arthur teamed Hauerbach with composer Rudolf Friml, a native of Prague who had studied composition with Antonin Dvořák. The lyricist and Friml were assigned to write something for a petite opera singer named Emma Trentini, who had been a great favorite of Oscar I. Because Trentini looked good dressed as a boy, Arthur stipulated that the story should involve cross-dressing.

Half borrowing from Shakespeare's *Twelfth Night,* Hauerbach provided a story about an Italian street singer, desperate to escape New York and her drunken guardian, who dresses as a boy to take a job aboard a yacht bound for Bermuda. Onboard she falls in love with the fiancé of an heiress. Eventually she not only wins the man but becomes an opera star.

Hauerbach cemented himself in Arthur's good graces when he fiddled with a 1915 musical called *Katinka* (scored by Friml), which looked to be a disaster when it was previewing in Morristown, New Jersey's Park Theatre. Hauerbach quickly rewrote the book as the show transferred to Broadway. As Hammerstein recalled in an oral history, *Katinka* cost about $25,000 to mount and had been pulling in less than $6,000 a week. After the rewrite, its gross more than doubled. The show ran for 220 performances and went on to do "great business" in Australia and New Zealand.

Hauerbach again changed his surname amid the anti-German sentiment of World War I, and it was as Otto Harbach that he became Hammerstein's writing partner. Making up the rules as he went along, his instinct was to honor story above all else. "Libretto means 'little book,' and, for opera, that book was usually a pamphlet to give you the outline of the story," he recalled in his own oral history. "But in a play with music, that play has to be carefully worked out as to plot and storyline and character, as though it were a play without music."

For models, Harbach had the light satirical plots of W. S. Gilbert as well as Americanized versions of Viennese operetta, such as Arthur's first producing venture in 1910, *Naughty Marietta,* set in a frantic fantasy of late eighteenth-century New Orleans. The story is a hot mess of governmental intrigue—the players include the colony's governor, his enslaved mistress, farmers, Indians, pirates, a Yiddish-speaking servant, and French girls sent by their king to marry colonists. The only thing I can say for sure about the plot is that sorting it out will induce a headache.

In the popular theater there had been earlier attempts to marry story and song, as in what some consider the first musical play, *The Black Crook,* produced in 1866, the year after Richard Wagner premiered *Tristan and Isolde*. Because a quick synopsis cannot do this story justice, I submit John Kenrick's description of the plot from his online encyclopedia *Musicals 101:*

> *The Black Crook*'s hodgepodge plot stole elements from Goethe's *Faust,* Weber's *Der Freischütz,* and several other well-known works. The evil Count Wolfenstein tries to win the affection of the lovely villager Amina by placing her boyfriend Rodolphe in the clutches of Hertzog, a nasty crook-backed master of black magic (hence the show's title). The ancient Hertzog stays alive by providing the Devil (Zamiel, "The Arch Fiend") with a fresh soul every New Year's Eve.
>
> While an unknowing Rodolphe is being led to this hellish fate, he selflessly saves the life of a dove, which magically turns out to be Stalacta, Fairy Queen of the Golden Realm, who was masquerading as the bird. (Still with me?) The grateful Queen whisks Rodolphe to safety in fairyland before helping to reunite him with his beloved Amina. The Fairy Queen's army then battles the Count and his evil horde. The Count is defeated, Satan's demons drag the magician Hertzog down to hell, and Rodolphe and Amina live happily ever after.

In fact, the secret of *The Black Crook's* success, or so Hammerstein speculated in a review of a 1950 book called *Musical Comedy in America* by Cecil Smith, was dumb luck. When New York's Academy of Music burned down in 1866, a French ballet troupe it had engaged arrived and was left hanging. The manager at another theater, Niblo's Garden, got the idea to incorporate the French troupe into a Charles M. Barras melodrama that it was about to premiere. That production was "quickly lost in the shuffle of two hundred female legs," wrote Hammerstein. In other words, the barely attired female form overtook the less shapely story, a formula that would later be perfected by producer Florenz Ziegfeld, born the following year as if on cue. A conflicted clergyman from the time, quoted by Cecil Smith and again by Hammerstein in his review, describes the key to America's first musical-comedy hit:

> The immodest dress of the girls, the short skirts, undergarment of thin material allowing the form of the figure to be discernible; the flesh-colored tights, imitating nature so well that the illusion is complete; with the exceedingly short drawers, almost tight-fitting, extending very little below the hips; arms and neck apparently bare, and bodice so cut as to show off every inch and outline of the body above the waist. The attitudes were exceedingly indelicate—ladies dancing so as to make their undergarments spring up, exposing the figure beneath from the waist to the toe, except for such coverings as we have described.

This much-enjoyed aspect of the musical, which includes display of the male form as well, remains to this day.

In 1920 Hammerstein began a frenetic immersion into the world of professional musical theater, writing three shows in one year. In January, he debuted as a Broadway book and lyric writer for a production called *Always You*, written with neophyte composer Herbert Stothart. Dissatisfied with the show during tryouts, and despite Oscar's protestations, producer Arthur brought in a comedian named Ralph Herz to enliven the proceedings. The *New York Times* noticed that the lyrics were "more clever than those of the average musical comedy."

Seeing the show in front of an audience for the first time, Oscar was dismayed that no one seemed to get a first-act joke he thought was funny. In the second act he "got a big shock" when the audience laughed at "a line that wasn't funny at all, a line I had never expected them to laugh at." When he analyzed the laugh, he found that it depended on another line that had been spoken in an earlier scene. "This proved a remarkable fact," wrote Hammerstein, only half facetiously. "The audiences—the fools—were following my story. I started to learn then that even though they may be neither thrilled nor gripped nor uproariously amused by a story, nevertheless they follow it, and when it doesn't hang together, nothing hangs together."

Hammerstein and Stothart regrouped with Harbach for another musical, *Tickle Me,* starring Frank Tinney, a comedian who had been quipping in blackface since he was boy. His gimmick was that he used no demeaning accent and showed little recognition that he was in fact wearing cork. In *Tickle Me* he played a property manager for a movie studio called Poisson Picture Corp., which sends him to Tibet to film a sacred bath ceremony. The show did sound business; it toured after playing 207 performances, mostly due to the great popularity of Tinney, who "corked up" at the top of the show but played the rest of it clean-faced ("to give the audience a chance to see how good-looking he is," said *Munsey's Magazine*). At this time other white blackface actors were also excising the more grotesque mannerisms (e.g., the eye rolling and shuffling) that had marked performances of Blackness since Thomas Rice unveiled Jim Crow. Some singers, like Sophie Tucker and May Irwin, sang songs in "Negro dialect" but without makeup in order to interpret lyrics in what they saw as a deeper and more modern manner.

With Arthur producing, Hammerstein went to on write a stream of undistinguished shows that came and went. *Jimmie* was Oscar's third show in 1920. In 1921 he wrote a straight play with Frank Mandel, *Pop,* which closed out of town. The following year Arthur produced another show for Tinney, *Daffy Dill,* in which the comedian again appeared only briefly in blackface. This show is notable because Oscar cowrote the book with Guy Bolton, who—according to an account by Oscar's grandson Oscar Andrew—commenced an affair with Oscar's wife, Myra, that lasted several years. Oscar enjoyed a little revenge later that year. He wrote a show called *Queen O' Hearts* for which he cast the diminutive Edna Hibbert to play a shallow, romance-obsessed character named Myra whom everyone called Mike, just as with the real Myra.

In 1923 Hammerstein and Harbach teamed up again for what would be their first hit, *The Wildflower,* produced by Arthur. *The Wildflower* told the tale of a fiery Italian girl who must hold her temper for six months to inherit a fortune. It produced a hit dance song, "Bambalina," and ran for 477 performances. Stothart and Vincent Youmans wrote the music, and they must have been surprised to read in the *New York Times* that the show featured "the most tuneful score that Rudolph [*sic*] Friml has written in seasons."

The following year the librettists wrote a musical with the actual Friml (and Herbert Stothart), which they called *Rose-Marie*. A love story set in the Canadian Rockies, this show turned out to be an enormous international hit and made Hammerstein quite wealthy. It ran on Broadway for 557 performances, produced five road companies, and enjoyed similar success in London, Sydney, Melbourne, and Paris, where it ran for 1,250 consecutive performances.

If we saw the show today we would almost certainly not recognize its innovations, but it did have them. Hammerstein said people laughed at him when he said he was writing a musical with a murder in it, so unheard of was that plot point. Further, Hammerstein and Harbach believed they had crafted a score so essential to the drama that they included this note in the program: "The musical numbers of this play are such an integral part of the action that we do not think we should list them as separate episodes."

The show produced a breakout hit song—"Indian Love Call"—which sold a million copies when it was recorded by Nelson Eddy and Jeanette MacDonald, who starred in the 1936 film version (one of three). The number was in fact incorporated into the story in an organic way. Rose-Marie teaches her sweetheart, Jim Kenyon, the supposedly Indigenous love call—"When I'm calling you-oo-oo, oo-oo-oo"—which is "traditionally" sung out by a Native while standing on a boulder near a valley with a lovely echo. If the singer's sweetheart reproduces the oo-oo's in response, then he knows she is smitten with him as well. Later in the show, Rose-Marie and Jim will signal each other with the love call when they are separated.

Cheesy as that scene might sound, it shows that Harbach and Hammerstein were working to remove the seams between score and story. They realized that one technique was to write songs that critics call diegetic, meaning music that is sung or played by the characters within the action onstage. *The Sound of Music*, for instance, is filled with such numbers: as when Maria teaches the children the basics of music ("Do-Re-Mi"), or when the children perform "So Long, Farewell" for the guests at a dinner party, or when Captain von Trapp sings "Edelweiss" onstage at a festival. Critics in 1924 did not mention diegeses, but they did enjoy *Rose-Marie*'s buffet of feminine beauty. "There is a seemingly endless array of costumes," noted the *New York Times*, "tasteful, dazzling, colorful; there are platoons and platoons of chorus girls—75, the rapid calculators have it—tireless, graceful, beautiful."

Harbach and Hammerstein took each story seriously, no matter how trivial the project. "He taught me to think a long time before actually writing," said Hammerstein. "He taught me never to stop work on anything if you can think of a small improvement to make." Even if they were the only ones who cared, the men constantly tried to solve the puzzles of motivation and character. Hammerstein said that Harbach "never wanted a song to be put in unless it was germane to the story. He never wanted a comedian to interpolate jokes that didn't belong in the story. However he didn't always win his battles. Very often the producer and the comedian and the director would conspire and overrule him, and the audience might laugh at the joke he'd objected to, but no one knew how dearly one might pay for the wrong joke in the wrong place." Under Harbach's guidance, Hammerstein began to see slapdash story as an existential threat to the development of the musical. "Because every play has a character, a soul of its own, when you are inconsistent with that character, you're in great danger," he wrote. Betray the story and you kill the show.

As he matured Hammerstein continued to integrate songs into the mechanisms of plot with ever-greater precision. If *The Sound of Music* is not Rodgers and Hammerstein's best musical, it is certainly their most diegetic. A particularly effective example occurs just after Captain von Trapp, at the urging of his fiancée, is about to fire the governess Maria. She takes the occasion to implore him to be a better father by seeing each of his children as individuals. Just as she finishes her plea, the Captain hears the angelic voices of his children singing "The Sound of Music" in harmonies Maria has taught them. He turns and listens, as if in a trance. In this moment, he reconnects with something he lost when his wife died: his role as a father. Then he joins them just as they arrive at a key change, singing, "I go to the hills / When my heart is lonely"—a consummation of music and story that many try for and few achieve. (PS: Maria does not get fired.)

Born Siegmund Rosenberg in 1887, Sigmund Romberg arrived in New York in 1909, at first working as a pianist in cafés and in restaurant orchestras. Eventually he was key in bringing operetta to American audiences, encasing romance in waltz time, delivered by string sections so industrious they could whip cream. His music so embodied the spirit of Vienna that the world forgot he was from Hungary. When in 1922 the *New York Times* noticed that his name "had been appearing in theatre programs with increasing frequency," the editorial staff decided to investigate his background and pronounced him Austrian.

Romberg's *The Student Prince,* written with librettist/lyricist Dorothy Donnelley in 1926, was the longest-running Broadway show of the 1920s—clocking in at 608 performances, it beat out *Show Boat* by a good three dozen. It tells the story of Prince Karl Franz, heir to a Teutonic kingdom, who studies incognito at a Heidelberg university. He falls in love with Kathie, the young server at a local biergarten. Then the time comes for him to perform his duty to family and country and marry the princess to whom he is engaged. He's a moral man, so he feels he can't proceed unless Kathie makes it OK for him, which she does. (After a visit from the princess, Kathie agrees to break up with Karl Franz for the good of the kingdom.) This story of interclass romance and lower-class sacrifice moved Broadway audiences to tears.

While *The Student Prince* was being performed in nine American cities as well as London, Romberg teamed up with Hammerstein and Harbach to write *The Desert Song.* As Hammerstein remembered it, he got the idea when reading a newspaper account of the troubles of the Riff, an Amazigh ethnic group in the mountains of Morocco. His timing was good. Actor Rudolph Valentino, whose good looks in *The Sheik* made moviegoers swoon, died that summer at age thirty-one from perforated ulcers, and his distraught fans nearly rioted at his funeral. People wanted the florid, Arab-accented romance they associated with his films, and Hammerstein and Romberg gave it to them.

The Desert Song follows a Frenchman living in Morocco. By day he is merely Pierre, the butterfly-loving son of a French general. But at night, disguised as the Red Shadow, Pierre galvanizes the Arab rebels fighting French forces (led by his own father) in the desert. The heroine, who feels only sisterly toward Pierre, is helpless to fend off the Red Shadow's charms. *The Desert Song* joined *The Student Prince* as one of the great hits of the decade, and three film versions were made (each with slight plot alterations). The show survived until it was no longer possible to stage most operettas with a straight face. In 1987, when New York City Opera revived *The Desert Song,* critic Donal Henehan reported that the audience took the show to be pure camp and hooted at certain lines. How else to approach a work, asked

Henehan, based on "the thesis that all women yearn to be carried off into the desert by a masked outlaw"?

Audiences of 1926 were untroubled by such a fantasy, and *The Desert Song* gave Hammerstein a third hit. He was now the father of two: Alice, born in 1921, and Billy, born three years earlier. Ready to step into his role as a successful man of the theater, he and Myra bought a plot of land on Long Island's Manhasset Bay, near where F. Scott Fitzgerald had set *The Great Gatsby*. There they built a grand 6,500-square-foot house in the Tudor style. The huge living room included a stone fireplace and French doors. The second floor featured bedrooms and a solarium. Throughout the house, windows looked out on the bay where Oscar and Billy swam every morning.

Working with Hammerstein, Romberg shook off much of his syrup. Together the men wrote five shows and three movies, and today virtually the only Romberg songs still performed are from those projects—"Lover, Come Back to Me," "When I Grow Too Old to Dream," and "Stouthearted Men." Eight years older than Hammerstein, Romberg was not able to sustain a relevant career into the 1940s, though he continued writing film scores and incidental music for movies.

On other stages, straight plays were wading into a new American realism. Hammerstein would have been paying attention in 1924 when Eugene O'Neill was forced to defend *All God's Chillun Got Wings* before it even opened at New York's Provincetown Playhouse. The play depicted the breakdown of a marriage between a Black man and an increasingly unhinged white woman; in a sense this disintegrating family was a warm-up for the autobiographical *Long Day's Journey into Night* (O'Neill named the characters in *All God's Chillun* Jim and Ella for his own parents, James and Mary Ellen). The playwright cast Mary Blair and Paul Robeson as the couple. Robeson, twenty-six, was a magnetically handsome former football star and class valedictorian at Rutgers University who went on to earn a law degree at Columbia. He was destined to be a symbol for the country's slow progress toward racial equality, a complex role he would understandably come to see as a burden.

Inevitably the country's racial tensions overshadowed those depicted in the play. The Ku Klux Klan sent a threatening letter to O'Neill when word got out that the play depicts a white woman kissing the hand of her Black husband. This was too much as well for other arbiters of morality such as

William Randolph Hearst's newspaper *New York American,* which led the charge against the Provincetown Playhouse; the periodical served as a mouthpiece for John S. Sumner, the secretary for the Society for the Suppression of Vice, who warned that "such a play might easily lead to racial riots or disorder," a claim the paper then picked up on as a reason for authorities to shut down the production.

Not able to find a legal way to do this, New York mayor John Francis Hylan decided to throw a wrench into opening night. A clerk telephoned the Playhouse several hours before opening with the news that City Hall would not grant work licenses to the eight children scheduled to appear in the play's prologue.

The show went on anyway, with director James Light reading the prologue for the audience. The *Times* reported that "any expectation that the production of the play would be attended by a public demonstration or protest against its subject matter proved mistaken," a neutral sentence that nonetheless manages to convey the paper's pro-theater stance.

In his own defense O'Neill raised the question "What is the theater for if not to show man's struggle, whether he is black, green, orange or white, to conquer life?" He added that a dramatist "creates his own world, and he uses the human soul, all life if you like, for his keyboard. If he isn't a sound creative architect, his structure crumbles." This was quite similar to Hammerstein's thinking about his own musical plays.

At first young Robeson stepped easily into his public role, telling the *Times* that we would soon see more roles written for African Americans. "There are, of course, white actors who play Negro parts cleverly," he said, referencing the still-ongoing practice of blackface, "but in the serious rendering of Negro psychology, they are not comparable to Negro actors."

In the next two years Robeson veered away from plays in order to dedicate himself to plumbing his great vocal gifts. He performed a series of concerts, both private and public, in which he lent his rich baritone to Negro spirituals, a genre much appreciated in the early days of the Harlem Renaissance. These songs, most by anonymous bards, proved the lie of the Jim Crow character by displaying the extraordinary forbearance and dignity it took to simply go on living amid the daily insults to body and soul. James Weldon Johnson, writer, poet, lawyer, and the head of the NAACP throughout the 1920s, published *The Book of American Negro Spirituals* in 1925; he considered such compositions "unsurpassed among the folk songs of the world and, in the poignancy of their beauty, unequalled." The following year, he published a second, equally popular volume.

The shepherding of the spiritual from the slave quarters to the stage was part of a pan-racial movement to create fleshed-out representations of African Americans—what the Harlem Renaissance called the New Negro. Composers of the new sound included Scott Joplin, W. C. Handy, and the Noble Sissle–Eubie Blake and Will Marion Cook–Paul Laurence Dunbar songwriting teams, all of whom wrote irresistible popular tunes that traveled where the artists themselves could not safely go. White artists absorbed Black music and responded with a respect and sensitivity notably absent in the decades before. In 1924, George Gershwin debuted his *Rhapsody in Blue,* which he described as "a musical kaleidoscope of America—of our vast melting pot, of our unduplicated national pep, of our blues, of our metropolitan madness." Some Black critics, like the pioneering culture writer J. A. Rogers (originally from Jamaica), liked what Gershwin was doing; writing in *Dance Lovers Magazine,* Rogers called *Rhapsody* "a harmonized and thoroughly delightful Jazz," though the debate about Gershwin's homage to, influence by, or appropriation of African American music would grow more complex in its century and even more so in the next.

In 1925, Hammerstein published a piece in *Theatre Magazine* that traced the history of the musical from John Gay's 1728 *Beggar's Opera* to Gilbert and Sullivan and the Viennese operettas. Though he said he saw the latter as "imitated to death," he continued to write them for at least another decade. "We became sick and tired of hussars with high patent-leather boots and capes full of gold braid," he wrote. He saw his own show *Rose-Marie* as an operatic musical comedy and not an operetta, though we might be hard-pressed to see the difference. Still, he was yearning toward what might come after operetta: "What will it be? Will it be a return to a lighter vein—or will we become even more serious, more legitimate as to drama and more operatic as to music? Is there a form of musical play tucked away somewhere in the realm of possibilities which could attain the heights of grand opera and still keep sufficiently human to be entertaining?"

The answer to that question was almost in utero, as it were—*Show Boat* would not debut for another two and a half years.

Prefiguring *Show Boat* by fourteen months was the 1926 jazz-inflected Broadway musical *Deep River* by a white team, composer W. Franke Harling and lyricist Laurence Stallings. Stallings's book borrowed from Lafcadio Hearn's writings about nineteenth-century New Orleans voodoo ceremonies to add atmosphere to the main tale of two white men vying for the favors of a woman at Louisiana's Quadroon Ball (essentially a showroom for mixed-race mistresses). *Deep River* is noteworthy as a musical about race featuring a multiracial cast, though it disappeared after thirty-two performances, perhaps because it was, as Brooks Atkinson wrote, "verbose," "leisurely," and "slender." But Atkinson also saw that the show "point[ed] the way to a rich mine of American drama."

During his moment in the sun, Harling explained his musical idiom by saying he wanted to "emphasize" that "jazz is not a thing to be deformed and travestied in cheap dance halls, but to be taken seriously as a new rhythm, a new contribution to music, the most important in the last hundred years."

In fact, the jazz from those "cheap dance halls" has far outlived the score of *Deep River.* "Lifting up" African American music by enshrining it in palaces of white culture often meant leaching out its life due to blind condescension. Gershwin struggled to find the right way of merging what was in him with the music he loved. In a June 1926 piece for *Theater Arts* magazine, he asked the question "Does the American spirit voice itself in 'coon songs'?" He continued, trying awkwardly to appeal to culture gatekeepers: "I note the sneer. Oh, I hear the highbrow derision. I answer that it includes them. But it is more. I do not assert that the American soul is negroid. But it is a combination that includes the wail, the whine and the exultant note of the old mamy [*sic*] songs of the South. It is black and white. It is all colors and all souls unified in the great melting pot of the world. Its dominant note is vibrant syncopation."

Gershwin believed that America's music could lead the way to true integration and that he would be part of that change:

> I do not know what the next decade will disclose in music. No composer knows. But to be true music must repeat the thoughts and aspirations of the people and the time. My people are Americans. My time is to-day. Of to-morrow, and of my to-morrow, as an interpreter of American life in music, I am sure of but one thing: That the essence of future music will hold enough of the melody and harmony of to-day to reveal its origin. It will be sure to

have a tincture of the derided yesterday, which has been accepted to-day and which perhaps to-morrow will be exalted—jazz.

In 1920 Kern enjoyed his biggest hit with *Sally*, written for the *Ziegfeld Follies* star Marilyn Miller. A lithe dancer, Miller began to resent Ziegfeld's affection and obsessive control during *Sally*'s two-year run, and the couple parted ways. Rival producer Charles Dillingham snapped up Miller and put her in a production of *Peter Pan* (a part immortalized in the 1950s by another alliteratively-named actor whose incandescence did not transfer to film, Mary Martin). Dillingham then appealed to Kern to write a follow-up to *Sally*. To that end, Harbach brought the twenty-nine-year-old Hammerstein to Kern's Bronxville house to discuss the project, probably in 1924.

The forty-year-old Kern, having fulfilled his young promise, was stepping into his full, rather large personality. Fastidious about clothes, he favored silk ties and ascots, tailored shirts and fashionably baggy pants. He was considered a fabulous conversationalist and is frequently described as owlish, as he was short and wore round glasses and a serious expression. He veered between the impish and the aggressively acerbic. One night, leaving the Brown Derby restaurant in Hollywood, he met a large crowd waiting to catch a glimpse of actor Robert Taylor. In his high-pitched voice he screamed, "YOU HEATHENS! Get out of our way!" and the crowd fell back. He enjoyed upsetting formality. At the end of one dinner party, he rose from his chair without the pants he was wearing when he sat down. According to the orchestrator Robert Russell Bennett, "Anytime he could cause a gasp of surprise, his life was a success. He brooked no nonsense"—except his own—"and only a fantastic sense of humor saved him from being a little tyrant." Playwright Marc Holstein described him as "the spirit of Ariel and Puck and Falstaff." His low tolerance for boredom prompted stunts that showed off his imperious deadpan. The producer Max Gordon remembered strolling with Kern and some friends in London when they came upon a group of workers laying the foundation for a public building: "He announced that plans for the construction had been canceled. Everyone, he said, could go home. And they did." Later, Hammerstein described him as "the most entertaining man I ever met."

Harbach saw an immediate affinity between Hammerstein and Kern. Hammerstein did not at all mind Kern's domineering manner, or even his belief that the importance of music far outweighed that of lyrics in a musical comedy. The younger man appreciated Kern's work ethic and found his personality endearing. They bonded over a dozen opinions, like hating the specialty acts that producers insisted they insert into musicals. Over the years they exchanged long letters full of details about whatever show they were working on, missives that reflect a deep affection they camouflaged in pretend gruffness. "I've just finished talking to you on the phone and I'm about to phone you again and I think I've had enough of you for today," wrote Hammerstein. Upon his second son's birth, Hammerstein wrote, "Dear Jerry: Yes his name is Jimmie. Do you want to make anything of it?" Kern, at the end of one of his letters, wrote, "Well, you brought all this drool on yourself." Hammerstein once said that Kern "had a greater grip on my whole being than anyone else I have known." Their bond was deep, and Hammerstein was at Kern's side when the composer died.

And so the three men—Kern, Hammerstein, and Harbach—teamed up to write a musical for the people who'd loved *Sally*. They called it *Sunny*. Sure enough, Dillingham saddled his writers with a number of specialty acts. Jack Donahue, a dancing comedian, came to Hammerstein's house to show him the routine he wished to be incorporated into the story. The creators also had to accommodate Cliff Edwards, known as Ukulele Ike, whose contract stipulated that he perform between 10:00 and 10:15 each evening.

Dillingham and his star were equally uninterested in story. Oscar remembers summing up the *Sunny* plot for Miller as she listened politely, after which she had only one question: "Mr. Hammerstein, when do I do my tap specialty?" Dillingham answered, "No problem, Oscar, just work it into the book." (Hammerstein collected stories of showbiz obliviousness. He recalled telling Ziegfeld about a major change he was making in *Show Boat* and seeing a faraway look in the producer's eye. While Hammerstein was in the middle of a sentence, Ziegfeld called to a chorus girl, "I liked the way you had your hair done yesterday.") Happily, *Sunny* was also a hit, largely because people could not get enough of Miller. She was a sensation and, at $3,000 a week, the highest-paid female star on Broadway.

Kern went on to write another musical with Harbach in 1926, *Criss Cross*, a showcase for star Fred Stone, an antic dancer from vaudeville and the circus. But when the composer found the book he was sure would undergird a real, important American musical, Kern called Hammerstein. What Harbach thought about that is lost to history.

CHAPTER THREE

The Invention of the Musical

IN A 1947 COVER STORY on Hammerstein, *Time* magazine described the shows *The Desert Song, New Moon,* and *Show Boat* as the lyricist's "triple triumphs" from the 1920s. "There was nothing very revolutionary about any of these shows," read the piece. "But they were charming and carefully dreamed." One doubts the writer in fact saw these shows, because this is like saying that three top songs of 1963—"Surf City," "My Boyfriend's Back," and "A Hard Rain's a-Gonna Fall"—were all catchy tunes.

In the realism of its story and emotional landscape, the urgency of its theme, and the intertwining of its music and characters, *Show Boat* was light years ahead of those other two long-lost hits. It was the first musical that successfully wove the stories of formerly enslaved people into its main narrative. In fact, it is the most revolutionary show in the history of the genre.

Before he finished reading Edna Ferber's novel, Kern decided he would turn *Show Boat* into a musical. It had an irresistibly picturesque setting and "a million dollar title," he told Hammerstein in the summer of 1926. Hammerstein read it and then "we each did independent scenarios and found that we had practically the same layout for the story," he recalled in a 1956 letter to writer Elizabeth Rider Montgomery. Hammerstein immediately became enamored, later recalling that he and Kern "fell hopelessly in love with it. We couldn't keep our hands off it. We had ourselves swooning." They visited an actual show boat docked on the Chesapeake Bay, dined with the cast, and stayed for the show. Hammerstein was not as enchanted as Ferber had been by the troupe's amateurish acting; in fact, he found it awful, and the two men left before the final curtain.

Ferber names her fictional boat the *Cotton Blossom,* giving it an aura of Southern charm, hospitality, and obliviousness to the workers who picked the crop. She describes it as a large, unwieldy vessel that travels to towns along the Mississippi River and its tributaries, bringing glamour along with performances of popular nineteenth-century melodramas like *Lady Audley's Secret* or one of the many dramatic versions of *Uncle Tom's Cabin.* The novel looks with fondness and nostalgia at the floating stages that were past their prime at the time of Ferber's writing. At the same time, the author shares a wink with the reader over the hucksterism of the enterprise. The boat's captain, Andy Hawks, hangs huge banners boasting of "One Thousand Seats!" (in reality six hundred) and a "Ten Piece Band" (actually six).

Primarily focused on the 1870s and 1880s, the novel follows Andy's daughter Magnolia Hawks from her girlhood on the boat, through her marriage to and abandonment by the gambler Gaylord Ravenal, to her return to the stage and to the *Cotton Blossom* as a mature woman. It was a best-selling work of popular fiction, but with a backbone. Beyond Ferber's valentine to a provincial and bygone form of show business, she examined miscegenation in the post-Reconstruction south, writing at a time when several states—Arkansas, Florida, Louisiana, Mississippi, Texas, South Carolina, and Alabama—had reinstated laws against interracial marriage that had been dropped after the Emancipation Proclamation. Several states enacted laws that were known individually as the "one drop rule," based on a eugenics theory that defined whiteness as not having even one drop of Black blood (i.e., any Black ancestry whatsoever). When Ferber published *Show Boat,* it was illegal in thirty states to marry a person of another race; sixteen upheld these laws until 1967, when the Supreme Court finally declared marriage one of the "basic civil rights of man."

While a pivotal scene exposes the senseless cruelty of anti-miscegenation laws, the novel itself remains unselfconsciously racist sentence by sentence. This dichotomy might be explained by something Ferber told the *New York Times* in 1945. "Every one of my books had a theme deep in it that was very important to me," she said. "I should say every book except *Show Boat,* which hadn't any theme, which was just fun."

The author may have had reason to forget parts of the novel. Early on she describes how, when the *Cotton Blossom* arrives in a new town, its band played merrily on the ship's deck while the local people "hurried down the streets, through the woods," and "invariably some magic-footed Negro, overcome by the music, could be seen on the wharf executing the complicated and rhythmic steps of a double shuffle, his rags flapping grotesquely about him, his mouth a gash of white." When the cook Queenie ("that mass of ebon royalty") and her husband Jo ("charming and shiftless") leave the *Cotton Blossom* at each season's close with their $300 pay, they do so in style, with "Queenie in a clean new calico, proper jeans for Jo, hats on their heads, shoes on their feet, but each spring they returned penniless in rags and slightly liquored." Ferber adds that "they were as faithful to [Captain Andy] as their childlike vagaries would permit."

Hammerstein and Kern, recognizing an opportunity to more fully imagine the lives of Queenie and Joe (they added the *e*), enlarged those roles significantly. In the musical, Queenie is the first character to speak. She's immediately accosted by Pete, the boat's engineer: "Hey there, nigger. Where y'all get that broach you're wearin?" His aggression doesn't rattle her. Queenie has seen it all, and besides, Windy, the ship's trusty pilot, is watching nearby. In fact, he's so shocked by Pete's words that he takes his ever-present pipe from his mouth. Queenie is imperious with Pete, fingering her pin with obvious pleasure as she replies, "You mean dis scrumptious piece of jewelry?" Pete gets louder and meaner: "Where'd you git it, nigger?"

The audience will soon understand the nature of this encounter, which demonstrates how the sanctioning of injustice emboldens the worst in and among us. The broach, it is revealed, was an unwelcome gift from Pete to Julie, the show boat's star, who is happily married to leading man Steve. When the couple enters, Steve and Pete argue and come to blows, a crowd gathers, and Captain Andy fires Pete. To get revenge, Pete notifies the sheriff of a case of "illegal miscegenation" aboard the *Cotton Blossom*. He has somehow discovered Julie's secret: she is mixed race. Her marriage to Steve, who is white, is therefore illegal. When the sheriff arrives, Julie's heritage is laid bare in a riveting scene that, in Hammerstein's version, includes Joe and Queenie as onlookers.

Hammerstein also fleshed out another interest shared with Ferber—the alchemy through which theater mines reality from obvious artifice. One night a "backwoodsman," who pays for his ticket with Confederate coins, attends the play on the *Cotton Blossom*. Like those fabled first moviegoers who fled when they saw footage of a train pulling into a station, the backwoodsman mistakes a scene in *The Parson's Bride* for the actual molestation of a young woman. Outraged, he aims his gun toward the stage and causes havoc. Hammerstein used the novel's show-within-a-show aspects to fashion his own essay on the power of belief, a theme that would become central to his work.

Ferber's Captain Andy is a lover of life, a gourmand, a generous and restless spirit who happens also to be a great father and a good, if challenged, husband to the formidable Parthy. To Andy's attributes Hammerstein added talent, making him a director and true man of the theater, however amateurish his domain. (One frequently cut but utterly charming scene has Andy take the stage and act out all the parts when his actors flee from the gun-toting backwoodsman.)

Hammerstein smoothed out the wildness in Ferber's Magnolia, or "Nola," making her a slightly less interesting young woman. But she grows significantly in the second act. In fact, she is the first female protagonist in musical theater to age from ingenue to mature woman, supporting herself and her child after her husband abandons them.

That husband is the dashing Gaylord Ravenal "of the Tennessee Ravenals," a man who always appears "sartorially and tonsorially flawless when dishevelment and a stubble were inevitable in any other man," according to Ferber. After Ravenal, known as "Gay," spots Nola, he allows Captain Andy to coax him into playing opposite her on the *Cotton Blossom* stage. Kept apart during the day by the hawkeyed Parthy, Gay and Nola play their love scenes on the boat with such passion that they become the hit of the Midwest. Once they marry, their union only increases their fame.

After Andy drowns (a death cut by Hammerstein) and Parthy takes over the boat, the couple and their young daughter Kim depart, drifting from town to town and card table to card table. Ravenal, still fastidious about his dress, leaves Nola and Kim alone in a hotel most evenings. Magnolia never knows if they will have to abandon their rooms that very night or if she will be escorted to a fine restaurant and given a fur coat (the latter which will surely disappear after Ravenal's next bad run). In the book he counters his wife's complaints with retorts like "You should have married a plumber" or

"Don't be like your mother." Worried about her daughter's education and financial future, Magnolia plans a return to the stage. What ends the marriage is the threat of an imminent visit from Parthy, which sends Ravenal away. He can't bear to see his life though his mother-in-law's eyes.

Working for the first time without a collaborator on book and lyrics, Hammerstein's early drafts cleaved so closely to the novel that his adaptation had a wooden quality. But he benefited enormously from what at first seemed like a substantial blow—Ziegfeld postponed the opening. *Show Boat* would *not* have its debut along with the beautiful new theater the impresario was unveiling on Fifty-Fourth Street and Sixth Avenue. The almost yearlong delay, though, gave Hammerstein the time to return to his text again and again with clearer vision. Eventually he developed a superb sense of how to spin the novel's various strands into a tight and thrillingly theatrical web.

The musical's first hour approaches perfection. In that short time, we meet and understand the emotional temperament of all ten main characters. Furthermore, Kern introduces their attendant musical motifs, which (like the characters themselves) merge and separate and rearrange in a complex aural tapestry, tied together by underscoring that adds depth and mood at every turn. Music quickens the drama in innovative ways. For instance, when we meet Ravenal, he is ambling near the *Cotton Blossom,* mulling over his itinerant life, so free and untethered and yet at times deeply lonely. Just as he admits he "sometime[s] wonders where's the mate for me," his thoughts are interrupted by the sound of someone haltingly practicing the piano. The little melody gets incorporated into Ravenal's song, telling us that Magnolia, the unseen player, has already entered his consciousness.

For that first golden hour, through the scene in which Magnolia and Ravenal step into the roles vacated by the expulsion of Julie and Steve, a listener may be hardly aware of the difference between music, lyrics, and dialogue.

Recalling the process of writing *Show Boat* years later, Hammerstein said, "I threw everything away, all the traditions I knew, and I allowed the novel that I was adapting to dictate my course." But he also made changes, and every alteration to Ferber's story pays off—he promotes Julie from character actor to star and slots Ellie (Elly in the book) into the secondary role of comedian (a position the character passionately protests as if she knew of her demotion). Hammerstein also embroiders the closeness of Nola and Julie, making them more like sisters, which heightens the devastation of Julie's ouster from the *Cotton Blossom*.

Prior to 1927, wrote Hammerstein, "both the operetta and the musical play were written in a kind of code." "The talk between the songs was usually almost telegraphic, and, according to certain phrases that you heard again and again in operetta and musical comedy, one knew that the author was trying to get to the song as quickly as possible. He was safe once he reached that island. The dialogue was the hardest part for the audience to take in. In *Show Boat* the characters, I think, for the first time spoke more like human beings."

Hammerstein scoured the novel for scenes in which characters literally sang, which offered opportunities to incorporate music organically. He focused especially on Magnolia's love of the spirituals she learned from Jo. That familiarity serves her well later when Ravenal abandons her and she seeks work in the theater, where minstrelsy is popular. In the novel Magnolia distinguishes between spirituals and the minstrel numbers that white people refer to as "real coon songs," which she does not perform. Hammerstein's Magnolia makes no such distinction. The song she learns, from Julie rather than Joe, is "Can't Help Lovin' Dat Man," which is in fact neither kind of tune. At first she performs it up-tempo while doing a sinewy cakewalk, so that the song resembles a minstrel number (in the 1936 film version, Irene Dunne's Magnolia performs another number, "Gallavantin' Around," in full blackface). But later, when she is broke and trying out at Chicago's Trocadero Club, Magnolia slows down the song, which is at heart a ballad, the story of a woman who knows she will never leave her man. Hammerstein had a soft spot for these kinds of torch songs and the tragic beauty of the heroines who sang them. ("What's the Use of Wond'rin'," written for *Carousel* in 1945, is a masterpiece of the genre which, in time, attracted controversy. It is in fact a tribute to masochism.)

Julie virtually disappears from the novel after her expulsion, though Magnolia does glimpse her in the background at a notorious brothel. Hammerstein brings Julie back to the fore in the second act for more suffering and self-sacrifice. She appears as a faded nightclub singer who happens to work at the Trocadero and sees Magnolia's audition. Understanding that her old friend must be in financial straits, Julie leaves the club, telling the stage door attendant she is going on a "spree" and that the director should hire the woman who was just singing.

Because Hammerstein tinkered with *Show Boat* throughout his life—rewriting, rearranging, adding, and cutting scenes and songs for the 1936 film version and for several stage versions—there is thought to be no definitive text. (For the 1951 MGM Technicolor version starring Ava Gardner, producer Arthur Freed ordered numerous misguided changes to the carefully constructed plot, best symbolized by that film's gigantic, ornate, steam-powered *Cotton Blossom,* a ship that, in the novel, had no power whatsoever and was pulled along by two tug boats from dock to dock.) Eventually the musical's original ending—which is peak Hammerstein—was restored, and it remains a deeply emotional masterpiece of theatricality.

In Ferber's novel, Nola never sees Gay again after he leaves her. Their daughter Kim becomes an actor like her mother. Captain Andy drowns in the Mississippi, and Parthy takes over the *Cotton Blossom*. One night, with Nola backstage, Kim takes her curtain bow at Broadway's Booth Theater and receives a note informing her that her grandmother has died. She and Magnolia travel to the *Cotton Blossom,* docked in Tennessee, for Parthy's funeral. As soon as Nola steps aboard, she feels that she has returned home. The novel ends with Kim, about to return to New York, turning to see her mother standing on the boat's upper deck, "tall, erect, indomitable," silhouetted against sky and water. Kim cries, "Isn't she splendid. . . . . There's something about her that's eternal and unconquerable—like the River."

Hammerstein's ending, instead, is about community, continuity, and redemption. He refused to kill Andy, whom Ravenal comes to visit on the *Cotton Blossom* after a twenty-three-year absence. The gambler, now sixty-five, has been chastened by life and looks it. He tells Andy he wants to see Nola again and meet his grown-up daughter, who, as in the novel, has become a Broadway star. Andy telegrams the women and asks them to return to the Natchez dock on which the show began, and they do.

With "Make Believe," their love song, playing softly in the background, Nola and Gay see each other. Ravenal is unsure, unsteady. Magnolia simply says his name, as if it's a sweet surprise to reconnect. Now the chorus is quietly humming "Ol' Man River." An elderly woman approaches the couple and says, "I was here on the levee the day you were married. My, how excited we all were. That was a real love match. Well, glad to see it turned out well and you're still happy together. Goodnight." We, the audience, were also at the couple's wedding. That the woman does not know what happened in the intervening years touches the couple and the audience. Ravenal and Magnolia take each other in. Though he seems ready to receive it, she speaks no word of reproach. Forgiveness rather than reunion hangs in the air. Now Joe is singing, "I gets weary and sick of trying" just as Magnolia spots their daughter and points her out—"Look Gay, there's Kim"—and the large chorus takes up the line, "But ol' man river, he just keeps rolling along." It is a thrilling consummation of music and narrative, of dialogue and lyric, of past, present, and future. An epic story ends on an epic emotion, and the musical is born.

Not surprisingly, Hammerstein and Kern each believed it had been his idea to write "Ol' Man River." The Mississippi River is ever present in the novel. By the time she is eight Magnolia "had fallen into and been fished out of every river in the Mississippi Basin from the Gulf of Mexico to Minnesota." The Hawks family lives on the river, drinks its water, and eats its catfish. Andy loses his life in it.

Hammerstein biographer Hugh Fordin reports that, initially, Kern did not see how a river song would be intrinsic to the story and resisted writing it, just as Hammerstein would later resist writing the title number for *Oklahoma!*—emblematic songs are not, in fact, relevant to creators' primary concerns, which revolve around plot and character. Fordin says that Hammerstein studied Kern's score and suggested taking some of the banjo music from "Cotton Blossom" and slowing it down to a dirge. This was the springboard from which Kern started on the song, which they assigned to Joe, thereby promoting an intriguing but minor character and evolving the work's thinking on race.

Kern told friends that he formulated the melody to "Ol' Man River" after hearing Robeson's speaking voice—"those organ-like tones"—in a 1926 play called *Black Boy*. It was one of the first songs Kern and Hammerstein completed for *Show Boat*. Critic Alexander Woollcott recalled getting a "frantic" call from Kern in late 1926 asking for Paul Robeson's phone number. That same day Kern took his new song and drove uptown to Harlem, where he played the number on Robeson's piano. Paul sang while his wife, Essie, listened. Kern couldn't wait for Hammerstein to hear Robeson's rendition; he asked the singer to drive back downtown with him. Unfortunately, Woollcott's story ends with Paul and Essie haggling over cab fare for Paul's return trip. There's no record of Hammerstein hearing Robeson that day.

Because of the delayed opening—Ziegfeld christened his gorgeous new theater in February 1927 with the more conventional *Rio Rita*—Robeson did not take the role of Joe immediately, as he was booked for an international concert tour that fall. In fact, while the cast of *Show Boat* rehearsed in October, Robeson was singing spirituals at the Salle Gaveau in Paris, where five hundred hopeful concertgoers were turned away. At the show's finale, the audience (which included novelist James Joyce) refused to let the singer leave the stage; he gave a full hour of encores.

According to Robert Russell Bennett, who saw an early draft of "Ol' Man River," "It was thirty-two not wholly convincing measures that sounded to me like they wanted to be wanted. In the first place, it starts with two harmonically powerful and self-reliant bars and then comes to a mud puddle and doesn't know where to put its feet for the next two." Bennett only warmed to the song when he heard Hammerstein's lyric, telling Kern, "Gee, that's a great song!" Kern responded sharply, "You didn't say that when I gave it to you before." Bennett writes. "He knew as well as I did that it wasn't a song at all until Oscar came in with the words. Reading them for the first time I was convinced that he was sent here to be a poet."

Early in the show, Joe sings the song as he sits on the dock, looking into the water and meditating on what he sees as its equanimity in the face of all the turmoil on shore:

Dere's an ol' man called de Mississippi
Dat's de ol' man dat I'd like to be
What does he care if de world's got troubles
What does he care if de land ain't free?

Kern's melody uses the pentatonic scale, with five instead of seven different notes per octave. The composer did the same for another, if lesser, song of uplift, "Look for the Silver Lining" from *Sally*. In fact, many spirituals are written using this more constrictive scale. Hammerstein kept Joe's words simple, employing repetition and little rhyming, guessing that the audience would listen more deeply when they understood they were not waiting for the next rhyme. Rhyme bestows sense, the feeling of completing a puzzle; Joe is grappling with a reality beyond sense, beyond articulated meaning. In the chorus, Hammerstein allows himself only near rhyme:

> Ol' man river,
> dat ol' man river
> He mus' know sumpin,'
> but don't say nuthin'
> He jes' keeps rollin'
> He keeps on rollin' along.

Joe projects onto the river some of his own characteristics, primarily an endurance full of grace and mystery. As the sole Black man among the play's major characters, he has access to varieties of human experience not available to the others. He knows more than he wants to know and, like the river, is unable to express his knowledge—not due to his own limitations, but because his experience is inexpressible, literally unspeakable. Still, he owns it; it is a part of him. Whatever comfort or strength he might acquire in this communion with the river is translated through the mournful surge of the melody, which goes where the lyrics cannot (and do not try).

"Ol' Man River" brought out in both Kern and Hammerstein a quality neither had yet exhibited, and one they would not summon again. The song stands apart from other anthems of endurance Hammerstein would write with Richard Rodgers for white characters, like "You'll Never Walk Alone" and its weaker cousin, "Climb Ev'ry Mountain." Unlike those songs, "Ol' Man River" offers no promise of relief except death, no other side of the storm where the "sweet silver song of a lark" awaits, and no assurance that if you keep hope in your heart you will again be made whole. Joe sings:

> Let me go 'way from the Mississippi
> Let me go 'way from the white man boss
> Show me that stream called the river Jordan
> That's the ol' stream that I long to cross.

Part prayer, part soliloquy, "Ol' Man River" acknowledges suffering that remains out of frame. In writing it, Kern and Hammerstein offered a deep bow to the Negro spirituals that Paul Robeson spent years showcasing, songs in which the biblical river Jordan serves as the crossing from slavery to freedom and from life to death. With this song, Kern and Hammerstein

Paul Robeson in *Show Boat*. The great singer and actor was burdened with being a symbol for the country's slow progress toward racial equality.
Courtesy of Photofest

played a central role in opening American popular music to any subject under the sun.

Robeson first played Joe in the 1928 London production, and New York finally saw him in the spring of 1932 in the first of the show's many revivals. Ferber thought it too soon to bring back the show but went to see it nonetheless, mostly so she could catch Robeson's version of "Ol' Man River." She captured her experience in a letter to Woollcott: "I have never seen an ovation like that given any figure of the stage, the concert hall, or the opera. It was completely spontaneous, whole-hearted, and thrilling. . . . That audience stood up and howled. They applauded and shouted and stamped. . . . The show stopped. He sang it again. The show stopped. They called him back again and again. Other actors came out and made motions and their lips moved, but the bravos of the audience drowned all other sounds."

Robeson would be forever linked to the song; it was what audiences always wanted to hear him sing. By the time of the 1936 movie version, though, Robeson's portrayal already seemed out of date; leading African American writers did not approve. Marcus Garvey's magazine wrote that Robeson was using his "genius to appear in pictures and plays that tend to dishonor, mimic, discredit and abuse the cultural attainment of the Black Race." After seeing the film, dancer Bill Robinson ribbed Robeson's wife, Essie, in a letter: "Tell Paul that we saw *Show Boat* twice; just to hear him sing and to get the new way of shelling peas." Robeson left the country soon after, spending four years mostly in Europe and the Soviet Union, where he felt less racial animosity. "Here I am not a Negro but a human being for the first time in my life," he said.

When he returned home Robeson began to alter the lyric in performance, changing "I'm tired of living and scared of dying" to "I must keep fighting until I'm dying." Hammerstein was not pleased. His original line says as much about the human condition as is possible in eight words, and Robeson's replacement did not. The lyricist issued a statement in 1949, saying, "As the author of these words, I have no intention of changing them or permitting anyone else to change them. I further suggest that Paul write his own songs and leave mine alone."

Indeed, Hammerstein's lyric has resounded through the years. In his book *Who Should Sing "Ol' Man River"?* Todd Decker documents how often it was recorded during the civil rights struggles of the 1960s. And in a 2015 *New Yorker* essay about songwriter and performer Sam Cooke, David Cantwell also drew a connection between "Ol' Man River" and the great protest songs of the '60s. Cooke recorded the song on his debut album in 1958, six years before he wrote "A Change Is Gonna Come," with its Hammersteinian lyric "It's been too hard livin', but I'm afraid to die."

Says Cantwell, "'Ol' Man River' was intended to evoke minstrel songs of ante-and post-bellum America—while subverting their sympathies." In the melody he finds shades of Stephen Foster as well as Dan Emmett's "Dixie." "In this way the song provided a crucial bridge in popular culture between the nineteenth and twentieth centuries," in essence "forcing 'Dixie' to switch sides." Cantwell continues:

> One way of reading this story is to note that racism isn't the only thing that lingers in America. Musical forms also persist. Sometimes, the old tunes will be tools that we can use—recycled or repurposed, sampled for the dance floor or shouted in a crowd, to aid in work that still needs to be done. "A Change Is Gonna Come" . . . was a long time coming, its genesis stretching a hundred and fifty years and longer, from "Blowin' in the Wind" to "No More Auction Block," from "Ol' Man River" all the way back to "Dixie," and through countless other songs and people besides. Listen to the record today and you can hear a story that's ongoing.

Interviewed by Arnold Michaelis in 1959, Hammerstein recalled how unlikely it was, in 1927, for Ziegfeld to produce a show like *Show Boat*. "He had never done a play with a story before," said Hammerstein. "And I think that before we opened, he expected *Show Boat* to be a pretty big bore, and he thought all that story stuff would be cut out and what would remain would be the pretty costumes and scenery and the girls and the comedian. And I know that the night before we opened in Washington he was very discouraged and nervous and started to lose his patience."

Ziegfeld had started out as a huge fan of the show, or at least of Kern's, writing, "This is the best musical comedy I have ever been fortunate to get hold of." But he discovered later that he had overestimated the comedy part, and he blamed Hammerstein for the project's seriousness. He sent Kern the following telegram dated March 3, 1927:

> I feel Hammerstein not keen on my doing *Show Boat*. I am very keen on doing it on account of your music but Hammerstein book in present shape has not got a chance except with critics but with the public no, and I have stopped producing for critics and empty houses. . . . I am told Hammerstein never did anything alone. His present layout too serious. Not enough comedy. . . . If Hammerstein will fix the book I want to do it. If he refuses to change it or allow anyone else to be called in if necessary, you and he return the advances.

This conveys something of the pressure on Hammerstein at this pivotal moment. But in fact Ziegfeld's long delay in opening the show in New York—from February until, it turned out, late December 1927—was crucial to *Show Boat*'s success. During that unexpectedly free time Hammerstein underwent the revelation of his life, an event that opened him up to every feeling in the human lexicon, as only falling in love can do.

Later that March Hammerstein sailed on the *Olympia* to direct a production of *The Desert Song* in London. As Myra would be joining him later, he boarded the luxury liner joined by his trusty lawyer and boyhood friend Howard Reinheimer. Just before saying his goodbyes, Reinheimer introduced Hammerstein to a couple he knew onboard—businessman Henry Jacobson and his Tasmanian-born wife, Dorothy. The latter was twenty-eight years old, athletic, slim, and tall, with thick chestnut hair, blue eyes ("soul-filling" in Hammerstein's words), strong cheekbones, a turned-down mouth, and a regal bearing. Hammerstein was at once smitten. Perhaps he felt an impulse to turn his life upside down, given that he was engaged in the deepest work of his career and knew he had not plumbed its depths.

On his first morning at sea, Oscar, who always started his day with exercise, walked the deck. He passed Dorothy, also strolling, and they exchanged hellos. He kept going but soon after passed her again; this time they laughed as they acknowledged each other. The third time he passed her, she was sitting on a deck chair, and he asked if he could sit by her. Immediately they both felt the frisson of a meaningful and illicit encounter. He told her about the show he was going to London to direct, and she admitted she wasn't a fan of operetta, where "people seemed to sing down each other's throats." They shared their stories and found they each had Scottish blood on their mother's side. Dorothy's father, Henry Blanchard, was a British sea captain who spent most of his life between Tasmania and Melbourne, where Dorothy was raised. When she was seventeen she married another sailor, William Thomas Meikle, who went off to serve in France and did not come back. Five years later Dorothy alleged desertion and filed for divorce in August 1922.

That same month Dorothy left Melbourne for London, thinking she might try acting. Her agent sent Ziegfeld her photo, and he hired her for the *Follies,* though her mother begged her not to take the part. She turned down Ziegfeld but went to New York anyway, where she landed a small role

Tasmanian-born Dorothy Blanchard Jacobson (*left*) played the part of smoke on an ashtray in a Broadway revue until, understandably, she grew bored. She and Oscar married in 1929. They were photographed (*right*) on their return from their honeymoon.
Left: Courtesy of the Hammerstein family; *right:* Courtesy of Library of Congress

in André Charlot's 1924 revue while also understudying the star, Beatrice Lillie. Dressed in gray chiffon, Dorothy played the part of smoke on an ashtray. Understandably, she soon became bored. To Oscar she admitted that she'd been a bit disappointed that theater life was not as "wicked" as she'd imagined it. This offhand comment inspired one of *Show Boat's* most delightful numbers, "Life upon the Wicked Stage," sung by the similarly disappointed Ellie.

Oscar and Dorothy spoke as much as possible throughout the voyage, and he confessed that his work up until then had not satisfied him. He wondered aloud if he could ever achieve what he wanted, which was to capture something real in a musical. It's not known whether he thought *Show Boat* might be that musical. Once docked in London, the couple continued their discussions in Green Park. Then Myra arrived. Perhaps intuiting what was going on, she immediately confessed to Dorothy that she had left a lover in New York and asked Dorothy if she had one, too, which no doubt increased Dorothy's sympathy for Oscar.

When everyone returned to New York, Oscar went back to working on *Show Boat*. Sometimes weeks would go by with no word from Ziegfeld, and the waiting was hard. Then, in the summer of 1927, Dorothy discovered she was pregnant. She decided she must give her marriage another try, so she told Oscar she could no longer see him. Oscar was devastated. He buried himself in work, taking on two more operettas: *The New Moon* with Romberg and *Golden Dawn*. The latter Arthur commissioned to inaugurate his own new theater, Hammerstein's, a basilica-like showcase on the ground floor of a thirteen-story building. Built as a tribute to Oscar I, the theater featured towering arches, a huge dome, and stained-glass panels that depicted operas produced by the impresario. Arthur also ensconced his father's silk top hat and a hand-rolled cigar in the building's cornerstone (which surely goes unnoticed today by visitors to the theater's current occupant, *The Late Show with Stephen Colbert*).

Golden Dawn opened Hammerstein's Theatre a month before *Show Boat*'s premiere at the nearby Ziegfeld. Like *Show Boat* it featured Black and white actors together onstage. Oscar cowrote the book with Harbach, and Arthur hired Emmerich Kálmán in Vienna to compose the music along with Herbert Stothart. Wanting the show to be a family affair, Arthur tasked Reggie with overseeing the nonmusical staging.

Set in colonial East Africa in 1917, *Golden Dawn* is a terribly odd show today, though it fit into the evolving operetta market of the time. It features a love affair between a white planter and Dawn, a young woman believed to be African. The crowning reveal in its convoluted story is that Dawn is in fact white, making possible her happy marriage to the planter. Arthur employed African Americans for the chorus, but he hired the Australian Robert Chisholm to play the lead Black character, Shep Keyes, in blackface.

As for thinking seriously about race or African culture, the musical does not at all. As Kate Edney writes in a New York Public Library blog post about *Golden Dawn:*

> The first racist trope is that a black man who considers himself equal to white men is villainous—a trope or archetype embodied by the character of Shep Keyes. In the plot and character outline for the musical, the description of Shep is worth quoting at length. He is "a negro of dominating force with some little education. His cleverness, his shrewdness, his fists and his whip have made him the leader of the colored workers. He arrived about a year

> ago, from nowhere. He seems to know a great deal about America and has been known to utter such words as 'Harlem,' '135th street,' and 'Pullman Porter,' words quite beyond the intelligence of the native African negro." . . . Shep, with his hinted-at urban roots, attempts a direct assault against accepted social norms and is clearly the villain as a result.

Oscar was working on *Golden Dawn* as he was finishing *Show Boat*. I'm guessing he was simply giving Arthur what he asked for in terms of story. The critics liked the songs and the singing of opera star Louise Hunter as Dawn, but they recognized that the plot was a mess. Walter Winchell dubbed it *Golden Yawn*. Atkinson reviewed the building, calling it "a Gothic theater which breathes a cathedral air," and he ended by saying he hoped the theater would become an institution. Although Arthur lost the theater a few years later in the Depression, in a way Atkinson's wish for it came true. It would later be home to *The Ed Sullivan Show* (and therefore to the Beatles' American TV debut in 1964) and to *Late Show with David Letterman*. When Stephen Colbert took over the *Late Show* in 2015, he and his team uncovered several original architectural details, including the gigantic dome on which Colbert's show projects digital images (one of which is the original pattern, which was overseen by Arthur Hammerstein in 1927).

Since Oscar was so downhearted when writing *Golden Dawn*, I scoured the score (thanks to Amy Asch's *Complete Lyrics of Oscar Hammerstein II*) for signs of a lost soul, and I found some moony lyrics. "I need your consolation / Just a touch of tender demonstration . . . I'll let no one console me but you alone" goes the song "Consolation." And there's this, from "Here in the Dark":

> Here in your arms I'd while away eternity
> Here's the end of time and space—
> There's no other place,
> There's no other world
> When you're with me.

Show Boat rehearsals began in September for a November 15 opening at the National Theatre in Washington, DC. On opening night, when the curtain rang down for intermission, the audience was quiet for five seconds—an eternity—during which Ziegfeld was sure he had been right that the damned thing *was* too serious. But the silence was broken by wild applause; the audience had simply been momentarily stunned by what they'd seen.

There was no ovation, however, at the final curtain, because the spectators were exhausted. At that point the show ran almost five hours, and people were aching to get home. Robert Russell Bennett recalled looking down at his watch "with such tired eyes that nobody should quote me, but I saw it as seventeen minutes till one a.m." The *Washington Times* critic said it was 12:40. Hammerstein and Kern instituted cuts for the next day's matinee. For the following few weeks they hardly left their hotel rooms in DC, Cleveland, and Philadelphia, subsisting on room-service steaks and Worcestershire sauce as they further trimmed the show.

Finally, the show was set to open at Ziegfeld's 1,600-seat theater on December 27. That evening, Brooks Atkinson went to see *Paris Bound,* a Philip Barry play at the Music Box. He figured he could catch up later with the new Kern show. Nine blocks north the Ziegfeld's grand art deco exterior was dramatically lit, and the audience mingled in front of a billboard touting "a new musical comedy." They no doubt expected a standard opening number—an unnecessary song that tells the audience to relax and stop talking as latecomers take their seats.

Instead, when the lights went down, the first sound the audience heard was a heavy, prolonged minor chord—a dirgelike call to attention. Then, an overture lush with gorgeous melodies. Despite bright bursts of the "Cotton Blossom" tune, the medley was dominated by the recurrent dark thread of a song called "Mis'ry's Comin' Aroun'," a musical approximation of dread, beautifully rendered. (The song was cut for time after DC but stayed in the overture.)

The curtain rises on a sight previously undepicted in musical theater: Black men loading and unloading heavy items on the levee. As they work and sweat in the imagined hot sun, the first words the audience hears are the following:

> Niggers all work on the Mississippi
> Niggers all work while the white man plays
> Loadin' up boats with the bales of cotton
> Gettin' no rest till the Judgment Day.

On come the white folk, dressed in light linens, carrying pretty silk parasols, strolling, chatting, and flirting. All they have on their minds is a good time. *Their* chorus sounds like a typical Ziegfeld opening:

Cotton Blossom, Cotton Blossom
Captain Andy's Floating Show!
Thrills and laughter,
Concert after,
Everybody's sure to go!

Had the musical started with this white chorus, it would have ended with the wedding of Magnolia and Ravenal. But it started with the Black chorus. Though a few Broadway musicals had featured multiracial casts before, they had kept the choruses segregated. None had offered the stark and telling juxtaposition that opens *Show Boat*. The first thing this show says is that Black and white realities coexist, and neither one is possible without the other. This is a sea change in musical theater. We have gathered here tonight, this opening suggests, to address the character of our country.

The best way to experience this merging of song and story is certainly not the 1936 film version of *Show Boat*. Though both director James Whale and Hammerstein attempted to make the film as close a record of the original stage version as possible, a contemporary viewer will be distracted, if not affronted, by racial stereotypes. Aproned and sporting a white kerchief on her head, Hattie McDaniel as Queenie is the very image of Aunt Jemima, a stock character that originated in minstrel shows of the 1880s. McDaniel was criticized for taking on so many of these roles, but her acting is quite compelling. (In the original stage production Queenie was played by Tess Gardella, a white actor in blackface who went by the stage name of Aunt Jemima.) Queenie constantly refers to Joe, played by Paul Robeson, as lazy, and, as if to give her accusations credence, Robeson seems to walk, talk, and think at a glacial pace. Other details, such as the way the actors in the Negro crowd wave excitedly at the *Cotton Blossom*, are cringe-inducing. Further, the songs' pacing will sound stiff and stodgy to contemporary ears.

However, thanks to the efforts of John McGlinn, a conductor and historian, there exists a version of *Show Boat*, recorded in 1988 for the EMI/Angel label, that plunges the willing listener into the fullness of this extraordinary moment for the American musical. As any fan of cast albums can tell you, the purely aural is an intense delivery system for story. Great recordings distill a show's meaning because, absent visual stimulation, the listener hears more deeply. Minute care and attention are usually brought to such recordings because the show's creators know they will be the best document of that live show (which is why cast albums are usually so much better than film soundtracks). In fact, it was the popularity of *Oklahoma!* in 1943 that produced the first widely purchased cast album, bought by more than a million fans, many of whom listened until they memorized every nuance. Hammerstein and Rodgers commented on this phenomenon in the liner notes for the 1958 soundtrack recording of *South Pacific:*

> Just as stage pantomime and ballet have developed ways of telling stories without words, so have record albums like this one created in recent years the newer art of telling a story to the ear without benefit of what the eye can see. . . . If you find, as we do, that these records are unusually "alive," if the personalities of the singers and the characters they play seem to emerge as you listen to them, it is because the songs were recorded with as much concern for their dramatic significance as for their vocal and orchestral performances.

McGlinn surveyed all the available iterations of the score and, using Bennett's stunning arrangements, put together the definitive version of the complete score (though not necessarily of role interpretation, which is ever shifting; for me, Frederica von Stade makes a stuffy Magnolia and I much prefer Rebecca Luker in the 1994 recording of Hal Prince's production). McGlinn restored the numbers that had been cut between the show's progress from Washington to Broadway and from later productions, including essential dispatches from the world of Queenie and Joe like "Mis'ry's Comin' Aroun'" and "Hey, Feller." McGlinn also restored Hammerstein's magnificent original ending, which director James Whale had severely trimmed.

To underline the seriousness of the project and the show's cultural import, McGlinn cast mostly opera singers for the major roles, featuring von Stade, Teresa Stratas as Julie, Jerry Hadley as Gaylord Ravenal, and Bruce Hubbard as Joe. From the musical theater he cast Paige O'Hara as Ellie, producing the most entertaining version of "Life upon the Wicked Stage" that I have ever heard. And casting silent film star Lillian Gish as the old woman who approaches Gay and Nola in the restored finale viscerally links the recording to the 1920s.

Finding the first arrangement for "Ol' Man River," McGlinn told the *New York Times,* "was like cleaning off an old painting and finding the original colors." Over the years, performers responded to the song's innate grandeur with extravagant production values. There is no better example of the cognitive dissonance of this approach than Frank Sinatra's rendition in the 1946 MGM tribute to Jerome Kern, *Till the Clouds Roll By.* Sinatra—a slim thirty-one-year-old in a white suit, white bow tie, and white shoes—is surrounded by a hundred musicians and dancers on a huge white pedestal that seems to float in clouds. Everything is white, including large kettle drums and long garlands of flowers trailing the female dancers. "Originally it wasn't a huge bombastic number but a simple folk song with sustained strings, a little oboe and bells," said McGlinn.

Like anyone who produces *Show Boat,* McGlinn ran into what he calls "the obstacle of the show": the intersection at which an African American demand to be portrayed with dignity collides with a white artist's attempt to represent race relations as they existed at a given time. I think it's worth noting that if *Show Boat* finds itself today in the crosshairs of a debate about racist works of art, it is because Hammerstein and Kern were among the rare commercial writers moved to examine aspects of their own country they found shameful.

Reviewing the London production for the *Amsterdam News,* J. A. Rogers objected only to parts of the show. He called *Show Boat* "one of the most snappy and sparkling plays I have ever seen" and declared, "Rarely have I laughed so much." He thought the white lead actors were "unusually good," but he saw the character of Joe as a "lazy, good-natured, lolling darkey that exists more in white men's fancy than in reality." He noted that the only way forward was for African Americans to write their own plays, though he predicted that "it will be a long time before this is done."

Audiences, theater artists, and scholars continue to debate a work so rich. Todd Decker, who has written two invaluable books on *Show Boat,* argues that, as decades pass, new productions bring with them new styles of acting and dancing, which in turn allow directors to tell different narratives within the larger story. Just as the vocal frills of an actor playing Hamlet from the early twentieth century sound intolerably stiff to us in 2023, many aspects of the original *Show Boat* would no doubt seem racist now. However, the show—unlike the novel or movie—is malleable. A director or actor who sees Queenie as multidimensional can give us a Queenie without condescension, whom we can recognize and understand today.

Of course, the first problem facing any new production is the first word of the musical. Hammerstein used the N-word in that position as a declaration of intent, for what author Jody Armour calls the "jagged-edged N-word's unparaphrasable power." In Hammerstein's lifetime, he allowed the substitution of "darkies," "colored folks," and the completely denuded "Here we all work on the Mississippi." I wish he had said what he thought about the following questions: Can we create meaningful works about our past by altering the language that people used? Does softening the language risk softening the outrage the language should provoke in us?

For McGlinn, the answer was clear. "'Nigger' is a hateful word," he told the *New York Times,* "but it's there for shock value, to stun an audience and make them think about what conditions were like in those days." When he reinstated the N-word for his recording, his African American chorus withdrew from the project in protest. Under deadline pressure, McGlinn asked the Ambrosian Chorus, a British group singing the white chorus, to perform both parts. Bruce Hubbard remained in the role of Joe. "The way the word was used once is not fiction but fact," he said. "Blacks today may want to forget the past and build on the future, but we should never lose our sense of history."

In *"Show Boat": Performing Race in an American Musical,* Decker concludes that *Show Boat* was "first in a line of shows that used music and dance to explore what it has meant to be black *and* white in America." He goes on to say that Hammerstein's book displays an awareness that concepts of whiteness and Blackness are equally performed and conditioned by social realities. He calls the show "the most important musical ever made," an attribute that "necessitated its remaking again and again."

After *Show Boat,* the world went on apparently unchanged, even in places you might think would have taken note. In the February 1929 issue of *Theatre Magazine,* for instance, the writer and producer Laurence Schwab penned a piece called "How to Write a Successful Musical Comedy," in which he advised, "Do not attempt too much sophistication . . . as only comedy which is written and played in broad strokes is successful." Schwab was known for writing the book to *Good News,* a "hotcha" musical (Schwab's word), which means it was high-spirited and centered on college romance. With a toe-tapping score by B. G. DeSylva, Lew Brown, and Ray Henderson, it preceded *Show Boat* on Broadway by a mere two and a half months and enjoyed great success.

Schwab, who also sold Hammerstein the land on which he built his Long Island estate, had the opportunity to argue his theory with Hammerstein; together, along with Frank Mandel, they cowrote *The New Moon,* the 1928 Sigmund Romberg operetta that would be the composer's last big Broadway hit. (Of that show Hammerstein later remembered attending the 1927 Philadelphia tryout and overhearing an audience member say, "They can never fix this one if they work for the rest of their lives.")

One subject we know Schwab and Hammerstein discussed was Myra Finn. Discreet Oscar would not have talked about his wife with a colleague unless he was off-balance, and indeed he was in early 1928. Dorothy was heavily pregnant and still refusing to see him. Myra now knew about the affair, and she promised to make his life unpleasant if he pushed for a divorce. Hoping to help, his friend Leighton Brill told him that Myra had indeed been unfaithful to him. Oscar turned to Schwab, who confirmed that Myra's infidelities were widely known.

The news that everyone around him knew about Myra, combined with Dorothy's desertion, flattened Oscar. He missed the September opening of *The New Moon* and committed himself to Alice Fuller Leroy's Leroy Sanitarium on Sixty-First Street and Madison Avenue. This was a new kind of hospital meant for wealthy folks that was run like an intimate hotel. There Oscar was subjected to hydrotherapy, meaning he was given cold baths and wrapped in sheets. There were also warm packs and hours of enforced rest. He returned to a version of the coping technique he'd invented after his mother's death: he recited the names of baseball players as a mantra to pull himself through.

Perhaps eager to be released from the cold baths and isolation, Oscar discharged himself after only two weeks. He emerged to find that in his time away his problems had rather sorted themselves out—Dorothy went dancing with him, and Myra was ready to negotiate a divorce.

Twenty-five years later Hammerstein would write a fond and funny version of Myra in Ado Annie, the girl who can't say no. In the original Riggs play, Annie is shy, awkward, and not at all bright, a hick on whom Laurey takes pity. Hammerstein changed her utterly, giving her a firecracker wit and making her so boy crazy that when a fella comes a-courtin' she thinks of "that old golden rule" and does for him "what he would do fer me." It's interesting to note, however, that an earlier fictional Myra was the acquisitive, unappealing Jenny in *Allegro,* which we'll get to in another chapter.

In November Oscar attended the premiere of *Rainbow,* his musical about gold miners working their way from Missouri to San Francisco in 1849. Youmans wrote the score, and Busby Berkeley choreographed. The show broke new ground by featuring murders in both the first and second acts. Interestingly, Hammerstein's collaborator on the book was Laurence Stallings, the librettist and lyricist of *Deep River.* According to Hugh Fordin, it was Stallings who suggested they work together. And though audiences stayed away from *Rainbow* and it closed within a month, Brooks Atkinson noticed the show's ambitions. After a second visit, he wrote, "No musical play with a spacious historical theme has been produced with so much artistic integrity." About its prompt closing he wrote, "The present commentator is unwilling to believe that such a broad-gauged swapping of yarns about an American epoch deserves failure in what the braggarts describe as the capital of the world theatre."

Despite the setback, Hammerstein was finding steady ground because he was at last free of his marriage. Dorothy, though, got brutal news. Her husband, Henry Jacobson, said that if she were to end their union, the couple's four-year-old son would stay with him. Dorothy would keep Susan, only seven months old, with her. Even on those terms, she determined she had to go.

To obtain a quick divorce in 1929, those who could afford it traveled to Nevada, which required only a six-week residency to legally end a marriage. So, from January through part of February 1929, Dorothy Jacobson established herself at the Riverside Hotel, *the* spot in Reno for sophisticated divorcées-in-waiting. Beset by anxiety, the couple experienced this as their most intensely emotional period. Oscar was at work on the East Coast, and he poured out his passion, as well as doubts and quicksilver jealousies, in a series of letters to Dorothy. With a lover's instinct, he started tentatively:

> Dear darling:
>
> I hope it doesn't annoy you when I write with a pencil. I hate a pen. I don't feel as tho I'm quite myself with a pen.

He recalled the last outfit he saw her wearing—a "white frock held up with devilishly provocative shoulder ends"—and the memory rattled him so much he forgot the word "straps." Sweetly, he signed off with "Good-bye for a little while, dear wife," though they were not yet married.

For the rest of his career Hammerstein fetishized the state of being on the threshold of a relationship, a heightened condition whose delights he never tired of reliving. From "A Kiss to Build a Dream On" to "All the Things You Are" to "So Far" to "I Have Dreamed," he was a poet of the anticipation of joy. And it should come as no surprise that the future author of "Some Enchanted Evening" penned a rapturous love letter. In a January 1929 missive to Dorothy he wrote, "You have punctuated the last two years of my life with many, beautiful, breath-taking moments. This afternoon's adds to the string—I will never forget kissing you good-bye. I felt so tender, so protective that I didn't dare yield to that funny impulse I have to cry about you. You were being so brave and I knew every word you weren't saying. Oh, thank God for you and the beauty you bring to me."

They were inventing the nicknames and private language they would use their whole lives. For the tiny Myra, who stood five feet tall in heels, they used the hilarious code name of Jumbo. For their most *intime* gushings, they sounded like any other happy couple: "Oh, my baby, baby, baby," wrote Oscar. "Wouldn't that irrelevant outburst look silly to anyone but you!"

In laying out the groundwork for what he expected from the marriage, Oscar showed himself to be a man of his time rather than a visionary on human autonomy or gender equality. He had firm ideas about how a man and a woman, but particularly a woman, should behave. In his longest and most florid letter (dated only "Saturday"), he said that "every day, many times a day I think of things I'll do to make you happy and make you feel like the queen you were born to be," enumerating the forms his worship would take. In the next paragraph he addressed Dorothy's apparently close friendship with a man named Bill Mellen, who told her that "all husbands—new, ex- or otherwise—are perfect asses." This "flippant comment," Hammerstein wrote, proves that Bill "is in love with you. . . . I say all this with the full realization that he is a fine man." He ended with a direct confession that prefigures the possessive Will Parker in *Oklahoma!*: "I love you. I am jealous. All the other men in the world must be as specks. If they grow to blots, they must be stamped out. That's my platform. If you vote for me, you vote for that policy—please don't forget that—and don't forget I love you to the exclusion of all else. I want us to give each other EVERYTHING—or the show's no good."

By January, Oscar was counting down the days until the end of their estrangement and looking forward to "the best of all possible worlds"—when they would at last be together, never again to leave each other's sides. "Dear, we must literally keep the rule of never spending a single night away from each other—even when it involves inconveniences," he wrote.

This was understandable given their history—Oscar was traveling without Myra when he met Dorothy on the deck of the *Olympia*. Ten years after their marriage Oscar remained touchy if Dorothy did not stay in close contact while on the road; in June 1939 she was in London and piqued her husband's ire by not writing. He scolded her by letter:

> There are new flowers in the garden, and all the bushes on the right side of the drive are now in bloom, but it is all obscured in a milky fog just now, very much as your absence bedims my normal joy of living. You have not done much to brighten this dimness. Since you left you sent me one radio-gram, and then a second (after I forced it out of you by my radio-gram to Milton). I don't understand such fundamental neglect. I have worked out several possible explanations but I don't like any of them.

By March 1929 Dorothy had served her time in Reno, and the lovers briefly reunited. Just before their May wedding, however, Oscar went alone down to Palm Beach, Florida, to work with Kern on a show called *Sweet Adeline*.

Life was good. Back at work with his favorite writing partner, Oscar wrote to Dorothy, "I know other good showmen, but when they have an opinion they express themselves so awkwardly that you have to puzzle out what they are driving at. Jerry is an intelligent analyst who can give clear reasons. This lightens my burden considerably."

Kern had recently sold his prized book collection, including first editions of Dickens, Thackeray, and Hardy, and purchased a yacht, *The Show Boat*, which Edna Ferber herself christened. When the two men were not working, they fished or sailed. Oscar floated in premarriage bliss. He wrote to Dorothy from Palm Beach:

> I've been away from "Old Broadway" so long [it had been six months] that I am quite thrilled by the activity I have barged into, and to realize again how important I evidently am. I know you are unsympathetic with that side of me, but with all my good resolutions about only doing two shows a year, when I see Ziegfeld, or Arthur, or Frank, and they talk of plots, and possible actors and actresses to engage, and where to get the scenery painted, and when I hear Kern, or Gershwin, or Romberg play pretty tunes to me, I start to race ahead breathlessly with the possibilities behind each suggestion. Even if I didn't get any money for it, I'd want to meddle in everything, and get ideas, and watch for the way they hit audiences in their final form. . . . My dream is to settle down with my beautiful wife, with my beautiful girl, and aim only to write masterpieces, or nothing. It will be lovely if some of them are masterpieces, and if they're not, I'll still be the happiest man in the world.

Hammerstein naturally wanted to express the large emotions he was experiencing at this time, and one of the results was a song called "Why Was I Born?" He wrote the lyric for Helen Morgan, the original Julie in *Show Boat.* Morgan's trademark as a torch singer was to suffer nobly while sitting on a piano ("Nobody Wants Me" was her signature number). While Hammerstein was ostensibly writing to Morgan's woeful quality, "Why Was I Born?" is more befitting a philosopher than a brokenhearted lover. I was curious how this song, which seeks to ask and answer the mother of existential questions, fit into *Sweet Adeline,* a musical about a Hoboken waitress who becomes a singing star at the turn of the century. In fact, Hammerstein barely attempts to fit it into the show, which focuses on the dating and mating of a group of young people who never emerge as distinct characters. In one scene Adeline decides she must march from the beer garden where she works to a nearby theater in order to demand that a member of the acting troupe stop flirting with her sister. The actors take one look at her, decide she must be in their show, and hand her a song: "Why Was I Born?" Though barely integrated into the play, it's a unique song, unusual in its metaphysical yearning.

■ ■ ■

Oscar and Dorothy tied the knot on May 13, 1929, at the Belvedere Hotel in Baltimore, joined by a small cadre of friends. The couple looked remarkably elegant. Slim Oscar, with his soulful eyes and contented smile, was dressed in a wide-breasted suit, his hair lightly brilliantined, and Dorothy wore a long-sleeved white dress with a garland of flowers around her shoulders. In classic Reggie fashion, Oscar's younger brother missed the wedding entirely—he was seeing a girlfriend off on an ocean voyage and failed to disembark before the ship left port.

Oscar, Dorothy, and one-year-old Susan set up house in the Weylin Hotel on East Fifty-Fourth Street. The stock market crashed that October, but it took a while for well-off people like Oscar and his friends to feel it. Some of them were fruitfully engaged in the movie musicals of the 1930s and therefore were never hard hit by the Great Depression. Though he worked throughout the decade and enjoyed a couple of noteworthy stage successes, Oscar grew increasingly aware that he was no longer in great demand. And so, for Oscar, the 1930s would present more of a spiritual struggle than a financial one: he was always working, but never on something that mattered.

CHAPTER FOUR

Dark Decade

IN THE WAKE OF BLACK TUESDAY—which kicked off the great stock market crash of 1929—Hollywood concerned itself with how best to meet the country's psychic needs. At the same time the studios were still puzzling out how to capitalize on the success of 1927's feature-length talkie *The Jazz Singer,* and they decided, as if in joint agreement, that musicals were the answer. Days after the crash, virtually every librettist and songwriter working on Broadway received an invitation to go west. In early December, Oscar, Dorothy, and baby Susan boarded the *20th Century Limited* at Grand Central Station for the twenty-hour trip to Chicago, where they switched to the *Santa Fe Chief* for an additional forty hours of luxury travel to California. Soon to join them were Sigmund Romberg, Jerome Kern, Otto Harbach, Richard Rodgers, Lorenz Hart, and a score of others.

For some reason Warner Bros. teamed Hammerstein with Romberg, and Harbach with Kern. Hammerstein and Romberg found the studio's offer to their liking—four operettas over two years, $100,000 per man per score, and the ads would feature their names over that of the stars. With an offer like that, you could not only ride out the Depression with ease but also shape the course of the emerging musical-picture genre.

Oscar began his tenure in Hollywood with total commitment. He turned down a request to write a stage show for his Uncle Arthur, who was not pleased and complained in a January 1930 letter to Harbach, "Oscar has practically given me to understand he will not write again for Broadway. People forget so readily of days when they were assisted in preparing their future. Enough said."

Rodgers and Hart also landed at Warner Bros. The pair had broken through in May 1925 with *The Garrick Gaieties,* a show billed as "a bubbling musical satirical revue of plays, problems and persons." What began as a two-night fundraiser for the Theatre Guild morphed into a sensation. At the conductor's podium Rodgers watched the audience "cheering, yelling, stomping, waving and whistling" as the show ended. He turned back to the musicians and had them reprise the number that had caused the audience's euphoria, a song called "Manhattan." "The cast sang it, the musicians sang it, even the audience sang it," he recalled. "After about ten curtain calls, the house lights went on, but still no one wanted to go." Today "Manhattan," a paean to the charms of all five boroughs, remains a standard. Rodgers was only twenty-three years old; Hart, thirty.

The following year the pair debuted two more addictive songs: "Mountain Greenery" from the second installment of *The Garrick Gaieties,* and, from a show called *The Girl Friend,* a miracle of a tune called "Blue Room." Simplicity itself, the melody has an unhurried beauty, capturing the enchantment of lovers who want nothing more from life than to be together. While the lyrics come off as informal and conversational, Hart had put much thought into conjuring just the right nonchalance. After speaking with another young lyricist named Ira Gershwin at a Writers Guild meeting in March 1926, Hart was eager to follow up, writing to him, "It is a great pleasure to live at a time when light amusement in this country is at last losing its brutally cretin aspect. Such delicacies as your jingles prove that songs can be both popular and intelligent."

Rodgers was sixteen when his brother's friend took him one block from his family's home on West 120th Street to meet Hart at the West 119th Street brownstone the lyricist shared with his parents. That Sunday Rodgers played some of his own compositions on the Hart family piano. He'd been influenced by the comic operas his mother loved, such as *The Merry Widow, The Spring Maid,* and *The Chocolate Soldier.* "This is what I was weaned on, and these were the happy moments in my childhood," said Rodgers, who grew up in a house of constant turmoil. His quick-tempered father, Will, hated his in-laws, who lived with the family. "People literally didn't speak to each other in that sad house," wrote Rodgers's daughter Mary, "except when they were screaming." Her father recalled, "And I turned to this, this kind of melodic construction, the way you turn to food."

Hart said he loved Rodgers's melodies. The lyricist shared his ideas about the relationship of words and music, what kinds of thoughts and emotions could be expressed on the stage, and what kind of music would be needed to support them. The pair dissected the Princess musicals and shared their dissatisfaction with the current crop of shows. "He felt that musical shows were cowardly, responded only to formula, and said nothing," Rodgers recalled.

And so began a twenty-four-year partnership that produced twenty-eight stage shows and more than five hundred songs, dozens of which fans and critics refer to as timeless.

Socially Hart was ebullient, an antic spirit; Hammerstein said he was "always skipping and bouncing. In all the times I knew him, I never saw him walk slowly. I never saw his face in repose. I never heard him chuckle quietly. He laughed loudly and easily at other people's jokes, and at his own, too." Mary Rodgers had a distinct visual memory of him smoking a big black cigar and rubbing his hands together energetically, a trademark gesture of his. (Theresa Helburn also recalled him "beating his hands as he walked up and down.") "Because of his height," wrote Mary, "I thought of him not only as younger than Daddy (though he was, in fact, seven years older) but almost as a child. He certainly had a child's sense of delight and irresponsibility."

Hart lavished gifts on friends, though some sensed a compensatory component in his generosity, as if he did not expect his affection to be returned without bribes. Hart had a handsome face and brilliant, dark eyes, but, standing slightly less than five feet tall and sporting an oversized head, he did not like his own appearance. He was a closeted gay person who disappeared into alcohol-soaked debaucheries with increasing frequency. Even at the start of his partnership with Rodgers, Hart was frequently missing in action. He could never focus on writing before noon. He would say he had to go downstairs for a cigar and proceed to vanish for the rest of the day. The youthful Rodgers accepted that half of his job was to locate Hart and keep him from drinking. Rodgers found "it was never wise to leave him alone because he would simply disappear and would have to be found all over again." At times Rodgers would force Hart to sit and play tunes to stimulate

Richard and Dorothy Rodgers in the 1930s.
Courtesy of Photofest

him. "Larry would not write the word 'hello' unless I was in the room with him," said the composer.

In 1930 Rodgers married another beautiful Dorothy, a well-to-do young lady who had just turned twenty. Their parents were acquaintances; in fact, Dick had first spied Dorothy Feiner when he was seven and she was still in her baby carriage. Dorothy grew up in New York Jewish high society; the parties she attended were covered in the newspapers, her family traveled extensively, and she bought her clothes in Paris and her shoes in Rome on "exhausting day-long safaris," said Mary. With her swan's neck and wavy brown hair, large eyes and slim figure, Dorothy radiated impeccable taste and poise. And she was categorically in love with her composer. Each added to the other's considerable glamour. They married at the Feiner apartment at 270 Park Avenue on January 12, 1930.

They were the couple everyone wanted to know. On their honeymoon

Elsa Maxwell, famed host to international society, threw a party in Rome and introduced them to barons and counts. From there they went to the French Riviera and then Paris, where they dined with Alexander Woollcott and continued to party with Maxwell's famous friends. Dick was already quite the jetsetter and counted Lord and Lady Mountbatten and Prince George among his acquaintances. The Prince of Wales let it be known he was a great fan.

Mr. and Mrs. Rodgers installed themselves in London's Marylebone neighborhood, near Regent's Park. "It drove Mummy crazy," wrote Mary, "that Larry Hart, having been invited to the wedding, came along for the honeymoon." It took Hart, living on the top floor, just two days to flood the couple's townhouse when he forgot to turn off the bath. Dorothy soon found out she was pregnant, and the couple returned to New York, where her doctor (Dick's brother Mort, an arrangement she found humiliating) recommended bed rest. Dick then traveled solo to Los Angeles to make his first film, *The Hot Heiress*. For Dorothy, the bicoastal arrangement only increased the difficulties and insecurities of a new marriage.

After scoring the film, Rodgers sailed from New York to London, where he joined Hart to finish a musical called *Ever Green*. Mary estimates that her father was bringing in about $5,000 a week at this time. These were the days when the rich made the four-day journey from New York to London in high fashion aided by a full service staff; moreover, such voyages were often just as much about pleasure as business. Both Oscar Hammersteins met future wives on ocean liners, and Dick and Dorothy had reintroduced themselves as adults in 1926 aboard the RMS *Majestic*. On this summer night in 1930, Dick dined at the captain's table—a mark of status that came by way of engraved invitation—drinking brandy and conversing with an attractive woman. He returned to his cabin alone and wrote to Dorothy on the ship's fine stationery, "I'm absolutely livid with desire and I'd give my soul to have you in this room at this moment. Then, I'd feel safe. As it is, I'm afraid. . . . I'm afraid of something inside that's raising hell with me. . . . I know that at this moment if I slept with someone on this boat that I'd tell you about it and you'd understand."

The letter alarmed Dorothy, who tried to call but was unable to connect as phone lines were unreliable on the high seas. The couple was still discussing the incident the following month when Dick referenced it in a letter from London, where *Ever Green* was in rehearsal: "I can't explain it completely because I don't quite understand it myself. You know that moral precepts play small part in my life; my instincts certainly haven't changed, that I rely on you for complete understanding for that sort of thing. Nevertheless, here I am as you last saw me: your faithful loving husband." He had a way of alarming and reassuring her within the space of a few sentences.

Dick reported diligently on the famous people who filled his days and nights: Noel Coward and Gertrude Lawrence sang his songs at a party with Prince George and the king of Greece; he ran into Greta Garbo at lunch; and then there was the night that Tallulah Bankhead stayed in his hotel until 3:30 a.m. doing imitations. Dorothy grew impatient with his absence, his late nights, and his name-dropping; they quarreled via letter about his return until finally he agreed to sail home in late October, missing the opening of *Ever Green* and whatever parties attended it.

Meanwhile, Hammerstein, leading a harmonious home life in Los Angeles, was happy with his and Romberg's first film musical, *Viennese Nights,* a tale of thwarted romance stretched out over a lifetime. In March 1930, he reported to his lawyer Howard Reinheimer, "There is no question but that we have made a big hit with everyone, from the assistant prop boy up through Crosland, Koenig, Zanuck and Warner. It is also equally certain that they have made a hit with me."

In November Warner released the film, which captures the moment that operetta succumbed to its death due to advanced artificiality. By this time, the studios were already rethinking their mass investment in the musical. They had hired a raft of songwriters and were waiting to see if any musical spaghetti stuck to the wall. When nothing did, it was the end of the "gold rush," as Oscar called the period from 1929 to 1931. At least Hammerstein and Romberg got two musical movies made in that period, however forgettable they might be. Kern and Harbach watched as Warner Bros. released their film, *Men of the Sky,* without any music at all.

In January 1931, unaware of impending doom, Hammerstein pitched ideas to Jack Warner for a third film, which he called *Hear Interest.* He clumsily attempted to move the project forward by writing Warner that, since he hadn't heard from the producer in two weeks, he considered himself "free to consider it accepted, according to the terms of our contract. . . . Please give it to Darryl [Zanuck], if you have not already done so. We should like to hear any ideas he may have on the story before going ahead with it."

Instead, Warner phoned Hammerstein and asked pointedly if he really wanted to fulfill his contract; as an alternative, he offered Hammerstein and Romberg $100,000 each *not* to make the remaining two films. This news came just as Oscar and Dorothy welcomed a new baby, James, who would be known as Jamie and, later, Jimmy. They were also hosting Billy and Alice periodically, depending on Myra's unpredictable peregrinations. Now living in Beverly Hills, Myra had a new husband whose name Hammerstein could never recall. His instinct was good because the man was soon history, and Myra never again remarried.

Sorting out his next move, one thing was clear: Hammerstein no longer wanted to work with Ziegfeld, who was aggressively pursuing him for a new musical. He assured the producer that he was reading four novels a week and "also trying to cook up an original plot," but so far had been unsuccessful. "It's easy enough to build up a conventional ready-made operetta story but I don't think that sort of thing stands a chance today," he wrote, stalling for time. He informed Ziegfeld that he was searching for something "unique and new, with at least one compelling idea in it" or else "it is useless for us to spend our time and money and risk all the heartbreaks that attend a failure." Ziegfeld persisted: "I do hope we will get another 'Show Boat.' I know they are hard to get, but I feel sure that if anyone can get one, you can. . . . I am very anxious to get something definite about a show for next Fall, and you know, you and Jerry promised to write it for me."

Hammerstein instead got to work on *Free for All,* a new show with music by Richard Whiting about the son of a California millionaire who gets involved with a group of radicals from Stanford University. The audience hated it; accordingly, it opened and closed in less than two weeks in September 1931. But the show is notable for several reasons—it reveals that the thirty-six-year-old Hammerstein found American Communists, a group he would later be suspected of joining, comically absurd, and it also shows that Sondheim was right when, many years later, he said Hammerstein knew nothing about psychiatry. *Free for All* represents Hammerstein's sole attempt to write a wacky comedy in the mode of George S. Kaufman and Morrie Ryskind, whose *Animal Crackers,* starring the Marx Brothers and Margaret Dumont, had just been released as a film. Lastly, *Free for All* is one of his least discussed works and therefore overdue for a second look.

The play opens in the Palo Alto home of millionaire Stephen Potter Sr., a copper and oil baron. While the servants set up for a dinner party, Potter's dining room is invaded by a group of undergrads singing "La Marseillaise."

These kids make up the staff of *Free for All,* the radical biweekly published by the university. They have come to challenge Potter's capitalism and convince him to send them all to the mother ship, Soviet Russia. There, at "its very source," says the ringleader Marie, the group will "learn the principles of Sovietism, and spread them in bloodless revolution over these fair United States." Marie has just been expelled for penning an article calling for "trial marriage," in which she argued, "You wouldn't take a vacuum cleaner without a demonstration, why a husband?" Her plan for Russian relocation has all the students living in a commune where men and women sleep in separate buildings and "those who feel the marriage urge shall live together for one year." She and her ideas have caught the interest of the millionaire's son, Steve Jr.

As the students present their cause to Potter in the dining room, for some reason Steve Jr. enters disguised as a Greek waiter. The only one in the group who recognizes him is Anita, who's in love with him and only pretending to be a Communist so she can be around him. Steve Jr., however, finds Anita too possessive; he tells her, parroting Marie, "I can't give myself just to you. One woman has no right to own one man, nor one man, one woman!"

Anita suspects, rightly, that Steve Jr. is more passionate about free love than about Communism. She's hoping that *her* dad, a successful psychiatrist (famous for conversion therapy that is said to "turn a dress designer into the toughest top sergeant in the marines") can help Steve overcome Communism and his "work Phobia." Unfortunately, the boy is not a serious student, which, in the view of Anita and Potter Sr., might make him a low wage earner. Other than free love, his only other substantial interest is in magic, which he reads about and practices quite a bit. Of course, in the end he will employ a magic trick to straighten out the plot's complications.

Finally Potter Sr. and Anita win the day, and Steve Jr. is domesticated. Anita tells him he must get "a real job," adding, "If we ever get a house and two automobiles, and everything else that goes with it, I want it to be because we worked for it, not because your old man gave it to you"—an apt summation of the meritocracy Hammerstein believed America should be.

The play ends on a recognizable Hammersteinian note. Potter tells his son, "Don't you be afraid to be laughed at. Every great idea started as a crazy dream." In terms of message, *Free for All* winds up hitting the same notes as the finale of *Carousel* fourteen years later. Potter is a precursor to that show's graduation speaker, the one who instructs the kids, "Try not to be skeered o' people not likin' you—jest you try likin' them."

Next Hammerstein reunited with Romberg to write *East Wind,* a tangled melodrama that moves from Saigon (now Hồ Chí Minh City) to Paris. Despite strong out-of-town reviews, New York was noncommittal about *East Wind.* Atkinson could barely rouse himself to hold his pen—after dismissing the comic character as "hardly funny," he ended his review by saying, "The girls are OK." The play closed after twenty-three performances.

The normally buoyant Oscar was rattled. First Jack Warner had cut ties, and now he had racked up two Broadway flops in a row. He considered a retreat from stage and screen entirely, writing to Myra he was "certain that my recent succession of musical comedy misfortunes has opened the gates to a career which is more to my liking, and I am embarking on it eagerly and happily—flushed with failure, you might say." He revealed he was writing a novel, though he quickly assured her he was being pragmatic about it: "I am wary enough to have chosen a subject that would make good stage material, so that if the publishers reject it I shall have nevertheless a complete scenario which could be dramatized with an additional month's work."

But that novel never got written. In 1933 Hammerstein sold *Sweet Adeline* to Warner Bros. and told Myra that "after commissions are paid my share is $8,000, which postpones digging into my small capital a little while longer."

Through their letters, Oscar and Myra exchanged selective tidbits from their lives, both underplaying their own spending. Myra noticed that her ex's constant calls for economizing didn't seem to apply to himself and Dorothy, whose Fifth Avenue apartment sat empty while they lived at Sunny Knoll, their house on Long Island, where Oscar was back at work with Kern on a show called *Music in the Air.* Oscar had bought Myra out of her half of the house, the first trophy of his youthful success. She knew well the property's amenities: swimming pool, tennis court, guesthouse, and private beach.

As the entitled son of an adoring mother, Hammerstein couldn't help thinking that his ex-wife would be pleased about his well-ordered life. He confided to Myra that he had contemplated renting Sunny Knoll for the summer but didn't think the profit could justify all the upheaval. After all, he wrote, "I have such a marvelous study there, with all my reference books catalogued, and the furnishings so cheerful that I really believe my work gains a great deal." And what was good for his work was good for Myra, wasn't it?

Still, he could never go for too long without delivering a lecture. "Living on my capital—now a shrunken nugget—I will not continue long on Fifth Avenue," he wrote. He advised her on exactly how much money she should withdraw from the child-care fund ($25,000 a year) constantly reminded her that this reservoir might at any time dry up. He told her how to invest her own money (conservatively) and what interest rate she should accept: "On small sums of capital it is not important whether you get 3% or 7%. Safety is all that counts." Whether she followed his advice, we don't know.

The children had reported to him that Myra and her soon-to-be former husband lived in a large home in Beverly Hills. He congratulated her briefly before pivoting back:

> I know that rents are very, very low now, but isn't it rather expensive to run a home as big as that? I sound like an old maid, don't I? I admit to a selfish anxiety. It is essential to my peace of mind that you and the children are secure. If you spend no more than $10,000 a year, you're taken care of for seven years. By that time Billy and Alice are both grown up. Keep to this rule and nobody will have to worry. Meanwhile I might make a little money, who knows? And if I don't, your husband might. But don't count on either.

In 1933 Sunny Knoll suffered a small flood, which gave Oscar and Dorothy a chance to redecorate, a talent of Dorothy's that would blossom into a successful profession. Dorothy had never particularly liked the Tudor mansion her husband built with his first wife and was eager to put her mark on it. And Oscar reassured Myra that her former home was being well cared for: "The first insurance made it possible to completely redecorate, and the 'depression' made it possible to buy gorgeous furniture at auction for next to nothing. And it really looks wonderful." The quotes around "depression" and Hammerstein's lack of interest in the people from whom he was buying cheap furniture is jarring, for it seems incompatible with the progressive he was to become.

Hammerstein unintentionally revealed something about his intellectual journey in a 1958 interview when he described the monarch in *The King and I* as a man who was "born a conservative and became a liberal."

In fact, this description does not at all apply to King Mongkut, who served twenty-seven years as a Buddhist monk debating canonical issues before he ascended to the throne at age forty-six. Hammerstein is referring to his own growth. Shortly after Hitler's rise to power, Hammerstein would experience a call to political engagement that only grew stronger with each passing year.

Back in 1932, Hammerstein had the idea to write about the office of a music publisher—an atmosphere ripe with organic song opportunities. Kern joined him for *Music in the Air,* the story of an unsophisticated couple from the Bavarian countryside who goes to the big city, Munich, to try to get a song published. There, they both become involved with glamorous figures from the world of operetta. In the end, they discover that they belong back in the country and love each other after all. Hammerstein enjoyed writing about "the passionate and irrational people of the theater," and he loved working with Kern. The project provided "sweet refuge for me after my two recent failures and my unfortunate excursion to Hollywood," he wrote.

He was also jazzed by the show's concept: all the songs were to be "introduced as alleged folk music or refrains from a play that one of the characters was writing." Hammerstein thought of the show as "my own very special darling." In 1946, after writing *Oklahoma!* and *Carousel,* he told a reporter that *Music in the Air* was the favorite of all his shows. Though he never repeated that sentiment, it demonstrates how thoroughly he enjoyed working on the project.

Despite the setting, there was nothing Teutonic in the score, which had a fresh, modern sound, one that signaled the show was almost a spoof. Kern had fashioned an affectionate homage to the operetta that was distinctly *not* an operetta; the show featured charming baubles like "The Song Is You" and "Ev'ry Little Star," a song that became a hit again in 1961 when Linda Scott released it as "I've Told Every Little Star." And the show was a success, running for 342 performances starting in November 1932.

When *Music in the Air* opened on Broadway, critic Brooks Atkinson was thirty-eight years old. He went on to preside over a golden age of theater and journalism, and he won a Pulitzer in 1947 for his work as Moscow correspondent. He would be remembered for helping audiences process the thorny, mature plays of Eugene O'Neill as well as the sui generis work of Tennessee Williams and Samuel Beckett. At this point in his career, he was growing impatient with shows meant to be nothing more than diversion, no matter how diverting they might be.

Hammerstein and Kern at the time of *Music in the Air.*
Courtesy of New York Public Library

In his second piece about *Music in the Air,* Atkinson clearly had *Show Boat* on his mind. He wrote, "Mr. Hammerstein and he [Kern] have discovered how musical plays, which used to be assembled, can now be written as organic works of art." He recalled the primitiveness of the form pre–*Show Boat:* "When you remember how frantically troupes of corybants used to rush into dull spots of musical comedies, and how the first comic used to strut up to the footlights with a bagful of gags, you begin to value the integrity of *Music in the Air.*"

Atkinson made an unusually direct, almost personal appeal to Hammerstein and Kern to concentrate on moving the art forward. "In the long battle for a coherent form of musical drama, Mr. Kern and Mr. Hammerstein have won the first victory. Since it is not a formula, it cannot be repeated or varied," he wrote, again referencing not the musical at hand but *Show Boat*. He urged the duo to keep to their difficult path. "When they sit down together to write another musical drama they will have to make a fresh start on a clean slate," he wrote. "Bleak as that project may appear to them as practical men of the theater, it is the inevitable result of creating a genuine work of art in which music, fable and acting are perfectly blended."

It would take Hammerstein eleven long years and a new writing partner to realize that project.

In the meantime, Hammerstein decided to shake things up with a change in residence: he would direct *Music in the Air* at His Majesty's Theater in London. He and Dorothy set up house in Weybridge, Surrey, just outside the city they both loved. They took Billy and Susan while Myra traveled with Alice to Vienna. On the ship Myra met Margit Sereny, an actor whose daughter Gitta (later a significant author on Nazism) was the same age as Alice. Myra left Alice in Austria in the care of the Serenys while she sailed on. Margit, who later married the economist Ludwig von Mises and wrote a memoir, recalled taking in Alice for more than a year. "Alice had suffered greatly from her mother's divorce, and it took all my love and care to make her smile again," she wrote.

Meanwhile, on the suggestion of music publisher Louis Dreyfus, Hammerstein visited Berlin at the end of 1932 to see a new operetta by composer Paul Abraham. *Ball im Savoy* opened at the Großes Schauspielhaus in the very last days of the Weimar Republic, on December 23. Like Hammerstein, Abraham was searching for ways to modernize operetta, and he infused his score with jazz and tango. He'd had a breakout success in 1930 with *Viktoria und ihr Husar,* and now his work was all the rage. The *New York Times* Berlin correspondent C. Hooper Trask loved *Savoy* and called Abraham "Central Europe's most popular composer." It was also the final few weeks of his life as he knew it.

Hammerstein just started adapting the operetta when Hitler became chancellor at the end of January. His version, *Ball at the Savoy,* opened in September 1933 at the Theatre Royal, Drury Lane. Given the situation in Germany, audiences were not in the mood for the romantic intrigues of a marquis and a marquise at a masked ball, particularly one imported from Berlin. The *New Statesman and Nation* saw in the show "the vulgarity of pointless luxury and spineless energy." The *Daily Mail* wrote, "Why Mr. Hammerstein thought it worthwhile to adapt this stolid German story is puzzling. Why he should have chosen it as the framework for a costly spectacle is beyond understanding." In fact, Abraham was not German but a Hungarian Jew, and his two librettists, Alfred Grünwald and Fritz Löhner-Beda, were Austrian Jews. Just months after the show's Berlin opening, Grünwald fled Berlin for France and Abraham went to Budapest, then Paris, then Havana, and finally the United States where he eked out a living as a pianist and eventually lost his bearings. In 1946, he was found conducting an imaginary orchestra in the middle of a busy intersection and wound up in Creedmoor, a Queens psychiatric hospital. Ten years later some friends brought him back to Germany, where he spent his final years.

In the States things had gone from bad to worse. Between 1930 and 1933, more than nine thousand banks closed, effectively disappearing $2.5 billion in deposits ($36 billion in today's dollars). At the same time a terrible drought hit the middle of the country, which, combined with farming practices that had depleted the topsoil, created the Dust Bowl. The environmental catastrophe displaced hundreds of thousands of farming families, suffocated livestock, and caused red snow to fall from the sky. Especially hard hit was the panhandle of Oklahoma, which was only just recovering when Hammerstein wrote his musical about the state ten years later.

Hammerstein soldiered on from the London suburb as Hitler cemented his power and curtailed civil liberties. The lyricist reunited with Kern to create *Three Sisters,* an original story about the romantic lives of siblings traveling the British countryside with their widowed father. At the same time, Kern was trying (unsuccessfully) to focus Hammerstein on the film version of *Sweet Adeline*. The days of Kern's being the duo's more powerful partner were ending. "I am now spending my time chasing Oscar in and out of Drury Lane and round about London trying to wheedle material out of him," wrote an irritated Kern to a friend. *Three Sisters* opened on April 19, 1934, to an unenthusiastic British press. The *Daily Herald* accused Hammerstein and Kern of trying to be "terribly English." The *Morning Post* said that "everything rings false." It seemed like the entire world was in a sour mood. The show closed in six weeks—the shortest run in the history of the Drury Lane. Hammerstein's dream of riding out the Great Depression in London was not to be. Kern was fed up and declared he was going back to Hollywood "for good."

■ ■ ■

This time it was Metro-Goldwyn-Mayer that lured Hammerstein to the West Coast, with a cozy $2,000-a-week deal. Contracted to perform "general adaptation work," he returned in 1934 and mustered the same optimism as when he came to work at Warner Bros. five years earlier. That hadn't turned out so well, but this time might be different.

He wrote with careful but definite confidence to Myra in May of 1934 about his new job: "My six week contract has much more purpose than meets the naked eye. They have told me frankly that this is an experiment. If they like me and I like them this is a mere prelude to a new contract, and I am to be groomed as supervisor of all their musicals. Big stuff you see, but I am not allowing my hopes to run away with me. So many strange things happen and don't happen out there."

Now that he could no longer claim looming poverty as an excuse, how could he convince Myra that a job with MGM was not a green light for excessive spending? "I won't even start to go into the incidental expenses of moving the whole family out here, and the continued burdens of a standard of living absolutely demanded by my business position," he wrote in a letter one senses was met by eye-rolling. "In Hollywood, above all other places, their psychology is to think a man unimportant and undeserving of his money if he lives in a modest hovel and does no entertaining—tho god knows I do as little as possible, since it never entertains me either to give or go to parties."

Dick and Dorothy Rodgers and Larry Hart were also back on the West Coast, all living in the same house in Beverly Hills. That is, until Dorothy, having endured a miscarriage and continual ill health, returned to New York to recover through the fall of 1932 and again in the summer and fall of 1933. Letters between the couple show a pattern of wifely reproach followed by Dick's specialty: mixed-message reassurance. Dorothy came home miserable one night after dinner with her in-laws. Her father-in law, Dr. Rodgers, kept exclaiming how well Dick was doing on the West Coast, how everything was going his way. Perhaps he was trying to boost her mood, but it felt to Dorothy as if her problems didn't matter. She left before dessert and cried in the cab ride home, all of which she later related her husband. He wrote back:

> Naturally, darling, Pop would tell you how happy I was here. In the first place, all he knows is that the work is going well, and I couldn't very well cry on his shoulder over my loneliness. Then (and you obviously realize it too, according to your letter) he evidently doesn't mind your knowing that I'm doing pretty well without you. I'm goddamn sick for you. I got sex hooting up my sleeve like an old bastard and I just won't hop into somebody's bed to relieve myself as though I had a stomach-ache.

Almost all of Dick's letters from this period begin by briefly acknowledging a grievance from Dorothy, such as this one from August 3, 1934: "I've been pretty depressed after your letter which came this morning. I've never read such a complete tale of unhappiness in my life. You said that you've forgotten people could laugh and be silly. Is it that bad, baby?"

Rodgers often dined out with aspiring young actresses, and he was well aware that Dorothy would hear about these dates one way or another. Preempting those discoveries was a smart way of conducting the business of being Richard Rodgers. In 1933 he reported to his wife, "Had dinner at the Russian Eagle with this Baxter girl, took her to the Bowl to hear a very bad all-Wagner concert" (like Hammerstein, Rodgers disliked the storytelling in opera). He continued, "Then we went on to the 50–50 club which was empty. It was a quiet evening and pleasant enough, as these things go, but I've discovered that I don't feel comfortable with any other girl." Dick was always in the process of learning this lesson.

The Rodgerses were back in New York for the birth of their second child, Linda, in March of 1935. Dick continued to shuttle between New York and Hollywood, but unlike Hammerstein he kept up a steady stream of theater hits. In 1936 he and Hart debuted *On Your Toes,* which became known for being the first musical to integrate a ballet—"Slaughter on 10th Avenue," choreographed by George Balanchine—into the plot. The following year Rodgers and Hart had another hit with *Babes in Arms.*

Nineteen thirty-seven saw Dick back in Los Angeles while Dorothy kept house in New York. His correspondence from that year is a litany of consoling and bragging. From March 1937: "Awfully sorry about your vacation." April: "Larry and I had lunch today at the Vendome. Next week dinner with Max Gordon at the Beverly Derby joined by George Jessel, Chico Marx, Larry Schwab, George Kaufman." May: "I'm sorry you're not having more fun. Off to Hornblow's for lunch. Last night after the Hearst party, Leila and Phil took me to Carole Lombard's for cocktails and there we joined Gable, Irene Dunne and Gail Patrick." Later that month: "Your surprise that people like you in spite of the fact that I'm away still amuses me. . . . The Marches gave a party last night which I finally discovered was in my honor." Even later in May: "At the Fields party, the Gershwins, Sam Harris, Moss, the Hammersteins, a flock of others. . . . I also have a beautiful Steinway here in the hotel which the studio sent me for free!" The following week: "Baby darling, when I mentioned Ginger [Rogers] last night on the phone you said, 'Please be good.' I beg you, darling, don't think of things like that. We've gone over seven years without hurting each other and I love you more now than I ever did before. Let's put things like that out of our minds and remember what we have."

I doubt Dorothy Rodgers ever got over "things like that."

As for their time in Los Angeles, Rodgers and Hart summed it up for *Time* on September 26, 1938, when the magazine put them on the cover with the title "The Boys from Columbia." "During the past three years they have continuously—except for one lone week—had a smash hit on Broadway," reported the magazine. "Of their six pictures, they vote *Love Me Tonight* the best. Once they worked for fifteen months at MGM and turned out only five songs." Then they quote Rodgers, who expresses a classist superiority that only the wittiest of the Algonquin set—which he was not—could pull off. "Hollywood's trouble is stupidity, not malice," he said. "And you can no more resent stupidity in a movie director than in an elevator boy."

Meanwhile, in June 1934, Oscar and Dorothy Hammerstein rented a house with a tennis court at the top of La Brea Terrace. Every day a chauffeur-driven Rolls Royce whisked Oscar to work at MGM.

Though Hammerstein disliked parties—Kern dubbed his move toward the exit "the Hammerstein glide"—he and Dorothy were not antisocial, and they met with other transplanted New Yorkers for cocktails, badminton, and other assorted games. And the company was good; among their crowd were Robert Benchley, Dorothy Parker, Marc Connelly, and Harry Ruby. Whenever Hammerstein ran into Richard Rodgers, they were happy to see each other. Though they led their private lives in almost diametrically opposed ways, they felt a mutual affinity, perhaps some harmonic convergence yet to be unveiled.

Despite a remarkably consistent string of failures, operetta was still something the studios could not quit, and Hammerstein's first assignment at MGM was exactly what it had been with Warner Bros.—to write an operetta with Romberg. This one was based on a story by Vicki Baum about a doomed romance between an Austrian royal and a ballet dancer. *The Night Is Young* included one of Hammerstein's first songs dedicated to lifelong love, a pretty thing called "When I Grow Too Old to Dream." He gifted Dorothy the copyright; in little more than a year it provided her with enough money to buy a lovely French provincial house in Benedict Canyon.

Both Dorothys made reputations as interior designers. Dorothy Hammerstein built a thriving West Coast business in the 1930s. Her signature, in her words, was to add a "slight dash of vulgarity," which meant interrupting a mix of early American and British pieces with a few bright red Asian elements. She ran a Beverly Hills store with a salon in the back where a cook prepared luncheon for important clients like songwriter Dorothy Fields, actor Norma Talmadge, and producer Pandro Berman. In 1939 Jules Stein, the president of Music Corporation of America, hired Dorothy to supervise the interiors of MCA's opulent new building, designed by pioneering architect Paul Williams. Her idea was to soften the traditionally male power center by installing as much natural fabric as possible, such as hand-woven drapes, throughout. "I tried to make the chairs look like a symbol of welcome instead of an invitation to death," she told the *Los Angeles Times*.

The career of Dorothy Rodgers started more modestly with furniture restoration in 1935, but she eventually expanded into interior decoration, housekeeping (inventing the Johnny Mop and a new dress pattern called Basically Yours), and all aspects of home entertaining, including flower arranging, menu planning, and dinner-party etiquette. In the 1960s she published two books on these topics that offer a window into the life of Mrs. Richard Rodgers, the cynosure of upper-class hosts. She gave her readers access to royal dining rooms, reporting, for instance, on how the Duke and Duchess of Windsor entertained in their Paris home—they used Chelsea porcelain, surrounded their soup tureens with arrangements of fruits and flowers and vegetables, and offered cigarettes from jeweled gold and enamel boxes.

I've heard it said that the two Dorothys had very different styles—Hammerstein more welcoming and informal, Rodgers a stickler for things staying in their designated places. However, comparing photos of their Upper

East Side bedrooms, one can't help noticing they look remarkably similar. Both women slept in carpeted chambers that featured wooden four-poster beds with canopies made of patterned fabric that spills over onto other furnishings (chairs for Rodgers, love seat and curtains for Hammerstein). For lighting Hammerstein chose candelabra wall sconces while Rodgers went for bedside lamps. Through the late 1940s and '50s millions of women saw these homes in newspapers and magazines and copied them down to the chinoiserie fabric and the Biedermeier writing table; in effect the Dorothys dictated upper-class urban style for almost two decades.

After the success of *Oklahoma!,* Oscar persuaded Dorothy to quit working. In November 1943 he told director Rouben Mamoulian that he'd convinced her "to retreat from the cares of her business, because there is little satisfaction in it these days. She can make lots of money (which she can't keep) but the aggravation of labor and material scarcity takes away all her fun." He did not want her to be drained of good humor by work—in 1944 he wrote Leighton Brill that she was "working very hard but having little fun because of the constant irritation." But she kept returning to her work; in the 1950s Dorothy decorated Mary Martin's Manhattan apartment as well as the Australian embassy in Washington, DC.

Back in Hollywood, Hammerstein was determined to succeed this time. He imagined he might guide studios in the art of movie musicals not as a writer but as a producer. He saw that his boss, Louis B. Mayer, treated producers with more respect than he treated writers, and he certainly paid them better. In a letter to Myra, Hammerstein tried on a producerly attitude: "Since it is usual to call in several writers on a picture (and I am beginning to see virtues in the idea), it is hard for a writer to build up an individual reputation as he does in the theater. Hence the producer, as the captain of the team, runs off with the honors."

And Mayer seemed to dote on him. "For some reason or other," Oscar wrote Myra:

> I have made a big hit with Louis B. Mayer. He looks upon me as a kind of protégé and keeps talking about grooming me as a producer, telling me to take my time and learn the business at his expense. So I'm in a very good spot so far and (barring one of those big Hollywood upheavals or fickle switches of sentiment which I imagine are not infrequent) I may remain out here and

> develop into an important factor. It seems faintly flamboyant to talk that way now when I am only a tyro and woefully lacking in the mere knowledge of the names of picture actors, writers and directors (I've only seen about four pictures a year, all my life), nevertheless I feel I have good qualifications for this kind of work.

In his optimism Oscar performed one of many mitzvahs for his brother Reggie, who had followed him back out to Los Angeles and gone to work at the Hal Roach Studio in 1934. By March the following year Reggie was again out of work, so Oscar wrote to Reinheimer with an idea. He proposed to the lawyer that they create a position in London, where his brother could scout for talent: "[Reggie] clicked there better than any place he has ever been, he has good connections, he is well thought of, and he is happier there. Until he gets a job I shall naturally have to carry him, as I am doing here." Oscar proposed paying his brother $200 a week. "The thing can be made to look legitimate," he wrote, ending with "the rest of the clauses I leave to your own legal invention."

Hammerstein's dream of a sheltered career at MGM was short-lived. The studio brought in two other screenwriters on *The Night Is Young* to punch up the film's comedy, and eventually they removed Hammerstein's writer credit altogether. In the spring of 1935 MGM did not renew his option. In a May 1935 letter to Reinheimer, Hammerstein seemed to accept that the West Coast was not his friend. Moreover, he was realizing that if he wanted to have control over his work, he belonged in the theater:

> Mind you I have no false illusions about the hazard of the theater, nor is my memory so short that I don't realize what a haven Hollywood seemed last year after being buffeted badly in New York and London. But after being here a year I know that outside of money there is nothing to feed on here. You may say money is a good thing to feed on, and certainly it is an essential. But there are other things a man needs, most of all he needs the impression that he counts for something in the work he's doing. He also must feel that the work is worth doing. The set up here is against that.

In the summer, though, Paramount picked up Hammerstein's contract on a nonexclusive basis. While waiting for a studio assignment, Hammerstein returned to New York, where he again teamed up with Romberg and book writer Frank Mandel on an operetta called *May Wine*. The play chronicles the love life of Johann Volk, a philosopher who sports an Einstein-like shock of hair. They adapted the plot from a treatment by Erich von Stroheim and Wallace Smith (which Smith published as a novel called *The Happy Alienist* the following year).

This forgotten musical is notable for one line, delivered by Volk's assistant Vera, who is secretly in love with the philosopher. She finds out that his bride is a con artist and warns him, "You're in love with something that doesn't exist. A madman's dream!" At that, Volk smacks her across the mouth. Her answer is triumphant: "Ah! That didn't hurt at all!" While the smack is in the source material, Vera's response is original to *May Wine*. Hammerstein wrote, "That didn't hurt at all!" Ten years later, in *Carousel*, Hammerstein again employed the idea of abuse made painless by love in a depiction that haunts the musical to this day (as we'll see).

"A conscientious attempt to produce a popular operetta shorn of the excrescences and stock appurtenances," wrote Atkinson of *May Wine*, sounding in a bit of a stupor. Not one memorable song emerged from the score.

Hammerstein returned to Los Angeles, still waiting for an assignment from Paramount. Carl Laemmle Jr. at Universal saw an opportunity: his studio's 1929 attempt to transpose *Show Boat* into a hybrid talkie-silent film had been a debacle, and now he wanted to do it properly. Playwright Zoë Akins provided Laemmle with an adaption, but after three drafts he was still not happy with her script. He asked Hammerstein to meet with British director James Whale (of *Frankenstein* and *The Invisible Man* renown), who had started in the theater, and the pair got on well. Hammerstein completed his adaptation in the first three weeks of November 1935. Starring veterans of the stage show—Paul Robeson, Helen Morgan, and Irene Dunne (who had played Magnolia on the road)—the film got rapturous reviews, and Hammerstein, too, was happy with it. Later he told interviewer Arnold Michaelis, "Few picture versions have been as faithful to the original as this one."

Even before the release of the film, the new *Show Boat* buoyed Hammerstein's mood considerably. Writing to Howard Reinheimer in January of 1936, Oscar again reported with confidence that he was in Paramount's good graces. When he offered to postpone his contract until the spring, he told Reinheimer, the studio "thought my attitude very generous and sporting but they wouldn't hear of my leaving." So stay he would. "I have decided after a great deal of thought that this is the place for a writer to earn a living," he wrote, completely reversing course from his letter to Reinheimer months earlier. "There is so much demand for material that once you are established as a screen author—as I believe I am now—there is nothing to stop you from getting as near to an assured income as any man can expect in my business." He instructed Reinheimer to sell the house on Long Island: "Tell [the realtors] I am more in a mood to talk turkey than ever before. I really want to make my home out here."

That same month he was scrounging for ideas, asking book publishers, "Have you anything that might interest me as a possibility for adaptation? I am searching for material with which to make a screen musical."

Since they were shuttling the kids between them, Oscar and Myra shared their childrearing views in letters, each using their old nicknames. She was Mike and he was Oc or Ock or Ockie. She was ranging all over Europe; he was commuting between New York and LA. In his handwritten missives, Oscar veers between who he has been and who he is trying to be: a breadwinner who takes care of everything—his ex-wife and children, his new wife and child, and the next generation of movie musicals. He was careful to mention Dorothy as little as possible and their young son, Jimmy, not at all. Still, some part of him seemed to want to share his hopes with Myra, and even to impress her, which conflicted with his attempts to downplay his income. (He and Myra would renegotiate support payments throughout the decade.)

At the start of 1936 the children were living with Myra, and the truth was Oscar didn't miss them all that much. He saw no reason not to let them stay with her for a while. When he talked to them, he got the distinct feeling they were bored. As the months went by, though, the separation tugged at him. He was shirking his responsibility. He wrote to Myra to send Billy, now thirteen, to him and Dorothy for the summer. Myra agreed but was beset by anxiety. Hammerstein's life was more lavish than hers and his home filled with interesting people. What if her son liked it better there? What if Billy, like Hammerstein, fell in love with the talented Dorothy?

To transfer her anxiety onto Oscar, Myra adopted the role of Billy's protector, the parent who understands the boy best. Billy had certain expectations and needs that an absent father would not be aware of. Indeed, Billy was a directionless boy—spoiled, moody, difficult to motivate. She must have known it would irritate her ex-husband, but she wrote Hammerstein a list of dos and don'ts for how to treat Billy. Hammerstein, responding crisply, did not take the bait: "I regard him as my son who wants to see us after a long separation—as I want to see him. He is not someone's debutante daughter for whom I must arrange a series of 'coming out' parties."

Billy arrived in June 1936. Hammerstein was relieved to find him on his best behavior as he tried to fit himself into his father's new life. Hammerstein saw Billy's complete lack of ambition (so much like Hammerstein's brother Reggie) in generous terms for the time being. He confided to Myra, "Somehow, he doesn't really expect to be good at anything—and he hasn't that vainglorious pride most boys have, that silly determination to excel. I wish he had. I'll do all I can to give him some of it—I've always had a little excess of it myself."

While they reported back and forth about Billy, Myra took the opportunity to pour out her melancholy to Oscar. She felt she was "drifting into middle age without having first lived," a dig at the years they'd spent together. He wrote her back in a spirit of benevolence, offering careful but not intimate support:

> First, you are nowhere near "middle" age. You are a young woman and will remain so for some time. Second, it seems to me you have "lived" a great deal—seen a lot of the world, experienced a lot and learned a lot. Who, of the girls you knew at nineteen, have "lived" more than you? Edna Keller? Rose Backer? Ruth Adler? Florence, Lilly, or any of the others you met later? And balancing all things, do you consider that any of these are better off than you now? Maybe you do. It is a question of a sense of values. I would not hesitate in preferring your own outlook, your comparatively comfortable state of wealth, your freedom, your intelligence and your two children to the uneventful, stodgy assets of the above named.

Hammerstein's radar for self-pity was sharp. He was no doubt on the watch for it in himself. Hollywood was again testing his native optimism, and he responded by designing a set of rules to guard against wallowing. He tried them all out on Myra. His letters to her let us glimpse the formation of a philosophy, a belief in the art of bouncing back, which would infuse the musicals he would soon write with Richard Rodgers. Don't dramatize yourself, he urged Myra. Pull yourself out of yourself. If you do, he writes, "a world much bigger than you and your problems will assert its existence to you. New places will fill your mind with thoughts of new things—without any effort on your part. I shall not go on. It will seem too much like 'selling' the idea to you. But I do believe it all so sincerely."

Oscar and Dorothy took over Billy's education and enrolled him in a Los Angeles high school. Hammerstein was a dedicated if frustrated dad, not as disengaged as he sometimes seemed to the children themselves. He struggled with the number-one challenge of affluent parents—how to make his children feel gratitude for all they'd been given. "I'm going to be much stricter with him than I've ever been," he vowed to Myra. "I've tried putting him on his own resources, and it's never worked. He is what I've never wanted him to be—a spoiled son of wealth. I'm going to make an heroic effort to cure him."

Oscar was fathering Alice from farther away, but he wanted just as much to impress his philosophy on her. When she told him about her disappointment while visiting the Panama Canal, he wrote back and modeled a better way of thinking:

> It seems to me that you both are pretty severe critics of new things, new places, and new experiences. I myself think that the mere fact of a thing being new and out of my ordinary course of daily living makes that interesting.
>
> Maybe you don't agree with me. You have a perfect right not to. You are yourself, and you don't have to be like me, and if you don't find something exciting it is silly to pretend that you do. But remember this: if you *do* find something exciting, it is silly to make believe you *don't*. Lots of people think it is very smart to seem unconcerned by things that delight other people. They think it makes them superior and above the ordinary weakling. People who say the world is a dull, flat place are very unlucky, because the world will always think that those kinds of people are dull.
>
> The best way to enjoy life is to be enthusiastic—and when you are enthusiastic don't be ashamed of it. Try to find things you like and don't waste too much time in telling people what you don't like. Nobody wants to hear it.

■ ■ ■

In the evenings, the Hammersteins ran into the Gershwins, Richard Rodgers, Oscar Levant, Cole Porter, Johnny Mercer, Arthur Freed, and Burton Lane, and they swapped stories about adjusting to the studio system. Hammerstein began to suspect that his lot in Hollywood was harder than that of his compatriots. Because his gift was for narrative integrity, Hammerstein was destined to be ground up by the filmmaking process; many of his friends, whose genius was for writing songs rather than the shows that contained them, fared slightly better. There were times when Hammerstein was thin-skinned. One morning he picked up the *New Yorker* and read a film review of *Show Boat* that did not mention his name. Livid, Hammerstein fired off a letter to critic John Mosher, who answered him respectfully, saying, "I felt that the work of Mr. Whale deserved commendation especially as he was the one new name hitherto unconnected with *Show Boat*. The whole matter boils down to a question of space." When Hammerstein sent a second letter of complaint, the critic was crisp: "I am interested in your second letter and still surprised that you have the leisure or the interest to pursue such a matter as this."

Around this time, Hammerstein completed the outline for a Paramount musical about the Pennsylvania oil rush of 1859. *High, Wide and Handsome* tells the story of a town that outwits the rapacious developers who plan to build a railroad on their oil-rich land and take all the profits. The film verged on outright anti-capitalism. The music was provided by Kern and the direction by Rouben Mamoulian, who would play a crucial role in the Rodgers and Hammerstein era. Preview audiences seemed to like the movie. Running into Hammerstein at the Riviera Country Club in Pacific Palisades, Paramount founder Adolph Zukor shook his hand and exclaimed, "That's the greatest picture we ever made!" A few months later, after the film opened to mediocre box office, Zukor walked past him as if they'd never met.

Hammerstein's instinct was to keep himself strong, disciplined, and engaged. He wrote every day and was equally devoted to exercise, especially swimming, tennis, and golf. When Dorothy Parker and Alan Campbell hosted the first meeting of the Hollywood Anti-Nazi League in the summer of 1936, Hammerstein was there, along with Donald Ogden Stewart, who was named president and quietly joined the Communist Party later that year.

Hammerstein, Parker, and eleven others formed the executive committee, with the Hammersteins hosting several meetings at their house. He saw that he was ideologically better suited to the writers, who had unionized and formed the Screen Writers Guild in 1933, than to the producers, who tended to lean rightward.

Nineteen thirty-seven was a gloomy year. Paramount did not renew its contract with Hammerstein in February, and he struggled to find work. In July, the songwriting community received the shock of shocks: thirty-eight-year-old George Gershwin died from a brain tumor at Cedars of Lebanon in Los Angeles. He'd been feeling unwell for a month, but no doctor had detected the cause. His music and presence had been so vital that it seemed impossible he could die. He embodied everything that was great about America—rising from poverty to stratospheric success, he merged what was seen as high and low culture. His music appealed to everyone.

Gershwin's body was put on a train for a New York burial; when it arrived, a thousand people lined the street on a rainy July 15 to pay respects to America's composer. That same day, the Los Angeles music community huddled together to mourn him at Congregation B'nai B'rith on Wilshire Boulevard. It was a mark of Hammerstein's standing that he was asked to give the eulogy when many other writers were closer to the Gershwin brothers, including Rodgers. Hammerstein spoke simply and from the heart, exposing something about his own personal moment. He opened with the following lines:

> We are all inadequate, muddling humans
> With hearts and minds woefully unequipped
> To solve the problems that beset us

And ended with these:

> In his honor
> They could try to appreciate
> And be grateful for
> The good things in this world
> In his honor
> They could try to be kinder to one another
> And this would be the finest monument of all.

■ ■ ■

In an attempt to regain the reins of his career, Hammerstein decided once more to shift his efforts to New York. Maybe he could apply what he had learned from studio executives to his first love, the theater. He would become a producer on Broadway. He returned to Manhattan, saw lots of shows, and got excited, writing Mamoulian, "New York has never seemed as thrilling, the theater never more alive. I've seen eighteen shows in two weeks."

His attempts at convincing his Hollywood contacts to invest in theater projects, though, received discouraging replies. David Loew, a producer at Universal, read one of the plays Hammerstein was considering and wrote, "I believe the second act is excellent and considerably better than the first, but I have decided that I wouldn't care to invest any money in any productions, whether musical or dramatic." Hammerstein soldiered on and produced three new plays on Broadway in the fall of 1938: *Knights of Song* (about the relationship of Gilbert and Sullivan), *Where Do We Go from Here?*, and *Glorious Morning*. The longest run of all these plays was twelve days. After seeing *Where Do We Go from Here?*, a comedy set in a college fraternity, Brooks Atkinson wrote, "To make it completely enjoyable, all they need is a play."

Bruised, Hammerstein wrote for comfort to his closest friend, Jerome Kern, who responded at once:

> Dear Oscar:
>
> There was an unfavorable reference in yesterday's (Monday's) Hollywood Reporter, so I was not unprepared for your telegram.
>
> I hate to be just perfunctory with a "Too bad, better luck next time" and there is really little one can say—except that perhaps two or three years of dolce far niente out here may have blunted the old, acute sense of dramatic values for the stage, which an incredibly short time spent in and around the theatre will undoubtedly resharpen.
>
> Your character and guts have been tested before this, and I know that these experiments, which just didn't happen to come off, are not going to permanently shake your confidence or cause you to temper your artistic honesty or lower your standards.

Over the coming months Oscar's letters betrayed cracks in his usually prideful self-presentation, the psychic equivalent of wearing frayed clothes to a meeting. He sent actor Buddy Ebsen a script and asked the actor to please return it if he didn't like it because he had no more copies. He responded to a downhearted letter from playwright Hy Kraft by confessing, "I will be another month on my play, and then I will have to do a picture to get some dough for current bills that are piling up alarmingly." He noticed when Billy Rose, who had once fawned over him, didn't bother to answer a telegram, which he complained about to his Uncle Arthur. People were whispering that working with Hammerstein was now the kiss of death. One story from that time has composer Lew Gensler coming into a party to find Hammerstein sitting alone in the den. "Where is everybody?" Gensler asked. "Maybe they heard I was coming," answered Hammerstein.

Even Reggie's regular pleas for assistance received a relatively cold shoulder. In June Oscar wrote to his brother, "I received your letter on my arrival here and appreciate the difficulty you have without any specific prospects in New York, but at the moment I can't think of anything that will help you out." He did, however, enclose a check. Reggie wrote back saying he was trying to get a job as a "glorified stage manager" with "Larry" (probably Schwab): "If you think I'm right, try to convince him that I am really capable and not the playboy that I believe he thinks I am." Perhaps sensing an end to the gravy train, Reggie wanted Oscar to know he was trying to be more responsible. He wrote that "being out of work as long as I have has taught me a few things too. My personality has been all wet and I'm going to try and change it. That might sound funny but in all my jobs I've made good but I'm not working. There must be a reason and I think that's it."

Despite his tightening finances, Hammerstein continued paying the rent for his Aunt Nettie and cousin Jean MacNaughton in Brooklyn. He also sent money, though less of it, to his pet causes. He wrote a lengthy letter to the United Jewish Welfare Fund in 1938 in which he sought absolution for his diminished contribution:

> I am writing this personal letter to you to explain that my making the amount considerably less than last year's donation arises not from any ignorance on my part of the direct necessities for which this fund is collected, but from the fact that what I have been called on to donate—and have donated—within the past 12 months has

> brought me to a point where I just cannot give any more. This, coupled with the fact that since December 1st I have not been on salary at any picture studio, having elected to spend my time preparing two productions for the stage next year.

At this time Hammerstein found himself more impatient than ever with his ex-wife. In Myra's behavior he continued to see the twin poles of disaster: self-pity and blame. The nursing of her wrongs made it impossible for her to look with optimism at the world around her. Increasingly he found her "deaf, dumb and blind" to anything but her own resentment.

He was riddled with self-doubt himself and trying desperately to hang on to patience, grace, and faith. If he allowed himself to wallow in wasted time and bad choices, to play the victim as Myra habitually did, it would bury him. It might even be said that we have Myra to thank for Oscar's upcoming role as the dean of American optimism. Her personality forced him to refine his theory that we control our destiny by controlling the way we see the world, and that therefore we make the world better by making ourselves better. If we can behave well or badly in any situation, why not chose the more positive option? This was a philosophy he would sell to the world, but he could not make Myra see it.

One day, after listening to Billy and Myra fight over the phone, Oscar's appeals took on a new urgency. He wrote to his ex-wife, "If Bill is neglectful he is at fault. And he is neglectful. The way to fix that is not to nag him! When will you get that into your head? Don't you see you only make yourself an unwelcome presence in his life? Let a few things go. Don't worry and fret yourself—and other people." He elaborated:

> YOU WORRY YOURSELF INTO TROUBLE . . . You fretted yourself right into the trap you're in. You fret yourself out of Billy's affection. Next time you feel like writing diatribes, don't. Try doing some work on yourself, and I guarantee that you will find less to complain of in your treatment at the hands of Billy—and everybody. It will be automatic.
>
> Believe me this criticism comes from my interest in you and my constant hope that you can <u>some day</u> shake off this unfortunate and very unattractive habit of complaint and resentment and trouble-stirring for those around you, but principally for yourself. Please do some *thinking.*

> God knows you've got a good sharp brain to do it with—clogged up by an illusion of persecution, as a motor can be clogged with carbon. GET IT OUT!

At the end of 1938, now back in New York, Hammerstein received a letter from Kern in Los Angeles, who was also feeling lost and fed up: "The situation now is past the joshing point and you and I both have to bang through with something powerful for the stage. We have both been much too long off the boards."

Hammerstein agreed. Moreover, he loved Kern's idea of writing something simple and fresh, in the mold of the Princess musicals, a show that celebrated the call of theater. Max Gordon would produce. The men started writing *Very Warm for May* in July of 1939 in California. By the fall they were in New York to cast and start rehearsals.

Very Warm for May gave Hammerstein a chance to do something he rarely did: write parody. His target was the kind of experimental theater he found pretentious and empty, and he was very funny on the subject. His story went like this. Threatened by some gangsters who are owed money by her father, Patsy hides out at the Connecticut estate of the Spofford family, where an avant-gardist named Odgon Quiler is using the family barn to stage his own play, starring Cutie Spofford, the young lady of the household. Quiler's play follows a pair of lovers throughout different time periods, and his innovative writing requires actors to play the roles of an old musket, a brook, a picket fence, and a willow tree. When Mrs. Spofford objects to one of her daughter's costumes, Quiler counters, "That is not a negligee, Mrs. Spofford. This young lady represents a molecular cell and it is from that standpoint I am judging the costume."

Everyone was excited about the show. Hammerstein's friend Leighton Brill thought Quiler's play-within-a-play would be "one of the funniest ever played on stage." Vincente Minnelli, who would go on to marry Judy Garland and direct great movie musicals like *Meet Me in St. Louis* (1944) and *An American in Paris* (1953), told Kern he wanted to join the production in any capacity. Max Gordon wrote to Hammerstein in July to say, "I am wildly enthusiastic about the show and have poured my enthusiasm into Jerry's heart and mind. He is sky high." And, later in July: "We settled with Minnelli to do designing of the scenery and costumes, lighting and general staging of the production numbers at $2500 and one percent of the gross. I think this is a great buy and I am certain that it will work out."

Kern was equally swept up. He telegrammed Hammerstein at Sunny Knoll and said, "Tried to phone you this afternoon after second reading because would not want you to sleep tonight without knowing that I think it's a knock out, easily the best embryo ever to come in sight and while I suppose it will never be properly played it cannot fail to be one of our tops. Congrats."

In *Very Warm for May,* Hammerstein's alter ego is a character called Johnnie Graham, a Broadway director surreptitiously called in to help make Quiler's production less awful. Johnnie interrogates Quiler about his choices—asking why a sofa and a chandelier mysteriously appear in a forest scene—but Quiler is defiant: "I don't want it to be clear! I don't believe in coddling my audiences. They must learn to find out for themselves what a play is about." Johnnie, who prefers his art coherent, answers, "I like things to be like other things—only much better."

Johnnie is an advocate for the straightforward, honest acting and writing that Hammerstein (having finally outgrown his attachment to the trappings of operetta) believed were the future. As he watches Cutie rehearse her number, Johnnie asks her why she is making a particular gesture:

JOHNNIE: What's it mean?
CUTIE: Nothing in particular. I've seen a lot of singers do that.
JOHNNIE: So have I.
CUTIE: What do you want me to do, stand here like a lamppost?
JOHNNIE: Nope. All I want you to do is to figure out what the words mean, and then sing them as if they were your own—I don't want you to move your hands or make faces except when the words give you a reason to.

Cutie tries again, but she can't help herself; she finishes the ballad with a dramatic sweep toward the audience and a big vocal flourish, which drives Johnny crazy. His admonishment to her is pure Hammerstein:

> You're making a bum out of the audience! You can't do that to them, you're cheating them! You're cheating them out of an illusion. That's what they paid for when they bought their tickets! But they'll get even with you! Don't kid yourself. They've got ways

> of getting even. They'll shift in their seats. They'll look at their programs. They'll cough! And it'll serve you goddamn right, for yelling at them in the middle of a tender scene. You see all you have to learn is one simple thing—sincerity. It's fundamental—like keeping your eye on the ball in golf—of course that isn't so easy either.

When the gangsters find their way to the Spofford estate, chaos ensues. They kidnap one of the actors, but rather than shut down that evening's performance Johnnie insists that the actors get in their costumes, which gives Hammerstein a chance to play on the theater's best-known adage:

JOHNNIE: Come on, get in your places there and go to work. There's a show that has to go on tonight.

PATSY: (firmly) The show does not have to go on!

(Pause. This is the first time in history that anyone has had the nerve to say this!)

JOHNNIE: Oh, doesn't it? There's going to be an audience out there, and—

PATSY: So what? I don't know any of them. Never met 'em. Don't give a damn for 'em!

In addition to delightful dialogue, the score showed Kern and Hammerstein in top form. Together they wrote fresh, contemporary love songs—"All in Fun," "Heaven in My Arms," "In the Heart of the Dark," and one that became a standard, "All the Things You Are," which was recorded by Tommy Dorsey's big band before the show opened.

Indeed, *Very Warm for May* did well with audiences in its pre–New York tour. Unfortunately, Max Gordon caught the show in Wilmington, Delaware. He found the play silly and demanded that Hammerstein remove the gangster subplot, tone down the character of Quiler, and fire Minnelli. Hammerstein was not in a fighting mood and did what Gordon asked of him. Suddenly the show lost its balance. People who saw it at the time said it was drained of all color. Robert Russell Bennett called it "a great show that was produced into a failure."

The revised script is disheartening to read. It has all the markings of a hasty rewrite. Jokes that once worked are dragged out and no longer funny. The story loses its shape and seems almost random. The dialogue no longer has its fizz. Even the ending seems like a first draft: "Everything's going lovely now, but hell might break loose again any minute," says a character. "This would be a good time to ring down the curtain, before they get in any more trouble"—and down comes the curtain.

Just before the show opened on Broadway, Hammerstein and Kern sat for a *New York Times* interview. They showed no signs of stress. Reporter Theodore Strauss described the differences in their demeanors. Kern spoke in "sporadic bursts," getting up and sitting down, opening doors and closing them, while Hammerstein's "speech is weighted, his smile slow. Massive of feature, tall and broad in body, he more resembles a construction foreman than writer of ardent verses for two in the moonlight." Strauss asked why they had stayed away from Broadway for so long—it had been eight years. Hammerstein gave a humorless answer about the intense competition from movies and radio, while Kern spoke of "the peculiar properties of the California climate," likening its denizens to the mollusk, which "opens and closes its mouth and lets the food flow in."

Brooks Atkinson saw no charm in the redone show. "There has seldom been a book that fought entertainment as successfully as the story of this musical play," he wrote. He could not make heads or tails of the plot and laid the blame squarely on Hammerstein: "Whether this is one of Mr. Kern's finest scores is hard to tell in the midst of so much literary confusion." He pronounced the story "singularly irrelevant."

Hammerstein's decade-long cold streak might have ended a smidge sooner if not for his own beaten-down ego and the terrible producing of Max Gordon. Though Gordon also produced Hammerstein's next musical, *Sunny River,* another failure, the lyricist never blamed Gordon or said a word against him. Moreover, when Gordon went through a depression the following year, he said Hammerstein offered him more help and support than anyone else.

The failure of *Very Warm for May* was a psychic blow. It had taken Hammerstein years to admit to himself he hated being a writer for hire in Hollywood, but he believed he still had a great talent for theater. Now he couldn't be sure of that.

When a collaborative artist loses the confidence to defend his instincts, he isn't in charge of anything he does. Hammerstein's closest friends noticed the unusual dejection in the lyricist's letters from this time. Uncle Arthur sent him the following scrawled letter: "Just a few lines; I received your 'lost his last friend letter'—what in hell is wrong with you, you sound as though you're licked. You were truly brave when you were with me, it made no difference to you in success or failure. Why should you have changed?"

Sigmund Romberg, to whom Hammerstein must have poured out his heart, wrote him a thoughtful and caring response. In the shore-up-a-friend section of the letter, Romberg introduces a phrase that Hammerstein would use in "People Will Say We're in Love" from *Oklahoma!*: "I am not trying to throw bouquets at you," wrote Romberg before saying, kindly and truthfully, "Out of one-hundred outstanding authors, writing dramatic plays, I don't think you'll find three who have the knowledge—the feeling and the sentiment to know how to write a book in which music is supposed to be interwoven with the music."

Hammerstein, though, would have bristled at Romberg's closing:

> Being hounded by critics isn't original with you, Oscar. Most writers, with very few exceptions, were hounded by the critics to the point of destruction. . . . Nature gives a writer something with which to withstand such blows. One throws it off—and we continue. I beg of you, never expect life to be the way you want it but come to the realization that in this rotten world, filled with lousy, stinking people, you have to take the other man as he is—and not as you want him to be.

Even in his darkest hour he would never have been willing to see the world as rotten and filled with lousy, stinking people. This was the kind of talk that drove him to madness. It was precisely what had made him rail against Myra for the past decade. Hammerstein wrote back, brushing off his own despair: "You know I never brood very long and I have done very little worrying over this season's misfortunes." He never gave up the idea that one day he would again be elated by a project and have the stamina to see it through. That buoyancy, so lost to him now, would in fact become the standard engine of the musical play. When the time came, Oscar would be able to access an almost childlike capacity for rapture, and it would be that quality that saved him and once again remade the form.

CHAPTER FIVE

Thus the World Broke Open

AT THE START OF A NEW DECADE, with war raging in Europe, Hammerstein made two moves on faith that severed his ties with Hollywood and reconnected him to himself. In 1940 he and Dorothy finally sold Sunny Knoll on Long Island, as well as their house in Benedict Canyon, and bought Highland Farm in Doylestown, Pennsylvania. They paid $23,000 for a three-story hundred-year-old farmhouse with a wraparound porch that stood on sixty rolling acres. If his career were indeed over, Hammerstein felt he at least could be happy living in this place.

According to Billy, Dorothy turned the farmhouse into a "highly decorated mansion" while Oscar acquired chicks, ducks, possibly geese, and cows. He took an interest in the animals and hired Peter Moën as farm overseer; Moën also tripled as the family's masseur and chauffer. At the start of the new decade Hammerstein spent many peaceful hours discovering every inch of his new home.

He later wrote to Billy about his relief on moving to the farm. "As far back as I can remember I always wanted to live in the country," he said. "Even in the city, if I saw an empty lot with a few weeds and a tree in it I was attracted by it. In your first year we took a small cottage in Far Rockaway in a street jammed with cottages but just across the street was a tall tree, and I used to sit on the small porch and look across at it and it made me thought-

Oscar and Dorothy Hammerstein in the 1940s.
Courtesy of Photofest

ful about life in the abstract as I sometimes get thoughtful listening to a symphony without actually hearing it."

In 1941 MGM came calling again—Frank Orsatti, Louis B. Mayer's fixer and putative procurer, offered the lyricist a two-year contract. This time Hammerstein turned it down. He explained his decision to agent Ralph Blum in November with perhaps too much information:

> After paying taxes and expenses, I would wind up with just about as much as I would staying right here and doing nothing. My income from sheet music and records (without new numbers) and from ASCAP and stock rights and radio rights on my plays amounts to about the same as I would net after a year's work in California. The slight balance would be consumed by extra expenses which I do not incur if I remain with my family on the farm. The only way for me to substantially increase my static income is to have a successful play on which there is no ceiling

> and against which there is no extraordinary charge, commissions or living expenses. This probably sounds fantastic to you but that is the way it adds up.

Instead, Hammerstein took on the only solo project he would write (other than the short-lived play he penned in 1919). The idea had been swirling in his brain since he saw Georges Bizet's *Carmen* in concert at the Hollywood Bowl in 1934 and discovered an opera he liked: "I found that Carmen was really the nearest to a perfect libretto that had ever been done, and I still believe that, with the exception of Wagner, Carmen is the best of the libretto. Although I'd seen it several times as an opera, I was never impressed with it so much before as I was at this concert." He later described it as "one of the only operas I've ever been able to stomach." (I believe his allusion to Wagner was perfunctory.)

The tale of a man driven to kill his untamable lover, *Carmen* employed a naturalistic form of storytelling and unusually earthy subject matter. Within ten years of its stage debut in 1875, Henri Meilhac and Ludovic Halévy's adaptation of Prosper Mérimée's 1845 novella became one of Europe's most popular operas. The Academy of Music hosted its 1878 American premiere, but it was the Met's 1906 production starring Enrico Caruso that cemented the show in the American repertory. Oscar I also had a significant success with a 1907 production at his Manhattan Opera House, a production that turned around the fate of that struggling theater.

Oscar II called his version *Carmen Jones,* transposing the story from nineteenth-century southern Spain to the contemporary American South, and he substituted Bizet's gypsies and military men for African American workers in a segregated World War II parachute factory. His idea for an all-Black cast owed something to Orson Welles's 1936 *Macbeth* as well as Gershwin's 1935 opera *Porgy and Bess,* which was successfully revived on Broadway in 1942 by producer Cheryl Crawford in the mode of a musical play. Hammerstein paused from writing *Carmen Jones* to pen a fan letter about Crawford's "thrilling" production to Ira Gershwin, who cowrote the lyrics. He described the "electric current" going through the audience that eventually exploded in "delirium." Ira thanked him for "the nice things you say." "I must tell you," he continued, "that the finest thing about it is what it tells me about you. Not that I didn't know it all along."

Before writing his new lyrics for Bizet's music, Oscar read Merimee's novella and consulted the published libretti in French and English. Then he placed the score on his piano and started listening obsessively to an Italian recording. "And, really, I had more pleasure than I've ever had writing anything," he wrote. "I took my time on it. There was no deadline. I loved what I was working on." He was thus engaged when he received a telegram on July 19, 1941, from Easton, Connecticut, which read:

> DEAR OSCAR HAVE YOU READ OR HEARD ABOUT A NEW SERIAL NOVEL OF MINE CALLED SARATOGA TRUNK RICHARD RODGERS WANTS TO MAKE A MUSICAL PLAY OF IT AND WE WOULD BE SO HAPPY IF YOU WOULD BE WILLING TO DO THE BOOK HOW DO YOU FEEL ABOUT IT
>
> —EDNA FERBER

Ten days later came another telegram, this one from New York:

> LARRY AND I SIT WITH EVERYTHING CROSSED HOPING THAT YOU WILL DO SARATOGA TRUNK WITH US
>
> —RICHARD RODGERS

These telegrams were not, in fact, the initial overtures to Hammerstein; Rodgers and Hammerstein had been quietly discussing collaboration since at least the beginning of the month. On July 6, two weeks before Ferber's telegram, Rodgers wrote to Hammerstein at Highland Farm, in media res, as it were:

> Ferber has been "acting up" and has been so impossible on the whole subject of the play that at the moment I am trying to decide whether or not I can afford to let myself in for what appears to be endless aggravations. I will let you know at the earliest possible moment. In the meanwhile you will probably come to some decision as to your own position. . . . . Even if nothing comes of this difficult matter it will at least have allowed us to approach each other professionally. Specifically, you feel that I should have a book with "substance" to write to. Will you think seriously about doing such a book?

Rodgers had come to the realization (again) that he could no longer work with Hart. The duo had produced a new show on Broadway every year from 1935 to 1940, but their dazzling twenty-four-year collaboration had become an emotional and logistical nightmare. Hart drifted further and further away from sobriety, from work, and from Rodgers. In 1937, when they were writing *I Married an Angel,* Rodgers wrangled director Josh Logan into serving as a babysitter for Hart, who was in Atlantic City avoiding writing any way he could (including teaching Logan a card game called Cocksucker's Rummy, in which cheating is required). Privately Hart referred to Rodgers as "a certain character back home with a sour apple face" and "the high-school principal." Logan saw that it was "agony" for Hart to sit down to write and that he "envied and therefore hated Dick's rugged self-discipline." Hart started writing only on the day the pair was scheduled to return to New York. Some of what he turned in was gibberish.

Rodgers had been actively casting about for a new partner since 1938 when he approached Ira Gershwin about working with him, but he came away from the encounter with the impression that Gershwin had lost his spark when his brother George died the previous year.

Saratoga Trunk would indeed be made into a musical, called *Saratoga,* without the participation of either Hammerstein or Rodgers. Their consideration of the project, though, was a bridge to what became the most meaningful collaboration in musical theater.

In its tenacious way, Hollywood still had one more humiliation to offer Hammerstein.

In September of 1941 Hammerstein attended the Hollywood Bowl production of *Rose-Marie,* his 1924 operetta with Rudolf Friml. He was appalled to find his dialogue cut in some parts, rewritten in others. No one had contacted him about these changes. Hammerstein shot off a letter to the newly formed Hollywood Bowl Opera Association, writing, "There is nothing I can do about it now except to express my surprise at such flagrant bad faith." He was answered by Association manager Tim Girton, who was not at all flustered by the anger of a has-been. "Before reading your letter of October 4," Girton wrote, "I expected it would contain words of praise, however, after reading your letter I find it contains nothing but criticisms. I believe that both you and Mr. Friml should be delighted to have one of your Plays produced by an Organization like the Hollywood Bowl Opera Association." Hammerstein's reputation in Hollywood was so low at this point that a functionary felt he could freely condescend to him without consequence.

As for defending what had been done to Hammerstein's libretto, Girton explained: "The re-writing of the script was in fine hands—Mr. Zeke Colvan and Mr. Milton Lazarus. They brought not only the script but also the music to where it is a credit to everyone connected with it." Colvan had been the production stage manager of the original *Show Boat,* and, because the physical show had been so complex, Hammerstein gave Colvan the credit of "director," even though Hammerstein himself had done the bulk of the work, as he told then-budding theater historian Miles Kreuger. That Colvan should now be credited for secretly "improving" Hammerstein's work would have been too much for the latter to bear.

Hammerstein's insistence on optimism skewed his judgment in Hollywood, preventing him again and again from honestly assessing his situation. In 1957, having finally absorbed this lesson, he sagely answered a letter from Lloyd Foster who asked him for his "best advice." "Develop the habit of being honest with yourself" was his reply. He continued:

> Being honest involves toughness and courage, courage for instance to admit what you are afraid of. Only when you admit the existence of a fear to yourself can you start making any advance toward conquering that fear. Honesty to yourself involves the finding out of what you really want in life as well as the things you really do not want. The truth about yourself is hard to find, but it is your duty to seek it. On no other basis can you erect a good life. Too many of us build our lives on self-created fantasies about ourselves.

Hammerstein knew he wanted to address the war in his work soon after the Japanese attacked Pearl Harbor. He had already penned a salute to America, a show called *American Jubilee,* for the 1939 New York World's Fair. When the Nazis invaded France in June of 1940, he impulsively wrote "The Last Time I Saw Paris," a lyric that Kern set to a melody of rue and sorrow. It was a song of mourning for prewar Europe that never mentioned the hard reality of Hitler or his troops on the ground. What went unsaid was what made the song special, and it became a hit by the end of the year.

Now Hammerstein approached Kern about another war song, though he was no longer seeking subtlety. Kern, who must have rejected the first lyric that Hammerstein submitted, wrote to him on January 19, 1942:

> Since you indicate that you are going to try again, it is only fair that I rush these reactions to you forthwith, even though unsigned. I just don't want to take part in producing a boastful, threatening, jingoistic roundelay. The very word "jingo" has gravelled the bejezus out of me, ever since I first encountered its doggerel generator. I have literally blushed for Britain every time I have seen or heard
>
> > We don't want to fight,
> > But, by jingo, if we do,
> > We've got the ships, we've got the men,
> > We've got the money, too.

The composer refers here to a British song that introduced the term "jingoism" in 1878, when the Russo-Turkish War threatened to spill over to the West. Kern suggested that Hammerstein might find "some composer who doesn't share my revulsion for the whole general scheme. . . . Sorry I couldn't thaw out your extremities with my usual warm enthusiasm for your art, indicated with my customary charm."

Instead, Hammerstein went to work on *Carmen Jones*. At the same time, he raised money for the war effort and for the National Urban League, an antidiscrimination organization. It would be seven months before he began writing *Oklahoma!*, which, though set in the first decade of the twentieth century, allowed Hammerstein to address the current moment in a way much more powerful than any patriotic song could.

The coming together of Rodgers and Hammerstein was a sweet relief for both men. They knew each other's sensibilities well enough that their artistic connection was fully formed the moment it began. "When we first started writing together," Hammerstein said, "we had no conversations on method." They had "no definite policy except one of complete flexibility." They went to work not on a Ferber adaptation but on the musicalization of a play previously produced by the Theatre Guild, *Green Grow the Lilacs* by Lynn Riggs. They discussed the mood and purpose of each song, and almost always Hammerstein penned the lyric first—a mark of the story's

Rodgers and Hammerstein together at last.
Courtesy of Photofest

prominence—although according to Oscar "in nearly all of our scores, there are at least one or two songs in which [Rodgers] wrote the music first."

It was a promising match, but not everyone saw it as a sure thing. Hearing the news, Robert Russell Bennett told Hammerstein, "You've got yourself another Vincent Youmans there," referring to the composer of Hammerstein's 1923 hit *The Wildflower.* What Bennett was saying about Rodgers we can extract from another of his observations about Youmans: "Something awful happens to very young people who see a lot of money coming in."

For his part, Rodgers revealed in a 1961 interview with Arnold Michaelis that he saw himself as the only successful person on the *Oklahoma!* team. Michaelis had asked for the composer's comment on an intriguing detail that Hammerstein had shared with him. The lyricist said that, over the years, he and Rodgers enjoyed a thought experiment about what they would have told each other if *Oklahoma!* had been a flop: "We would tell each other why it was a failure and how ridiculous we were to do what we did—to open the show with the best song in the show, for instance, to begin with. Who would do that? Forty minutes pass after the rise of the curtain before you see one chorus girl. There's no chorus. Who wants to go to that kind of a musical comedy?" Michaelis asked Rodgers to elaborate on Hammerstein's story. He went in an unexpected direction:

> Oh, yes, yes. There was nothing about *Oklahoma!*, absolutely nothing, to suggest success to anybody. The original play was a flop. *Green Grow the Lilacs*—very unsuccessful play. We were being produced by the Theatre Guild, and the directors of the Theatre Guild have said this publicly and in print that this was to be their last show, because it was going to be a flop and that would finish them. I'm not putting them out of business by revealing this because they have said it. Oscar had had nearly eleven years of failures. Mamoulian, the director, couldn't get a job. Agnes de Mille, who did the choreography, had done one job, *Rodeo*, and that's all. She was William de Mille's daughter; this was her claim to fame. Now, the only person connected with that show who had had success was me. But I was invalidated in everybody's mind because I had worked, for twenty-three years at that time, with Larry, and *I was now working with a failure* [emphasis mine], and I had to be bad, too. So every single element connected with this show had to spell failure.

Rodgers discounts *Show Boat* and all of Hammerstein's earlier work when he characterizes the pre-*Oklahoma!* Hammerstein as a mere technician: "I think to say 'The corn is as high as a elephant's eye' instead of what Oscar first thought of, which was 'cow pony's eye,' I think this is brilliant. And I think this is where the man starts to become an artist instead of a workman."

At this point, Hammerstein had been dead for a year. I do not believe Rodgers would have ventured this opinion during his collaborator's lifetime.

Hammerstein's long fight to keep bitterness and alienation at bay paid off in a burst of five words—"Oh, what a beautiful mornin'!" Recalling that time in a letter to Elizabeth Rider Montgomery, Hammerstein said, "This is one of the few songs that I wrote quickly. I would say that I finished it in about three days." He worked at a tall standing desk in Doylestown, writing with a soft pencil. Rodgers composed the melody in ten minutes, which likewise suggests the ease that presents itself after laying down a heavy burden. For these men at this moment there truly was a bright golden haze on the meadow. Their excitement for a new beginning infused the entire show with an exceptional light.

For research, Hammerstein sent Rodgers a book of folk songs from the American Southwest. "I opened the book, played through the music of one song, closed the book, and never looked at it again," said Rodgers. "If my melodies were going to be authentic, they'd have to be authentic on my own terms." At times Rodgers found his sound in the lyrics themselves. In "The Surrey with the Fringe on Top," for instance, Hammerstein's words suggested to Rodgers "both a clip-clop rhythm and a melody in which the straight, flat country road could be musically conveyed through a repetition of the straight, flat sound of the D note, followed by a sharp upward flick as fowls scurry to avoid being hit by the moving wheels."

In fact, playwright Lynn Riggs had relied on the music Rodgers overlooked: "My intent was to recapture in a kind of nostalgic glow, the great range of mood which characterized the old folk songs and ballads I used to hear in my Oklahoma childhood, their quaintness, their sadness, their robustness, their simplicity. . . . For this reason I considered it wise to throw away the conventions of ordinary theatricality—a complex plot, swift action, to try to exhibit luminosity in the simplest of stories, a wide arc of mood and feeling."

Hammerstein connected with this search for the elemental. "Dick and I talked for a long time before we accepted this revolutionary idea of not having any chorus girls in the first forty minutes," he wrote. His language echoes Riggs, who thought it wise "to throw away the conventions of ordinary theatricality." Hammerstein said he and Rodgers "tried very hard to obey tradition, to invent reasons why the girls should be on. We couldn't find any that didn't seem to hurt the character of the play we were adapting. So we opened the musical play very much as the play opened."

As had happened sixteen years earlier with *Show Boat,* the audience sensed instantly that this show was something they had not experienced before. The overture starts with the blast of a horn, then a whirr of violin strings as fast and high as a comet, before the orchestra gallops off into rousing melody. When the curtain goes up—silence. A mature woman in a bonnet churns butter; no one else is in sight. The backdrop is clearly country, prairie, somewhere sparsely populated (though after the title change from *Away We Go,* the locale was obvious). Then, a man's voice from offstage, sings a cappella:

> There's a bright golden haze on the meadow
> There's a bright golden haze on the meadow
> The corn is high as a elephant's eye
> And it looks like it's climbing clear up to the sky. . . .

Starting on such unembellished emotion lent credence to everything that followed. "It was like the light from a thousand lanterns," said Hammerstein about those opening moments in the theater. "You could *feel* the glow; it was that bright."

Hammerstein sometimes humblebragged that *Oklahoma!* was simply "a story about a girl deciding which man will take her to a box social." The girl is Laurey, and there is never any doubt she prefers the handsome cowboy Curly, who represents what is noble in the American character. Though he works by and for himself, he is deeply invested in the communal good. He wakes up seeking beauty and feeling gratitude. He is funny, kind, and generous but tough when he needs to be. He is alive and open to the world and creates goodwill wherever he goes.

And then there's the not terribly clean farmhand Jud Fry, who lives in the smokehouse and lurks ominously on the periphery; bringing firewood into the house, he stares at Laurey over breakfast "from under his eyebrows." She's afraid to ride alone with him and tells Aunt Eller he might "do sumpin' terrible. He makes me shiver ever' time he gits clost to me." At night, after she locks her door and fastens her window, she hears him "a-walkin' up and down out there under that tree outside my room."

Jud is a loner and a collector of pornography, an unnerving blot on the otherwise sunny depiction of territory folks and their future state. Knowing his customers, the peddler Ali Hakim offers Jud a novelty item called "The Little Wonder"—a kaleidoscope of "dirty pictures"—but instead Jud wants a "frog sticker," a similar device but with a hidden knife on a spring. Jud is both violent and inherently antidemocratic. In his best of all possible worlds, he thinks, "I'm better than that smart aleck cowhand / who thinks he is better than me." Fifty years later Stephen Sondheim wrote *Assassins,* an entire musical full of Juds. In 1943, however, Jud was a new kind of musical character: not a cardboard villain and evil schemer, but a disenfranchised man nursing a rage that inevitably finds a target.

Set "just after the turn of the century," *Oklahoma!* of course never alludes to World War II, which the country had entered fifteen months earlier. Combustion occurred, however, in the space between the story and the audience's feelings about their present moment. Agnes de Mille, who watched from the back of the orchestra section with Richard Rodgers on opening night, recalled the song in which the audience moved from excited to unmoored. It came early in the second act, with the whole cast onstage for a party. A farmer named Carnes, moved by a drunken love for his fellow man, toasts a community that has overcome differences to achieve cohesion just before the territory graduates to a state. Then comes the song "The Farmer and the Cowman," which refers to a historical enmity in which the farmer's need for fencing to control his property collided with the cowboy's desire to freely move his cattle. (This battle still rages in part of the American psyche; look at Cliven Bundy and his refusal to pay the federal government's grazing fees in southern Nevada.) In fact, the farmer's ascendency spelled an end to the cowboy's way of life, which is why the show ends with a married Curly settling down to plant a garden with "carrots and pertaters."

Carnes's well-intentioned toast devolves into a feud, with comic insults flying between farmers and cowmen. When these barbs spill over into a physical free-for-all, however, order must be restored for the sake of the community. That is why Aunt Eller grabs a gun from someone's holster and fires it over her head. The shot freezes men in mid-punch, and the partygoers look around to see if anyone's been injured. An armed Aunt Eller strides through the crowd, yelling in a voice that demands respect, "They ain't nobody goin' to slug out anythin'—this here's a party!" The guests hesitantly resume singing at gunpoint.

Perhaps it was the joke of a woman shooting a gun to demand an end to violence—showing Americans to be peaceful non-pacifists, a people not seeking violence but willing to use it to restore order—but when Aunt Eller shouted her line, the audience exploded in joy. Victor Hugo's credo that "in the theater, a mob becomes a people" comes to mind.

With the crowd still elated, Aunt Eller added one more verse, a distillation of democracy, which again ignited the audience:

> I'd like to teach you all a little sayin'
> And learn the words by heart the way you should
> I don't say I'm no better than anybody else,
> [pause]
> But I'll be damned if I ain't jist as good!

The story of *Oklahoma!* has been told in many volumes, but it bears repeating. The musical's triumph is the theater equivalent of *Rocky, Seabiscuit,* and *Cinderella* combined. As Rodgers said, the show came at a true do-or-die moment for the Theatre Guild, a producer of worthy stage fare since 1920. It had just suffered sixteen flops in a row and put its Fifty-Second Street theater up for sale. Its demise hung over the making of *Oklahoma!,* which held tryouts and rehearsed in the Guild's unheated quarters; dancer Vivian Smith recalled that the creators were bundled up in overcoats when she auditioned. Nor was the theater clean; Agnes de Mille and her dancers worked on filthy rugs in the foyer or upstairs in a badly lit room filled with boxes that, when moved, sent an avalanche of dust into the performers' lungs. "We all got catarrh," de Mille later said.

The Guild showed a desperate brilliance when it laid down its last bet on a musical about the American Southwest. In 1942, when contracts were signed, the two most popular Broadway musicals were Rodgers and Hart's *By Jupiter,* a knowingly silly show about a war between the Greeks and the Amazons; and *Star and Garter,* a burlesque revue starring Gypsy Rose Lee, Bobby Clark, a vaudevillian known for his painted-on eyeglasses, and Professor Lamberti, who chewed a huge wad of gum while playing the xylophone. Between the bombing of Pearl Harbor and the opening of *Oklahoma!,* audiences seemed to want nothing more than to escape reality.

The show previewed under the title *Away We Go* in New Haven while the Guild was raising money for the move to New York. Producers Helburn and Langner discovered that the very idea of their show repelled investors. MGM said it was categorically not interested in western musicals, and countless backer auditions ended with awkward comments such as "I don't like plays about farmhands." The son of playwright Phillip Barry saw the musical in Boston and phoned his father to urge him to invest. Barry demurred, saying that "*Green Grow the Lilacs* was one of the dullest plays ever written."

Too bad for Barry: *Oklahoma!* eventually paid $2,500 for every dollar invested. Somehow the Theatre Guild, which had begun by devoting itself to noncommercial American and foreign playwrights, produced the biggest hit of all time.

In Max Wilk's book *OK! The Story of "Oklahoma!"* de Mille talks about the time a musician struck a wrong note during the final dress rehearsal. Diana Adams, one of the dancers, winced in pain—"not annoyance or amusement," but "agonized concern," said de Mille. Richard Rodgers noticed. He told his choreographer that "never before had that look crossed a chorus girl's face." This is when it hit him that the entire company comprised dedicated artists—the business of making musicals was now fully professionalized. "Diana's expression marked the beginning of new era," said de Mille.

De Mille cast her most serious and talented students and allowed them to have their own distinct movements—her chorus did not dance in lockstep. "The lineup I put together was without parallel," she said. "These young women did not look like traditional Broadway chorus members." Richard Rodgers took one look at Bambi Linn, sixteen at the time with braces on her teeth, and said to de Mille, "Uh-oh. No." Even Theresa Helburn asked de Mille why they couldn't have girls who could dance and also had pretty legs.

"These were personalities, and they were soloists, and they had big, strong techniques," recalled de Mille, who herself used the term "piano legs" to describe a couple of her dancers. To please Rodgers and Helburn, de Mille cast two traditionally beautiful dancers "just for appearance['s] sake," and the pair clung to each other desperately, she said, "from pure loneliness."

Oklahoma! investors learned that they would not be able to procure a role for a girlfriend, a fairly widespread perk in the 1920s and 1930s. Hammerstein's correspondence file contains several letters from acquaintances vouching for the "poise and charm" of a young actor who really needed to be seen. "After you have seen and heard her I am sure you will think the same as I" goes one characteristic note. A similar request reads, "I would appreciate it greatly if you or your secretary would get in touch with her and arrange an audition at your convenience." Another gentleman added, "I do not usually go for brunettes at all, so you know this girl must be good."

Choosing from the young women already cast was, however, still allowed. De Mille recalled that hookups tended to happen as soon as the company left New York for a pre-Broadway tour. "The people who date up the girls arrange it out of town; they take them upstairs at the first stop," she told Max Wilk in 1990. "But when I was there nobody said anything to those girls in my presence." Still, she couldn't be everywhere at once. Linn, the teenager whose looks Rodgers had derided, became interesting to him in New Haven. De Mille said that "Bambi had a conversation with Dick Rodgers, and she said she wasn't interested in sex, and he was simply stunned. How can she say such a thing?" Her dancers were artists, said de Mille: "They didn't have time for that nonsense."

Oklahoma! underwent vital fine tunings on the road. In the process nerves were strained and arguments broke out, especially in New Haven, where the cast and crew were working around the clock. Wrote de Mille in her diary, "There's hell ahead, and unless we pull the show up very quick we are sunk."

Hammerstein alone remained visibly unperturbed. De Mille wrote, "He sat through the endless nights, quietly giving off intelligence like a stove. He never got angry, or nasty, or excited, but when people were beating their heads on the orchestra rail he made the one commonsense suggestion that any genius might think of if he was not at the moment consuming himself."

The show's next stop was Boston, which is where the creators renamed the musical and added a rousing harmonic vocal arrangement to the title song, the eleven o'clock number. This prompted a restaging from de Mille, who put in what became known as the "flying wedge" at the song's climax. Again, the entire company is present, this time for the wedding of Laurey and Curly. They sing "Oklahoma!" as a toast to the newlyweds, and the song peaks as the company spells out the name of the soon-to-be christened state, all the while moving downstage in a V-shape until they form a straight line at the very lip of the stage, as close as possible to the audience. When they tried out the new staging, conductor Jay Blackton could hear the audience at his back slowly going crazy. Once the team got this number just right, the whole show clicked into place.

Still, word on the street said their odds were shaky at best. A week before opening Oscar wrote to Arthur, "The show looks fine but Dick and I are keeping our fingers crossed until the New York opening is over." To Lynn Riggs he wrote, "If we can just make the hurdle over the first night grave diggers in New York, we will all be home." On the morning of their Broadway opening, Oscar and Dorothy took a walk in Doylestown. He confided to her that he did not know what he would do if the audience did not like *Oklahoma!* because it was the only kind of show he could now write.

Hammerstein did not have to wait for the reviews to learn his fate. About the opening night crowd, de Mille wrote, "They were roaring. They were howling." Oscar and Dorothy sat holding hands together in the fifth row while Rodgers and de Mille stood at the back of the house. The choreographer recalled the night in a note to Rodgers, written just two weeks before he died. In a cramped, unsteady hand, de Mille scrawled, "Dear Dick—Thirty-eight years ago you and I stood hand in hand at the back of the St. James waiting to see what would happen. Your arms were around me at the end of 'Farmer' and thus the world broke open." She added, "We are both broken now and badly dented if not daunted but we know we were right and we know what we are doing today and we can take joy in the knowledge."

Larry Hart was also in the audience on opening night. He had seen the show in New Haven before it gelled and couldn't have anticipated the mad joy that now gripped the crowd. Sitting with his mother in a box, he applauded, howled with laughter, and shouted bravos. At Sardi's after the show he embraced Rodgers and said, "This show of yours will run forever."

For her part Mary Rodgers, who was thirteen at the time, remembered the morning after: "My parents insanely excited as they sit with the seven big rave New York reviews spread out in the dining room. My mother is clapping her hands in delight, and Daddy looks—what is that?—happy. I thought it was a very good opportunity to ask them to let us go riding, which was expensive so they usually said no. They said yes."

Three weeks later Hart's beloved mother, Frieda, died. Her funeral had to be postponed until Hart could be found drinking in a nearby bar. Mary Rodgers wrote that her father suggested a revival of Rodgers and Hart's 1927 musical *A Connecticut Yankee,* "possibly to soften the blow of the huge success of *Oklahoma!*" When that revival premiered at the Martin Beck Theater in November, a drunken Hart stood in the back of the house loudly reciting the show's lyrics and had to be "escorted" from the theater. The next afternoon, Frederick Loewe found him sitting in the gutter outside an Eighth Avenue bar. Hart died four days later, from pneumonia, at Doctor's Hospital. The nurse who was with him reported his last words, which could have been a line from one of his lyrics: "What have I lived for?"

It's difficult not to contrast Hart here with Hammerstein, who asked a much better question: "Why was I born?" Again, here's how Hammerstein put it to an interviewer: "I don't know why I was born, beyond the fact that I know why everybody was born. Everybody was born to advance the life in this universe, the life that we all live."

Two months after *Oklahoma!* opened, Hammerstein contributed a piece to the *New York Times* in which he shared that his most pressing problem in adapting Riggs's play was its "shivaree scene" near the end. A shivaree (from the French *charivari*) is a noisy mock serenade forcibly visited on newlyweds after they have retired, a ritual that often turns rowdy and lascivious. The one depicted by Riggs (who spelled it "shivoree") is drawn out and awful. He describes the perpetrators as "disturbed and hysterical with conjecture on the marital scene they have come to despoil." As they raid the couples' bedroom, the men share drunken opinions about the bride like "She's a purty un, too" and "Got a face for kissin'!" followed by "And that ain't all, brother!" They drag Laurey and Curly out of the house and force them to climb a ladder to the top of a large haystack. They shout and throw things at them until Curly notices the haystack is on fire. Jeeter (Jud in the musical) has crept into the crowd and lit the stack with a torch. Curly leaps down onto Jeeter, and after a brief struggle Jeeter falls on his own knife and dies. Three days later Curly breaks out of jail, where he's awaiting trial, to visit Laurey and tell her his epiphany—he's going to become a farmer. When the federal marshal's men come to collect Curly, Aunt Eller shames them for siding with the "govament" instead of with territory folks and for taking a bridegroom away from his bride. The marshals agree to let Curly stay the night until the following day's trial. The play ends on that off-balance note.

Hammerstein determined he would shorten the shivaree and make it "lusty and boyish," "essentially good natured" rather than "smirky." There's no haystack (though it reappears in the film version), and the intruder's remarks are threatening but not as explicit. Jud arrives and, in the middle of the chaos, seizes and kisses Laurey. When Curly pulls him away, the men fight; Jud dies as Jeeter did, by falling on his knife. "I never had the slightest squeamishness or hesitation about this scene," writes Hammerstein. "The only honest way to grant Curly and Laurey a future of real fulfillment is to wipe out Jud."

Then there was the problem that Riggs left hanging. As Hammerstein put it, "Once our hero had killed a man, how could we get him out of that jam?" He decided that the community, led by Aunt Eller, would try Curly for Jud's murder "right then and there." He saw nothing pernicious in this act of frontier justice and its inevitable not-guilty verdict; to his mind the scene was "funny, but reasonably just and fair and common-sensible." Seven decades later, a director named Daniel Fish slowed down this scene significantly and cast it in a sinister light. Now there is nothing accidental about Jud's death—Curly shoots Jud through the heart at close range. The makeshift trial is neither reasonable nor fair; it is a clear railroading of justice. Fish forces *Oklahoma!* into a tragic mold, ending it on a bleak and bitter note.

With pistols and rifles adorning the walls of the set, Fish implicated the audience in the proceedings. His in-the-round staging, in which the actors addressed specific theatergoers, allowed us all to watch each other watching. Further dissolving boundaries at intermission, actors served small cups of under-spiced chili to anyone who wanted one. In Fish's *Oklahoma!* we are all part of a gun-crazed culture that scapegoats the disenfranchised and will overlook, in certain cases, those who take the law into their own hands.

The show was first produced at Bard College in the summer of 2015, three years after the killing of teenager Trayvon Martin by a vigilante, and at a time Americans were still absorbing the astonishing fact that the murder of twenty children and six adults at Connecticut's Sandy Hook Elementary School that same year had failed to produce a single act of federal gun reform. This first iteration of Fish's *Oklahoma!* also opened a year after twelve-year-old Tamir Rice and eighteen-year-old Michael Brown became two more names in the ever-growing list of African Americans killed by law enforcement and the Black Lives Matter movement took hold. According to an NPR report, police fatally shot at least 135 unarmed Black men and women between 2015 and the end of 2020. When Fish opened his production on Broadway in April 2019, these killings were on the minds of many theatergoers.

Among Fish's many ideas about the show, perhaps his most enjoyable was to countrify its sound. The strumming of banjos and mandolins and the twang of a steel pedal guitar made the score intimate, unpretentious, and fresh. Dressed for an informal hoedown, the youthful cast employed the vocal frills and rural inflections of country and bluegrass singers. The western music that Rodgers eschewed had finally made its way into the show. Line readings sounded utterly contemporary and served as a reminder of how funny Hammerstein was. His dialogue was riveting and charming. In the hands of actor Will Brill, "It's an Outrage"—Ali Hakim's screed against the current crop of shotgun weddings—was a well-structured comedy routine (and the only funny version of the song I've ever heard).

The production reveled in the attractions of its young, interracial characters, and within the triangle of Laurey, Curly, and Jud desire flowed in all directions. Fish also acknowledged a new generation's approach to gender fluidity and ambiguity: choreographer John Higginbotham reenvisioned the "dream ballet"—an explication of Laurey's emotional state in the middle of the show—as a solo dance for Gabrielle Hamilton, who appeared bald and nonbinary in a long T-shirt. Instead of presenting Laurey's fears and desires, as Agnes de Mille had done, Higginbotham invaded her id, sending Hamilton scuttling and galloping across the stage like a child scrambling for identity and form. This abrasive element further unbeautified the original *Oklahoma!* and claimed the show for contemporary times.

Ambitious in both conception and execution, Fish's *Oklahoma!* produced much excitement and controversy. The director shoehorned the ending of Sondheim's *Sweeney Todd* into the finale of a show once known for its "infectious gaiety," a phrase used by the original *New York Times* reviewer (Lewis Nichols, because Atkinson was reporting from China at the time). No one saw the overlay of Sondheim on Hammerstein coming. Anyone who knew the show and walked in on the finale would be mystified to see a blood-splattered Laurey and Curly, along with a raised-from-the-dead Jud, angrily bark the show's last bit of song ("Oklahoma! OK!").

The production alienated much of the old guard—the *Wall Street Journal's* Terry Teachout called it "a sneering burlesque of the most influential and beloved Broadway musical of the 20th century." Rex Reed in *The Observer* wrote, "It had to happen. The miserable fools who are hell-bent on changing the theater world by destroying timeless classics in a misguided effort to make them relevant, trendy and politically correct (whatever that means) finally got around to screwing up *Oklahoma!*" However, Ben Brantley in the *New York Times* called the production "wide awake" and posed the

Ideas of male sexiness on stage evolved from Alfred Drake's 1943 Curly (*left*) to Damon Daunno's 2019 Curly (*right*).
Left: Courtesy of the New York Public Library; *right:* Courtesy of Teddy Wolff

question, "How is it that the coolest new show on Broadway in 2019 is a 1943 musical usually regarded as a very square slice of American pie?" The production won a Tony Award for best revival of a musical (as well as for Ali Stroker's turn as Ado Annie) and excited a new generation of theatergoers who launched the hashtag #sexyOklahoma!

As someone who never tires of Hammerstein's best shows, I was surprised by the widespread surprise that *Oklahoma!* remained relevant and sexy in 2019. By this time New York audiences had seen significant revivals of *Carousel* (directed by Nicholas Hytner, 1994), *South Pacific* (Bartlett Sher, 2008), and *The King and I* (Sher, 2015), and each time reviewers had trouble believing that shows they had considered nostalgic Americana were pertinent, biting, and moving. Explaining his own interpretation, Daniel Fish said that he was not trying to change or push *Oklahoma!* but to "really hear it," leading critic Frank Rich to pose "a cultural riddle" in *New York* magazine: "If the darker show [Fish] illuminates was present in *Oklahoma!* at its inception, why and how did it get there, and how did it evaporate in the intervening decades?" The darkness was always there. But familiarity breeds indifference, and we simply stopped listening. Those who recalled the show as antiquated were not remembering it accurately. It took a shift in emphasis to reveal what was already there: a show about how scapegoating helps cement communities, how disenfranchisement incites violence, and how who and what we love is entangled with where we stand.

CHAPTER SIX

The Namesake

OSCAR HAMMERSTEIN II knew that by recasting *Carmen* as a musical about African Americans working for the war effort he would make the story newly relevant. But, as he wrote in his introduction to the published libretto, this was no "stunt." The recasting allowed him to explore his own developing ideas about civil rights and ask his largely white audience to do the same. The musical played for more than a year on Broadway and was revived soon thereafter. The *New York Tribune* called it "brilliantly translated" and "as wonderful and exciting as it is audacious."

Throughout his life Hammerstein felt *Carmen Jones* to be one of his finest works. At its out-of-town opening in Philadelphia, he saw "the most excited first night audience I have ever seen." After it opened, he wrote to Billy, "All the things I would have liked to be said about it have been said by press and public alike."

Writing the show also made good on a late-blooming gratitude and connection the lyricist felt for his grandfather, Oscar I. After sailing from Germany as a teenager, Oscar I dedicated his life to bringing first-rate opera to the good people of Manhattan. He met solid resistance to the form, including from a young Oscar II. In a 1945 letter to Alfred Knopf, the lyricist recalled being taken by his mother to an opera:

> I sat back in the well-cushioned orchestra chair—Grandpa built beautiful opera houses—and I found myself enjoying the lovely

> music coming up from the orchestra pit. But I was puzzled and disturbed by the accompanying action on stage. Sometimes the fat lady would look very sad, and there was no way of knowing why. Sometimes she laughed, but I wouldn't know what the joke was and I wished I did. It then seemed quite clear to me why Grandpa lost money on opera. Listening to people sing words you didn't understand wasn't much fun. That what I thought then. That's what I think now.

Featuring an uncomplicated yet sensational plot—woman seduces and then spurns man, man kills woman—*Carmen* was the rare opera that the adult Hammerstein admired. Georges Bizet, having been dead for sixty-eight years, was the perfect writing partner for a normally collaborative artist seeking at that moment to wrest back control of his career. The resulting work was a hybrid—half opera, half musical—and a daunting show to stage and cast; *Carmen Jones* called for more than one hundred singing actors at a time when there were few pipelines to the Broadway stage for African American talent. Max Gordon said he would produce the show but, unable to raise funds before the advent of *Oklahoma!*, dropped his option at the end of 1942. Once Hammerstein became a success again, Billy Rose read the script and declared, "Oscar, you've written the freshest musical anyone ever wrote and I want to produce it."

Married to vaudeville powerhouse Fanny Brice, Rose was a latter-day Ziegfeld, an impresario who loved large-scale extravaganza, particularly those involving female flesh in glittering settings. He had a finer appreciation for lyrics than did Ziegfeld—he was, after all, a lyricist himself, known for co-writing some charming popular songs such as "More Than You Know" (with Edward Eliscu) and "It's Only a Paper Moon" (with Yip Harburg). Also like Ziegfeld, his association with Hammerstein would produce the most serious and lasting work of his career. For *Carmen Jones* he raised $176,000—twice *Oklahoma!*'s budget—and wanted a visually striking but appropriately serious look. He turned to Hassard Short, known for innovative lighting design, whom Hammerstein had apparently forgiven for his role in *Very Warm for May*. Short was the minder Max Gordon brought in to oversee that show's disastrous rewrite.

Short's idea for *Carmen Jones* was to drench each setting, via light and fabric, in its own bold color: a yellow scene was followed by a purple one, then by a blue one, and finally the death scene was saturated in red. "Razzle-dazzle is the word—or one of them," reported playwright Leo Brady in a letter to his friend Walter Kerr. "Positively shocking colors like nothing you've ever seen anywhere." For his work on the show Short was profiled in the *New York Times,* which reported that "the primary colors used, with all their primitive qualities, were needed to bring out . . . the characters of Carmen Jones, Joe, Husky Miller, and all the rest."

The use of the word "primitive" here signals the problem that has always dogged *Carmen Jones:* is the show trading on harmful stereotypes and therefore inherently unworthy? The answer is not as simple and clear as it might at first appear.

With *Carmen Jones,* Oscar II honored his namesake by bringing one of his grandfather's favorite operas to a large American audience. He adapted *Carmen* not merely into English, but into folk English. As in many other projects, Hammerstein wrote in dialect to make the show as accessible as possible. He took the promise of verismo, updated it, and put it in a fraught and powerful American context. But to understand the importance of *Carmen Jones,* it is necessary to know a bit more about the lyricist's grandfather.

In their underemployed days of the 1930s, Oscar II and Uncle Arthur gathered material to make a film on Arthur's father, Oscar I. They interviewed actors, singers, stagehands, stage door attendants, and "Lord knows how many people" who knew him from the cigar business. The film never materialized, though in the 1950s Oscar II oversaw a published biography of the patriarch by J. Vincent Sheean. In that book's introduction, the grandson wrote, "It is ironic and sad and strange that I did not begin to understand or like my grandfather until the day of his death. But he was a strange man and so, perhaps, am I."

According to his naturalization papers, Oscar Hammerstein I was born on May 8, 1846, in Stettin, a prosperous Prussian city in the northwest of present-day Poland—a region that had only recently lifted its centuries-old edict barring Jews. He grew up in Berlin, the first child of Abraham Hammerstein, a successful builder and amateur violinist, and Berthe Valentin, who began teaching him to play piano when he was five. Ten years later, Berthe died, Abraham remarried, and Oscar left home. He bought passage to Liverpool, where he may have taken a clipper ship called the *Isaac*

Webb to New York. His name, however, does not show up on a manifest for that ship (or any other in that year or the surrounding years) at the National Archive, although his citizenship papers say he arrived in January 1863 at the age of sixteen. He found a room on the southern end of Greenwich Street, where he shoveled coal into the furnace in exchange for bed and board.

With the Civil War raging, employment for young men was plentiful. Oscar spotted an ad in a German-language newspaper calling for a "wide-awake young gentleman"; he applied for and landed the position. He started at two dollars a week at M. W. Menel & Bros Manufactory on Pearl Street, a cigar-making concern. He quickly learned the craft, swept floors, and studied English at night.

As soon as he acquired a few extra dollars and leisure time, Oscar became a dedicated theatergoer. In March 1864 he caught the Bryant Minstrels, an act made up of three Irish siblings who sang and played instruments in blackface. They were the first to perform Dan Emmett's "Dixie," which became the most popular song in the country—Abraham Lincoln loved it, and the Confederate States of America adapted it as its national anthem. Nine months later, Hammerstein was savvy enough to score a ticket to a one-night-only event at the Winter Garden on Broadway and West Third Street—*Julius Caesar* starring the brothers Edwin, Junius, and John Wilkes Booth. Five months after that, John Wilkes assassinated President Lincoln at another theater, in Washington, DC, shouting Brutus's line "Sic semper tyrannis!"

Oscar caught a full season of German opera at the Academy of Music on Fourteenth Street and Irving Place and became a regular patron there. Life was improving: he moved to a better address on Ann Street, an apartment he shared with coworker Adolf Blau; and he promptly fell in love with Blau's seventeen-year-old sister Rosa, who was petite, dark-haired, and striking. Around this time, he was also managing the Stadttheater in the Bowery. George Blumenthal, a child actor in those years, remembers Oscar directing the Christmas pantomimes, rushing about "on stage, in the front—and everywhere." He also wrote one-act comedies that were produced at the Germania Theater, also on Fourteenth Street and Irving Place. In 1874, he somehow found time to start a trade magazine, the *United States Tobacco Journal*. He continued tinkering with the mechanics of cigar making throughout his life, eventually taking out forty-four patents on devices that performed such neat tricks as stripping tobacco stalks in a new way or rolling twelve uniform cigars at once.

Rosa and Oscar married in 1868, when she was eighteen and he twenty-two. In their eleven years of marriage, she gave birth to eight children, only four of whom survived to adulthood—Harry, Arthur, William (Willie, father to Oscar II), and Abraham Lincoln Hammerstein. Oscar I was largely uninterested in his young sons; Arthur remembered his father returning home at night and going straight to the piano, which the children were not allowed to touch.

Rosa died nine days after delivering her fifth son, Edward, who himself was claimed by cholera before his first birthday. Oscar's sister Augusta, who had married and settled in Alabama, suggested he bring their younger sister Anna over from Berlin to help with the children. Something of a matchmaker, Augusta introduced both Anna and Oscar to their next mates. For her brother she picked a Selma acquaintance, Malvina Jacoby, a large, solidly respectable woman who was formidable even in her twenties. Oscar courted her in Selma and soon brought her back to New York as the second Mrs. Hammerstein in 1879. A stout, Margaret Dumont type who would be subjected to the kind of indignities the comedian suffered in multiple Marx Brothers movies, she bore Oscar two daughters: Rose and Stella.

The 1880s and 1890s were decades of extraordinary expansion for Oscar, who discovered that his tolerance for risk could be used to excellent advantage in real estate. He bought his first land parcel on 116th Street and flipped it a week later for a profit of $1,600. Then he bought more land. Malvina disapproved of the real-estate expenditures; if her marital troubles hadn't already begun, they did then. Oscar II remembered her as an overweight woman with a deep bass voice and a large mole on her chin. She frightened him, but he pretended she did not.

Poor Malvina. In marrying a man who seemed destined for greatness, she assumed that greatness would protect her and her family. She could not have imagined a husband with a complete disregard for financial security, or one who would sacrifice anyone and everything to feed his passion for opera. Oscar I's triumphs were glorious but fleeting, his decisions unilateral, and he swiftly alienated any business partners who dared to back him. His only long-term lieutenants were his brother-in-law Henry Rosenberg and his sons Willie and Arthur, but even his family had to sink or swim: the sons not willing or able to keep up, Harry and Abe, found themselves stranded in poverty and ill health. Oscar and Malvina divorced in May 1911 just before her death that same year. He then summarily cut off his daughters Stella and Rose, even though he had agreed to pay each young woman $100 a week for life. He was happy to explain his decision in theatrical terms to the *New York Times:* "I can only say that I have no intention of continuing to support grown-up children who are perfectly capable of supporting themselves. I have cut them off completely. . . . I have no desire to emulate the eccentricities and actions of the late, lamented King Lear."

Oscar was a short man, five feet three inches, with brown eyes that radiated intelligence. In his prime he was just stocky enough to connote wealth but not gluttony. He wore a mustache and trimmed goatee; his large, handsome head and gray-flecked hair were often seen beneath a top hat. He created the prototype of a flamboyant impresario; his dashing image marked by the black silk hat, frock coat, and ever-present cigar would appear in countless newspapers and magazines. Oscar fed his growing fame with a deadpan wit and an outsized personality. Many of his quips were eminently repeatable. For instance, when asked if there was any money in grand opera, he replied, "Yes, my money is in it." Vincent Sheean says that in his time he commanded more newsprint than anyone except Teddy Roosevelt.

Using money from his cigar inventions, Oscar was instrumental in establishing the neighborhood of West Harlem, building dozens of row houses and apartment buildings from 125th to 142nd Streets. At the same time he watched jealously as the city's Gilded Age eminences (the Vanderbilts, Astors, and Morgans)—after being effectively blocked by the older New York families from buying boxes at the Academy of Music on Irving Place—built themselves an opera house in 1883. The new Metropolitan Opera House, which spanned a block on Broadway between 39th and 40th Streets, ignited Oscar's ambition. Didn't his burgeoning Harlem neighborhood deserve an opera house as well? He decided he would build one and produce opera according to his own tastes.

Though he became one of the most famous men of his time, his path was tortuous and filled with setbacks. Producing requires financial discipline and working with others, skills he was too bullheaded and narcissistic to learn. For his first theater he hired famed architect J. B. McElfatrick but involved himself in the design, paying as much attention to the audience's comfort as to the splendor such a structure demanded. He opened the Harlem Opera House in September 1889, and it attracted all the attention he could have wished for. His venue became known for the plushest seats, the best acoustics, and the most democratic distribution of sight lines in the city. The *New York Times* deemed the interiors "pleasing in spite of their excessive gorgeousness" and called the entryway "one of the wonders of Harlem." Patrons entered through a frescoed foyer of Italian marble that led into a lobby featuring a spectacular staircase and the largest mirror anyone had ever seen. The color scheme was gold, rose, and sapphire blue.

When the theater was finished, Hammerstein realized he had forgotten to build a box office, a symbolic oversight that would please many theater historians over the years. His life was a series of fistfights, lawsuits, bankruptcies, love affairs, and fabulous wagers, all chronicled diligently in the pages of the New York dailies. Journalists and their readers were invested in his frenetic activity and effortlessly entertaining personality; he was an American original, a man who refused to take bunk from less intelligent rivals or corrupt officials. He scuffled with a police captain named H. D. Hooker—as best as I can make out, the officer arrested Oscar for running the Harlem Opera House without a license, but only after the impresario cut off his supply of free theater tickets. Upon Oscar's release he in turn demanded that Hooker be jailed for making an illegal arrest, a feud that ended in an outrageous courtroom scene in which Oscar pounded on a table and called Hooker a "coward" and a "scoundrel." The *New York Times* ran three stories on the kerfuffle, one subtitled "Oscar Hammerstein Does Not Intend to Be Bulldozed."

After the novelty of the Harlem Opera House wore off, however, Hammerstein found it difficult to book first-rate acts so far uptown; singers who could be choosey decided not to work there. His solution was to build an even larger establishment nearby on 125th Street, the two-thousand-seat Columbus Theater, in which he'd produce more popular light entertainment and thereby help finance his opera. But he realized quickly that New York did not need or want a theater district north of Central Park.

So south he went. He bought land near the spot where Macy's Herald Square now stands, and there he constructed the 2,600-seat Manhattan Opera House, providing an immense stage and good sight lines for most seats. In a mistake Hammerstein repeated throughout his career, the theater proved too large to sustain itself; after trying English, French, and American plays as well as comic and grand opera, Oscar had to admit his programming had not worked. He wound up losing the theater after a vicious and public feud with his partners.

On his third try to establish a new theater district, Oscar got the location right. In 1895 he bought three lots in Longacre Square, also known as "Thieves' Lair." The area was all but deserted at night, as the city's electric lights stopped at Forty-Second Street. By July 12, when Oscar toasted the birth of his first grandson, Oscar Hammerstein II, he had literally laid the foundation for what we now call Broadway. In November he unveiled New York's first entertainment complex, a colossus that spanned Seventh Avenue from Forty-Fourth to Forty-Fifth Streets, consisting of the giant 2,800-seat Olympia Music Hall for variety acts from all over the world, a smaller concert hall, and a legitimate theater called the Lyric, with eighty-four boxes and an orchestra section outfitted with wide, comfortable chairs. There was also a summer rooftop theater, the Wisteria Garden, that *Variety* called "easily the most ornate showplace of its day."

Once again, the huge Music Hall could not survive Oscar's impetuous programming. He quarreled with a popular French singer named Yvette Guilbert, whose American debut he had arranged, and replaced her with his own dramatic ballet titled *Marguerite.* Receipts at the Music Hall fell from $15,000 to $4,000 a week. He spent lavishly on his own compositions, and the newspapers applauded the scenery. They were indulgent about his comic opera *Santa Maria* in 1896, less so the following year with his *Very Little Faust and Much Marguerite.* He had a hit with Anna Held in the French opera *La Poupée,* which he mounted with Flo Ziegfeld until the two producers quarreled. Hammerstein then fired Held, who was Ziegfeld's mistress, and replaced her with his own, Alice Rose. Ticket sales plummeted. In 1897 came every producer's nightmare—a series of flops, followed by a rainy summer that hurt business at the usually reliable rooftop theater.

When the interest for the Olympia mortgage came due in November, two years after his grand opening, Oscar could not pay it. He tried a series of diversionary tactics, but he lost control of the complex in 1898 and filed for bankruptcy. The New York Life Insurance Company took possession—at which point he somehow convinced Malvina to help him retrieve light fixtures from the theater, landing them both in court. The $2 million he had raised was gone.

Oscar was now fifty-two and broke, reduced to sneaking into a bedroom he kept above the Olympia to retrieve $400 stashed under a pillow. But it turned out the theater world thought fondly of him, and no one wanted to see the most entertaining man in showbiz go under. Many performers loved him—they were the one group he always paid on time—and produced six benefit performances at various venues around town, raising $8,000. With that money Hammerstein bought another lot, this one on the northeast corner of Seventh Avenue and Forty-Second Street. To fund a theater there he took some remaining Harlem properties that he'd put in Malvina's name, transferred them back to himself, and liquidated them.

For the first time building without extravagance, Oscar salvaged bricks from a stable that had been on the lot and used the surrounding debris for insulation. He installed secondhand chandeliers, carpet from various hotels, and seats from a defunct theater. Ironically this modest new theater, called the Victoria, would be his only consistent moneymaker, thanks in part to his decision to put Willie in charge in 1904. The antisocial Willie, who rarely laughed or even smiled and didn't care much for the theater, turned the Victoria into a gold mine while his father kept a watchful eye on the receipts.

Next door Oscar built the Theatre Republic, another modest building, which he leased two years later to producer David Belasco. Similarly, he leased a third new Forty-Second Street theater in 1904 to Lew Fields, a popular comedian. (Lew's son Joe would team up with Oscar II fifty-four years later to write *Flower Drum Song*.) Leasing meant someone else figured out the programming, which freed Oscar to do what he was always waiting to do: stage a reentry into opera. To achieve this, he siphoned profits from the Victoria, an arrangement that tormented Willie before finally wearing him out.

Oscar opened his second Manhattan Opera House in 1906 at 311 West Thirty-Fourth Street. It was his biggest yet, a 3,100-seat auditorium that was wider and shallower than the Metropolitan's so that he could advertise even better sight lines. As part of his plan to challenge the Met on every front, he immediately sailed to Europe. He arrived unannounced at the Paris home

New Yorkers admired the pluck of Oscar Hammerstein I and were ready to help their David in his battle against the world's entitled Goliaths.
Courtesy of the Hammerstein family

of the world's most famous opera star, Australian-born Nellie Melba, whose voice was said to have unmatched purity. Somehow, he charmed her into coming to America for his 1907 season. From there Oscar went to Italy and achieved a similar feat with Italian conductor Cleofonte Campanini, whom he appointed artistic director. Then he came home and scoured New York voice studios for young, good-looking talent. He stole the singer Luisa Tetrazzini from the Met and hired other glamorous stars. What the newspapers called "the opera war" was on. And, whatever else it would mean for Oscar and his family, the war was good for the opera business.

In the Met's audience and on the board of directors were the crème de la crème of New York society, and every great international singer performed on its stage. But it was the upstart Oscar, with all his shenanigans, who captured the public. He was not part of the snobby elite; he stood apart as a passionate loner who risked everything to do what he loved. He was someone to root for. New Yorkers admired his pluck and were ready to help their David in his battle with the world's entitled Goliaths.

True to form, Hammerstein began his first season without a complete schedule and literally before the paint on the walls had dried. On opening night, December 3, 1906, crowds of curious New Yorkers began lining the sidewalks before their new opera house.

Oscar watched gleefully as his company cut into the audience for the Metropolitan Opera, which suffered its first loss in years. Many first-time operagoers bought tickets simply to see him—he was ever present in his black top hat, at the box office, in the lobby, pacing at the back of the orchestra. He watched performances from a wooden chair in the wings, stage right. He never took a night off and was never far away, sleeping in a little bedroom he furnished for himself off the balcony of the Victoria Theatre.

In his first two seasons Hammerstein imported three divas who generated much excitement: There was Nellie Melba as Mimi in *La bohème*. Then came the lithe young star of Paris's Opéra Comique, Mary Garden, who, as, an Egyptian courtesan in Jules Massenet's *Thaïs,* inspired a cult of young followers. Lastly, Hammerstein introduced the newly famous Luisa Tetrazzini to Manhattan in what became a legendary performance of *La traviata*.

But the Manhattan Opera's first enormous hit was its *Carmen,* featuring the strikingly original Clotilde Bressler-Gianoli in both 1906 and 1907. According to the *New York Times,* Bressler-Gianoli possessed "the allurement of sheer wickedness," and Richard Aldrich of the *Century Magazine* said the performance "was not pretty or graceful" but that it had an "emotional reality" that "deeply struck the few listeners of experience and judgment who were present." Sheean reports that Hammerstein's *Carmen* was "a stunning success" that sold out "every time it was announced."

Oscar I felt he was just getting started. As the *New York Times* put it, "He sighed for more worlds to conquer." He announced his plan to build an opera house in Philadelphia, which put an immediate strain on his finances. He also bought land parcels in Brooklyn, Boston, and Cleveland for future opera house locations.

From this overstep, the descent of the great Oscar was swift. He opened the Philadelphia Opera House in 1908 and was immediately overwhelmed by the expense of running two simultaneous seasons. He grew irritable and instigated a feud with a fascinating figure named Katherine Duer Mackay, an influential art patron and suffragette who had brought her wealthy friends from the Metropolitan to the Manhattan Opera House. (Her then five-year-old daughter Ellin would, against her father's wishes, go on to marry a Jewish songwriter named Irving Berlin in 1926. Oscar II considered writing a musical about the Mackay clan in 1929.)

That argument lost him about 40 percent of his box owners and alienated another Mackay friend, the conductor Campanini, who announced plans to return to Italy. This defection then caused subscriptions to fall precipitously. In January 1909, Oscar got in a fistfight with two reporters from the *New York Press,* landing him and Arthur and Willie in a courtroom where the brawl continued and Willie got hit in the face. According to Sheean, the impresario began to lose "his sense of reality toward the end of the 1908–1909 season," and his "genius for self destruction" found its full expression.

Arthur, hoping to save his father from yet another disaster, entered talks with the banker Otto Kahn, a German Jew who had emerged as the financial brain at the Metropolitan, which of course wanted to stop the annoying parvenu any way it could. Having risen spectacularly in a largely anti-Semitic haut monde, Kahn was a cautious man, discreet and low-key—the yin to Oscar's yang. He began negotiating with Arthur over the first months of 1910. Realizing their talks might continue for some time, Arthur became concerned that his increasingly distracted father might do or say something to upset the situation. He demanded Oscar leave the country, and, for the first time in his life, Oscar took orders and set sail for Europe in March. Arthur was able to extract an impressive $1.125 million from the Met on the condition that Oscar not produce opera in the United States for ten years. Arthur thought this was a win-win, since *he* had always hated opera.

The settlement was more than enough money for Oscar and his family to ease into a comfortable and well-deserved retirement, but that was not to be. Oscar took his penultimate stand in London, where he built his tenth theater, the London Opera House. When reporters asked him what he would open the new theater with, he answered, "With debts." He produced two seasons there, though his unique personality caused more of a stir than did his productions. He greeted theatergoers King George V and Queen Mary with a cigar in his mouth and an outstretched hand, saying, "How are you, King? I'm glad to see you," a line his grandson later borrowed for *Free for All*. His personal charm was such that the monarch was not offended. But Oscar's manners were famously erratic. When the American-born Lady Maud Cunard, known for talking throughout performances, attended his production of *The Children of the Don* along with the king of Portugal and some other chatty friends, Oscar sent an attendant to her box with the message "Mr. Hammerstein requests you to leave this theater at once."

In 1912 he closed the London Opera House. It was time for the sixty-six-year-old producer to return home and make a last batch of disastrous decisions. The first of these was to become enamored of Emma Swift, a woman in her early thirties he met on the transatlantic crossing whose beauty reminded him of his first wife, Rosa. It was a romance that would cause grief to his family in perpetuity and would prove fatal to Oscar himself.

Back in New York, Oscar dealt Willie a blow from which he never recovered: in March 1913 Oscar sold the Victoria's exclusive booking rights—an agreement that had for years insured Willie was the only producer of vaudeville in the Times Square area—for $225,000 to rival producers B. F. Keith and Edward Albee (whose grandson was the playwright of the same name). This ensured that Keith and Albee's Palace Theater would become the jewel of the circuit, replacing the Victoria Theatre as the nation's "Valhalla of Vaudeville." Willie at last got angry and quit the theater. He came back, but he was effectively dethroned.

Nineteen fourteen was a brutal year for Oscar I. Just as he completed his last theater—the ill-conceived Lexington Opera House—the courts said he could not produce opera there, even in English (the means by which he thought he could get around his agreement with the Metropolitan). He instead opened it as a movie house and sold it shortly thereafter. Three of his four sons died that year: Abe, who had a weak heart, in February; Harry, from diabetes-related complications, at the end of July; and Willie, who died suddenly in June. The cause was Bright's disease, an inflammation of the kidneys in which high blood pressure and stress play a part. It was this death that plunged Oscar into rare remorse. He knew that Willie had died without forgiving him, and he told George Blumenthal it was the worst thing that had ever happened to him.

Still, he could never stop himself from doing exactly what he wanted, and he developed no new fortitude in his final years. He married Emma.

Arthur, his remaining son, bought the couple a home in Monmouth County, New Jersey, which one suspects was just far enough away. The newlyweds quarreled often but managed to stay together until one summer day in 1919 when volatile Emma dumped a bucket of ice water on her seventy-three-year-old husband's head as he napped. Oscar staggered to a nearby train depot, where he collapsed. He died two weeks later at Lenox Hill Hospital. He had made Emma his sole heir, ensuring continuing legal battles between her and his surviving children.

Although Oscar I had shown virtually no interest in his grandson, the twenty-four-year-old Oscar II visited his namesake at the hospital just before he died. He sat silently, listening to the breathing of the unconscious man on his last day on earth. Then he left. Waiting for the elevator in the hospital corridor, he was approached by "a handsome, big-boned woman" who asked, "Aren't you Oscar Hammerstein's grandson?" He assented and she said, "I'm his wife." They shook hands and smiled politely before Oscar could escape to the elevator. He would hear from Emma many times before her story was through.

At first she lived in the Manhattan Opera House, refusing to vacate even after Rose and Stella regained control of the building and sold it. Eventually she went to live with a friend who, in 1922, notified the police when she went missing one day after leaving a note hinting at suicide. She was found wandering, and no one knew what to do with her. In 1930, she was selling apples on a street corner while living on ten dollars a week provided by the Association for Improving the Conditions of the Poor. She pursued Arthur in court for various settlements. However, as soon as Oscar II emerged as a possible money source, she redirected her energies, sending him many letters from obscure hotels reporting that she was about to be evicted or some other sad story. She ended up in Syracuse, New York, with relatives, where she died in 1946.

At the same time her stepdaughter Stella, who had a short stage career, besieged Oscar II with her own tales of woe. She wrote from the Hotel Commander, saying she was about to be locked out. She would work as a waiter if she could only get the job. She was staying with a friend but wished she had the courage to end her life. Oscar II called her "a born codger" but gave her money, eventually setting up recurring payments. In 1957 he wrote to his lawyer Howard Reinheimer, "I enclose a letter from my Aunt Stella, as usual I can only read about one word out of six. Maybe you can do better.

The only reason I bother you with it is that she seems to be saying that her contract with me is up and should it not be renewed, or something like that. It probably should be so that I can continue to help her and deduct the payments. Would you mind checking on this situation?"

Stella outlived Oscar, Arthur, and even Reinheimer. She died in Englewood, New Jersey, in 1975, at age ninety-five.

The artistic legacy of Oscar I has all but faded away. Nothing he wrote is still produced. Of his twelve theaters, only two still stand: the modest Theatre Republic on Forty-Second Street, renamed the New Victory, and his second Manhattan Opera House, which became the Hammerstein Ballroom and is now part of an entertainment complex. When Oscar I died, state senator and soon-to-be New York City mayor Jimmy Walker proposed that Times Square be renamed Hammerstein Square. The *New York Times* referred to him as "the immortal Oscar" in a front-page obituary, lamenting that "his death removes from the public eye one of the most interesting personalities the melting pot of American has produced." *Variety* called him "the world's most picturesque impresario, a man whose spectacular and vivid ventures have attracted the limelight so frequently that his personality and name must be indelibly impressed upon theatrical history for all time." Today, though, even theater people will be hard-pressed to say exactly what it was he did.

But Oscar II knew, and he also knew that his grandfather had been especially fond of *Carmen*. Still, it was an uncharacteristic choice for the lyricist. Nowhere else in Hammerstein's work do you find a freethinking heroine with no discernable moral center. (Other nominees would be *Oklahoma!'s* Ado Annie, but she is simply a high-spirited, pleasure-loving girl; and *Allegro's* shallow, unfaithful Jenny, though she is meant to be one-dimensionally awful. Interestingly both characters represent different sides of Myra Finn.)

Hammerstein began *Carmen Jones* shortly after the Pearl Harbor attack, when his patriotism and his sense of community were at their most intense. If Bizet's Carmen was fated to die as punishment for her sexual liberation (as so many feminist critics have declared over the decades), Carmen Jones must die because her actions are destructive to the fabric of her community. She is Jud Fry, only charismatic and sexy. In fact, Hammerstein worked on both characters at around the same time.

Like Bizet's Carmen, like Mérimée's Carmen, Carmen Jones is violent. When a coworker at the parachute factory reports her for lateness, she jumps on the tattletale, tearing out her hair, squeezing her throat, and bloodying her nose (in Mérimée she goes further, carving an *X* into her enemy's face). And Hammerstein adds to her crimes—Carmen Jones cares nothing for the war effort and publicly humiliates Joe for his ambition to become a pilot, an act for which the audience is not expected to ever forgive her.

Before Hammerstein brought African Americans into the equation, questions of misogyny and racism had already attached themselves to *Carmen*. In fact, Mérimée finished off the original tale with an epigraph from the Greek poet Palladas, translated into English as "Every woman is as bitter as gall. But she has two good moments: one in bed, the other at her death." That pretty much set the tone.

Mérimée's narrator is a French writer traveling through Spain when he meets both Don José and the bewitching "Gypsy" named Carmen, who tells his fortune and steals his watch. Later, when Don José is jailed for Carmen's murder, the Frenchman goes to see him and hear his story. This narrator eagerly shares with readers his knowledge of the itinerant Romani people. "Something in their eyes," he reports, "can only be compared to that of a wild creature." When they are young, he tells us, the women may "pass for attractive in their ugliness, but once they reach motherhood they become absolutely repulsive. . . . The filthiness of both sexes is incredible . . . They are cunning and make their living off of the credulity of others."

Bizet and his librettists dropped the narrator, thereby alleviating some of the original misogyny and racism. But Bizet's Carmen still embodies a colonialist view of the wanton sexuality ascribed to "the Orient" and the lower classes, as well as the freedom, desire, and disgust they inspired. In her 2012 essay "The Politics of Color in Oscar Hammerstein's *Carmen Jones*," Melinda Boyd notes that "as neither Bizet nor Hammerstein were ethnographers, Hammerstein's *Carmen Jones* is about as authentic a representation of African American culture as Bizet's Carmen was of Spanish culture—that is to say, not very."

Bizet fleshed out the plot significantly, adding Don José's innocent girlfriend Micaëla and the bullfighter Escamillo, who become Cindy Lou and Husky Miller, respectively, in *Carmen Jones*.

Still, something at the core of *Carmen* transcends most of what dates and disfigures it. Bizet and librettists Meilhac and Halévy gave us a hero who is blazingly alive, incapable of doing anything she does not want to do, even if it leads to her death. She is a fantasy of ultimate human freedom in female form—and, as such, the ultimate threat to patriarchy.

Carmen made her operatic debut at the height of the conservative Victorian era, positively shocking audiences. According to musicologist Susan McClary, "We see her rolling up these cigars on her bare thigh. And none of that kind of explicit sexuality had been on the operatic stage at all. And to have this woman who smokes and does exactly what she pleases just blew everybody's mind."

And Carmen survived long enough to be reinvented by the #MeToo movement: in 2018 Italy's Teatro del Maggio Musicale Fiorentino staged a *Carmen* that ends with the character as perpetrator rather than victim—Carmen shoots Don José with his own gun—while that same year London's Royal Opera had her get up after being stabbed to death and shrug at the audience just before the lights go out.

Carmen Jones on Broadway received virtually unanimous acclaim, even among the few African American critics working at the time. Miles Jefferson, whose column "The Negro on Broadway" appeared in *Phylon* (a journal started by W. E. B. Du Bois), found the lyrics "ingenious and ingenuous at the same time—quite excellent in their own right," adding, "The results indicate how much talent the Negro performer has." Writing in the *Amsterdam News,* Dan Burley saw in the show's choreography an advance over some of the old clichés: "The things Negroes are 'expected' to do in the theatre are conspicuous by their absence; there is no tap dancing, no crap games, no 'amen, Lawd,' no hand-clapping and shouting, praying and bowing and scraping. Instead there are marvelous ballets danced with precision, grace and dignity, as well as high skill by some of the best colored dancers in the country."

Hammerstein found particularly sweet the notices that acknowledged his tribute to the world of Oscar I. In the *New York Herald Tribune,* Howard Barnes wrote that Hammerstein opened "infinite and challenging horizons for the fusion of two art forms," and he went so far as to say, in a time-traveling mind twist, that *Carmen Jones* showed what "*Carmen* might have been had it achieved a more perfect balance of theater, spectacle, song and dancing in the first place." In the *New York Times,* Lewis Nichols began his rave playfully, referencing Oscar I's great rival: "Possibly it is a little soon to be tearing the bricks from the Metropolitan Opera House as an indication that institution has outlived its usefulness."

For the show's actors, every one of them new to Broadway, the glowing reviews were double-edged. Olin Downes, classical music critic for the *New York Times,* pointed out that the performers are "amateurs and showed it," noting the stiff acting of "the Joe of the performance we saw" (not bothering to name the actor) and of Glenn Bryant as Husky Miller, who, the critic reminds us, works as a police officer as his day job. In his next paragraph Downes switches course and criticizes the cast for being over- rather than undertrained: "We were considerably disappointed in one thing of which we had expected a great deal. This was the prevailing self-consciousness and a degree of restraint in much of the acting and nearly all of the dancing. A performance by Negroes—yes—and they do a highly credible job! But it was not a Negro performance in the natural creative way of that race of born actors and musicians that we had expected to see. There was evidence of too much white man's training in it all."

One aspect of the show was not debatable: *Carmen Jones* was a great employer of Black talent on Broadway. The NAACP reported that the "number of shows with Black performers steadily increased from three in 1940 to twenty eight in 1946," and another study stated that 1946 saw more than five times the number of African Americans hired for Broadway plays and musicals than in any year before the Second World War. That *Carmen Jones* was a hit encouraged other producers to stage shows with African American casts. And in the following decade, Hammerstein would create a similar pipeline to the professional stage for Asian actors in *The King and I* and especially *Flower Drum Song.*

To find his cast, producer Rose hired John Hammond, producer of *From Spirituals to Swing,* a pair of sold-out Carnegie Hall concerts. George Jean Nathan described the casting process, writing that Hammond "penetrated into the lairs of bellhops, chauffeurs, chicken-kitchen cooks, policeman, photograph developers, crap game professors, stevedores, steer-busters and countless other such bizarre haunts to find what he and Impresario Rose wanted." Hammond—who later produced Bob Dylan's first two albums and is credited with "discovering" the seventeen-year-old Aretha Franklin—hired not only much of the cast but several Black musicians for the *Carmen Jones* orchestra as well.

■ ■ ■

In his introduction to the published libretto, Hammerstein exhibited racism of which he is entirely unaware, as well as his sometimes-disastrous impulse to overexplain: "I want to establish that my choice of Negroes as the principal figures in the story was not motivated by any desire to pull an eccentric theatrical stunt. It is a logical result of my decision to write a modern American version of *Carmen*. The nearest thing in our modern American life to an equivalent of the gypsies in Spain is the Negro. Like the gypsy, he expresses his feeling simply, honestly, and graphically. Also as with the gypsy there is rhythm in his body, and music in his heart."

The condescension Hammerstein displays here bleeds into the show in all kinds of ways. How could it not? That Hammerstein sometimes wrote in dialect, both for Black and white characters, was not at all unusual in the nineteenth and twentieth centuries; so did Mark Twain, Harriet Beecher Stowe, William Dean Howells, Zora Neale Hurston, Paul Laurence Dunbar, and Harper Lee, to name just a few. Still, Hammerstein's original text has several cringe-inducing lines deeply embalmed in stereotype, including these written for Cindy Lou, Joe's girlfriend:

> I is skeered.
> O Lawd! I is skeered!

Some of his lyrics, not surprisingly, are also problematic. In "Beat Out Dat Rhythm on a Drum" (Hammerstein's version of Bizet's "Gypsy Song"), Frankie, standing in for Every Black Woman, is sent into paroxysms of desire by tambourines and "frenzied guitars"; in the song's tribal refrain she hears a "thumpin' underneath the music" which is "all I need to start me off." The at-the-ready sexuality of Frankie and her friend Carmen is deeply enmeshed in their "wild" African souls. The problems inherent in that white male fantasy would be debated and derided for years to come.

In 1954 director Otto Preminger made a film version of *Carmen Jones* starring Dorothy Dandridge and Harry Belafonte. Like the Broadway musical, the film was a cultural milestone at the time; its progressivism, however, had more to do with the fact that it starred two Black actors than from any social message the story itself conveyed. Under the extraordinary headline "Negros in a Film," Bosley Crowther's *New York Times* review is rife with conflicting arguments, all of them racist: "It has long been a gripe of this reviewer that a race of people as wholesomely endowed with talents for singing and dancing as the Negro people should be so infrequently given opportunities to perform on the screen." He determined that, though "vigorous" and "vivid," the juxtaposition of opera and Negro life did not in fact cohere: "It's not right. It's emotionally superficial, inconsistent with the depth of its theme, and is musically false and incongruous, as far as the natural rhythms of its characters are concerned." After referring to the twenty-seven-year-old Belafonte's character Joe as a "boy," Crowther concluded that this story of a "mighty hero who is corrupted and led astray by the two-timing woman from up-river" is "a profound and poignant theme . . . in the Negro culture."

Riding to the rescue came James Baldwin, who was moved to write an essay titled "*Carmen Jones:* The Dark Is Light Enough." "The implicit parallel between an amoral Gypsy and an amoral Negro woman is the entire root idea of the show," he wrote, a fact that Hammerstein frankly admits to in his introduction to the text. Baldwin continues:

> But at the same time, bearing in mind the distances covered since *The Birth of a Nation,* it is important that the movie always be able to repudiate any suggestion that Negros are amoral—which it can only do, considering the role of the Negro in the national psyche, by repudiating any suggestion that Negroes are not white. With a story like *Carmen* interpreted by a Negro cast, this may seem a difficult assignment, but Twentieth Century Fox has brought it off. At the same time they have also triumphantly *not* brought it off, that is to say that the story *does* deal with amoral people, Carmen *is* a baggage, and it *is* a Negro cast.

In other words, *Carmen Jones* and its makers expect to score points for liberality while simultaneously offering a view of Blackness that is false at its core. And there's no denying that the defects Baldwin identifies in the film apply to the musical play as well. Baldwin calls the characters "ciphers" and notes the show's "total divorce from the realities of Negro life." As for the dialogue, Baldwin thought that "Negro speech is parodied out of its charm and liberalized, if one may so put it, out of its force and passion."

By setting *Carmen Jones* in an all-Black universe, Hammerstein unwittingly magnified his lack of knowledge of that universe, a breach he was able to disguise more effectively in his other multiracial shows (*Show Boat, The King and I,* and *Flower Drum Song*) with their message of universal humanity. As for *Carmen Jones,* the critic Hilton Als commented, "The show is a figment of Hammerstein's imagination, and he is to blame for what's stupid about it."

Any contemporary director who might consider taking on *Carmen Jones* will wrestle with a text that seems patronizing in a way that *Porgy and Bess* does not (though Gershwin's work has its own appropriation issues). When Jude Kelly, artistic director at London's Royal Festival Hall, produced *Carmen Jones* in 2007, one critic wondered, "Do you really need a designated black-cast piece in order to showcase black talent?" Another wrote, "Rather surprisingly, the Southbank Centre seems wholly unaware that any socio-political issues might be raised, and has assembled a cast of black people who conscientiously talk as if they were slaves or ex-slaves in *Gone with the Wind.*"

So it was a surprise when John Doyle, a sixty-five-year-old Scottish director best known for his pared-down productions of Sondheim in which the actors double as musicians, unveiled a highly praised *Carmen Jones* at New York's Classic Stage Company in 2018. It was the first major New York production since a 1946 City Center redo produced by Billy Rose. Doyle, who is white, earned his bona fides for the project when he delivered a brilliant restaging of the musical *The Color Purple* in 2015, which led critics to write that they felt they were seeing the 2005 work as if for the first time. In the words of its star Cynthia Erivo, he "unlocked" the text.

Doyle was able to do something similar for *Carmen Jones.* His strategy was simple and brilliant. Just as he reduced the cast from one hundred to ten, he stripped the musical of dialect, asking the actors to translate their lines into contemporary speech. He pronounced his own ignorance and leaned on others to educate him. In this way Doyle found a way to respect both Hammerstein and the people best able to bring out whatever truth the text might hold. *New York Times* critic Ben Brantley called the show Doyle's "most unexpected act of reclamation," and he was not alone in finding the production "sublime." He added, "The doomed title character and the people whose lives she damages often seem as timeless as the beautiful and damned of Greek tragedy."

Whenever writers use what they consider a race's inherent characteristics as the root of a character, they inevitably reinforce stereotypes, positive

Oscar the First's Carmen (Clotilde Bressler-Gianoli from 1906, *left*) and Oscar the Second's Carmen Jones (Anika Noni Rose from 2018, *right*).
Left: Courtesy of Wikimedia Commons; *right:* Courtesy of Joan Marcus

or negative. Hammerstein admitted quite clearly that he was guilty on that count. At the same time, he tried to find transcendent human truths in the story of *Carmen Jones*. Whether or not this is possible became the question underlying every thoughtful review of Doyle's production. In the *New Yorker,* Hilton Als called the musical "bizarre and politically archaic," but he was also dazzled by the performance of Anika Noni Rose in the title role and begrudgingly approved the production. "I can no longer imagine anyone else as Carmen," he wrote. "Having the all-black cast drop the 'dem' and 'dose' bullshit," he continued, "releases the actors from the need to perform blackness; they are characters, who, in addition to being black, are sexual, or jealous, or lost, or all three at once." So, it seems, in his imperfect way, Hammerstein might have been on to something all along.

CHAPTER SEVEN

Don't Be Afraid of the Dark

IT WAS NOT RODGERS OR HAMMERSTEIN but film producer Darryl Zanuck who had the winning idea for how the pair should follow the triumph of *Oklahoma!* (though Sam Goldwyn offered a suggestion—"You know what you should do now? Shoot yourself!"). Zanuck thought the pair should make a musical film of *State Fair,* a popular slice of Americana from 1932 by Iowa-born novelist Phil Stong. The story was slight; it followed the household of a farmer, his wife, and their two teenage offspring as they get ready for the event of the season, the Iowa State Fair. The critics saw Stong as an authentic and vibrant voice of rural America, but his writing had the folksiness of Mark Twain with all his teeth removed. Fox had already made the book into a 1933 nonmusical film starring Will Rogers as Abel Frake, the farmer who has high hopes that his gigantic hog, Blue Boy, will take top prize at the fair. His wife, Melissa, harbors a similar dream for her mincemeat pie. The teenage siblings, Wayne and Margy, want to find romance.

For Margy, Rodgers and Hammerstein wrote "It Might as Well Be Spring," a song loved by singers for its symbiosis of music and lyrics. "I'm as restless as a willow in a windstorm / I'm as jumpy as a puppet on a string" is paired with a melody so skittish you can feel the yearning and tension that will lead to an imminent bad decision. The opening verse is particularly charming; it describes adolescence as economically as has ever been done, with a self-deprecating turn that is pure Hammerstein:

> The things I used to like
> I don't like anymore
> I want a lot of other things
> I've never had before.
> It's just like mother says
> I sit around and mope
> Pretending I am wonderful
> But knowing I'm a dope.

The film was a hit, but one could argue that Zanuck did the men no favor by guiding them to this work at this time. If today Rodgers and Hammerstein are unfairly invoked as the authors of meaningless Americana, it is as much because of *State Fair* as anything else. Twentieth Century Fox took a work with little depth and no conflict and smoothed out its rough edges. *State Fair* is more wholesome than a college sweater with elbow patches and an embossed letter, which is what Wayne wears throughout the film. As Margy, Jeanne Crain is dewy-eyed and personality-free (Elia Kazan, who directed her four years later in the film *Pinky,* described her as having "an emotional passivity").

Back in Hollywood, Rodgers watched the dailies and felt his old ambivalence return. Just before the film's release he wrote to Josh Logan, "This, for instance, is symptomatic of the whole job: the little girl from the farm [Crain] is dressed in very fancy dirndl clothes and the boys [the film producers] have proceeded on the theory that if the woman's bosom is attractive to an audience, she will be ten times as attractive if her bosom is ten times as big. They've taken a cute little kid and stuffed her out so that she follows her chest across the screen all evening. But don't get me wrong—I hate Hollywood."

Hammerstein, too, disliked an early cut of the film and wrote a long letter to producer William Perlberg in June full of suggestions for improving it. "My over-all disappointment was the fact that the story and the characters were presented with less realism than I had anticipated and the picture emerges as more of a 'musical comedy' than I hoped it would be," he wrote. His detailed notes on how to fix the film were virtually all ignored.

While Rodgers and Hammerstein were writing *State Fair,* Theresa Helburn suggested the men adapt Ferenc Molnár's *Liliom,* which had its American premiere at the Theatre Guild in 1921. Both men at first said no—they simply did not want to write a musical about a Hungarian suicide. In May of 1944, the pair canceled a trip to Hollywood to finish work on *State Fair* when Hammerstein suffered an attack of diverticulitis. The subsequent operation may have elicited a light shock of mortality just before the lyricist's fiftieth birthday. In finally taking on *Liliom,* which became *Carousel,* the men wrote not only their darkest and deepest work, but one that served as a corrective to *State Fair.* Once they changed *Carousel's* setting from Budapest to New England, they were writing back-to-back musicals about young love taking hold on the fairgrounds of an American town. But *Carousel* was full of everything *State Fair* lacked: danger, death, and meaning.

Carousel also counteracted *Oklahoma!,* which had focused on a couple and a country on the rise, looking toward the future with expansive optimism. Instead, *Carousel* focused on a pair who, despite loving each other, lacked the ability to dig their way out of meanness and brutality. In fact, the couple would slide into a mire from which relief could only come in retroactive forgiveness and redemption in the afterlife. For Julie Jordan and Billy Bigelow, happiness on earth was not in the picture.

Oklahoma! succeeded despite bucking every trend. *Carousel* was—and remains—a complete oddity. A musical about a brute who figures out how to be human only after he dies, and even then just barely, simply should not work.

But Molnár had found poetry in Liliom, the bad boy of the Budapest fairground, the sexy roughneck who attracts wayward servant girls to his merry-go-round. When he falls for an utterly unguarded young woman, he feels the first stirrings of human engagement; however, he doesn't get to travel far down that path. Now called Billy Bigelow and Julie Jordan, the lovers marry. When he is unable to find work, Billy lashes out and hits Julie, and his judgment never evolves; his best plan to care for his unborn child is to rob a rich man. When he botches that, he stabs himself rather than go to jail, and he dies crying out for Julie. But his story is not over. Billy next finds himself before a heavenly tribunal, one set up especially for suicides who depart having left things below undone. An overseer allows him to return to earth for one day to do something for his widow and now fifteen-year-old daughter, Louise, but he bungles that as well, striking his daughter's outstretched hand as she points the way for him to leave.

Molnár made audiences feel something for this irredeemable abuser, a man who wanted to but never could be better than he was. And, despite their initial rejection of the project, Rodgers and Hammerstein themselves were eventually seduced by *Liliom*. In December 1944, the two men met at Hammerstein's townhouse to discuss adapting Molnár's play. They decided to view the project's unlikely nature as a welcome challenge; after all, they thought, look at how that dubious prospect *Oklahoma!* had turned out. "This is not a high-minded policy of ours, it's just a device for not getting bored ourselves and not boring our public," said Hammerstein. Rodgers came up with the idea of setting the story in a New England coastal town, where Julie and her friend Carrie work at a mill. The setting inspired Hammerstein:

> I began to see an attractive ensemble—sailors, whalers, girls who worked in the mills up the river, clambakes on near-by islands, an amusement park on the seaboard, things people could do in crowds, people who were strong and alive and lusty, people who had always been depicted on the stage as thin-lipped puritans—a libel I was anxious to refute. As for the two leading characters, Julie with her courage and inner strength and outward simplicity seemed more indigenous to Maine than to Budapest. Liliom is, of course, an international character, indigenous to nowhere.

Still, he felt stymied by what he called "the tunnel" of the second act, meaning Liliom's crime, his death, and the hopelessness of Molnár's ending, in which the antihero blows his chance at redemption.

The men had been discussing an aria for Billy for the moment he finds out he is to become a father. Rodgers suggested that the character start by imagining a son; then, in the middle of the song, he realizes he could be the father of a girl, at which point he is flooded with protective feelings. This gave Billy a path to redemption, a subject that interested Hammerstein. Now he could begin. Billy's epiphany was translated into "Soliloquy," an extended monologue unlike any musical-theater song that had come before.

"Soliloquy" gives us access to a real-time shift in the protagonist's thinking. Because we share this with him, we understand Billy Bigelow and judge him less harshly than we might, allowing for a profound catharsis at the show's end.

As they continued to develop the story, the men multiplied Billy's chances at redemption; on his third try they allowed him to finally get it right. Hammerstein explained to Michaelis why he had to diverge from Molnár. "It wasn't the anxiety to have a happy ending that made me shy away from the original ending," he said, "but because I can't conceive of an unregenerate soul. I can't conceive of a dead end to any kind of existence."

In a separate interview Rodgers told Michaelis that he "held out" for changing the ending, though against whom he does not say. Here he displays, to my mind, a lack of depth and an assumption that Hammerstein's writerly problems were as easy to solve as musical puzzles were for him:

> I didn't want to touch it with the ending that it had. I felt that the ending was destructive and didn't say anything. The man coming back from limbo with the chance to redeem himself and his family, and he hits his kid, and then he goes back to limbo. I thought this was suicide. Not only in the theater, but as a philosophy. . . . And I held out for changing the ending. And this was very easy to do. All we had to do was have Liliom say to the child, "You have to live with people." And the child put her arm around another little girl, and they smiled at each other, and the curtain came down. And here was the philosophy completely changed.

Sitting before his heavenly judges, Billy is asked why he beat Julie. In a Hammerstein addition, Billy first corrects the questioner and downgrades his crime: "I didn't beat her," he says. "I would never beat a little thing like her—I hit her." Asked again why, Billy says, "Well you see—we'd argue. And she'd say this and I'd say that—and she'd be right—so I'd hit her."

Billy's understanding of his actions—that he hit Julie because she was right and he was wrong—came from Molnár, and it constituted the character's most honest and salient thinking. The idea that we fight hardest when we suspect we might be wrong was a concept that stayed with Hammerstein. He would return to it six years later in *The King and I.* This insight also informed Hammerstein's budding activism and defined his views of the international nuclear peril in the last decade of his life.

Rodgers believed that *Carousel* represented the pair's best work (Hammerstein suspected it might be the *King and I*). From its first moments the score shimmers with something rare, a blending of the sober and the light that would now be the province of the new kings of the form.

In place of an overture, with its promise of songs to come, the show opens with "The Carousel Waltz," a seven-minute orchestral piece Rodgers called "a composition in extended waltz form." It begins on a bittersweet pang that opens into a sloping, then swirling celebration of life, much like the story to follow. While it plays, the audience is treated to a wordless introduction to the characters and the setting—exactly what is shown in this pantomime is up to the director and varies in every production.

"You'll Never Walk Alone" is the jewel of the score, and it may be the pair's most durable song. Hammerstein showed the confidence to skirt the very edge of banality, using the simplest language possible—seventy-one words, all but five of them one syllable. The song's been sung at countless funerals and benefit concerts after every conceivable disaster. iTunes counts 250 covers of it. The first few notes alone can alleviate at least a drop of suffering by offering the possibility of strength and dignity. When you keep your chin up high—or hold your head up high, as many singers insist—the physicality of the action takes you one step outside yourself. Hammerstein gives you credit for simply going on when your heart is so heavy you'd rather not. And that credit marks one step out of darkness and toward rebirth and forgiveness, whether it's for yourself or someone else.

The story's tragic nature required an amendment in the tradition of treating the secondary pair of lovers as less serious. Since Billy and Julie are our focus, it is left to Carrie Pipperidge and Mr. Snow to be the couple who get it right—who know how to say "I love you" and treat each other with respect. Hammerstein allows himself a few jokes at their expense once they have been long married and pretend to be propriety itself, but overall they represent the good that love and commitment foretell.

As a young man, Mr. Snow is industrious and ambitious; he dreams of turning his herring boat into a fleet and overseeing a lucrative sardine empire. He's the anti-Billy: he's excited about life, he likes work, and he woos Carrie with his vision of wealth and security not for their own pleasure but so they can take on the responsibility of a large family. In their love song, they dream about a life so full and busy that the only time they'll be able to snatch a moment alone will be "When the Children Are Asleep." Here is a song truly outside the range of a writer like Larry Hart, who would live his life in a cycle of new love and heartbreak.

But this was the age of romantic courtships. Monogamy was in vogue. War brought the reality of separation and a premature knowingness about the nature of life and therefore of love. When wartime couples said, "Until death do us part," as my own parents did in 1945 (just before seeing *Oklahoma!* on their honeymoon), they knew that could mean next week. Therefore love songs of the era often have a gravitas that stands apart. As the singer Andrea Marcovicci pointed out in her concerts dedicated to the ballads of World War II, "There were no co-dependency meetings. People liked being dependent. They called it falling in love."

When Carrie and Mr. Snow are long married and prosperous with nine children, their fate is briefly contrasted with the lives of Julie and her fifteen-year-old daughter, Louise, both still unmoored from Billy's absence. Just back from New York, Carrie stops by to entertain Julie with a description of the Broadway shows she and Mr. Snow saw—she's more enthusiastic about *Madcap Maidens,* in which the chorus girls had "nothing on their legs but tights," than about *Julius Caesar,* in which "all the men were dressed in nightgowns and it made me sleepy." The everyday happiness and relative inanity of Carrie's comfortable existence casts Julie's loneliness in a romantic light. Despite her deprivations, Julie sees more, feels more, and knows more.

When Billy comes back to earth and approaches his unhappy daughter, she does not know him. He is merely a stranger who exerts a strange fascination. He tries to force a gift into her arms—a star he's stolen from the heavens—but Louise pulls away in fright, at which point Billy smacks her hand in frustration. A few minutes later, she turns to Julie with her burning question. In an early draft of *Carousel,* Hammerstein wrote these lines between daughter and mother:

LOUISE: But is it possible fer someone to hit you hard like that—real loud and hard—and not hurt you at all?

JULIE: It is possible, dear—fer someone to beat you—and beat you—and beat you—and not hurt at all.

Hammerstein realized that the image of a man beating his wife might close hearts and minds to Billy at this crucial point in the story. So he made a telling edit. The final version goes like this:

LOUISE: Has it ever happened to you? Has anyone every hit you—without hurtin'?

JULIE: It is possible, dear, fer someone to hit you—hit you hard—and not hurt at all.

As part of the show's finale—these words are said as the musical gears up for the reprise of "You'll Never Walk Alone," one of the most moving finishes in all of musical theater—the exchange is given special prominence. Hammerstein downgraded Billy's crime from a severe beating to a single blow so that the audience would not be robbed of *Carousel*'s emotional climax. Whether he succeeded is up to each individual viewer to decide.

Henry King directed the film version of *Carousel* (1956). Best known for *Song of Bernadette* (1943), Hollywood's earnest depiction of a Christian miracle, he brought a similar otherworldly stodginess to the musical. Starring Gordon MacRae and Shirley Jones, *Carousel* the film received the seal of approval by critics such as Bosley Crowther, who saw it as beautifully and carefully crafted. He couldn't get over how nice it looked. Crowther wrote that the film was faithful to the play in mood and spirit—despite the fact that it altered key scenes and veered from the soundstage to vérité street scenes in a botched attempt to serve the story's purgatorial aspect.

Like any movie, *Carousel* freezes the work in the era of its production. To the next generation, Billy Bigelow's costume of a knotted neckerchief and too-tight striped shirt no longer signaled danger and raw masculinity. As the years passed, the film started to look like a corny love story about a man in a strange getup who hits his wife, and the surreal tribunal near the end only made it all the more odd.

Carousel, it should be said, was not aging well in the decades after Hammerstein's death, when his work was largely overseen by his sons Billy and Jimmy, both of whom started out as assistant stage managers like their father. They graduated to producing and directing shows by Hammerstein and others, and both carved out credible careers. Perhaps inevitably, the handling of their father's enormous legacy overtook them both. (When Billy died in 2001, the headline on the *New York Times* obituary read, "William Hammerstein, 82, Director with a Famous Father, Dies.")

As stewards of the estate, the brothers saw it as their mission to keep new productions of the Rodgers and Hammerstein classics as close as possible to the spirit of the originals. This resulted in some excellent productions—such as the 1979 *Oklahoma!* that Billy directed on Broadway (starring Laurence Guittard and Christine Andreas)—but also in the fading of a brand that was not adapting to the times. By the 1970s, the hope for Broadway's future was Hammerstein's protégé Stephen Sondheim, whose worldview was less optimistic and whose early assessment of marriage (*Do I Hear a Waltz?, Company, Follies*) bordered on brutal. Then came the so-called British invasion of the 1980s, which swept Broadway with an overheated sensibility and a retreat from the relative realism and subtle mood variations that characterized Sondheim and the early Rodgers and Hammerstein. British hits like *Cats* and the French crossover *Les Misérables* pushed Rodgers and Hammerstein further into the remainder bin of culture. The longest-running show of the 1980s, racking up a stratospheric 12,500 performances, was *Phantom of the Opera,* a throwback to the hyperromantic plots and dazzling set design from the era of Friml and Romberg.

Ironically it was producer Cameron Mackintosh, leader of the British invasion, who set in motion a next life for Rodgers and Hammerstein. He donated about $2 million to Britain's National Theatre to focus on a classic musical of its choice. Director Nicholas Hytner remembers that he, Mackintosh, and the theater's artistic director Richard Eyre discussed a handful of shows they might remount.

It makes sense that it took a British company to revitalize a great American musical, in the same way that it makes sense that Taiwan-born Ang Lee directed *The Ice Storm,* the great film on 1970s U.S. suburbia. Often it takes someone close, but not too close, to see the bigger picture. Hytner's *Carousel,* first staged at the National in 1992, was a revelation. When the New York production opened at Lincoln Center in March 1994, Frank Rich, the most perceptive writer on musicals since Brooks Atkinson, had just retired his reviewing post at the *New York Times* to become an op-ed writer, and it was in that section that he published his impressions. He noted that *Carousel* had "disappeared in the 50's, when Hollywood and a thousand stock productions bowdlerized the show to fit the treacly conformist culture of a decade whose rigid dogma was sexless suburban family bliss." But here again was the oddest, darkest musical of the last century, a reminder that when they were "liberated by success to say whatever they pleased, Rodgers and Hammerstein chose to depict an American haunted by inequities and suffering." This was a show that "told the truth about its era." The audience cries at *Carousel*'s finale because "it realizes that it is up to us to break this country's unending cycles of social injustice and domestic violence." And, Rich found, "not even Rodgers and Hammerstein, the soothing parental figures we had always depended on, can bail us out."

Jan Clayton and John Raitt in *Carousel*'s famous "bench scene" from 1947 (*left*). In 1994 director Nicholas Hytner put Billy (Michael Hayden) and Julie (Sally Murphy) on the ground for a much earthier interpretation (*right*). Looking on is Audra MacDonald as Carrie.
Left: Courtesy of Photofest; *right:* Courtesy of Photofest / Joan Marcus

I spoke to Hytner about his approach to that unforgettable *Carousel.* "One thing we British know is that there is no such thing as a revival," he said. "We don't use that word here. One doesn't 'revive' *Hamlet.* Every production is a new production, because no show is merely the text or merely the music; those who perform a show create half of it. So that's the position from which we started. We looked at the text as if it had arrived new on our desk."

To prepare for the production, Hytner and his designer Bob Crowley toured coastal Maine, focusing on Castine, a village on the Penobscot Bay. They saw a town defined by a hard, no-nonsense approach to life and a Spartan kind of beauty. The two men also drew on the dramatic moodiness of painters Winslow Homer, Grant Wood, and Andrew Wyeth, particularly Wyeth's *Christina's World.* They made the circle (the shape of a carousel) their prime visual motif, echoed in the set's full moon, the huge clock at the

mill where Julie works, and the little hill on which Billy and Julie court; the round shapes underline the eternal forces at work in the story. In an interview with the *New York Times,* Crowley called the circle "the most basic human symbol" and added, "The show isn't about a carousel. It's about the world going round."

Hytner injected into the setting a bit of "central European grotesque" from Molnár's Budapest, where the "carnival is a place for thrills and sex, and there's danger in the festivity." All of this imbued his *Carousel* with a gravitas viewers felt from the show's first moments. As the audience hears "The Carousel Waltz," injustice and toil seemed to hang from the clock that oversees the mill-working women, an instrument so huge it would crush them if it fell. When the clock strikes six, the women, too young to be full-time drudges, leap up and remove their smocks. Now they are just girls heading to the local fair. On a turntable, another circle, the set moves from grim to tawdry, from day to night, to the fair that will be their evening's entertainment. We learn quickly and wordlessly that Billy has a volatile sexual relationship with the older Mrs. Mullin who runs the carousel. We also sample the fair's attractions: an Uncle Sam on stilts, a bearded lady, and a bear being whipped by his trainer. Inescapable cruelty is a hallmark of this place and time.

Hytner paid great attention to the way poverty grinds down even the young. Billy Bigelow and Jigger, his criminal accomplice, appear embalmed in dirt and sweat; as the play goes on, they grow more haggard. By the second act Billy (played by Michael Hayden both in London and New York) appears debauched, older, his eyes smeared from alcohol and meanness. His menacing of women—he throws Mrs. Mullin to the ground and threatens to smack Julie's friend Carrie—illustrates how poverty perverts love and spawns misery from which none can escape.

Because they are buffeted about by forces beyond their understanding, Billy and Julie's courtship seems like an act of nature. They find themselves alone together after the fairground closes, and Billy gruffly asks Julie how much money she carries. She disarms him by saying she'd happily give him whatever she has. This triggers Billy's hidden tenderness, which rarely rises to the surface.

Once they've begun this dance, they have to finish it. No matter if they're interrupted—first by Mrs. Mullin and then by the mill supervisor, a pompous, upright citizen who gives Julie a last chance to return to her dorm before curfew. They will both lose their jobs to stay together and continue their conversation, an act that feels to them like blessed autonomy no matter how ill advised.

Hammerstein shifts from the external reality of the couple's wooing to their interior thoughts, from advance to retreat, from dialogue to song and back, in a seamless nine minutes that became known as "the bench scene" because *Carousel's* original director, Rouben Mamoulian, staged it on and around a bench. We see and they see, too, that on this windless, still night, Julie and Billy are very much like the blossoms that float down from the trees of their own accord. Making a guess about the descent of the blossoms, Julie says, "Just their time to, I guess," but Billy's mouth is over hers before she can finish the thought.

"We hadn't grown up with a reverence for benches," said Hytner, who with Crowley stripped the stage of the iconic prop, leaving nothing but the moon and a mound of earth that seems to trace the planet's curve. In this scene, the set and the play conspired to take us beyond the confines of our physical universe.

In a 1956 letter to Otto Harbach, Hammerstein thanked his former mentor for an insight that helped him look at writing in a new light. It was on "a day thirty summers ago when we were sitting in your garden," wrote

Hammerstein. The men were at work on *The Desert Song* and experienced a kind of artistic epiphany, or at least Oscar did: "We were stuck. We had been rejecting each other's ideas for a couple of hours. Every road we had explored had become a dead end. We sat in mute frustration, staring in opposite directions. Then you broke the silence: 'Oscar,' you said, 'we are not going to create this song. This song exists right now. It is somewhere in the world. Our job is to find it.'"

The courtship of Billy and Julie has that quality of already existing, of being transcribed from nature, artless and perfect.

After Billy stabs himself, Julie and the rest of her party stumble on the scene; she holds him while he dies. Her cousin Nettie suggests singing a song she knew in school, and Julie tries, tentatively beginning the slow, hymnal progression of "You'll Never Walk Alone." But she is too overcome to get very far. Nettie's strong voice takes up the song. Hammerstein loved this technique—having one character start a song and another take it up—which embodies his belief in the transitive properties of hope and optimism. In *South Pacific,* for example, Nellie Forbush commits herself to taking care of Emile de Becque's children when he goes missing on a reconnaissance mission. She is full of worry but calms herself by singing "Dites-moi" to the children; she forgets the French lyric and falters, but our hearts soar when we hear de Becque finish the line for her just before he enters.

Ultimately, *Carousel* is a treatise on the messiness of forgiveness. If Julie is capable of forgiving Billy for his abuse, does that mean the audience is expected to forgive him as well? Because of where Hammerstein places Julie's controversial line—"It is possible, dear, fer someone to hit you—hit you hard—and not hurt at all"—just before the reprise of "You'll Never Walk Alone," the thought gets tangled up in the great emotion of the ending.

Twenty-five years after he staged the scene, Hytner told me he regretted not excising those lines from the musical. "Those words should not have been said on the stage because they are a lie," he said, with passion. I suggested that since Billy is long dead when Julie speaks those words to her daughter, they cannot be construed as enabling further abuse. The director would not have it: "It is an appalling truth that people feel that way, but . . . to put those words in the show's climactic moment is a huge blot on that text. It's outrageous and unforgiveable. It should be cut."

Perhaps. Hammerstein uses Julie's dialogue to launch the play's crescendo, thereby signaling, if not approval, acknowledgment of the messiness and the durability of love. Of course, one sign of a culture's evolution is the rejection of tropes that did not seem offensive to their original audience. And yet it bears repeating: it is possible to be swept up in *Carousel*'s conclusion, to appreciate its verismo, to weep for Julie and for Billy, and still decry spousal abuse. When I viewed a video of Hytner's production at the Lincoln Center library, I saw something the director may have forgotten, a gesture that makes an enormous difference. Billy, who watches Julie say those words to Louise, shakes his head "no." That directorial choice offers the audience not only Hytner's own comment on the text, but an important amplification of Hammerstein's attempt to show Billy's awakening comprehension. And it gives a contemporary audience permission to be swept up in a powerful tide of forgiveness.

In 2018 the bench was back, along with some of the sentimental trills that Hytner had stripped away. That year American director Jack O'Brien restaged *Carousel* for Broadway starring Jessie Mueller as Julie and the African American actor Joshua Henry as Billy, a role originally written for and until this production virtually always played by a white actor. While in the past O'Brien's nontraditional casting might have provoked some commentary, especially since Billy is a violent man, there was little mention of it when the show opened in April. Six months earlier the *New York Times* had broken the story of producer Harvey Weinstein's decades-long abuse of women in the film industry, which launched the #MeToo movement and a rethinking of everything we had accepted as the social status quo for women. In this climate, it was Julie's stubborn defense of love that generated most of the public commentary.

The director, though, couldn't decide what to do about the ending. He kept Julie's lines in, cut them during previews, then reinstated them but had the women speak them quietly, as if no one would notice.

There is no question that Hammerstein saw nobility in Julie—the sacrifice of her own body and dignity—and wanted the audience to see it as well. The reason audiences still cry at *Carousel*'s end is that its true subject is the overwhelming power of love, both happy and tragic. Today, our tears fall as an answer to the ever-evolving question: Can we forgive ourselves, each other, and the artists who still have something to say, no matter how imperfect we all might be?

CHAPTER EIGHT

They Toil Not

IF THE COLLABORATION of Rodgers and Hammerstein was like a love affair right out of the gate, its remarkable success depended on the fact that it was *not* a love affair. Richard Rodgers admitted as much when he first spoke to Hugh Fordin, Hammerstein's biographer, in 1976. The composer was almost apologetic. "I'm not sure how much I can help you," he said. "I never knew whether he liked me or hated me."

On Rodgers's fiftieth birthday, Hammerstein wrote an appreciation of his partner in which he offered a cunning tautology: "At the age of fifty you are Dick Rodgers. I think that is a very good thing to be." Not exactly gushing. The men always, though, signed their letters to each other with "love."

Since their collaboration was a lucrative second professional "marriage" for each of them, they instinctively tried to shield themselves from the forces of estrangement. Certainly they knew the plight of Gilbert and Sullivan, who each harbored the opinion that he was the more talented of the pair and ended their lives not speaking to each other. (In 1938 Hammerstein produced a play about them called *Knights of Song*.)

Rodgers and Hammerstein were experienced enough to know that partnerships run on a finite supply of goodwill, so they used distance as their friend. For the most part, they worked separately. As Hammerstein explained to Arnold Michaelis, "We discuss and plan together then we go off to our various homes. And I sometimes phone a lyric in to him when he is in Connecticut and I am in Pennsylvania."

With Hart, Rodgers had been the high school principal, insisting on work not play. Now he was the one who hid the dimensions of his drinking. He was the insecure one who wondered what he meant to Hammerstein, and who sometimes felt his partner's attempt to lead a purposeful life as a kind of reproach. On top of that, people preferred Hammerstein; he was warmer, more empathetic, funnier, he could discuss a wider range of subjects, and women knew they could chat with him without having to fend off advances.

One assumes that Hammerstein kept mum on their differences. Everyone in the theater knew that Rodgers was a roué—he met few young actresses he did not want to know better—just as later everyone knew he was a high-functioning alcoholic. While in Rodgers's day this behavior was often excused as just good fun, today we have a keener awareness of its consequences and costs. We know as well as Richard Rodgers did that some young women in need of a job would feel they could not say no to so powerful a man. Whether we imagine these women as scheming careerists or as noble Fantines matters not.

Mary Rodgers wrote of her father, "I think it was the owner of the Alvin Theatre [now the Neil Simon] who gave him a key to a room of his own upstairs: a place he could take girlfriends anytime he wanted, which was quite often." Mary found out about many of these liaisons years later. "Some volunteered the information," like John Steinbeck's wife, Elaine, who before her marriage was an assistant stage manager on *Oklahoma!* "Daddy apparently had a big thing with the original Tuptim in *The King and I:* Doretta Morrow, the whitest Burmese slave princess ever," Mary reports. One day her father convinced Morrow to overstay her break, making her late for an understudy rehearsal. "He promised to cover for her but didn't and she was fired. Shitty way to treat someone you supposedly cared about. To say nothing of your wife," wrote Mary.

We will never know if Hammerstein judged his writing partner for these abuses of power; if he did he went to the grave with it. And of course neither man wanted their fantastically successful association to end by anything other than death. In that, and much else, they succeeded.

With their third hit in a row (including *State Fair*), it was time to cement power by instituting some of the lessons they'd learned in the years of struggle against the Hollywood system. There, they'd worked with producers who had only a vague idea of how to use artists wisely; consequently, much money was wasted on bad guesses and mediocre films. Back in New York, their own domain, Rodgers and Hammerstein thought they could do better.

Hammerstein had had no luck in 1938 when he produced three new Broadway plays, all flops, but now every door seemed to be open. Rodgers had previously coproduced two musicals: *Best Foot Forward* with director George Abbott, and his own musical with Hart, *By Jupiter.* The men now made a plan—they would alternate yearly between writing a new musical and producing someone else's show. It didn't work out as neatly as that but they started off strong, producing the cozy family drama *I Remember Mama* (featuring a twenty-year-old Marlon Brando) in 1944, which ran for 713 performances.

They opened a small office in the RKO Building at Rockefeller Center and began looking for other plays to produce. Also in 1944 they established a music publishing company called Williamson Music—both of their fathers were named William, another cosmic coincidence that seemed to bless their collaboration. (Said Rodgers, they'd "be suckers" if they didn't publish the *Oklahoma!* score themselves.) In addition, they bought the film rights to their first musical. They grew richer and savvier; in a few years they would own 100 percent of what they wrote, and they grew adept at the art of ruthless negotiation.

Critic John Lahr argued, in 2002, that their business sense informed Rodgers and Hammerstein's commitment to the well-constructed show, which devalued the talent of individual performers and was less expensive to produce. Lahr, son of the great comedian Bert Lahr, wrote, "Anarchic, freewheeling frivolity that traded in joy—in other words, in the comedian's resourcefulness—was renounced for an artful marriage of music and lyrics that traded in narrative. Seriousness replaced sass. Big names were no longer needed to carry the show; the show itself was the star." If Hammerstein was solving the problem of musical narrative, he was doing so at the cost of idiosyncratic performances. Rodgers and Hammerstein would now, in Lahr's view, become the theatrical equivalent of Henry Ford's assembly line: "In show-biz terms, Rodgers and Hammerstein had hit the mother lode. They had engineered the musical equivalent of the interchangeable part, which insured a sort of quality control. Improvisation was no longer an element, and the musical was now, in principle, anyway, infinitely repeatable.

Rodgers and Hammerstein were not just a sensation—they were a corporation."

I believe Lahr was in part responding to (and misunderstanding) a comment Hammerstein made to interviewer Arnold Michaelis in 1959: "I found out early in my career that I preferred to write musical plays that did not depend on stars, because then you owned the play, you owned a piece of musical and literary property that was detached from personalities and you could play it anywhere."

Lahr saw this as a mercenary impulse, but it originated in an aesthetic concern. Only in hindsight did Hammerstein see the de-emphasis on stars as lucrative, and even then it was an insight rather than a guiding philosophy. (Lahr also never warmed to Sondheim, whom he found disapproving and sour.)

And of course Rodgers and Hammerstein no more killed comedy, improvisation, and star power than movies killed theater. Things shifted, no more. But it is true that the pair took the reins in all matters of economics, and they did indeed incorporate, appearing all-powerful to the stage artists of their era.

Behind closed doors, Rodgers relied on Hammerstein for advice about every aspect of their business and in some cases his personal life as well. Whether it involved who should publish their work in book form or if the pair should musicalize *Of Mice and Men* or whether Rodgers should try to repair the relationship between his wife and her doctor, the composer asked and Hammerstein answered. His advice was straightforward, brief, and practical. Hammerstein enjoyed being the elder brother as much as he had enjoyed being mentored by older men earlier in his career (and just as he enjoyed mentoring Stephen Sondheim later). Through Shakespeare's seven stages of man, Hammerstein found grace in every role.

One also gets a sense from their letters that Rodgers sometimes imitated Hammerstein, as if he were trying to pass for a man with the kind of substance people perceived in his writing partner. For instance, Hammerstein often spoke of how he always cried when he heard the song "The Surrey with the Fringe on Top." When Michaelis asked the lyricist about this, Hammerstein said, "I don't cry at sadness in the theater; I cry at naïve happiness. The fact that two people are looking forward with great anticipation to a ride in a surrey to go to a dance makes me cry. Of course, the extreme and almost-bone-headed youth of the two characters arouses my sympathy." Speaking to Michaelis two years later, Rodgers said something similar. However, read closely, he seems to be crying about other people crying about the work he produced:

> The first time I saw *Oklahoma!* in London and the girl put her head on his shoulder, there was a murmur over the whole audience, and I started to bawl. And this is a very good moment, nothing sad about this at all. Here was the transfer of *Oklahoma!* from New York to New Haven to Boston. Now it's in London, and look what happens. The reserved English, you know, are falling apart over a little bit of a point that we had conceived years before. Well, to me, this is very, very emotional.

By the end of 1943, Rodgers and Hammerstein entered a new social class, and their incomes would grow and grow. How much did they make in the late 1940s? Many publications gave up trying to estimate and referred to the amount as equivalent to the U.S. Department of the Treasury. During a truckers' strike in 1946, a popular wisecrack was to wonder how Rodgers and Hammerstein would get their money to the bank. In the 1970s, Agnes de Mille said their longtime fixer Jerry Whyte estimated they each took in about $30,000 a week at that time. "That didn't include their ASCAP earnings or anything," said de Mille. "It was $50,000 a week at least. Like today a million a week" (actually it would be the equivalent of $150,000 in the mid-1970s, or $760,000 a week today). She then added, as she always did on this topic, "Of course I got no residuals of any kind."

After *Oklahoma!* Rodgers and Hammerstein accepted this mantle with a sense of responsibility, as good liberals of their time. Oscar wrote to Billy in December 1943:

> Big as my income was in the late '20s it looks as if I will make more in 1944 than in any other year of my career. You understand, naturally, that only a small part of this remains mine—80 to 85% will go to build planes, destroyers, etc. and help repair boats that recline on reefs. But, God knows, I don't kick. I'm in favor of these taxes, for the good of the nation and the good of my own soul. . . . . All in all, your old man is sitting pretty, at last—after some struggle, and not a few disappointments.

Rodgers also believed in paying his taxes. His daughter Mary said, "They never cheated on income tax. Not because they didn't want to get caught but because they didn't think it was the way to behave."

And now these good citizens stepped up their producing game. *I Remember Mama* was performing well and would continue until the summer of 1946, an almost two-year run. It was time to oversee a musical—not one of their own, but another great American story nonetheless. Dorothy Fields came up with the idea to adapt the life of sharpshooter Annie Oakley. Since she loved working with Jerome Kern as much as Hammerstein did, the men approached him to supply the music. Rodgers sent Kern a telegram: "It would be one of the greatest honours in my life if you would consent to write the music for this show." At the same time, Hammerstein asked Kern to coproduce a new staging of *Show Boat*. By several reports, Kern was thrilled that Hammerstein was bringing him along on the crest of this new wave. He missed Broadway. Producer and director Edwin Knopf threw a goodbye party for the Kerns the night before they left Los Angeles for New York, and friends say the composer was the happiest he'd been in years.

Jerome and Eva flew east and spent their first weekend at Highland Farm with the Hammersteins. Returning to New York on Sunday, Kern visited his parents' graves in Brooklyn. On Monday, November 5, having a few hours to kill before chorus auditions for *Show Boat,* Kern had just left the St. Regis to shop for antiques when he collapsed on the street. He carried no ID and so was sent to a hospital for the indigent on Welfare Island (now Roosevelt Island), under the Queensboro Bridge. An enterprising nurse found his ASCAP card and called that office with a description of the unconscious patient. Someone reached Hammerstein and he rushed to the hospital where he found "a zealous priest hovering there to administer last rites." Kern remained unconscious, but Hammerstein said he "was responsive when he heard my voice or Eva's." Hammerstein called in his doctor, Harold Hyman, who declared that Kern has suffered a cerebral hemorrhage, and the patient was moved to Doctors Hospital. Oscar and Dorothy took a room there, and Oscar remained by Kern's side for three days. If Kern could still perceive at the end, his last earthly experience may have been hearing Hammerstein gently sing him a love song they'd written together, "I've Told Ev'ry Little Star."

Eva asked Hammerstein to speak at the service. As he told his daughter Alice, "I doubted whether I could go through with it, but agreed to try. I didn't quite make it. I sort of went to pieces at the end and never finished the last sentence." His brief eulogy concluded:

> We all know in our hearts that these few minutes we devote to him now are small drops in the ocean of our affections. Our real tribute will be paid over many years of remembering, or telling good stories about him, and thinking about him when we are by ourselves. We, in this chapel, will cherish our special knowledge of this world figure. We will remember a jaunty, happy man whose sixty years were crowded with success and fun and love. Let us thank whatever God we believe in that we shared some part of the good, bright life Jerry led on this earth.

The next order of business was to find a new composer for the Annie Oakley musical. Hammerstein approached Irving Berlin, who at first protested he knew nothing about "hillbilly lyrics." Hammerstein assured him that he only had to drop the final "g" from most of the gerunds. Like Kern, Berlin was flattered by the wooing of Broadway's reigning geniuses; he accepted the offer, and the result was *Annie Get Your Gun*. This mammoth hit racked up over a thousand performances and became one of the biggest moneymakers in the Rodgers and Hammerstein catalogue. It's the only musical of Berlin's that is still regularly produced today.

Whereas once he could not gain traction no matter how hard he worked, Hammerstein now seemed infallible, though he never felt that way. He worried that his new position and new responsibilities might conspire to keep him from doing the work he loved. He channeled his anxiety about his new status into a 1947 musical called *Allegro*. His most autobiographical work, *Allegro* offers us a window into Hammerstein's perception of his own privileged childhood and his first marriage to Myra Finn, mother to Billy and Alice.

Allegro turned out to be Rodgers and Hammerstein's first Broadway failure, though it had an interesting afterlife. Given that Hammerstein was trying to find a way to fix the show until he died, *Allegro* has acquired an almost mythical reputation as a profound work that could have been but never was.

Adding to the show's mystique, Hammerstein had working beside him the seventeen-year-old Stephen Sondheim, who for twenty-five dollars a week served as his assistant. "It was a seminal experience in my theatrical life," Sondheim recalled years later. "I typed the script and got coffee. I listened to Agnes de Mille maltreat singers, and I watched the growth of this quite remarkable show" (de Mille, he said, treated only the dancers well). "I might not be quite so attracted to experimental musicals if I hadn't gotten my feet wet with *Allegro*," said Sondheim. Later he told Frank Rich, "A friend of mine said that I've spent my whole career trying to fix *Allegro*."

Hammerstein was writing a cautionary tale for himself with *Allegro*. Speaking to *Time* as its cover subject in 1947, he called it "the first play I have written," although it was not his first musical with an original story, nor even his first play. He added, "It's the first time I have put myself into a show."

His initial vision was a production of the utmost simplicity. He told Arnold Michaelis, "I was thinking of college theater—I was thinking not only of Broadway, but the colleges very much need properties that they can do. I evolved a play without any scenery, just props, chairs and table and so forth, to sort of supply the scene. I borrowed from the Greeks the chorus idea, and then found that I could do other things with the chorus. I could provide the audience with insight into character, which I did, and it came off quite well in spots."

Like his protagonist—a small-town doctor who gets railroaded into treating rich city dwellers and their questionable ailments—Hammerstein was pressured to forgo his dream of simplicity for *Allegro*. Todd Purdum reports in his book *Something Wonderful* that Jo Mielziner's sets weighed eighty-five tons and were moved on synchronized motors on five giant tracks. It was a curious irony that Rodgers and Hammerstein, with all their power at this moment, could not get the production they wanted. This in turn hurt the work's message, making *Allegro* a self-fulfilling prophecy of failure.

Allegro follows Joe Jr. from birth to age thirty-five. Like Hammerstein, Joe receives a warm welcome to the world; his grandma and mother find his every goo and ga proof of brilliance. They think, like Hammerstein's own grandma, that he arrived on the earth looking aged, as if he had been here before. They hope he'll become a doctor, like his hardworking dad, Joe Sr., who seems to be the only physician in their unnamed small town. Watching Joe grow up is the delight of the family's days.

As a kid, Joe joins his dad on his rounds, and it turns out he does indeed have the makings of a doctor—either that, or an overweening need for adult approval, another Hammerstein trait. Young Joe exclaims, "Dad had to use the kitchen table to operate on the kid. Boy, was I scared! Nothing in the world mattered except saving a ten-year-old boy I'd never seen before. Gosh! Who would want to be anything else but a doctor!"

Eventually Joe does join the family practice. However, he allows himself to be pulled so far in the direction of glittering yet trivial prizes—wealthy clientele, prestigious titles—that he risks losing touch with what makes him happy and gives his life purpose. In fact, none of this ever posed a problem for Hammerstein, in part because his sense of meaningful work was entwined with his sense of accessing an audience's emotions—his artistic and commercial ambitions were in sync.

On the other hand, Joe's single biggest mistake is marrying the wrong woman. This was something with which Hammerstein had experience. He was twenty-two when he married Myra, an inveterate flirt, unrelentingly shallow, and completely wrong for him. Their height disparity might have been a tip-off: she was five feet and he six two. They looked like a mixed-gender Mutt and Jeff.

In *Allegro,* Joe Jr. marries Jenny, his childhood sweetheart. Jenny sees doctoring as thankless work. She pressures her new husband to take a more lucrative job in her father's coal and lumber business—though in the second act her dad will go broke and move in with the couple. At that juncture Jenny switches her ambition for Joe to big-city medicine. She wants them to move to Chicago, where she could have a beautiful house, servants, and lovely dresses. And, like any good femme fatale, Jenny slides herself into her victim's lap or down at his feet before cooing some version of "But whatever happens, Joey, it's got to be you who decides."

Joe's mother, Marjorie, feels strongly that practicing small-town medicine is a noble calling and the right one for her son. Just before the marriage, the fiancée and mother have it out. Jenny doesn't see happiness for herself "as the wife of a starving doctor" and tells Marjorie, "I've got things inside of me too." (One thinks of Rose's line in Sondheim's *Gypsy,* "What I been holding down inside of me, if I ever let it out . . .") After they argue, Jenny exits while shouting at her future mother-in-law, "Try and get him away from me! You just try!" Marjorie walks to a chair, clutches at her chest, and tries to yell for help. She dies, killed by Jenny's awfulness.

Some might have thought the show died with her.

But Hammerstein was striving for something greater than these clunky scenes betray. He had in mind iconic rather than melodramatic slices of life. His first inclination to strip the stage bare was meant to underline that *Allegro* was about an Everyman and the dangers of success in any field at any time.

In its attempt at allegory, *Allegro* closely followed the fashion of Thornton Wilder's *Our Town,* which had debuted nine years earlier and featured no set and only minimal props. Both stories begin in the first decade of the twentieth century—just far back enough to exploit a nostalgia for a supposedly simpler time. Both Wilder and Hammerstein were interested in how the ordinary functions of human biology, like mating, can overwhelm us with their meaning—the meaning of life, if you will. But the more cerebral Wilder had a genius for underwriting; he could lead an audience to the brink of epiphany and let them stumble, blinded by tears, to a place where they see their lives from a philosophical height.

Hammerstein could do many things brilliantly, but underwriting was not one of them.

In *Allegro* chorus members form a literal Greek chorus, commenting in unison on and analyzing the action as it is happening. Though the technique obviously harks back to ancient drama, it was something new for musicals and therefore a primary reason *Allegro* became known as Rodgers and Hammerstein's experimental work. Several observers noted that the show's failure was so painful that *Allegro* ended Rodgers and Hammerstein's risk-taking period. But arriving nine years after *Our Town*—a work so similar that virtually no review of *Allegro* fails to mention it—how experimental was it really?

Still *Allegro* offers its share of innovative moments. Hammerstein sometimes uses the chorus in creative ways—such as when it heralds the news of Joe Jr.'s birth to the town, comically highlighting the way we think our personal milestones are important to the rest of the world. Similarly, when the chorus speaks the thoughts of the preverbal Joe Jr., who perceives adults as "those things with the big heads," it serves a helpful narrative purpose and is charming as well. But once Joe Jr. can speak, the chorus becomes obsolete, telling us things we can clearly see for ourselves. For instance, when Joe and Jenny say goodnight, the stage directions say that Jenny looks at Joe "with an expression that would make it obvious to a more sophisticated escort that she expected to be kissed." Any actor could telegraph this to an audience in a millisecond. But here the chorus whispers Joe's thoughts:

"What do you suppose Jenny would do if you kissed her?" Few plays can recover from telling the audience what it already knows.

In the same vein, at the marriage of Jenny and Joe, the chorus delineates what should hang in the air unsaid, chanting:

> A change has come over us.
> The simple word,
> The commonplace words,
> And the two serious children listening—
> A change has come over us!
> The whispered jokes,
> The "cracks" that seemed funny
> A few moments ago,
> Aren't funny anymore!
> This is not time for the humorous skeptic,
> Or the gloomy prophet.
> This is a time for hope.
> These children desperately
> Need our hope!

This is describing why chocolate is delicious to a child from whom you withhold chocolate.

Ernest Hemingway, like Wilder a master of understatement, famously described his method as a "theory of omission": "If a writer of prose knows enough of what he is writing about he may omit things that he knows and the reader, if the writer is writing truly enough, will have a feeling of those things as strongly as though the writer had stated them. The dignity of movement of an iceberg is due to only one-eighth of it being above water."

Aesthetically speaking, Rodgers and Hammerstein preferred to hit the iceberg full-on, and never more so than in *Allegro*.

Because it is about an American Everyman, *Allegro* reveals what Hammerstein thought to be givens in the human experience, thus exposing his own blind spots more than any universal truths. *Allegro* is so blithe in its assumptions about gender roles that it could have been written before its author was born. The play opens with Marjorie in bed with her newborn, looking dreamily contented. Nearby is the chorus to tell us "this is the happiest day of her life, except for her wedding day." Marjorie never learns enough about doctoring to offer an opinion on her husband's cases; however, she is always at the ready with unmitigated support, usually in the form of secret messages she receives from the universe. When her husband cannot find the cause of a patient's trouble, Marjorie responds, "You'll pull her through. I have a feeling." Joe Sr. is not so sure. No diagnosis has so far panned out. "At this moment I haven't the faintest idea what to do for the lady," he confesses. Marjorie simply puts her hand on his. "You'll beat it," she says, "I have a feeling about it."

This loving dynamic is celebrated in a song, "A Fellow Needs a Girl":

A fellow needs a girl
To sit by his side
At the end of a weary day
To sit by his side
And listen to him talk.
And agree with the things he'll say.

I'm guessing this song failed to charm some female members of the audience. Things get better when Joe replaces Jenny (after finding she has been unfaithful) with Emily, a nurse who cares about people's welfare.

Billy Hammerstein saw a direct link between the limitations of some of Oscar's female characters with the lyricist's premature loss of his mother. "She was always the perfect woman in his mind," Billy noted many years later. "In his plays all of the women are too perfect," he said, noting particularly the songs "What's the Use of Wond'rin'?" from *Carousel* and "Something Wonderful" from *The King and I*. "In all his love songs the woman devotes herself completely and she can do no wrong. Always the ideal woman who will stick with the man no matter what he does. This came from his idealization of his mother."

Allegro is at its most clear-eyed and delightful when commenting on the behavior of the one-percenters, a group to which Rodgers and Hammerstein now belonged. Hammerstein seems to feel as much chagrin as pride that he is economically on par with avaricious industrialists. He is clearly in a watchful mood for the rationalizations and magical thinking of the privileged.

The title song condemns the unexamined life. Sung by the good guys—Joe, Emily, and their friend Charlie—the song is their response to the firing of a nurse who had been agitating to reduce daily staff shifts from twelve to eight hours. Feeling their own rebellion brewing, the three friends enact a giddy parody of the rich folk that they serve:

> Hysterically frantic,
> We are stubbornly romantic
> And doggedly determined to be gay!
>
> We spin and we spin and we spin and we spin,
> Playing a game no one can win,
>
> The men who corner wheat,
> The men who corner gin,
> The men who rule the air waves,
> The denizens of din—
>
> The girls who dig for gold,
> And won't give in for tin,
> The lilies of the field,
> So femininely thin,
> They toil not, they toil not,
> But oh, how they spin!

This is the kind of social commentary at which Hammerstein excelled: recognizably true and spooned out softly enough so that each member of the audience can be sure it's about someone else. Later, when he tried to analyze what he had gotten wrong in *Allegro*—or what the audience had misinterpreted, though he swore one should never blame the audience—he said the show was misperceived as advertising the virtue of small town or country life over urban values. Like Sondheim would do in his juvenile musical *Climb High,* Hammerstein was instead expressing anxiety about a successful man's ability to lead a meaningful life. The pitfall of such a theme is that it requires judging those who do not find their way to what the author identifies as meaningful.

Opening nights were never easy for Hammerstein. Given the personal nature of *Allegro,* this one was particularly hard. He sweat so much that he needed a change of clothes afterward. Dorothy removed her rings as he twisted her fingers in an agony of suspense. "It's like jumping off a precipice," he says. "It's like a nightmare about being caught naked in public." He admitted hating those audience members who did not pay strict attention. "I really feel like killing them," he told the *Saturday Evening Post*. He always watched the bored ones and followed them out of the theater to overhear their comments. (Six years later, he took revenge on audience chatterers in a song called "Intermission Talk" from *Me and Juliet*.)

In 2009 the Rodgers and Hammerstein Organization produced a star-studded recording of *Allegro* (distributed by Sony) featuring Broadway royalty Audra McDonald, Laura Benanti, Patrick Wilson, and Liz Callaway, accompanied by a fifty-piece band and the original orchestrations by Robert Russell Bennett. Listening to it, I was struck by a charming song of which I had been only vaguely aware. It comes at the top of act 2, just after the stock market crash. Jenny, wearing a "plain house dress" according to the text, is hanging laundry while trying to be nice to her dad, Ned, who has lost his business and is now living with her and Joe. Ned tells his daughter she should feel lucky that her husband makes a decent living. Jenny's answer is pure Jenny and probably pure Myra Finn as well: "Decent living! If I thought that was all we'd ever have, I'd just as soon die!"

Jenny's mood is enlivened by the entrance of three friends, all wearing "cheap print dresses." The women take a moment to drool over a *Vogue* magazine photo of a chinchilla wrap, "the dreamiest coat you ever saw." One of them notices a sermonizing story on the page opposite titled "Money Isn't Everything," and this amusing mixed message is not lost on the group.

Once they start their song, "Money Isn't Everything," Jenny transforms from acquisitive brat to a sharp-eyed wit in the manner of Dorothy Parker, equipped with a perspective she exhibits nowhere else in the text:

Oil tycoon and cattle king
Radio troubadour,
Belittle the fun that their fortunes bring,
And tell you that they are sure
"Money isn't everything!"
Money isn't everything.
Money isn't everything—
Unless you're very poor!

In this song Jenny is not a spoiled child who will lead a fine doctor astray; she is merely young and dreaming of pleasure, a cousin to the appealing teenagers in *Bye, Bye Birdie* who sing of all the living they've got to do. The lilt of three-quarter time—and no composer got more range out of the waltz than Richard Rodgers—lends a playful sensuality to Jenny's dreams of luxury. In this song, a stern morality tale gives way to what we suspect are the writers' true feelings. You can hear Rodgers and Hammerstein's personal pleasure and pride in the kinds of goodies they now bestow on their own wives, just as you can sense a fine appreciation of the habits of their own glittering caste. Just look at the details they pick:

> Money isn't everything—
> If you're rich, you pay
> Elizabeth Arden to do your face
> The night you attend a play.
> Feeling like the bloom of spring,
> Down the aisle you float,
> A Tiffany ring, and a Cartier string
> Of pearls to adorn your throat. . . .
> To your creamy shoulders cling
> Ermines white as snow
> Then on to cafes where they sway and swing,
> You go with your wealthy beau.

Senator Joe McCarthy, who would soon launch an investigation into Hammerstein's political affiliations, must have missed *Allegro:* the man who wrote this song was clearly not a Communist. Hammerstein worried that the show might be misunderstood as a criticism of capitalism when a theater in Finland wanted to stage it in 1948. He wrote to Swedish producer Lars Schmidt:

> I suppose it will be all right for "Allegro" to be played at the Kansan Theatre in Finland. We of course would have to own the translation and control it as in all other countries. The only thought that occurs to me in connection with Finland is that the theme of "Allegro" might easily be turned against us as a social criticism of life in the United States under the crushing heel of capitalism. What about this? What is the temper of the Finnish Theatre and how much is it dominated by the Soviet?

■ ■ ■

The two Dorothys standing next to their husbands (the Hammersteins, *right;* the Rodgerses, *left*).
Courtesy of Photofest

When the two Dorothys converged in 1943, each harbored doubts about the other. Agnes de Mille, who described herself as "quite good friends" with Dorothy Hammerstein, said her pal was well aware of Rodgers's womanizing. While *Carousel* was in previews out of town, Dorothy H. told the choreographer that she dreaded Rodgers's influence. "Ockie's going to be different," she worried. "Dick is just altogether different in his way of life and his approach to women and everything. It makes me very nervous. And we are locked together."

Mary Rodgers saw with clarity the Dorothys' similarities and differences: "These were two wives who adored their husbands and who would have done everything they could to see that there wasn't a problem." She admits that her mother, with the better education and class bona fides, felt superior to Dorothy Hammerstein, whose "whole life was more self-indulgent and more giggly and more frivolous and less guilt-ridden and, to me, certainly more fun, but probably with much less fine values in the long run.

I mean my mother may be difficult, but she's sure as hell ethical. As much as she possibly can be, she is a very decent human being. She's honorable as much as she can possibly be."

Both Dorothys played their wifely roles with careful deference. When a reporter for the *New York Herald Tribune* asked Dorothy Hammerstein if she helped her husband, she said, "He'll always sing a lyric to me first and if I notice a word sticking out, he'll invariably say that was the one that bothered him. But help him, no. I hate wives who say they advise their husbands." Richard Rodgers described his Dorothy in a 1959 *Holiday* magazine interview titled "The Nicest Guys in Show Business": "I love satire but I couldn't write it. I would find it just as impossible to live with a wise-cracking wife as I have found it extremely possible—and extremely agreeable—to live for some twenty-eight years with a lovely, gentle, sweet, quiet, soft-spoken gal who knows what the score is." In 1962 he elaborated on his views, telling the *Ladies' Home Journal* that the essential component of femininity is to be "as little like a man as possible. I think you can follow this line of thought from the purely physical aspect to the mental one in which the aggressive woman becomes less feminine because aggressiveness is essentially a male characteristic."

Away from her husband, Dorothy Rodgers constructed her own public identity; she did not self-present as gentle, sweet, or quiet, and was the opposite of soft spoken. If being an American homemaker were a competition, Dorothy Rodgers wanted the world to know she had won it. In her 1964 book *My Favorite Things: A Personal Guide to Decorating and Entertaining,* she admits that she got a late start on acquiring such skills, because "when I should have been learning cooking and sewing, I was being propelled through museums and chateaux during summers abroad." Once she set her mind to it, she caught up with and surpassed all comers, and that would include Dorothy Hammerstein, who may have beaten her to a career of interior design but would now be outshone by sheer industry. Three years later Dorothy Rodgers published a second book, *The House in My Head,* in which she paints a life of abundance and glamour. Her works provide evidence that people with the most status suffer the most status anxiety.

Dorothy Rodgers's in-town staff consisted of "a cook, a waitress and a chambermaid," and one senses she was not an easygoing head of household. Vigilance was what kept life above average. "I have known the same cook in two vastly different households," she wrote. "In one, the food she produced was indifferent, in the other, superb." She invented a remote-controlled bell to keep by her side at dinner parties, signaling the staff to appear as if by magic when they were needed. (Dorothy Hammerstein used the more mundane foot pedal.) No detail was too small to escape her notice, and she had definite opinions on all aspects of entertaining—for instance, a host might mix pink napkins with blue, but the stemware must always match perfectly. She also has advice for entertaining foreign visitors ("Don't serve pasta to an Italian or curry to an Indian") and somewhat catty insights on wardrobe ("I'm convinced that no one who needs a size larger than twelve should wear tapered pants except on the beach; they really only look well on slim long-legged people").

Whatever Dorothy Rodgers's husband might be doing in his off hours would not diminish her power and prestige. Nor would she acknowledge any rumors. If she so much as strayed near the subject of a young actress, she let her position speak for itself:

> In my decorating days, I once agreed to do an apartment for a girl in one of Dick's shows who had never had a home of her own and who didn't really know at all what she liked or needed. She wanted "a pretty place" but could give me no hint about her favorite colors or styles or atmosphere. I got the same sort of noncommittal reply to every question I asked. Desperately searching for just one decisive answer, I said, "Well, at any rate, I can estimate how much furniture you'll need to put books in. Do you have many of them?" "No," she answered, "but I'm going to get some. How many do you think I'll need?"

As Dorothy Rodgers was an expert on the hosting habits of the American rich, so was her daughter Mary on child-rearing.

"It was an era of nurses, and she was a very unaffectionate mother," Mary recalled in an oral history recorded in 1982 by Columbia University. Mary had no memories of being held or read to during childhood. She recalled being alone with her dad once; it was the "hot and awful" summer of 1935 and Rodgers took her to Tavern on the Green for ice cream. "My father's idea of what to do with a child was to squeeze it a lot, to say hello twice a day."

At this point the family lived in two apartments at the Carlyle Hotel, and Mary remembers thinking, "I cannot wait to get out of here and be a mother because I can do it better than she's doing it." (Mary went on to have six children.) She was sent first to the Horace Mann School and then to the Brearley School in Manhattan. Linda was a more self-contained child, but the sisters bonded over their common plight: "We used to talk more than anything else about our parents—which was the only thing for a long time that we really had in common: how much we hated growing up in that house."

De Mille found Rodgers's marriage to Dorothy to be "a fearsome thing. He could be quite indifferent and rather cruel. She was so perfect in all her housekeeping, impeccable. And she couldn't bring the children up, I mean there was no love in the home." Said Mary, "What I wanted, desperately, was my parents' affection, but it wasn't there to be gotten. Or I didn't know how to get it."

Mary recalled the sensation of, early one morning, lighting the organdy curtains in her bedroom with a match. "I was a little startled," she said. "They went whoom!—you know—an explosion of flame." She ran to the next room and got her nurse, who got her father, who stamped out the flames. She explained that she had been sleeping when she smelled smoke. Her father told her he would have a hotel employee who was an arson expert look into it, and then let her wait. But he never disciplined her for her crime; discipline was Dorothy's department, and she had outsourced this one to him.

At the Hammerstein home Oscar also practiced the noblesse oblige style of 1940s upper-class fathering; one paid attention to the children when the schedule permitted. As his daughter Alice recalled it, "When we stayed in Doylestown we had certain times that we could see him. He would take a walk, but we weren't allowed to go, because he was probably talking to his characters." He and Dorothy breakfasted together and then he disappeared into his study. "We weren't allowed to go there unless we made an appointment," continued Alice. "But he would come down for lunch, and then we might play some croquet after that. He'd go back to work and he'd come for tea. And then I guess he went back and got dressed for supper."

According to Billy, Oscar did not seem to notice "when we were sick as kids, like when I had bronchial pneumonia when I was eleven. He isolated himself physically. He didn't want to experience any discomfort. It was a family joke." Billy recalled one dinner when Oscar got up himself to refill his own water glass and the family burst into applause.

Interviewing Billy in 1990, Max Wilk tried to inject a cuddly note into Oscar's parenting. "People make Oscar sound so somber," said Wilk. "He was never reticent about saying something emotional, about saying I love you in a loud clear voice." Billy would have none of it. "He couldn't say it himself, though," the son countered. "All his emotion came out in his work. The only emotion he expressed at home was anger. He was totally undemonstrative. This made for a wonderful body of work but a frustrating home life for everyone."

Billy had another theory: that his father could enjoy his feelings for his children more fully when he was alone. In a letter to Josh Logan just after his father's death, Billy wrote, "He was embarrassed by emotional demonstration and I think it not insignificant that Billy Bigelow is alone in his soliloquy of exhilaration over his unborn child, Anna alone when she talks back to the King, the King alone in his puzzlement, and what's-her-name alone with her nervous anticipation of life—as jumpy as a puppet on a string" (he's referring to Margy in *State Fair*).

In a 1954 letter to Billy, Oscar offered a mea culpa of sorts when he described his own father:

> Just as I took for granted that I loved him because he was my father, I also took for granted that he loved me because I was his son. I believe now that he loved Reggie and me very much, but he was shy in his love. It is a trait in most Hammersteins (if you believe in family traits as I cannot avoid doing) that they are shy in their expressions of affection, and in their shyness they are rather gruff about it and adopt a clumsily humorous attitude toward not only the deeper and tenderer emotions, but indeed to the formal amenities of life.

Oscar did take time to teach the kids to throw a ball, play tennis and board games, and, in a sense, be wary of their opponents. He tripped Billy with a stick while they were ice-skating together. "He was a ferocious, mean-spirited but funny competitor who, if he got you at a bad spot on the chess board, would hum or tap his fingers, anything to make it harder for you to concentrate," said Billy. "There was nothing low that he wouldn't do to you. He wanted to win."

Hammerstein's competitive edge may have softened by the time he raised his younger son Jamie, who grew up to be a fierce athlete. (When Jamie died in 1999, playwright Simon Gray remembered his near-professional skill at tennis, golf, swimming, diving, and ping-pong, at which he tormented Gray with his "lethal combination of good manners and swift reflexes.")

Oscar and Dorothy welcomed a steady stream of visitors to the farm; the stability of their marriage provided shelter for those needing equilibrium. Reggie, for one, was a frequent guest. Mary Rodgers remembered Oscar from that time as "a big, rumpled guy with a full, friendly mouth, gentle eyes, a soft voice, and badly pockmarked skin that made people think he'd be sympathetic. Dorothy was a great-looking Australian dame with blazing red hair—dazzling Rinso white when she was older—regal posture, a slightly down-turned mouth, a happy laugh, or sometimes a naughty-little-girl giggle to make sure you knew she knew she'd said something reprehensible, which she frequently did."

Sondheim recalled that during the war years "the house was virtually an orphanage as well as a home." Said Mary Rodgers, "Steve was one of the semi-orphans and sad strays with rotten parents that Ockie and Dorothy were always quasi-adopting." Dorothy invited the daughters of two friends to stay for months, as she did for her niece Jennifer Watanabe when Jennifer's half-Japanese father, Jerry, was interned at Ellis Island. (In 1949, the Hammersteins joined with Pearl Buck to establish Welcome House, an adoption agency to find families for Asian and part-Asian children born in the United States whom other agencies could not or would not place.)

The twelve-year-old Sondheim frequently biked over from his mother's post-divorce house four miles away. Janet Sondheim, known as Foxy, had consulted with Dorothy Hammerstein about decorating the San Remo apartment she shared with Stephen's father, Herbert, though Sondheim says that was never arranged. But it was through this connection that Stephen met Jamie Hammerstein, who was one year and one day younger. Stephen visited the Hammersteins at Highland Farm often. In that first summer of 1942, he chose to stay there instead of going off to camp, which put him in the historic position of being on the scene the moment Rodgers and Hammerstein began to discuss a collaboration.

Almost immediately Sondheim endeared himself to Hammerstein by teaching him chess, a game he grew to love. (In 1951 Hammerstein wrote to a friend, "I started chess late in life, and my teacher was an eleven-year-old boy. It took me three years to be able to beat him, and now we play pretty even. Of course he is much older now, and something of a genius—I hope.")

Sondheim was "overwhelmed by the extraordinary serenity" of the house in Doylestown. "The huge living room was dark and cool and chic, the atmosphere unhurried. Not reverent—there were too many children for that—but unhurried, promising that every wound would be healed and that boredom would be dispensed with forever." He also called it "a place of material as well as spiritual comfort." Highland Farm was a working grange. "It was a non-show biz life," added Sondheim. "Gertrude Lawrence did not swan in for the weekend."

The boy at once took to Hammerstein's "laconic" wit. "I remember standing in front of a window with him looking at the rain," Sondheim told me. "I said, 'It's really coming down.' He said, 'That's because it's heavier than air.'" Dorothy, Sondheim said, "had a soignée elegance" and "was a big fan of Stephen Leacock [a Canadian humorist]. She was mischievous, known for saying things like, 'Hold my purse, dear, while I get married.'"

Oscar and Dorothy were aware of "Stevie's" challenges on the home front and offered a sympathetic and discreet ear. Foxy was not cut out for parenting. By all accounts, she was an impossible narcissist—controlling, vindictive, flirtatious, and a world-class social climber. Sondheim said his mother was torn by her desire to be close to the Hammersteins and her jealousy of them. She told her son she was going to sue the family for "alienation of affection."

"We discussed my home situation every time I was at their house," recalled Sondheim. "They would always ask me how things were at home. They tried to explain my mother's behavior without either defending her or attacking her."

Foxy enrolled her son in the George School, where Jamie went, making it easy for Sondheim to begin "infiltrating the house," as he himself put it. The boy's relationship with his mother reminded Jamie of Edward Albee's *Who's Afraid of Virginia Woolf?:* "Even at the age of twelve he could be as bitchy as she was. They were incredible, the way they could dish it out. I didn't understand it, then or now."

It must have been unnerving for Jamie how much his friend and his father had in common. Like Oscar, Sondheim skipped ahead two grades, in his case kindergarten and seventh grade, and so was the youngest in his class. They both suffered from acne as teenagers and still bore some of the scars. Both loved games and were extremely competitive, with Sondheim teaching Hammerstein chess and Oscar teaching Stephen bridge. They also shared a love of crosswords and the Puns and Anagrams feature in the *New York Times*. "The whole idea of words, my interest in words qua words, came from Oscar," said Sondheim.

One year younger than Sondheim, Mary Rodgers also was drawn to the warmth in Doylestown: "I had daydreams about my parents dying in a tractor-trailer crash and my immediately being sent to live with the Hammersteins," wrote Mary. "They looked like so much fun to me. They really left you alone, and they laughed a lot." As time went on she decided this was a "grass is always greener" fantasy, having noticed that "there were all kinds of problems" with the Hammersteins as parents. "Dorothy was practically neglectful," she said. "I could have done with a little benign neglect in my life, but she really didn't pay an awful lot of attention." This may also explain why they were so open to having other people's children around: they didn't sweat the details.

Mary was present at one Sunday lunch in Doylestown when Oscar was in a mocking humor. She remembers him picking apart some opinion of either Jimmy's or Billy's. "Whatever it was, it was devastating," she said. Sondheim also remembers cutting remarks that Oscar directed at his sons: "He was better with children when they reached a rational age. Perhaps he felt a bit threatened by their physicality and impulsiveness, by their illogic, and his best defense was irony. Sometimes the irony lurched into sarcasm, and when it did, the victims were more likely to be his flesh-and-blood children than we outsiders."

Sondheim has often said that if Hammerstein had been a geologist (or some other occupation), he, too, would have become that. I asked him about that since I found it hard to believe he would not have somehow found his way to music. He agreed but added that he had seriously considered a career in math when he was at Williams College. "Still," he said, "I didn't want to be a composer before I met him. When I was at prep school [the George School], I suddenly wanted to write songs for school. Just being around Oscar made me want to do it. I met him when I'm eleven or twelve and then suddenly, at fourteen or fifteen, I start writing musicals."

Whether they knew it or not, the Hammersteins were hatching the next generation of musical-theater artists in their Doylestown living room.

Mary Rodgers and Stephen Sondheim met there and became fast friends. (Actually, Mary fell instantly in love with Sondheim. She wrote, "I don't think he thought I was as bright as he was, and he was right. . . . But at that moment I thought I would never be as infatuated with anyone again. Which turned out to be true.") Later Mary introduced Sondheim to Hal Prince, her boyfriend at the time. Her parents were not thrilled with the match: "I remember at one point they told me that Hal was never going to succeed; he was going about everything in the wrong way."

Sondheim has often described the life-changing master class he received when Hammerstein gave the young composer notes on his musical *By George,* which was produced at the George School in 1946. Hammerstein called it, dryly, "the worst thing I've ever read." He spared the fifteen-year-old author nothing. "He pointed out everything that was wrong—the characters weren't developed, the scenes weren't real, the songs had no beginning and end," recalled Sondheim. "He also explained how a lyric must have clarity of sound and clarity of thought, and that a song should reveal the character to the audience." Hammerstein also helped Sondheim understand that he shouldn't try to copy his mentor or anyone else.

When his parents divorced, Sondheim was sent to the New York Military Academy, which he liked. "I felt that I knew what was going to happen next," he said, vaguely alluding to some other chaos. "There were schedules and an enormous kind of regimentation. Emotional order." He touches on his difficulties in a comment as short as it is devastating: "If it hadn't been for the Hammersteins, I really don't know where I would even be, if I'd even be alive."

CHAPTER NINE

You've Got to Be Taught

AS PRODUCERS, Rodgers and Hammerstein decided to remount the most influential American musical that preceded their collaboration: *Show Boat*. The revival opened for a brief run at New York's City Center in September 1948 and then toured the country. Brooks Atkinson saw this as the moment to declare that the musical had become "immortal" and "part of our cultural heritage." He called Kern the "perfect internationalist," reporting that he had heard music from the show in Shanghai, Singapore, and the Soviet Union, and he noted that *Show Boat* and *Oklahoma!* were "the two finest musical plays in modern American theatre." He called Hammerstein "the king of lyricists." In the twenty-one years that had passed since *Show Boat*'s debut, though, a profound shift had occurred in the critical community—African American writers now had better platforms to voice concern over aspects of the show that they found to be racist.

Lee Newton, a critic at the *Daily Worker* (a newspaper published by the Communist Party USA), challenged Hammerstein to prune the show of racial stereotyping. Much as J. A. Rogers did when he reviewed the original London production for the *Amsterdam News*, Newton began with praise, noting the "lovely and enduring songs" and calling the show "a permanent institution in the American theater." But he said there were aspects of the musical that abetted leading racists of the day, singling out John Rankin, a

Mississippi representative who enjoyed using the word "niggra" on the floor of the House and legislated accordingly. Then Newton got to his appeal:

> Yet I have a hunch that you would be happier about *Show Boat* if it was changed just a bit. I'm not talking about your theme, your fundamental storyline, the songs, etc.: the changes I'm referring to would not in any way affect the structure of *Show Boat*. They would, in most cases, be a simple matter of omission.
>
> I mean omitting all the Uncle Tom business, the Negro as a shiftless, lazy good-for-nothing—the Negro as the object of patronizing ridicule. Why retain these blemishes in a show which will be seen by many more Americans in the years to come—including impressionable youngsters—who will more easily absorb the patronizing attitude toward Negroes simply because of the memorable songs that go with it?
>
> I don't believe that either of you are consciously propagandizing Jimcrow. To the contrary, those who should know, say you're on the liberal side of the fence. Why help the Rankins and the other monstrosities on our national scene?

Speaking in their new role as creative and commercials leaders of the American theater, Rodgers and Hammerstein cowrote a reply, also published in the *Daily Worker*. They offered a defense of the inviolable right of artists to depict human behavior as they find it. First, they assured Lee that their own ideas about "Jimcrowism" and "Uncle Tomism" coincided with his: "Our difference lies only in our belief that no rule of thumb or blindly followed shibboleths should govern us in handling this question." They continued:

> We deplore the evil of stereotypes in fiction on the stage and on the screen—the crap-shooting, razor wielding Negro, the crafty and penurious Jew, the pugnacious whisky-drinking Irishman. All these are on their way out as stock characters. When races are invariably symbolized by these types, the result is not only harmful but it is likely to make dull entertainment. We ourselves have been active in the past in movements to educate authors in the necessity of putting an end to these characterizations as exclusively representing their races.

On the other hand, we would be the last to advocate the theory that never again shall a Negro character gamble or be lazy or that never again shall a Jewish character be anything but honest in any business dealing, that never again shall an Irish character raise his fists. We both believe that the evil of stereotype lies in its exclusive use. We believe all races should be represented by their good types as well as their bad types, that all races should be regarded as having their share of imperfections as well as virtues because this is the truth.

Rodgers and Hammerstein concluded that *Show Boat* "does not pretend that there is no segregation in the South. It acknowledges the existence of this evil and while making no direct comment, its attitude on the issue is definitely and dramatically expressed by the story itself."

This prominent debate in the Communist Party's newspaper occurred on the cusp of the Cold War. President Harry Truman had already announced his intention to "contain" Communism, and Joseph McCarthy was serving his second year as a U.S. senator; two years later he began blacklisting a secret band of Communists that had supposedly infiltrated the State Department. During those uneasy years, anyone who fought publicly for integration, civil rights, or an end to "Jimcrowism" was smeared as a Communist or Communist sympathizer. *Show Boat* star Paul Robeson—who fourteen years earlier had visited the Soviet Union and declared that "here I am not a Negro but a human being for the first time in my life"—was already under investigation and Hammerstein himself would soon be caught in a web of accusations and associations. Rodgers, on the other hand, did not raise any alarms.

At this moment Rodgers and Hammerstein were casting about for their next show. The idea to adapt *Tales of the South Pacific*, a novel in stories by a relatively unknown English teacher named James Michener, was first brought to the team by Josh Logan. This move by Logan would define his legacy and haunt him till the end of his days.

Coincidentally Michener had been raised in Bucks County and had taught at the George School. At age thirty-three he joined the navy and was stationed on an island in the New Hebrides, where he took the opportunity to explore the region and write stories. In these tales Michener focused on how quirky personalities managed the profound day-to-day shifts that war brings. Logan read *Tales of the South Pacific* while he was adapting with Thomas Heggen the latter's novel *Mister Roberts,* another book of war stories from a young, unheralded writer.

Having served as an intelligence officer himself, Logan found in both books a new kind of war writing not bound up in traditional notions of heroism. They captured what Logan thought of as "*my* war, the boredom and idiocy of it."

In 1938, while directing the Rodgers and Hart musical *I Married an Angel,* Rodgers had handed Logan the impossible job of babysitting Hart and getting him to write. Rodgers hired Logan again to direct *By Jupiter* in 1942, and for this Logan was especially grateful; the director had recently been released from a psychiatric hospital after a bipolar episode and was worried he would not work again. Logan was also drafted into the army that year and quickly proved he could contribute more by distracting the troops than fighting by their side. He codirected Irving Berlin's *This Is the Army* on Broadway and in London and was eventually assigned to Special Services, which meant he organized touring "jeep shows" that entertained the troops in Europe.

When he was about to be released from the army in 1945, Logan stood in a lengthy line for the pay phone at Camp Kilmer in New Jersey; he used his one call to contact Richard Rodgers. He was eager to get started on directing *Annie Get Your Gun,* the new musical written by Kern and Dorothy Fields and produced by Rodgers and Hammerstein. Rodgers had sent him a letter a few weeks before the Japanese surrender saying he had "reason to believe" the war would soon be over, adding to the air of omnipotence Logan believed was collecting over Rodgers and Hammerstein. "Had someone slipped Dick Rodgers a hint about the atom bomb?" he wondered.

Logan was only half joking; he had become fixated on Rodgers, and, after the success of *Oklahoma!* and *Carousel,* on Hammerstein as well. For people in the theater industry, having the chance to work with Rodgers and Hammerstein was like securing one of Willy Wonka's Golden Tickets. *Annie Get Your Gun* was a huge success, producing a litany of hit songs and a run of more than one thousand performances on Broadway and more in London. At the start of 1946 Rodgers and Hammerstein had three Broadway shows still running from their original productions—*Oklahoma!, Carousel,* and *I Remember Mama.* Over the course of the year *Annie Get Your Gun* and

Happy Birthday opened, along with a Hammerstein-directed *Show Boat* revival and limited-run productions of *Desert Song* and *Carmen Jones* at City Center. Altogether, Rodgers and Hammerstein were responsible for eight shows on Broadway in a single year, a record that still stands (to the best of my knowledge).

Inevitably their spectacular success attracted envy and the kind of unhinged behavior that attends any large concentration of wealth. They regularly received requests for money from relatives, old friends, strangers, and sometimes colleagues who felt they had been slighted.

One example of this was a letter Rodgers received from John O'Hara, whose idea it had been to turn his *New Yorker* stories about a disreputable character named Joey Evans into the 1940 musical, *Pal Joey,* which became Rodgers and Hart's most enduring show. O'Hara wrote ostensibly to congratulate Rodgers for the sale of *Annie Get Your Gun* to MGM for $650,000. He may have consumed several drinks (one of O'Hara's biographies is titled *The Art of Burning Bridges*). In this remarkable missive, O'Hara reminds Rodgers of a dinner they and their wives had shared at the Brevoort in Greenwich Village during which he, O'Hara, proposed a musical on the life of Annie Oakley and laid out the plot for "a perfect musical comedy." He continued:

> I have been making inquiries and I must say I am very glad that you have purchased a vast estate in Connecticut and have a triplex apartment on Park Avenue and your two lovely children are going to an expensive finishing school and having dances at Christmas time. We are doing as well as can be expected. Belle has had all her teeth out owing to lack of dental care and our little daughter's belly is all swelled up which the visiting nurse says is on account of her not getting the right things to eat, like milk, but we can't complain so long as we have so many good friends. I am working nights now, making changes at the Mott Avenue station of the Lexington Avenue subway and if you are ever in that neighborhood from 10 p. m. to 9 a. m. why don't you come down and say hello? But I guess you are pretty busy. . . .
>
> Best wishes to your beautiful well-dressed wife and happy well fed children. You can always reach me at this address unless we are evicted next week, or you can get in touch with me through

Louis Nizer, of Phillips, Nizer, Benjamin & Krim, Paramount Building, Times Square, New York City.

As ever,

An expert at avoiding confrontation, Richard Rodgers pretended he thought the letter was a joke. In 1951 he received another angry missive from O'Hara, this time protesting an inequity regarding credit on *Pal Joey*. Rodgers wrote back, "I thought at first you were sending me another funny job similar to the 'Annie Get Your Gun' letter, which I still treasure, but that evidently is not the case." Rodgers ended his letter thusly: "I will not telephone you at Quogue 305, as you suggest, because I don't want words with you. Instead I send my love to Belle, Wylie, and you."

After *Annie Get Your Gun* Logan jumped at the chance to direct Rodgers and Hammerstein's next producing venture, a play by Anita Loos called *Happy Birthday*. The show went badly at the pre-Broadway opening in Boston, and Logan and Loos were called to a meeting in Hammerstein's hotel room with both the producers. Logan expected to hear they were closing the play. Instead, Hammerstein calmly said, "Let's fix it" (Rodgers added, "By Monday"). Logan was overjoyed and later wrote, "To me, those words were straight out of Beethoven's Ninth."

Robert Russell Bennett, who provided the play's incidental music, said that night they "all sat in a big circle and Hammerstein in his quiet friendly way just tore the whole play to shreds. He took out whole characters from the story, changed the order of scenes, practically gave us all the job of writing a new show in some twenty hours." Thrilled by their professionalism, Logan recalled his relief: "What had made me think they would abandon the play! I don't think I had ever seen dogged pride and fixed determination played in unison before." The eleventh-hour fixes worked. *Happy Birthday* moved to Broadway and ran for a year and half. "I vowed secretly to be as emotionally tough as they were that night," wrote Logan.

Except he could never be tough when negotiating with *them,* the golden pair.

When *Allegro* was previewing in New Haven, Logan went to see the show. He wrote Hammerstein two long letters, on September 4 and 6, with extremely detailed suggestions about how to fix *Allegro*. In the first he explained the feverish nature of his missive: "It's just that I'm jealous as hell of the director that gets a chance to work on a show with the inspired conception this show has." Logan saw the show a second time and elaborated in his second letter: "Believe me, Oscar, this is not idle play-making on my part. Whether this is the solution or not, I feel that you are in more trouble than evidently most other people feel." He offered to come see the show again when it moved to Boston the following week, reiterating, "I'm afraid I have indicated to you and Dick that I am just a jealous bastard who feels that he's been left out of the show. I hope you believe that my jealousy is the jealousy for you two and your success. I have a much clearer idea of how to fix the show than I have been able to put on paper." As it turned out, these letters were an audition for the roles he would get to play in *South Pacific:* not only as director, but also collaborator. His dream come true was the ultimate "be careful what you wish for."

Soon after that Logan was readying *Mister Roberts* for its Broadway debut. In January 1948 Hammerstein caught a preview in Philadelphia; he stayed to talk with Logan and mentioned that he and Rodgers were searching for their next project. Logan blurted out his enthusiasm for *Tales of the South Pacific*. Despite having promised producer Leland Hayward that he would keep the Michener stories under his hat, Logan had also mentioned them a few days earlier to Rodgers at a party. The composer took a note and forgot about it, but Hammerstein immediately read the stories and paid particular attention to the one titled "Fo' Dolla" as Logan had advised. In the meantime, *Mister Roberts* opened and became one of the biggest hits of 1948.

Once Hammerstein made it clear he liked Michener's story and wanted to build a musical around it, Logan had no choice but to tell Hayward that Rodgers and Hammerstein were interested in the project. "Idiot bastard!" said Hayward, who hadn't wrapped up negotiating the rights to the book. He knew that Rodgers and Hammerstein would muscle in and want a majority share of the project—which, of course, they did. The next day "with a dark, grey face," Hayward informed Logan that Rodgers and Hammerstein "won't do it unless they own 51 percent to our 49 which assures them the final say." Logan's answer: "Let's give it to them. They're not the fairest, but the best."

"At that moment I had such an adolescent worship for Rodgers and Hammerstein that I didn't care what they demanded, and foolhardy as I was, I forced Leland to give Dick and Oscar the final say on *South Pacific*," wrote Logan, who was slated to direct. "I don't think in his heart Leland ever forgave me. Later on, I couldn't forgive myself." Logan was determined to enter the enchanted circle; with *South Pacific,* he would find out exactly what it would cost him.

A few months into his adaptation of Michener's stories Hammerstein got stuck, having completed only the first scene and some lyrics. In a June 1948 condolence letter to Dorothy, whose mother had just died, a young Sondheim asked how the work was going: "Is Ockie still in the 'groping' stage (to use his phrase)?" Hammerstein always had trouble constructing original stories, and the book's anecdotal nature proved especially difficult to transform into a unified play. Rodgers asked Logan if he might help; the director phoned Hammerstein, who admitted only that he felt stymied by his ignorance of military etiquette. "I know nothing about army behavior or how a sergeant talks to a general," he told Logan, who offered to come to Doylestown and assist. This offer was accepted. Sometime that summer Logan arrived with his wife, Nedda Harrigan, and the two men hashed out the plot. Logan realized, he wrote, "that Oscar was holding onto our talks, like a man grappling up a cliff." Logan suggested that they improvise the characters. He used his Dictaphone to record their efforts, with Hammerstein playing Emile de Becque and Bloody Mary and Logan taking the roles of Nellie Forbush and Lieutenant Cable. With Logan there Hammerstein got out of the mud, and the story flowed.

Logan and Harrigan stayed in Doylestown for ten days; that week and a half turned into a lifetime of disagreements about credit and money. Given how his sense of self-worth was bound up in his admiration for the pair, Logan could never let it go. His battle endured past the deaths of both the lyricist and the composer, at which point Logan and Harrigan took the fight to Dorothy Rodgers and Bill Hammerstein.

Josh Logan met Harrigan when he cast her in a 1940 production of *Charley's Aunt.* He took one look at her—"an astoundingly beautiful woman, darkly radiant, with an exciting body"—and said, "'Holy Christ. Who are you?'" Harrigan came from musical-theater royalty; her father, Edward, was a director, a playwright of immigrant life, a songwriter, and half of Harrigan and Hart, a popular variety act that was a major influence on George M. Cohan. Nedda was the first to tell her husband he must get a cowriting credit for his work on *South Pacific,* but he couldn't bring himself to ask for it.

Nedda brought Logan's lawyer and doctor into the conversation. They also insisted that Logan had gotten himself in an impossible situation and needed to act, if for no other reason than his mental health. Nine years earlier the director had suffered a manic-depressive episode so severe he had been forcibly hospitalized; no one wanted to go through that again. When he finally raised the issue to Hammerstein, Logan was so nervous he almost had a seizure. "The rug before me seemed to split in two, while the floor below it yawned open, revealing a terrifying chasm fourteen stories deep," he wrote. "I could feel a great wind sucking me down into it, and then it all slowly closed in as I began. 'Oscar, I think I should get half credit for the book.'"

"Oscar's face was immobile," wrote Logan, though he detected a slight blush. "After the briefest of pauses Hammerstein answered, 'I wish I'd said it first. I'm sorry you had to. Of course you must have credit. After all you wrote it as much as I did. We'll work out the exact credits later.'" Logan was ecstatic.

What transpired over the next twenty-four hours between Rodgers, Hammerstein, and the lawyer Howard Reinheimer could be taught as a master class on how power protects itself. The question of what exactly the team owed Logan morphed into what the smallest concession was that they could make. When Hammerstein returned to Logan's apartment the following day, as Logan recalled, his demeanor was tense and his words sounded rehearsed. "In order to keep me from feeling penalized by your demand," he said, "I will agree to the following arrangement." Logan was struck by the word "penalized"; what could that mean? Hammerstein went on to say that they would acknowledge Logan as cowriter of the book; however, in all ad material for *South Pacific* his "directed by" credit would no longer be the same size type as theirs but only sixty percent thereof. As Logan was visualizing this, Hammerstein delivered the death blow: "That's the only possible way we can go on. Of course it goes without saying that you won't get anything whatsoever of the author's royalties."

Logan could see pain in Hammerstein's face as he added, "Josh, Rodgers and Hammerstein cannot and will not share a copyright. It's part of our financial structure. Including you would weaken our position. My partners feel this strongly. It's impossible, Josh."

If Rodgers and Hammerstein and Reinheimer ceded that Logan was a cowriter when they gave him a "written by" credit, then he would be due

Josh Logan (*left*) and Richard Rodgers (*right*) at a rehearsal for *South Pacific.*
Courtesy of the Estate of John Swope and Craig Krull Gallery

half the book writer royalties—1.5 percent of the gross receipts. Denying him that was strange, especially since the men had been friendly colleagues for years. Given Hammerstein's initial acknowledgment of Logan's contribution, the final decision almost certainly came from Rodgers. As his daughter Mary recalled, "The bible in our house was never sell your copyrights. Daddy used to say it was like selling your birthright."

Beyond that, Rodgers seems to have enjoyed sticking it to Logan for some reason never articulated. As Logan pointed out many times over the years, Hammerstein was happy to share a writing credit with Joseph Fields ten years later for *Flower Drum Song* and to accept that the writing of *The Sound of Music* would be entirely by Russel Crouse and Howard Lindsay (though Hammerstein was ailing at the time).

I believe that Logan's worship incited a kind of disdain in Rodgers. As Mary put it, "Before *Oklahoma!* Rodgers was just a songwriter." Now he was part of an empire, and he wanted to feel his power by exercising it over someone to whom it really mattered. Rodgers continued to torture Logan in odd ways over the years; he never rectified the initial financial injustice, while at the same time he pretended he took little interest in business matters. In a 1960 interview with the Canadian Broadcasting Corporation, for example, Rodgers said that he "insists on leaving contractual matters, booking, and other negotiation to men he has hired for that purpose." He added, "I'm not a businessman. I'm a bad businessman. I hire people to do it for me. . . . At this moment I couldn't tell you the salary of anyone in this office." In fact, his letters over the years show that Rodgers paid close attention to every aspect of the business. The following year Arnold Michaelis asked Rodgers if he took pride in being, as Logan put it, "the toughest businessman alive and at the same time writing music that made people cry." Rodgers denied this outright:

RODGERS: I would like to go into this illusion because a good deal of it disturbs me. People think I'm a businessman. People thought Larry was a nut, which he was, and Oscar was a poet, which he was. And I was the guy who transacted the business, made the deals, knew how to count. All I can tell you is that this is all a lie.

MICHAELIS (laughing): Well, Oscar himself said that you were the businessman.

RODGERS: Well, Oscar didn't tell you the truth.

MICHAELIS: Well, who was the businessman?

RODGERS: I've got any number of people in this office who do my business for me. I've got a lawyer whom I can talk to on this: [picks up and hangs up telephone receiver]. I've got accountants who do all the adding up. I don't know the salary of one person who works for me.

MICHAELIS: Well, Dick, I think it's an achievement to get the reputation of being a good businessman without being one.

RODGERS: I don't care for this reputation.

Eventually the injustice done to Logan was known throughout the theater community, contributing to prevailing sense that there was something unholy in Rodgers and Hammerstein Inc.

Agnes de Mille also spoke all her life about being robbed for her work on *Oklahoma!* She had accepted a $1,500 fee at a time when no one expected the show to pay out large profits. In 1951 she visited the Hammersteins in Doylestown and spoke to Oscar about rectifying the situation. On a walk around the farm, he assured her of her value; by this time he had learned how to appear sympathetic while ceding not an inch. "Dick and I have talked about this and we recognize that you're not like other dancers or directors, that you do more than just direct dance. You do things that amount to playwriting. But *if* we recognize you and your rights, what about the music arrangers? What about the scene designers?" And that was the end of that.

Both Logan and de Mille came away forgiving Hammerstein but not Rodgers. In a 1990 interview with Max Wilk, de Mille remembered Hammerstein as "a wonderfully sweet, warm man." She added:

> I think he was greedy, like Dick. Immensely. But he was wise, and he was very interesting to talk to. Extremely. Dick wasn't a bit. He could only talk about two things, sex and business. Not sex in the abstract, which can be pretty fascinating, but, "Are you fascinated by me? How 'bout it, kiddo?" You can get to the end of that subject pretty fast. And Dick didn't listen. He would listen to a conversation to see how he could give it the coup de grace, to make a quip, a quotable quip, sometimes quite funny and smart, and he would decapitate the subject at hand.

Logan says he saw "an enormous change" in Rodgers around the time of the *South Pacific* negotiations: "He became, almost in front of our eyes, a monument. He was so sought after that he had to closet himself in his office and dictate letters daily in order to handle his business affairs and to fend off the many people who wanted to sap his talent. To me, his fun seemed gone." De Mille wrote, "His piercing black eyes grew as opaque as an Aztec's, his face expressionless." Mary Rodgers added that "she had a "very peculiar feeling that gradually over the years he changed from somebody who had a wonderful time to somebody who had a terrible time." He did suffer, she said, from "depression and alcoholism and various things that he always wanted to keep secret and the family always tried to keep secret."

South Pacific ran for a record-breaking five years on Broadway. It won the Pulitzer Prize as well as ten Tonys; it toured nationally and internationally and for decades was a staple of regional, community, and high-school theater groups. The original cast album sold one million copies and held the top spot on the charts for sixty-nine weeks. Sheet music sales exceeded one million in the first four months of the show's run, and overall profits topped $5 million even before the movie rights were sold. But Logan got no cut.

Logan had a big personality. His depressions were deep and his mania made him feel superhuman. But when he hit his sweet spot, with just the right amount of sparkle, this made for deep friendships and brilliant work. The relationship he fostered with Hammerstein was particularly pleasurable for both men. Hammerstein's letters to Logan show him at his most relaxed, intimate, and chatty.

In 1949 Logan hired Billy to work as an assistant stage manager on *Mister Roberts,* and Hammerstein was grateful: "My fretting son was up for dinner last night. Piercing his protective pessimism, which he wears as a Turkish woman wear her veil, I am led to suspect that he is secretly elated and optimistic about all the people he is working with." In 1953 Hammerstein wrote Logan about a discovery made while reading British writer G. K. Chesterton:

> Maybe I feel dull because I have just read such a bright quotation from a man whose wit I envy, Gilbert K. Chesterton. Here is what he said: "Angels can fly because they take themselves lightly" Isn't that great?
>
> Does it make you sore when you see words like that and realize the awful truth that you did not write them? Magazine articles call me that "nice, modest, unenvious O. H." When will they discover the scowl behind that benign mask? I confide to you that I loathe G. K. C. for having found these words and put them together. There they were all the time and I might have done the same.

Hammerstein never wrote to Rodgers just to share an enthusiasm. Their letters consist mostly of pleasantries and business. In his autobiography Logan wrote, "Oscar was one of the best friends I ever had and . . . along with Irving Berlin, the most talented, the man with the greatest range."

Even the normally tight-lipped Rodgers confided in Logan, writing him about his guilt for not having served in the war. He admitted feeling badly for "being able to sit comfortably on one's plush behind while other men are wallowing in mud. I had never discussed this question with Oscar but at lunch the day after the Japs threw in the sponge Oscar said to me, 'this is the first time I have been able to think of *Oklahoma* and *Carousel* without feeling like a son-of-a-bitch.'"

Meanwhile, Nedda Harrigan and Dorothy Hammerstein grew quite friendly, especially once Dorothy took over the decorating of the Logans' River House apartment in 1948. It was a spare-no-expense renovation, with the Logans paying $255 ($2,900 in today's dollars) for a coffee table with black lacquer finish, the same amount for a pair of Italian armchairs, $297 for a club chair and ottoman covered in red quilted faille, as well as silver sconces, glass lamps, and Chippendale mirrors, all custom-made. It was the year of *South Pacific,* and there was plenty of optimism and (for the time being) money to go around. (In fact, at this time Hammerstein sent his ex-wife, Myra, a large and unexpected sum; she wrote to him saying, "I was quite bowled over & at a loss for words. It has made such a difference, both in my comfort and my peace of mind.")

Many gifts and letters were exchanged over the years between the Logans and the Rodgers and the Hammerstein households. Between expressions of love and friendship, however, the *South Pacific* situation remained remarkably alive for the Logans. A major flare-up occurred seven years after Hammerstein's death when a revival of the show opened at the New York State Theater of Lincoln Center, where Rodgers was president and producing director. Nedda and Josh noticed that, in the program, Logan's cowriter credit was only 40 percent as large as the names Rodgers and Hammerstein (not the 60 percent stipulated in the original agreement).

For Logan and Harrigan, the 20 percent difference in type size triggered all the old resentment. A flurry of letters passed between the couple and Rodgers, with some missives from attorneys thrown in for good measure. Harrigan was incensed. She recounted facts that no one disputed—that it was Logan who brought the Michener stories to the attention of Rodgers and Hammerstein, for instance—as proof that her husband had been cheated. Rodgers answered her on June 15, 1967, assuring her the incorrect type size was a mistake that will be "rectified immediately." He apologized for causing her "so much anguish." And then he added a sentence that is not true: "Incidentally, I was present when Josh asked for book credit and said he was not interested in royalties."

This was too much for Logan, who sent off a long letter to Rodgers again detailing all the wrongs that had been done him and adding a new one. He said he had been pressured to sign the unfair *South Pacific* agreement by a Reinheimer associate named Irving Cohen, who had issued an ultimatum. "If I did not sign the contract in two hours, agreeing to give up all rights to copyrights, . . . I would be replaced as director of SOUTH PACIFIC," wrote Logan. He implored Rodgers to search his memory and added, "I cannot let you go on believing a rosy fantasy."

Rodgers responded on July 11, assuring Logan that the program and house ads had been corrected with Logan's name now in the agreed-upon size. In addition, he told a story meant to demonstrate that Logan would be well advised to acquire a sense of humor like Rodgers had:

> Incidentally, I have a poster advertising the moving picture of "Oklahoma!" for its production in Poland. The director's name is there and the names of all the actors in very clear Polish. Rodgers and Hammerstein are nowhere to be found. I have hung the poster in the hallway in the country [house] because the design is beautiful and because I find something funny in the fact that our own names are not there. All I can do, Josh, is make every effort to see that your name is given proper prominence wherever it is possible for us to do so.

In fact, Rodgers had been incensed at various times over acknowledgement issues, most notably when he believed that director Rouben Mamoulian was claiming credit for several staging ideas in *Oklahoma!* that had come from him and Hammerstein. He demanded that producers Theresa Helburn and Lawrence Langner put a stop to it.

On and on it went, with Logan getting angrier and angrier. Possibly through a subconscious desire to further torment his old friend, Rodgers cut Logan completely out of the story when he penned a short essay for the album liner notes of the 1967 Columbia Masterworks edition of *South Pacific,* saying that the idea for the show had been brought to him and Hammerstein by Leland Hayward and Richard Halliday, Mary Martin's husband (who had not been involved).

One can only imagine Logan reading this essay. He wrote to his attorney H. William Fitelson, "I realize that Richard Rodgers might be slightly off his rocker, what with the disappointment he has had recently, but how on earth could he make such a mistake?" Indeed, Rodgers had been racking up disappointments and hardships. Even while Hammerstein was alive the composer's alcoholism had landed him in the Payne Whitney Psychiatric Clinic in the summer of 1957 (more on that in an upcoming chapter). Then, shortly after Hammerstein's death in 1960, Rodgers fell in love with actor Diahann Carroll and wrote a show for her, *No Strings* (1962), contributing both music and lyrics. Everyone in the theater noticed his inability to keep his hands to himself when he was around his lead actor, and his penchant for dalliances was now seen by many as sad. Meanwhile Dorothy Rodgers, according to Rodgers's biographer Meryle Secrest, was hospitalized at this time, and Rodgers told friends that her X-rays showed "absolutely no difficulty of any kind beyond the adhesions she's been so proud of for the last ten years."

No Strings was a hit, but Rodgers floundered afterward. He announced a new partnership with lyricist Alan Jay Lerner, whose *My Fair Lady* (1956) became the first show to surpass *Oklahoma!* as Broadway's longest-running musical. But once they started working, Lerner kept disappearing on him just as Larry Hart had, an insult on a whole new level given Rodgers's stature by that time. Then the composer teamed up with lyricist Sidney Michaels to write a new musical for Diahann Carroll based on the life of the Egyptian queen Nefertiti. However, Rodgers then fell out with both Michaels and Carroll, who was angry that Nancy Kwan was cast instead of her to star in the film version of *No Strings* (which was never made). Rodgers was finding it wasn't as easy to get along with everyone now that Hammerstein was gone.

In 1964, Rodgers became the producing director at Lincoln Center. In the large and unforgiving 2,586-seat New York State Theater (now the David Koch Theater), he produced summer musicals, starting with *The King and I* starring Darren McGavin. To inaugurate his august new post, he wrote a piece for the *New York Times* that showcased his personality's wooden aspect. He didn't sound like he was having much fun: "I firmly believe that the musical theater—possibly the most imaginative form of nonobjective theater we have—can have a long and prosperous life if it continues to express the honest thoughts of creative men and women who are unafraid of taking a chance on new ideas, and have the ability to translate these ideas into meaningful theatrical terms."

But Rodgers did not produce new musicals at Lincoln Center; he followed *The King and I* with *Carousel, Annie Get Your Gun,* and *Show Boat*. In 1965, he entered a writing partnership he hoped would give him new relevance, joining forces with the thirty-five-year-old Stephen Sondheim to write

Do I Hear a Waltz?, an experience he later described as "ghastly" (also more on that to come). That takes us to Rodgers's Lincoln Center production of *South Pacific* that caused the brouhaha with Logan. At the moment he accidentally attributed the idea for doing the show to Richard Halliday instead of to Logan, Rodgers was in court with both Halliday and Hayward for cutting them out of the profits on *The Sound of Music* soundtrack album. This lawsuit originated when Leland Hayward ran into Rodgers at a party. One assumes liquor was flowing. Rodgers turned merrily to Hayward and said, "What about that check we received for the first picture recordings?" Hayward asked, "What check?" As a producer of the stage version of the musical, Hayward would have been owed royalties. Halliday and Hayward then successfully sued Rodgers and Hammerstein Inc. for $1 million for the eight million records already sold. Rodgers appealed the ruling and lost. In September he and the Hammerstein estate paid out $1.1 million to Halliday, Hayward, and other *Sound of Music* backers.

But Logan maintained cordiality, perhaps because his emotional investment in the relationship had been so great he couldn't let it go. He was still capable, under extraordinary circumstances, to feel his old love for Rodgers. He and Nedda dined with Dick and Dorothy in January 1979, and it was obvious that Rodgers would not live much longer. Logan wrote to him the next day:

> I began to realize all over again that you gave me a lifetime career in our profession. You took a chance on a legitimate and young director for I MARRIED AN ANGEL; then later when I had just been released from four months in a mental hospital you took a bigger chance by asking me to direct BY JUPITER. . . . You invented me, Dick, as a musical director, and as I write these words I am as moved as I was when talking about you on the stage at the Y, when I choked up and could not continue.

Rodgers died in December of that year. But Logan and Harrigan's grievance flared up in one last gasp of outrage in the summer of 1983, probably instigated by some financial crisis. Missives were sent to Billy Hammerstein and Dorothy Rodgers asking them to reconsider the original agreement on *South Pacific*. These hit a dead end. Billy wrote, "Josh, in 1949 you signed that contract. I looked at it today and it states in clear, clean language that you will receive credit as co-author of the book and that any contribution you may make becomes the property of R&H as part of the copyright in the work. There is no possibility of changing those words. It may have been possible at another time but certainly not beyond the lives of Dad and Dick."

To the end Logan felt robbed, and not just of money: "My name had been so minimized that I lived through years of having people praise *South Pacific* in my presence without knowing I had had anything to do with it." Still, it remained the most important collaboration of his lifetime. Logan was moved to write to Dorothy Hammerstein around the time of her eighty-seventh birthday: "When Oscar died he was 65 years old, and I am now 77. When we worked together in 1949, he was 54 and I was 41. We accomplished a lot together, and as I said before to you, that ten days in Doylestown was the high spot of my life." Two years after that, in 1988, Logan died on Hammerstein's birthday, July 12.

On those eventful ten days in Doylestown, Hammerstein and Logan teased out the musical's themes from two love stories in Michener's *Tales* and filled in holes with characters borrowed from elsewhere in the book. They zeroed in on the revelatory experience of living overseas for two cosseted young Americans. From Main Line, Philadelphia, and Otolousa (changed to Little Rock), Arkansas, respectively, Lieutenant Joe Cable and nurse Nellie Forbush both fall for islanders—he for a seventeen-year-old Tonkinese girl, she for a French plantation owner. They are soon forced to see their lovers through the racist eyes of the folks back home. This proves shattering for them both, but especially Cable, culminating in his song "You've Got to Be Carefully Taught," an impassioned indictment of how racism is passed from parent to child as surely as any gene. Cable's fury—and the reason the song works as something other than a harangue—comes from his discovery that the poison is in him as well. He cannot bring his love home to Philadelphia nor can he stay forever on Bali Ha'i, the beautiful island that's always disappearing in a mist, rather like the short lifespan of blind love, or a vision of a world without prejudice.

Reaction to this, Hammerstein's angriest song, was mixed at the time. Some fans wrote to say it was too "on the nose," "too blunt," and "too much like pure, harsh propaganda." Lieutenant Commander Thomas MacWhorter opined that the lyric "gives the audience the same let-down feeling as if the show were abruptly halted for a double-barrel three-minute commercial. It's like drinking a scotch-and-soda and suddenly swallowing the ice cube!" He suggested cutting the song. Hammerstein answered:

> Please forgive me for not agreeing with you. . . . I am most anxious to make the point not only that prejudice exists and is a problem, but that its birth lies in teaching and not in the fallacious belief that there are basic biological, physiological and mental differences between races. . . . I believe I get the point of your letter very clearly and I realize very well the dangers of overstating the case. But I just feel that the case is not fully stated without this song. I wish it were true that all these things are accepted by the public. You say "the theme is wearing thin," but in spite of this, I see progress being made only very slowly.

Some questioned the song's premise; Brooks Atkinson pointed out the reverse theory of civilization, which says that "overcoming hate and fear is what we have to be taught. Not the other way around." And yet the song was impossible to ignore and to this day serves as a reminder that the country is always redefining itself, its character, and its values, usually in reference to racial animus. There are always people who feel threatened by and who fight the very idea of diversity, while others, like Hammerstein, see it as a cornerstone of our identity.

When *South Pacific* played in Atlanta during a 1953 national tour, two state legislators introduced a bill to ban works that "had an underlying philosophy inspired by Moscow." Representative David C. Jones explained that "You've Got to Be Carefully Taught" justified interracial marriage and as such was a threat to the American way of life. Phoned for his reaction, Hammerstein said he did not think the legislators were "representing the people of Georgia very well."

"The American way of life" was exactly what Hammerstein wanted to examine in 1949, at a moment when middle-class white Americans felt secure in their country's economic and military power. *South Pacific* asked that we reject the myth of our superiority and look within. Its most pointed question is delivered by de Becque, whom the Americans ask to undertake a dangerous scouting mission that "might turn the tide of war in this area." An officer pleads with de Becque, "We are asking you to help us lick the Japs It's as simple as that. We're against the Japs." De Becque answers, "I know what you're against. What are you for?"

"He waits for an answer," writes Hammerstein in the text. "They have none."

As Jim Lovensheimer points out in his book *"South Pacific": Paradise Rewritten,* the navy officers in the show frequently use the words "Jap" and "Nip" to describe the enemy, which was common during the war. However, it is virtually impossible to tell whether Hammerstein was acknowledging the irony of the officers' xenophobia in the larger context of *South Pacific;* in the middle of a war, xenophobia can seem like sanity.

In 1949, institutionalized racism was a fact of life. In the absence of federal anti-discrimination laws, the map of the United States was a patchwork of inequity. Children recited "liberty and justice for all" at segregated schools in twenty states. Thirty states prohibited mixed marriage, and only eighteen states had made discrimination in public accommodations illegal. Fourteen states permitted or required segregated railroad cars. Fifteen million African Americans needed to consult state statutes to find out where they were allowed to sit or drink or ride or go to school.

South Pacific issued a call to root out what was poisonous in the soil of our national identity. The show brilliantly reassures us of our essential decency, and only then does it make its statement—that, unless we are vigilant about the enemy within, our decency as well as our democracy can be lost. And the country loved it; Americans responded ardently when asked to be better than they were. Hammerstein knew how to challenge with one hand and give tribute with the other.

The result for audiences was an overwhelmingly moving celebration of America's unique possibilities as a beacon of decency. But to achieve that effect, Hammerstein and Logan had to clear out some of the book's messier complexities. One needs a clean surface on which to project such large emotions.

Reality is more real in Michener because it is more specific. The nurses stationed on the island are not the fun-loving young women of the musical; in fact, they feel a constant physical threat, both from the islanders and the GIs themselves. Attacks on nurses were "grim, hushed up affairs." Michener writes. "With thousands of men for every white woman . . . it was to be expected that vague and terrible things would occur." Hammerstein sweeps this under the rug. The navy men who sing "There Is Nothing Like a Dame" are in awe of American womanhood; they may be horny, but they are wholesome.

Hammerstein's de Becque has two small, adorable children; in the novel he has eight daughters with four women of three different ethnicities—Javanese, Tonkinese, and Polynesian. De Becque keeps all of this from Nellie until they are engaged to be married. Michener's Nellie finds herself shocked, and for a surprising reason: "Emile de Becque, not satisfied with Javanese and Tonkinese women, had also lived with a Polynesian. A nigger! . . . He had nigger children."

Hammerstein's Nellie, on the other hand, says nothing of the kind. In an early draft she was permitted one use of the word "colored" to show her small-town racism, but even that was deleted during rehearsal. (Director Bartlett Sher restored the word in his great 2008 production at Lincoln Center.)

And yet Michener's book, too, is at times simplistic. For instance, his Nellie overcomes her racism after lying in bed and thinking about it for a little while. In the musical the change takes time and is prompted when she finds out that de Becque is off on what may be a suicide mission. Hammerstein teases out the conflict, almost to the point of melodrama. His de Becque loves Nellie so much he essentially loses the will to live when she rejects him. That's why he volunteers to scout Japanese movement on a nearby island. When Nellie finds out he is gone she realizes how wrong she was. As penance, she installs herself in de Becque's home—apparently raising his kids with the help of servants—which is where he finds her upon his return.

In *South Pacific,* Nellie is "stuck like a dope / with a thing called hope," but in Michener she is more of an actual dope. The first man she dates is a snobbish Princeton student named Bill Harbison, who "never in a hundred years" would have "noticed her in the States. She wouldn't have moved in his crowd at all." But given that "pretty white women" were "rarities," he has no choice but to make a move on her. They date for a while and make out until one night he attacks her: he tears at her dress and bra and "claw[s] at her underwear" at which point she grabs a coconut and smashes it on his head. Still, there is a next date, during which she tells him she is desperately in love with him and asks if there's a chance they'll ever marry. He tells her he is already married.

Hammerstein had a precise sense of just how much specificity could be sacrificed without losing the audience's emotional investment in the space of two hours and forty minutes. Nellie, of course, becomes a friendly and admired American Miss, except for that one thing she has about dark people. More to the point, the viewer's attention is never steered toward the larger system of oppression that enables de Becque to import cheap labor from Tonkin to work his plantation and have his pick of island women. It's the same system that drives Bloody Mary to offer her daughter to Lieutenant Cable (and what if the girl *didn't* fall instantly in love with him?). Did Hammerstein whitewash the truth for commercial purposes, as some of his critics suggest? Or is Hammerstein's uncanny ability to balance the light and the dark exactly the device that allows him to persuade people to face the world's ugliness, even while giving us hope that we can redeem what is worst in our nature and culture?

Robert Russell Bennett remembered seeing tears in the eyes of both Rodgers and Hammerstein on opening night, April 7, 1949. For "the first time in my life," Hammerstein wrote, "I was not jittery at a New York opening. My wife and I sat in two aisle seats in the 9th row and enjoyed the play almost as much as if it were someone else's." Checking in with the show a month later, Hammerstein wrote to Logan, "The advance hovers somewhere between $400,000 and $500,000, and the audience hovers up around the chandeliers throughout most of the performance."

In the summer Hammerstein sent Logan another excited update:

> The audience behaved like a large group of people who had all met somewhere else and said, "Let's all go over to the Majestic Theatre and get drunk." Their behavior was irrational. They laughed at every joke. . . . It sounded more like a football game than a show. I am not sure but what, in some way, we combined all man's emotions into that play so that the reactions are somewhat like the combination of a big football game and a bull fight and grand opera and tragedy and comedy, the thrills of first love, fireworks on the Fourth of July and a soupcon of that exaltation which the Wright Brothers must have felt when their first mechanical kite left the ground. Now *I'm* drunk!

At the Library of Congress, the folder holding *South Pacific*–related correspondence overflows with ecstatic avowals. "I have never spent an evening in the Theatre to compare with our enjoyment of South Pacific" . . . "We never knew theater could reach such heights" . . . "Bookkeeping suddenly becomes so very dull that I think I'd give anything to be an usher at the Majestic Theatre!" . . . "Our night at the theater left absolutely nothing to be desired except to see this show again, again and again." Even Myra Finn had only good things to say:

> It is difficult for me to tell you how much I enjoyed S.P. the other night. It is easily the most satisfactory evening in the theatre I've ever spent. If satisfactory seems a general word I'm sorry, but it does express what I mean. The whole thing was so *easy* to see and hear. Never a moment of strain or embarrassment. . . . . It's odd to want to describe a middle aged somewhat portly man as "cute," but that is just what I want to do!. . . . I loved the whole thing—and should like to see it again. Let me know when I may.

In his third piece on the show, Brooks Atkinson wrote as if the musical had finally achieved its platonic ideal in *South Pacific*. The characters, he said, were not simply characters "but also figures of music." And "the music cannot be separated from the characters or the play."

Public intellectuals were equally swept up. Alfred Kazin contributed a piece called "We Who Sit in Darkness" for *Commentary* magazine:

> The audience at *South Pacific* never forgets that it is present at a fabulous occasion. Everyone in the theater feels this. . . . If we ever had doubts about what we were fighting for, we lose them here, and can instantly answer Pinza's weary "European" question—I know what you Americans are fighting against, but what are you fighting for? . . . Curiously this was the great theme in Henry James—the meeting between America and Europe, between the power of innocence and the depth of wisdom. But Henry James was too pessimistic, perhaps too morbidly conscious of what the world did to Americans, rather than of what American could do for the world.

Agnes de Mille forgot her financial grievance and told the men they were "our chiefest [*sic*] national pride and spiritual comfort." At the closing performance five years later, on January 15, 1954, a decision was made not to bring down the curtain when the show ended. The audience stayed, the actors stayed, and they sang "Auld Lang Syne" together. The gesture conveyed the sense that Americans wanted the meaning and mood of *South Pacific* to always be a part of them.

The simplicity that Hammerstein's critics hated—his respect for the unexceptional and his belief in our everyday power to access the divine—is all over *South Pacific*. Listening to the cast album or even watching the mad movie version, you will hear or see a young woman in summer clothes singing the phrase "I'm in love" thirteen times while swirling around, arms outspread, embracing the universe. Nellie performs this dance at the end of "A Wonderful Guy," a song in which the nurse describes herself as naïve, corny, normal, conventional (twice), trite, a cliché coming true. *South Pacific* could not have survived by "You've Got to Be Carefully Taught" alone. It says that being normal is good and reminds us that we can at any time or any place chose to be exceptional.

With their third remarkable Broadway hit (and their second musical to win the Pulitzer Prize), Rodgers and Hammerstein became a force too big to deny. A heavenly choir sounded, and their colleagues in the theater began to kneel before them. Screenwriter Nunnally Johnson wrote to Hammerstein, "The truly remarkable thing about you and Dick is that your successes always seem to please everybody, not only the people who love beautiful songs and a wonderful show, but also, astonishingly, your professional rivals and competitors, of which, thank God, I am not one. I believe that this almost universal happiness in your successes is one of the warmest and most wonderful things I have ever heard of in show business."

Enshrinement was sweet. Yip Harburg telegrammed, "THIS IS A SALUTE TO PERFECTION BRAVO AND HALLELUJAH AND THANKS FOR IGNITING ME."

Hammerstein momentarily worried about the hosannahs. He responded to a *Time* magazine rave with the comment "No show can be that good." He heard from a radio personality named Ed Gardner who commented, "You're nuts. It is."

Oscar replied:

Dear Ed,

You're right. I am. It is.

Oscar Hammerstein II

■ ■ ■

Even before *South Pacific* became the second-longest-running musical on Broadway, after *Oklahoma!*, Rodgers and Hammerstein had reason to believe their vision of the country—their ideas about what values elevated and defined it—reflected the vision Americans had of themselves. In her book *Cold War Orientalism*, Christina Klein notes that "many contemporaries saw Rodgers' and Hammerstein's musicals as expressions of an authentically American national identity, a form of modern folk culture that formed an integral part of the nation's cultural heritage." Her work explores how these "articulators of America" arose at a time when the United States was assuming an ever-greater role on the global stage, and that meant Rodgers and Hammerstein would go on to exert an unusual influence in our understanding of affairs domestic and foreign in the 1950s.

Hammerstein worked actively to extend his cultural capital into the policy arena; Rodgers sometimes lent his name and went along for the ride, but never saddled up himself. In March 1950 Hammerstein, along with other members of the Writers Board for World Government, hosted a dinner that featured speaker Harrison Brown, a nuclear chemist who had helped separate plutonium from uranium for the Manhattan Project. Since then Harrison had become convinced that the best hope for global survival lay in America taking a leadership role in dismantlement, an opinion Hammerstein shared.

Without coordinated international intervention, nuclear capability would spell the end of the human race. "Can we doubt for a moment that Hitler in the desperation of defeat would have killed everything had he had it in his power to do so?" Brown reasoned. "It has been insinuated by several people, none of them scientists, that in stating life on earth could be wiped out, we are exaggerating. If I accomplish nothing else tonight, it would be to impress upon you that we are not exaggerating. We are deadly serious."

After listening to the speakers, the gathering was treated to a playlet called *The Myth That Threatens the World*, which Hammerstein directed and cowrote with Rex Stout and Clifton Fadiman. They defined the myth of the title as "the idea that nations can stay sovereign and stay at peace." This was the real beginning of the United World Federalists, which came five years after the founding of the United Nations, an organization that few in Hammerstein's circle believed had the power to do what must be done in the atomic age. The Federalists' mission was to articulate arguments that would enable people to see something larger than national interests. Performing that night were Henry Fonda (at the time married to Dorothy Hammerstein's daughter Susan), Eddie Albert, Marian Anderson, Brock Chisholm, New Jersey governor Alfred E. Driscoll, and Hammerstein himself. The Federalists hoped to use a new goal—avoiding nuclear destruction—to establish a consensus, revise the United Nations Charter, and set up a world constitution under which all governments would pool their arms into one organization called the World Government Police Force.

The Federalists said they did not expect Russia to sign on, but that it was better to have a partial world federation until such time as they could have a complete one.

Hammerstein argued cogently and much of his writing on the subject is effective. For instance, he characterizes most humankind as "zombies in a trance, sleepwalkers clinging to a dream from which they do not want to be awakened." The idea of a Doomsday Clock—a symbol of the present likelihood of a nuclear catastrophe given global geopolitical conditions—was only three years old (upon its founding by the members of the *Bulletin of the Atomic Scientists* in 1947 it was set at seven minutes to midnight; in 2022 it was pushed forward to one hundred seconds to midnight). Hammerstein and the Federalists were trying to bring home to everyday Americans the threat's urgency. Hammerstein wrote:

> What else are the zombies dreaming? They are dreaming that the very horror of modern warfare contains its own prevention, that the leaders, knowing what the results would be, would at the last minute always hold back from pressing the button. There is some validity to this theory, up to a point. Surely the completeness of such wholesale tragedy acts as a deterrent. Is it enough to satisfy us that we and our descendants will always be safe from the tragedy? Can we bet on the sanity of all leaders at all times in all nations?

Hammerstein also railed against labels like "idealist" or "dreamer" that conservatives deployed to discount ideas of disarmament and progressive betterment. His hero Nellie Forbush proudly proclaimed herself an optimist, as did Hammerstein himself. But he rejected the connotations his opponents drew from that word and its synonyms. In a 1950 speech he said:

> I am convinced that if this world is to be saved from the destruction that modern warfare promises, it will be saved by the people whom hard-headed men call "dreamers." . . . As you may have gathered, I am tired of this practical man, with the hard head—and a soft brain. I am tired of his patronizing smile when he calls me an idealist. He has a good-natured and tolerant way of disposing of you, by merely calling you an idealist, and in his kindly eyes there is an implication that he will forgive you, but that he has some secret that you don't know, because he is a practical man and you are not. All right, I am willing to believe this. Only, let him roll around with one practical idea—one plan for meeting the crisis that faces mankind today.

In striving to find a sane way to live in the world, Hammerstein proved himself, perhaps for the first time in his life, to be anti-traditional. He believed that the nuclear crisis was something entirely new in human affairs; solutions could not be found in the past. In a 1951 speech for the United World Federalists he wrote, "We live in a new kind of world where the attitudes of our ancestors are no longer relevant. We know now far more than they did about everything. We have no need to refer to our ancestors in consideration of our present situation. We need to refer to our own intelligence, to our own experience, to the world as it is now at this moment, and none of the old answers will do, quite clearly."

In this, his most intense period of activism, Hammerstein was of course attuned to the actions of his ideological opponents. He was horrified by blacklisting, and he publicly condemned the "loyalty questionnaire" that CBS made its employees sign in 1950. In the parlance of the time, he attended meetings by several organizations designed to "combat censorship" after the House Un-American Activities Committee began issuing subpoenas to theater and film artists, starting with screenwriters and moving on to actors, directors, and playwrights. Hammerstein was also part of the Freedom from Fear Committee, which raised money for the defense of nineteen witnesses deemed unfriendly to HUAC.

The Federalist cause was crippled by HUAC, whose work divided Americans not merely into the right and left but into "elites" (aka internationalists) and "traditionalists" (aka nationalists). HUAC was a referendum on the very idea of progress, and it targeted writers and other creators of culture because of their tendency to question the status quo, think beyond the local, and stand up to authoritarianism. The strong nationalist current that carried Joseph McCarthy was directly opposed to the Federalist belief that the world must come together to avoid destroying itself.

With the Cold War ramping up, McCarthy and HUAC argued that either you believed in your government wholeheartedly or you were a Communist and therefore a traitor. If you fought in any way for racial justice, you were a Communist and therefore a traitor. Their work was so rabid that it ensnared even the model citizen Oscar Hammerstein.

The FBI had launched a "security investigation" in 1951 and found that Hammerstein had been "affiliated with or participated in the activities of" seventeen organizations that had been "cited as Communist by either the Attorney General, the Congressional Committee on Un-American Activities or the California Committee on Un-American Activities."

Hammerstein discovered he was being investigated when he went to renew his passport in 1953 and was asked to sign the now-infamous statement swearing he was not now nor had ever been a member of the Communist Party. This he did, truthfully. But he was then granted only a six-month passport. To get a full passport renewal, he would need to submit a detailed report of his political beliefs to "the passport office," which meant, of course, to the House Un-American Activities Committee.

Hammerstein wrote the requested letter. He offered a full-throated defense that included the kind of preening and bragging he normally detested. He starts by establishing his "important business interests in England," which thereby make it "a hardship for me not to have a passport with the customary two years' duration." But that is not his chief concern, he says: "I am much more deeply troubled by the fact that my loyalty as a United States citizen has been questioned. For a man who knows that he believes in American Democracy, who knows that at no time in his life has he harbored the slightest inclination toward Communism, it is a humiliating experience to find suddenly that he is considered a 'security risk.' I want to clear this doubt that has been cast upon me."

He could not bear the suggestion that he would work against his country's best interests. But not once in his twenty-six-page letter does Hammerstein protest the tenor and tone of the committee's questions, its reliance on the accusations of anonymous informants and guilt-by-association techniques, or the vast overreach of its investigations. He remains focused on clearing his name.

Hammerstein goes on to explain in detail his reasoning for each of his associations and preemptively second-guess those that might raise alarm. Yes, he sent a check to "The Independent Voters Committee of the Arts and Sciences for Roosevelt" in 1944. And yes, the association has since been put on a list of suspicious organizations. But "I never got close enough to know whether this was justified but I remember not liking the whole flavor of the activities, and therefore I got out of it." In other places, he seems to almost cower: "If I have been careless in the past in lending my name to organizations with high-sounding titles, I no longer make this mistake. Today when I get requests for my sponsorship, I very carefully look over the names of other sponsors and do all I can to find out who and what is really behind the organization making the request."

Hammerstein compiles his many awards and honors, all the citations that prove what a good boy he was and is. He helped to establish the Stage Door Canteen (along with Nedda Harrigan) and became chair of the Music War Committee of the American Theatre Wing. He was also on the Writers' War Board, which coordinated efforts between writers and the government to place magazine and newspaper articles helpful to the war effort. He mentions citations received from the Massachusetts Committee of Catholics Protestants and Jews, the American Jewish Committee, and the Anti-Defamation League of B'nai Brith, as well as honorary degrees from Drury College and Dartmouth College. He offers that he voted for Republican Thomas Dewey in 1944 and that he himself is officially neither a Democrat nor a Republican.

After writing that he found it "hard to control my indignation at the suggestion that I would do anything to injure my country or expose it to danger," he goes on to "make a statement now of my views on Communism," which are very much in line with the Committee's:

> Communism is in my opinion the worst gold brick that has ever been sold to the underprivileged. The distribution of wealth may not have reached perfect justice. There is still privilege and there is still prejudice in our land. These defects are all being met, and

> having lived 58 years, I have seen vast improvements in my time, improvements in the attitude toward minorities. The Negro is not treated as well as I would like to see him treated, but he is surely being treated twenty times better than he was when I was a little boy. Our democracy obviously is working here, and the improvement is so apparent that I cannot understand why any American wants to reach out for a sudden and extreme disruption of the present system, in favor of a system which at its very best is an unknown quantity.

The FBI concluded that Hammerstein "does not appear to be in sympathy with communism at the present time." However, the Bureau kept an active file on him until 1956, when it wrote that "although [Hammerstein] is an extremely liberal individual, he is not a member of the Communist Party." The file was closed in 1959.

At the beginning of 1960 Hammerstein received a letter from a twenty-four-year-old student named Alan McGowan who was about to be questioned by the Committee about attending Vienna's International Youth Festival, believed to be a Russian-run Communist recruiting ground. McGowan asked Hammerstein to join him in a protest of HUAC's existence. The lyricist declined, writing, "I have many times disapproved of some of the procedures of the House Un-American Activities Committee. I believe, however, that for a group of citizens to attempt to stop its hearings is not only hopeless, but highly improper, and I will not lend my name to any such project." Hammerstein's battle with McCarthy was done.

A week after he got his letter from Hammerstein, McGowan testified before the Committee on February 4, 1960. He refused to answer questions and offered little more than his brief statement, which included a sentiment Hammerstein failed to make over the course of a twenty-six-page letter: "This committee violates the rights of all people called before it."

CHAPTER TEN

Women's Work

AS THE PLANET'S BEST MINDS WRESTLED with the threat of mutually assured destruction, no one created a pithier take on the subject than Hammerstein in this lyric for the King of Siam:

> Is a danger to be trusting one another
> One will seldom want to do what other wishes
> But unless someday somebody trust somebody
> There'll be nothing left on earth excepting fishes.

The King and I tells a version of the true-life story of Anna Leonowens, a thirty-two-year-old widow who came to Siam (now Thailand) in 1862 to tutor the royal children of King Mongkut, including the crown prince. She also taught English to wives and consorts and served as an unofficial secretary to the monarch. She later wrote about her travels in two books and many articles. Thirty years after she died, writer Margaret Landon plucked Leonowens from obscurity, an act for which Leonowens might have blessed or cursed her. Landon based her 1944 best-selling novel *Anna and the King of Siam* on the schoolteacher's life; in it she detailed how Leonowens went on to advise and influence the King, however unofficially, on matters domestic and international for five years.

Landon was doing missionary work in Siam when she discovered Leonowens's two memoirs, *An English Governess at the Siamese Court* (1870) and

The Romance of the Harem (1872), both of which were out of print in America. These books recount Leonowens's tale while also evoking the sights, smells, and customs of nineteenth-century Siam—from the floating shops and fantastic pagodas of Bangkok, twinkling at night with hundreds of covered lights, to the sprawling bows performed by the King's subjects as they prostrated themselves before him with five points of the body touching the ground (the forehead, both palms and both knees).

At 20th Century Fox, Darryl Zanuck made a 1946 film version of Landon's book, starring Rex Harrison and Irene Dunne. A few years later, Gertrude Lawrence acquired the rights with an eye to playing Anna in a musical adaptation, and she brought the project to Rodgers and Hammerstein. When the pair agreed to take it on, they did not set out to portray America as the good guys in a Southeast Asia–centered global struggle for dominance. And yet they managed to have something to say about it nonetheless.

When North Korea invaded South Korea in the summer of 1950, the Cold War looked as if it might turn hot. President Harry Truman sent air and naval forces to South Korea to "stem the spread of communism in Asia" and stepped up military aid to the French, who were fighting Communist Party forces in Vietnam led by Hồ Chí Minh. Thailand remained independent though firmly anti-Communist. As Christina Klein notes in *Cold War Orientalism,* Thailand was the only Southeast Asian nation that had not been colonized, was "not wracked by nationalist and communist-supported revolutions, and was thus seen by Washington as a dyke against the surrounding waves of de-stabilization."

In his correspondence from this time Hammerstein never mentions his thoughts on the intricacies of the Cold War in Southeast Asia. For him, the key to the musical was a minor detail in Anna Leonowens's story—a royal concubine's obsession with Harriet Beecher Stowe and her antislavery novel *Uncle Tom's Cabin.* Hammerstein elevated the importance of her obsession, and the musical's ennobling idea would be that the abolishment of slavery anywhere was good for human beings everywhere. In this way Hammerstein inserted into the story both the U.S. abolitionist movement and one of the most influential American novels ever written.

Hammerstein shared some common ground with Stowe, a writer born into a well-connected family who implored her compatriots to care enough to improve conditions in a country that dares to call itself democratic. (The two were also attacked for similar aesthetic crimes, but more on that in a bit.) Stowe represented the slaveholder as a horrific villain in the form of Simon Legree, but she took care to give white readers an entry point with Augustine St. Clare—a character meant to be seen as an essentially decent slaveholder who, because of financial pressure, feels forced to sell Uncle Tom and others when he says he wants to free them.

In *The King and I,* Hammerstein lent the main characters some of the ideas he was developing for the World Federalists. The final scene—when Prince Chulalongkorn announces he will abolish the most autocratic aspects of his father's regime as the King lies dying—embodies Hammerstein's hope that the twin forces of insight and empathy could aid in the fight not only for civil rights but also for nuclear disarmament. Americans responded to both *South Pacific* and *The King and I* regardless of whether they understood the scope of Hammerstein's intentions; his widely seen work helped pave the way for civil rights legislation, just as *Uncle Tom's Cabin* changed hearts and minds and helped lay the groundwork for the Civil War and the end of slavery.

Anna Leonowens has a prose style that leans toward purple, in keeping with much nineteenth-century writing. Her books are also structurally adrift, taking sudden and lengthy detours that go wherever the author's interests take her. She offers digressions into the various kinds of shells found by divers in the Gulf of Mannar, the history of the Siamese esteem for the white elephant, and various ceremonial rituals (like those involved when a young prince has his first haircut, when the King takes a bride, and when a royal wife presents a new baby).

No matter what detour she takes, Leonowens always returns her gaze to "the ladies of his Excellency's private Utah"—that is, the women of the harem (those who served King Mongkut and those who waited on and guarded them). As with imperial harems all over the globe, those who lived within had little (if any) access to the outside world, and few outsiders were granted entry. Leonowens was the first Western writer to spend significant time in this particular marble prison, and she felt the weight of that responsibility. She recorded with psychological acuity how women adapted (or didn't) to life there.

The most gruesome part of her story, however, is almost certainly an exaggeration (and one excised by Hammerstein). Leonowens writes that the concubine Tuptim, dressed as a boy, escapes the palace and becomes the student of a monk with whom she is enamored. Once discovered, she and the monk are arrested and publicly beaten. Leonowens begs the King to show mercy, as she had done successfully for other imprisoned women in the past. But Tuptim has insulted the King's pride and so cannot be spared. And here is where Leonowens likely diverges from the truth and elevates her own importance—the King orders that Tuptim's torture and death take place under the bedroom window of Leonowens, as a public rejection of her Western values. There Tuptim undergoes her fate with such dignity that the King comes to believe her claims of innocence. Later he erects two pillars commemorating her and the monk.

For this operatic staging, and for a variety of lesser crimes against plausibility involving alterations to her own biography, the writer's reputation took a surprising amount of groundfire decades after the musical debuted. An unexpected early sally came in 1970 from a Scottish radio personality named Ian Grimble. An amateur historian, Grimble explained to the *New York Times*'s Bernard Weinraub that Leonowens was "a squalid little girl," "one of those awful little English governesses" and "a sex-starved widow," who lifted her books from other sources (which he did not specify). King Mongkut, he believed, was a remarkable ruler who subsidized the building of Catholic and Protestant churches and was kind to his more than thirty-five wives. Leonowens, on the other hand, was a hysteric: "Her comments about [the King] have very strong emotional overtones. They are inconsistent from one page to the next and suggest a sort of love-hate relationship." He added, a little confusingly, "I have never heard of libel as brazen as Anna Leonowens' achieving such phenomenal success." He also had no love for Margaret Landon. "So many women authors love building up the image of the brave woman taming the man," he told Weinraub. "Isn't it dreadful that this happened to the awful little Anna and the King?"

Five years later, W. S. Bristowe, a naturalist who was doing research into the life of Anna's son Louis, found supposedly definitive proof that Anna was a serial fabricator. She said she was from Wales when she was in fact born in India, and not to a captain but to a sergeant or even an army private. Her mother was almost certainly half Indian—"a bit of the tar-brush in her veins" was how Bristowe put it. Further, Leonowens shaved three years off her age and changed her family name from Edwards to Crawford. She said her husband's name was Thomas Leonowens when in fact it was Thomas

Leon Owens (but the inscription on his gravestone reads Leonowens). Anna promoted her husband from a clerk at the East India Company to an officer. I would venture that all these fabrications may have been made in order to appear more employable.

Modern critics may be more forgiving if Leonowens rewrote parts of her autobiography to secure work. Not so for Grimble and Bristowe, whose vitriol reveal the durability of the misogyny and racism Leonowens was trying to dodge in her own time. She was a survivor who did what she needed to, and she lived an adventurous life that few women in her time could have managed. She married Thomas in 1849 and three years later they moved to Perth, Australia, where they opened a school for young women. They then moved to Penang in 1859, where Thomas died following a stroke. With few friends and two small children, Anna opened a school on her own in Singapore. It was there that she learned the King of Siam was looking for a governess, a job she applied for and accepted.

Historians say Leonowens in her books exaggerated her importance to the King, which is possible, though probably no more than did any other memorialist in frequent contact with royalty. Hammerstein, writing a fiction, was free to move his characters about as he saw fit; it was he who put Anna by the King's side when he dies (in reality she left Siam a year earlier), but Leonowens eventually got blamed for that and other alterations found in the musical.

In 2014 Alfred Habegger published *Masked: The Life of Anna Leonowens: Schoolmistress at the Court of Siam*. The author found corroborating evidence for several incidents in which Anna said she helped free unjustly imprisoned concubines. Among this evidence is a letter in which Mongkut encourages Leonowens to continue to petition for justice, which, Habegger writes, "she presently did with a persistence he had not foreseen." At the same time, Habegger doubts other details of her reporting that seem half-hearted or random. For instance, he asserts that one concubine could not have escaped, as Leonowens wrote, by swimming the Chao Phraya River. He describes this as "a claim impossible to accept once one has seen the river's width and rapid flow through Bangkok." But in the center of the city the river is less than five hundred feet across, the fierceness of its flow is dependent on the season, and numberless boats ply its waters at every hour of the day, any one of which could have picked up a stray swimmer.

Other of Leonowens's detractors likewise employ supposition-based evidence of the very kind they bash her for using. By the 1990s it was simply accepted that Leonowens was a fraud. Writing in the *New York Times* about a 1996 revival of *The King and I,* Stephen Erlanger says that Leonowens's work is "full of historical errors, beginning with the title of governess, since the King's diaries make clear that Anna was hired only as a teacher of English." Another *New York Times* reviewer in 2008 referred to Leonowens as a "gifted con woman."

Western observers have forever projected their own ideas about gender onto royal harems. In the eighteenth century, amateur historian Lady Elizabeth Craven visited the Ottoman Empire's Imperial Harem and found it a clean, orderly place where women were respected. At this time, Turkish women enjoyed property rights denied to their British counterparts, a fact that colored Craven's assessment: "I think I never saw a country where women can enjoy so much liberty and freedom from all reproach as in Turkey." She added, "A Turkish husband that sees a pair of slippers at the door of his harem must not enter; his respect for the sex prevents him from intruding when a stranger is making a visit."

If this sentence defies everything we know about harems and husbands, we should remember that the idea of the harem as a protective and pleasant place for women has a peculiar hold on the Western imagination. Chroniclers of all sorts have failed to see what to Leonowens was always paramount: however favored one or another concubine might be at any moment, to live in the harem was to be enslaved. As an absolute monarch, Mongkut's moods had enormous consequence for the women of his household. Leonowens tirelessly details the myriad ways his servants dealt with the isolation, idle hours, and whatever else might be required of them.

Almost upon her arrival Leonowens was a natural agitator for justice, and she repeatedly risked the King's ire and her own position to petition on behalf of women caught in some foul injustice. She first notices the fifteen-year-old Tuptim while the girl is working at her assigned task of pounding bits of pottery into material for the foundation of a new temple. She is struck by the girl's "delightful piquancy of ways and expression." Tuptim is "very artless and happy . . . as free as she was lovely," writes Leonowens, who is always appreciating the beauty of the women both young and old. A week later she spots Tuptim "lying prostrate on the marble pavement among other of the King's offerings," petitioners' gifts that he would "inspect on his leisurely progress toward the breakfast-hall." Months later Leonowens comes upon head wife Lady Thieng scolding Tuptim, who is sobbing and begging that she not be taken to the King that night for she is too ill. Thieng explains to Leonowens that the King will blame her if Tuptim fails to appear; he suspects her and the other wives of being jealous of the girl, who regularly hides when the King calls for her.

Of this scene Leonowens wrote, "I had never looked upon the sickening hideousness of slavery till I encountered its features here." In the harem she saw its "deformity" and "a darkness to which there is neither beginning nor end, a living which is neither of this world nor of the next."

In the decades before Leonowens visited Siam, two of the world's greatest writers—Alexis de Tocqueville and Charles Dickens—published indictments of human bondage on our shores, charting, as Alfred Kazin wrote, "the equanimity, indifference, and moral carelessness with which Americans everywhere managed to live with slavery." Both writers delineated what should have been obvious: that every American declaration of freedom and democracy was proven empty by the enslavement of millions of human beings.

Why did Harriet Beecher Stowe succeed in galvanizing a nation where Dickens, de Tocqueville, hundreds of slave narratives, and thousands of abolitionist pamphlets failed? Even sympathetic critics agreed that the book's influence was not necessarily due to Stowe's artistry—Dickens called the novel "noble" and "admirable," not prime literary values, and he went on to point out its "overstraining conclusions and violent extremes." Stowe herself downplayed her book's writerly qualities, describing it in an 1852 letter as "an instinctive, irrepressible outburst [that] had no more merit in it than a mother's wailing for her first born." In another letter from that same year, she revealed the unbearable thought that prompted the novel: "This horror, this nightmare abomination! Can it be in my country?"

Frederick Douglass wrote of *Uncle Tom's Cabin* that "nothing could have better suited the moral and humane requirements of the hour." It was the first American novel to sell more than one million copies, and countless spectators saw one of the unauthorized dramatic versions that toured the country. A probably apocryphal story went that Abraham Lincoln, upon meeting Stowe, said, "So you're the little woman who wrote the book that started this great war."

Almost a hundred years later, one of the twentieth century's most brilliant writers, James Baldwin, declared with great passion that the march for racial justice could not move forward without a day of reckoning for the fraud committed on the American people by Harriet Beecher Stowe.

The grandson of a slave, Baldwin was born in Harlem in 1924, at the height of the Harlem Renaissance—just when the designation "Uncle Tom" came to mean a Black man too oppressed to fight for his freedom. Young James was a dedicated reader, and he became obsessed, starting at age seven or eight, with *Uncle Tom's Cabin*. "I was trying to find out something, sensing something in the book of some immense import for me: which, however, I knew I did not really understand," Baldwin wrote. His concerned mother hid the book on a high shelf; when he climbed up and dragged it back down, however, she relented and let him keep it. "From that moment, though in fear and trembling, [she] began to let me go," wrote Baldwin in his book-length essay *The Devil Finds Work*. After spending three teenage years as a preacher in his stepfather's Harlem church, Baldwin began to trace a connection between religion and slavery. He saw evidence that Christianity helped enslaved people to accept their oppression, while for some churchgoing whites it provided a convenient way to believe they were still in God's good graces. This new understanding led him to reject Stowe and her eponymous hero. Tom was a slave who did not escape, who did not try to escape, who died so that others could escape. He left the matter of justice on earth to the Lord above. Baldwin wrote, "Because Uncle Tom would not take vengeance into his own hands, he was not a hero for me. Heroes, as far as I could then see, were white, and not merely because of the movies but because of the land in which I lived, of which movies were simply a reflection. I despised and feared those heroes because they did take vengeance into their own hands. They thought that vengeance was theirs to take."

Rejecting both vengeance and pacifism left young Baldwin little room in his search for an American identity. It was at this point, at the age of twenty-four, that he emigrated to France. Two years later he published the essay "Everyone's Protest Novel," turning his ire on Stowe herself. Her work was fueled by her religious faith, he argued, which meant that she was driven by the "panic of being hurled into the flames, of being caught in traffic with the devil." Her activism was selfish at its root; she was simply

Two women writers of the nineteenth century maligned in the twentieth: Anna Leonowens (*left*) and Harriet Beecher Stowe (*right*).
Left: Courtesy of Wikimedia Commons; *right:* Courtesy of the Library of Congress

"bargaining shamelessly before the throne of grace." Stowe's novel was written not from anguish but from "the terror of damnation," which Baldwin likened to the "spirit of medieval times that burned witches." Therefore "the protest novel, far from being disturbing, is an accepted and comforting aspect of the American scene, ramifying that framework we believe to be so necessary," much in the way religion did. In other words, *Uncle Tom's Cabin* only helped uphold the status quo.

Baldwin also declared *Uncle Tom's Cabin* a "very bad novel, having in its self-righteous, virtuous sentimentality, much in common with *Little Women.*" Baldwin believed that women, and the kind of emotional labor at which they tend to excel, could not move forward the great struggle for equal rights.

It should come as no surprise that it was female scholars who resurrected Stowe's reputation. She was vigorously defended starting in the 1980s by critics like Jane Tompkins, Ann Douglas, and Elizabeth Ammons, who saw *Uncle Tom's Cabin,* and the work of "sentiment" in general, as essential to the country's moral evolution. Jane Tompkins writes that "the inability of 20th-century critics either to appreciate the complexity and scope of a novel like Stowe's, or to account for its enormous popular success, stems from their assumptions about the nature and function of literature. In modernist thinking, literature is by definition a form of discourse that has no designs on the world. It does not attempt to change things, but merely to represent them. . . . Consequently, works whose stated purpose is to influence the course of history, and which therefore create a language that is not only not unique but common and accessible to everyone, do not qualify as works of art."

But before that—just a year after Baldwin declared Stowe and women in general less than useless in the fight for social justice—Rodgers and Hammerstein decided to make a musical about the vast reach of *Uncle Tom's Cabin*. And if Baldwin's attack carried the distinct odor of misogyny, *The King and I* celebrated a strong and independent heroine and employed a narrative method that resembled Stowe's. The antebellum novelist conceived her book as "an instrument for bringing about the day when the world would be ruled not by force, but by Christian love." The same could be said of Hammerstein, minus the word "Christian." He also appealed to reason by way of emotion, hoping to move Americans into responsible international citizenship. He, too, would be looked down on as a writer who dealt in mere sentimentality.

In Leonowens's story, it is not Tuptim but Lady Son Klin who becomes obsessed with Harriet Beecher Stowe. Son Klin is a royal consort who bore the King a son before becoming enlightened by literature and falling out of the sovereign's favor. She so admires *Uncle Tom's Cabin* that she frees her own enslaved women and begins signing her letters Harriet Beecher Stowe in honor of the "kind American lady" who taught her "the rights of her fellow creatures." With Anna's help, Son Klin translates Stowe's book into Siamese. But this is almost a footnote in Leonowens's story.

In a deft act of compression, conflation, and stagecraft, Hammerstein transfers the obsession with *Uncle Tom's Cabin* to Tuptim, who is so moved by the plight of the American slaves that she adapts the novel into a ballet featuring a highly personalized narration. She calls her work *The Small House of Uncle Thomas,* which was choreographed for the show by Jerome Robbins. In the musical Anna recommends that the King let Tuptim's ballet be performed for a delegation of dignitaries from Great Britain, as a display of Siam's high regard for culture. Neither Anna nor the King anticipate that Tuptim's work will be a protest against her own predicament enacted in the presence of her oppressor. As seen by the international visitors, though, Tuptim's ballet casts the King in the flattering role of an openminded leader who is willing to contemplate the evils of slavery.

Anna and the King both consider the evening a success, and the two of them celebrate by taking a turn around the ballroom floor in a number called "Shall We Dance?" Later that night, Tuptim and her lover are caught trying to escape the country; in a radical departure from the Leonowens's story, Hammerstein's King is unable to punish Tuptim. He has been softened by Anna's sense of decency such that he cannot bring down the whip on Tuptim's back, and so in his own mind he is mortally humiliated. He at once falls seriously ill, and the Kralahome (the King's prime minister and closest adviser) accuses Anna of destroying the monarch by infecting him with her Western empathy. In Hammerstein, the King must die so that a better world can be ushered in, thanks in large part to Anna.

The real King Mongkut was a more serious intellectual than the man depicted by Hammerstein. He studied science, geography, clockmaking, astrology, and linguistics. As part of his mission to combat the superstitious beliefs he felt marred Siamese spirituality, he was also an amateur astronomer. He spoke Pali, Thai, English, and Latin. His English, learned largely from American Protestant missionaries, was imperfect; however, it was good enough for him to communicate with foreign heads of state, none of whom spoke Siamese. He was interested in the advancement of technology and culture but bullish on the preservation of the monarchy and polygamy, which he thought important for joining together powerful families and building political alliances (and no doubt for maintaining the more private privileges of patriarchy). We may intuit some of these qualities and values in Hammerstein's King, but his background and cultural context remain shrouded.

There was no romance between the real Anna and the King, who was twenty-six years older and rather frail by that time. Hammerstein's King is in the prime of life and possesses a nimble mind but not necessarily the patience that scholarship would require. In public he is a proud authoritarian—his people see him as a bodhisattva (a reincarnated soul who chose to return to serve as an example of perfection), and he acts accordingly. Hammerstein does give his King the habit of relentless probing, a trait the lyricist thought important in a leader. In the song "A Puzzlement," the King even doubts his own doubting:

Shall I then, be like my father
And be willingly unmovable and strong?
Or is better to be right?
Or am I right when I believe I may be wrong?

This monarch also shares Hammerstein's belief that humans are most prone to violence when they secretly doubt the righteousness of their cause—just as when Billy Bigelow hit Julie Jordan because he sensed she was right and he was wrong. As the King sings:

And it puzzle me to learn
That tho' a man may be in doubt
Of what he know
Very quickly he will fight
He'll fight to prove
That what he does not know is so.

Hammerstein uses the cultural differences between Anna and the King to build an intelligible attraction. Much like the women in the harem, the King is impressed by Anna; he has never seen a woman demand her rights so regularly (or at all, really). And his acknowledgment that he needs Anna's help, though veiled in pride, is touching to her. They begin a flirtation by arguing about the virtues of monogamy versus polygamy. The King's logic is amusing—both to Anna and to us—in that it shows how thoroughly natural gender norms appear by their adherents. As he explains to Anna:

To fly from blossom to blossom
A honey bee must be free
But blossom must not ever fly
From bee to bee to bee.

In "Shall We Dance?" Anna explains British mating rituals to the King, and her attempt betrays a need to connect—she wants him to better understand Western culture because she wants him to know her. Whether that wish comes from affection, physical desire, or both is up to the individual theatergoer (and Hammerstein was forever cagey on the matter, not wanting to limit the audience's options).

Just after the triumphant dinner and ball for the Europeans, Anna agrees to teach the King to polka. But first she pauses to recall her own youth and the parties she attended in England, painting a picture of the charged moment just before a boy invites a girl to join him on the dance floor. This song (another of Hammerstein's many great tributes to incipient relationships) is also Anna's answer to the King's bee analogy. She describes the deliciousness bestowed on courtship by a world that values monogamy—a convention that, whatever else it may do, conveys a kind of grandeur to wooing, something the King has not experienced. The King understands this and, like Ravenal in *Show Boat,* is swept up in role-playing.

"Shall We Dance?" is another small Hammerstein masterpiece. Its execution is precise with not a wasted word, look, or breath. After a few comic missteps the King masters the dance; he places his hand on Anna's waist and asserts, "Come!" allowing her to experience the thrill of submission without relinquishing any of her actual power. The couple takes a whirl around the stage in a dance that stands in for their attraction's physical consummation. Critic Margo Jefferson called it "one of theater's most thrilling moments of East-West eros."

With *The King and I,* Rodgers and Hammerstein were for the fourth time the toast of Broadway. The musical opened on March 29, 1951, and ran for 1,246 performances, toured the country for a year and a half, and was embraced in London. In October Rodgers wrote to Hammerstein with a report on their unmatched portfolio: "South Pacific will do $50,000 this week in Chicago. The advance at the Majestic [*South Pacific*] is around $160,000, which, at the close of its third summer, is nothing sort of phenomenal. The St. James [*King and I*] now has an advance of over $270,000 and Morrie [Jacobs] tells me it's growing and should reach $300,000. The show is almost seven months old so I guess it would be hard to conceive of a bigger hit."

Darryl Zanuck again stepped in and produced the 1956 film for Fox, which was a cultural event. Newspaper and magazines could not run enough photos of Deborah Kerr and her voluminous dresses. Her Anna was meticulously starched and groomed, the black bow in her bun matching the one on her button-down bodice, the prim short bangs with every hair in place; in all this one senses the presence of assistants with brushes and combs just out of frame. Even her voice, supplied by Marni Nixon, seemed faultless.

The film enshrined a certain 1950s sensibility, a glossy idea of privilege combined with what Bartlett Sher calls "an almost insane amount of Orientalism." "Fresher and finer than it was on stage," declared critic Bosley Crowther, and the movie grossed more than $21 million and won five Academy Awards: for score, sound, art direction, costume design, and for its star, Yul Brynner.

The Russian-born Brynner, who arrived in the United States at the age of twenty-one, became internationally known as the embodiment of a fiery-eyed monarch short on temper and long on pride, but one who is always present and curious. It was a much more full-bodied and virile performance than the strangely effete one given by Rex Harrison in the 1946 film *Anna and the King*. Brynner won two Tonys for playing the King and devoted much of the rest of his career to reprising the role in stage revivals; he played his 4,625th performance a few months before he died in 1985. (Interestingly critics at the time did not see condescension in his portrayal; reviewing the original production, Atkinson wrote, "There are no villains. There are only human beings subject to the usual frailties of human nature. . . . Their impulses are good, but they are not masters of every situation. In the course of the evening they learn from each other.")

Hammerstein thought *The King and I* the best of their work. After seeing the movie in Australia while vacationing with Dorothy in 1956, he wrote to Rodgers, "I have a kind of humble feeling of not knowing how we did it. It has more wisdom as well as heart than any other musical play by anybody. It will remain 'modern' long after any of our other plays. It seems to me to be far in advance of them in its mental and emotional adulthood."

The show and movie, however, are still banned in Thailand, where officials find it insulting to the monarchy. Asian Americans have long felt ambivalent about the musical (as we'll see when we get to Rodgers and Hammerstein's next show about Asians and Asian Americans, *Flower Drum Song*). Interestingly, at a 2006 symposium about *Uncle Tom's Cabin* with historian Henry Louis Gates, critic Margo Jefferson recalled that *The King and I* served an important function in the African American community in the 1950s: "All the Black people I knew could see their situation aestheticized in the Asian/white situation. It was a respectful and a very useful way for us to assess our own situation."

Problematic though it may be, *The King and I* still enthralls audiences. It asks questions about the nature of human dignity. Moreover, the show takes what may be an obvious yet still necessary stance about the education of women in developing countries, both issues that have outlasted Yul Brynner's red harem pants. Theater directors Christopher Renshaw in 1996 and Bartlett Sher in 2015 came up with two different approaches for shoring up the work's historical bona fides. For Renshaw, who is British and lived for a time in Thailand, one solution was to fill the set with copies of Thai murals and designs taken from the Grand Palace in Bangkok, and he dressed his monks in appropriately colored saffron robes. His costume designer, Roger Kirk, procured Thai silk for Anna's hoop-skirted dresses, Thai sarongs for the ladies of the court, and Thai masks for the dancers. A dialect coach worked with the actors to speak English as a Thai who retained an accent would.

Twenty years later, Bartlett Sher felt a need to "strip the musical of its decorative varnish" and "get rid of the red and the gold." He expressed an abiding respect for Hammerstein's book, which he thinks is the strongest of all the Rodgers and Hammerstein shows. "Hammerstein was the genius in the team," he told me over breakfast near Lincoln Center. "He was the center of the cog. He made it happen." To help ease the problem of white representation, Sher cast Japanese film star Ken Watanabe as the King. Like the actual King, Watanabe's English was not perfect, which brought a jolt of "Will he pull it off?" to the production.

Watanabe was indeed kingly and charismatic in the role, though, in 2015, virtually every reviewer recognized the problems of authenticity and representation. When, in 2021, Paramount announced plans to make a new *The King and I* movie for contemporary sensibilities, Sravya Tadepalli published a piece in *American Theatre* saying she found this goal to be "far fetched." Reminding us that the original "reeks of white savior-ism and an imperialist gaze," she suggests making Leonowens "a mixed-race woman" whose "racial identity is a secret," which she reveals to the audience in a coda to the song "Hello, Young Lovers." Tadepalli adds that a new and "decolonized" plotline "need not be historically accurate, but would ensure that fictional elements do not perpetuate racist harms."

That same year, Steven Spielberg released a powerful film version of *West Side Story,* a musical about two New York street gangs in the 1950s, with music, book, and lyrics by three American Jews (Leonard Bernstein, Arthur Laurents, and Sondheim, respectively). Another Jewish American, Tony Kushner, supplied a refurbished book that tries to address the question of authenticity in the story's depiction of its Puerto Rican characters. Kushner made sure the film's depiction of Puerto Rican culture was historically accurate, and transposed some of the dialogue to Spanish. Other alterations were made—Ariana DeBose's Anita still greatly prefers "the island Manhattan" to her homeland, but she no longer wishes it to "sink back into the ocean." Still, when the film opened, at least a dozen critics in prominent publications took the occasion to question why anyone should revisit this work at all.

Hammerstein of course believed that we bipeds are able to understand each other's pain, and that artists are capable of capturing characters who are of a different temperament, gender, social class, race, or ethnicity from themselves. Once again, this idea is central to his view that we are, all of us, more connected than divided by our shared humanity.

Hammerstein rarely allowed himself to show, with anyone but Dorothy, the irritation he felt toward Rodgers. He couldn't help himself, though, one day in 1950. After struggling for a month with the lyric to "Tom and I," which became "Hello, Young Lovers," he was satisfied that he had captured something subtle and unique—a grief that is diffused by understanding its place in a continuum of death and renewal. This song is the apotheosis of all those eulogies Hammerstein had been called on to deliver (and the one he would soon give at the funeral of Gertrude Lawrence). Indeed, it is difficult to think of another song that achieves this particular poignancy. Hammerstein took the unusual step of sending the lyrics by special messenger to Rodgers. Hearing nothing back, Hammerstein stewed about it for days until the composer phoned to discuss some other matters. As he was about to sign off, Rodgers said, "Oh, I got that lyric. It works fine."

Livid, Hammerstein called a person who knew how impossible Rodgers could be—Josh Logan, who no doubt commiserated. In January of 1951 when Logan heard the almost-completed score for the first time, he wrote to both Rodgers and Hammerstein with praise, but his first order of business was to address this unusual song: "First of all, I think both musically and lyrically that HELLO YOUNG LOVERS is the greatest single dramatic song that I have ever heard in my life, and probably ever will. Up to this point my favorite had been that soliloquy in CAROUSEL, or perhaps IF I LOVED YOU, but this one seems to me at this moment to top both of them."

The song, with its appealing reverse schadenfreude, has had remarkable staying power. In a way it bookends all the songs Hammerstein wrote as paeans to a relationship's beginning—which now included "Getting to Know You," Anna's ode to her pupils. Hammerstein later connected that song's delightful truism—that "when you become a teacher / by your students you'll be taught"—to his most important disciple in a moving tribute, as we'll see in a future chapter.

For Tuptim and her lover, Lun Tha, Rodgers and Hammerstein wrote the crushingly beautiful "I Have Dreamed." This composition, too, engages the pre-conscious sense of fate Hammerstein felt was present in certain human connections. A direct line runs from *Show Boat's* "Make Believe" to "I Have Dreamed," in which the singer has so thoroughly imagined a love affair that he cannot tell where the dream ends and reality begins.

Hammerstein had been attuned to the supernatural melding of love and telepathy since his earliest days. He brought this enthrallment into his courtship: when he and Dorothy were still married to other partners he designated specific times for them to, though separate, gaze at the moon together. He immortalized the pleasure of this indulgence at the song's start:

Alone and awake, I've looked at the stars
The same that smile on you
And time and again, I've thought all the things
That you were thinking too.

He imbued Anna with knowledge that attraction affords us access to powers not available in everyday life. As she sings in "Hello, Young Lovers":

I know how it feels to have wings on your heels
And to fly down the street in a trance
You fly down the street on the chance that you'll meet
And you meet—not really by chance.

Rodgers and Hammerstein's take on geopolitics in *The King and I*—combined with the success of their shows abroad—elevated their status even further. They were artists who had created a unified definition of Americanness. Their productions made audiences feel proud of not only what the country was but what it could be—that beacon of hope and fairness for which we strive yet find so elusive.

When John Steinbeck saw *The King and I* he had a vision of a new Rodgers and Hammerstein musical that he might coauthor. Having written both *The Grapes of Wrath* and *Of Mice and Men,* Steinbeck was also a kind of national artist. While he had a deeply literary bent, the young Steinbeck had done manual labor and viscerally felt how the hoarding of wealth on one end of the economic scale causes inexcusable misery on the other. Like Hammerstein, he preferred a plainspoken style. Later, when asked if he thought he deserved the Nobel Prize in Literature, which he was awarded in 1962, he said, "Frankly, no."

Rodgers and Hammerstein had produced a stage version of Steinbeck's novella *Burning Bright* in the fall of 1950 that closed after thirteen performances, a rare failure for the producing team. But neither party faulted the other. Now Steinbeck was thinking about a real collaboration—one that, given the combined talents and interests of the three men, might produce a uniquely national musical. After all, between the three of them, they had enshrined the state of Oklahoma in modern American culture. On the notable date of July 4, 1952, Steinbeck wrote to Rodgers and Hammerstein from Positano, Italy, where he was writing a travel story for *Harper's Bazaar.* He made his pitch:

> Can't get the "King and I" out of my mind, the dignity it has and the stature and the tenderness and the reaching in both music and theme. I guess everybody tells you what to write. So I'm going to join the unselect group and tell you what to write. Boileau said there were three creatures worthy of literature: Kings, Gods, and Heroes. You can kind of transcribe that to mean that the only men worthy of literature are men who make their mark on the souls of men. We have one in our country who above all others has done this. Everybody has had a crack at him and I don't think anyone has done it yet. I begin to think you can't get deep into people without music. I mean the story of Abraham Lincoln. It's the whole country and the mark of him is just as deep or deeper now than it ever was. And nobody could do that story like you two. And there is no story I would rather help with. I think of it in this unique American form which you have so developed, the play with music.

He laid out the basic plot and suggested that the Lincoln-Douglas debates could be musicalized. He envisioned ending the show with the president's assassination in Ford's Theater. Steinbeck closed his letter with the following: "I can't think of anything better to do for you nor for me. That's all, now I've told you and I won't haunt you with it but I hope the subject begins to haunt both of you."

Writing back a month later, Hammerstein made it clear they were not haunted by this idea. He said they could give Steinbeck "no definite reaction" but suggested that the novelist come and talk to them in person, so "that the three of us can sit down and discuss it very carefully." He reported that he and Rodgers could not see the Lincoln-Douglas debate as a musical number; even though they "were keeping their minds open," it was his "instinct as well as Dick's that the thing has been done just too often." I would guess he recoiled at the prospect of working on a subject that came with such baggage and responsibility. Still, he closed the letter with the hope that the men could work together on something else; the result of that hope would be a musical called *Pipe Dream*.

CHAPTER ELEVEN

Cinderella and Other Myths

THE 1950S WAS THE DECADE of enshrinement for Rodgers and Hammerstein, which naturally created a next wave of doubters and naysayers. Some were envious and others simply harbored a different kind of taste, but after *The King and I,* just when the pair seemed invincible, the wheels of culture began their inevitable movement toward new modes of expression. Looking back at that musical, Hammerstein had said, "I have a kind of humble feeling of not knowing how we did it," which was not only characteristically temperate but also prescient. They would create only one more enduring theatrical hit, their last show, *The Sound of Music.*

By 1952 the pair decided they would forego producing in order to concentrate on their own work. Writing to Felicia Lamport, who had sent him her adaptation of a book called *Mink on Weekdays,* Hammerstein told her they "have retired from production—as far as other people's plays are concerned." Rodgers had long thought they should write a musical about a musical; Hammerstein was never taken with the idea (possibly because he had lent his thoughts on live performance to the character of Johnnie Graham in *Very Warm for May* and the outcome had been so dispiriting). But Hammerstein had initiated *Allegro* and felt he owed Rodgers. Therefore, the men embarked on their final original story, *Me and Juliet.*

The show takes place inside a theater well into the life of a long-running musical. Chorus member Jeanie is dating lighting man Bob, a cad with a violent temper, which everyone seems to know except Jeanie. Like Nellie Forbush and Anna Leonowens, Jeanie announces her brand of optimism in her opening song. But this time Hammerstein sees more than a bit of foolishness in the character. Jeanie is not the smartest. She wakes up feeling that "today will be a very special day" but is invariably disappointed; each night, after she's had her toast and tea, she begins to have a hunch "that tomorrow's going to be a very special day for me." What was spunky in Nellie and brave in Anna seems insipid in Jeanie. She lacks ambition and doesn't hope for much other than her very own piano. Larry, the assistant stage manager, secretly loves her and urges her to audition for a better role—the star's understudy—but she says she doesn't want to be an actor. She is in the show for the paycheck.

Me and Juliet offers some fun details about backstage life. A stage manager reprimands a chorus member for getting a tan on her day off, and a lead actor famous for his charm threatens to punch the conductor when a trombone oversteps his solo. Hammerstein also includes an exchange he witnessed as an assistant stage manager in the 1920s—a resourceful chorus boy swipes some mascara from an actress's eyelashes to disguise a hole in his tights. We see what happens just before the curtain goes up and after it comes down. Hammerstein indulges in a couple of self-referential jokes—Josh Logan and Yul Brynner are both parts of punchlines—as well as a critique of his own well-heeled audience. Called "Intermission Talk," the number greeted theatergoers when they returned from that break and guesses, a little rudely, at what they had just been discussing. Having spent years eavesdropping in the lobbies of theaters, Hammerstein chides theatergoers here for their consumerist concerns and not terribly astute drama criticism. Here's an example of the former:

WIFE: I don' think it's right
To be sulky all night
Over one little bill from
Saks!
BUSINESSMAN: What do I care if they
Balance the budget,
As long as they cut my
tax?

In an earlier number, however, Hammerstein bows to the anonymous, ever-changing crowds he'd spent his life courting, expressing a more contemplative view. Sung by Larry, the experienced theater hand, to Jeanie, who confesses to being afraid of the audience, "The Big Black Giant" reveals something about Hammerstein's commercial sense, which developed the way it did because he saw his connection to the audience as something important, primal, eternal. In "The Big Black Giant," the audience is an entity

Who looks and listens
With thousands of eyes and ears
That big black mass
Of love and pity
And troubles and hopes and fears
Will sit out there and rule your life
For all your living years.

Hammerstein adds this fillip, which sums up his belief in the ability of art to relieve and improve the human condition:

Every night you fight the giant
And maybe if you win
You send him out a nicer giant
Than he was when he came in.

When a romance develops between Larry and Jeanie, Bob's rage is terrifying. He is Jud to their Curly and Laurey. Perched on a catwalk, an inebriated Bob reveals his desperate need to feel superior:

It feels good
To feel high
High above a world of weasels and their lousy weasel talk.
A good drink, and you fly
Over all the things that frighten all the little jerks who walk.

Back on the ground Bob grabs Larry and his voice is quiet as he says, "If you ever try to move in on me with that kid, I—I'm telling you. . . . Something would happen to me. . . . I couldn't help killing you—not if I tried." Then, one night in the middle of a show, Bob swings a spotlight from the stage and shines it on Larry and Jeanie as they kiss in the wings. He drops a sandbag on a fleeing Jeanie and knocks a tray out of her hand. As in *Okla-*

homa!, the community comes together to protect the lovers against the rejected suitor. In this case, though, Bob becomes inexplicably rational when it is explained to him that the couple has already married.

Brooks Atkinson said, rightly, that the story had "no velocity." Still, because it was from Rodgers and Hammerstein, the show ran for almost a year. Eight months in, Hammerstein wrote to his Uncle Arthur, "*Me and Juliet* does not act like a champion. We have got back the $330,000 investment, and have made some, but I don't expect this to be a real smash like the others."

In a pre-opening interview with the *New York Times*, Rodgers said that in writing the show the pair had tried to avoid clichés about theater, such as the one where all the chorus boys are effeminate. "Try that one backstage at 'Me and Juliet' and you might get your arm broken," he remarked, demonstrating his natural ability to demean while offering praise.

Perhaps the most conspicuous event in the coronation of Rodgers and Hammerstein came in 1954, when General Foods celebrated its twenty-fifth anniversary. The company hired actor Ronald Reagan as its TV spokesperson that year and, as a gift to the American people that would double as a sure moneymaker, produced a lavish ninety-minute salute to the undisputed kings of Broadway. The program, which included scenes from *Oklahoma!, Carousel, Allegro, South Pacific, The King and I,* and their new show *Me and Juliet,* aired simultaneously on the era's four networks—DuMont, ABC, NBC, and CBS—something that had not been done before. It was perhaps at this moment, when Rodgers and Hammerstein allied themselves with the company that made frozen dinners, that they became more of a corporation than an artistic force.

This was also the decade in which Rodgers and Hammerstein made movies based on their four hit musicals, which would help cement their reputations, though not necessarily in the way they hoped. It was the time of color-saturated, big-screen extravaganzas, the vibrancy of which seemed like a partial solution to a dilemma Rodgers and Hammerstein faced concerning film: How does one transfer what is alive onstage to the daunting immortality of celluloid? It was not an accident that *The Wizard of Oz* (1939) and *Singin' in the Rain* (1952)—the freshest film musicals since the early work of Astaire and Rogers—were written for film and did not originate in the theater.

In truth the pair were not creatures of the cinema, and their attempts to translate what they had fashioned so perfectly for the stage were ham-fisted. The film versions of *Oklahoma!* (1955), *Carousel* (1956), *The King and I* (1956), and *South Pacific* (1958) offer certain pleasures; however, for those who have experienced the originals well produced in a theater, the movies can seem like beautiful butterflies pinned in a case. Still, all four were box office hits in quick succession.

By the time *Oklahoma!* was filmed, Rodgers and Hammerstein had established their own Hollywood concern, the Rodgers and Hammerstein Picture Company. No expense was spared in the embalming of this vital theatrical experience, starting with the two thousand corn stalks spaced far enough apart so that Gordon MacRae (as Curly) could ride his horse through them without being smacked in the face. For the set Oliver Smith designed a complete farm in Arizona's San Rafael Valley, which stood in for the forty-sixth state. *Oklahoma!* cost almost $7 million, making it the most expensive movie ever made at that time.

Robert Russell Bennett experienced a sinking feeling at an early viewing: "I have neither the equipment nor the desire to write a review of what we saw at the preview," he recalled. "Beyond wondering why a group of wise, experienced showmen would choose a darling little show of vignettes of little people to show off the world's biggest screen, I didn't even allow myself the luxury of an opinion."

For their part, Rodgers and Hammerstein always convinced themselves that their films were going to be great. They were easily enamored of flashy new technologies developed in response to television—for *Oklahoma!* it was widescreen, 70 mm Technicolor and stereophonic sound. Hammerstein believed the Todd-AO process (named for producer Mike Todd) "gave the story the visual scope, the big outdoor feeling it needed."

The most controversial effect in the filmed musicals was Josh Logan's use of colored filters in *South Pacific,* which the director first employed to suggest the hallucinatory qualities of Bali Ha'i. Though a good idea in theory, the novel technique ended up calling too much attention to itself. While filming, Logan feared it looked absurd one minute and was ecstatic about its potential the next. He dictated a letter to Hammerstein while shooting his first filtered scene on Kauai's Lumaha'i Beach to reassure his friend about the yellow filters implemented by camera operator Leon Shamroy:

> Fortunately, a set of dailies came through . . . and I can tell you now that they are history-making dailies. The only thing the matter with them is that in a couple of years we will hate them because so many people will be copying them! I can only describe them to you by saying that they are the most romantic scenes I have ever seen on film. They are something like a sanguine drawing or a copper etching. Nellie's face is soft around the edges, her lips, eyes and nose are clear—but the whole effect is of great beauty. There is even a suggestion of "evening" in the shots which adds to the meaning of the song.

Hammerstein decided to hope for the best. Just before the film's release he wrote:

> The device developed by Mr. Logan and Mr. Shamroy in "South Pacific" for changing the light and texture of the pictures when a musical number starts is a very important contribution. It is a kind of subtle acknowledgement that the literal reality of dialogue will be suspended for a moment while we pretend that people express their thoughts and feelings in song. It helps our imagination to find the truth that the fumbling prose used by most of us does not express, the poetry that sings inside all of us at certain times.

But by the time Logan had published his book *Movie Stars, Real People, and Me* in 1978, the filters were generally acknowledged to be an odd but amusing footnote in the annals of the musical, so much so that Logan opens the chapter about the filming of *South Pacific* by assuming everyone knows what he is referring to: "According to all rules of logic, they were in the picture because I wanted them there. Untrue! I hated them and will always hate them, but since I instigated them, I found myself powerless to do anything about them in the end but suffer." He then lays out a long story, spreading the blame around, as to how the filters happened. Logan ends his tale by saying, "The ghastly part of this story is that [the film] *South Pacific* turned out to be the most financially successful thing I ever did in my life. It made more money than all the rest of my pictures and plays put together. Unfortunately, that doesn't make me feel any better about it."

Truly, that musical was Josh Logan's blessing and curse.

But of all the Rodgers and Hammerstein films, *The King and I* has aged best, in part because it relies the least on techno-gimcrackery to translate theatrical magic. It is a straightforward filming, although it very much betrays the tastes of the time, which could be described as peak 1950s. The perfection of Deborah Kerr's image and her upright demeanor brought out the starchiness of the character; her Anna is more proper than brave, a woman sailing into another culture with a firm sense of the superiority of her own.

Playwright Christopher Isherwood, attending the film's opening with producer Charlie Brackett, wrote in his diary that night "I HATE Anna." He objected to "that sweetly smiling, gently snooty apostle of democracy and 'our' way of doing things. Hammerstein has written some of his vilest lyrics for this play—particularly the one about 'whistling a little tune' and 'Getting to Know You.'" The backlash, which saw Rodgers and Hammerstein as purveyors of cultural imperialism and sentimental schlock (and which would blossom after *The Sound of Music*), had begun.

In 1953, a year after Hammerstein had turned down John Steinbeck's idea for a musical about Abraham Lincoln, he was on his way to London to oversee the opening of *The King and I* at Theatre Royal, Drury Lane. He received another letter from Steinbeck enclosing pages from his new novel, *Sweet Thursday*. This was a sequel to *Cannery Row*, based on Steinbeck's days spent hanging out with a quirky marine biologist named Ed Ricketts and his ragtag community living in the empty lots and flophouses of Monterey, California, where the fish canneries used to be.

I believe the fifty-eight-year-old lyricist saw himself in the show's lead character, Doc (based on Ricketts). Although Doc is an eccentric who lives in the makeshift lab he runs, he and Hammerstein share a way of looking at the world. He is the center of his community and freely distributes dollars and wisdom to an oddball cast of characters who love and protect him. "He was beloved and preyed on by his friends, and this contented him," wrote Steinbeck in the novel. "For he remembered the words of Diamond Jim Brady who, when told that his friends were making suckers of him, remarked, 'It's fun to be a sucker—if you can afford it.'" And Steinbeck might just as well have been writing about Hammerstein (and how he saw himself) in this description of Doc: "All in all, he had always been a fulfilled and content man. A specimen so rare aroused yearning in other men, for how few men like their work, their lives—how very few men like themselves. Doc liked himself, not in an adulatory sense, but just as he would have liked anyone else. Being at ease with himself put him at ease with the world."

Sweet Thursday was, in its way, a perfect vehicle for Rodgers and Hammerstein. They were taken with Steinbeck's marginalized, troubled, yet decent characters, and they hoped that focusing on them might once again push the boundaries of the musical as a form.

Although Steinbeck focuses on a group living on the edge of respectability and in the shadow of vagrancy laws, they all watch out for one another; their community holds together through a general and innate sense of goodness. Case in point, Doc's friends decide he is lonely and engineer a plan to throw him into the arms of Suzy, a young woman they would like to see retire from her life as a prostitute. Fauna, the brothel overseer, is like a den mother to her workers. She is kindhearted and gives the women lessons in table settings, grammar, and deportment. She makes sure they get a balanced dinner: beef stew, creamed carrots, and Jell-O for dessert. When one of her brood makes good—which means marrying a wealthy and respected male—Fauna posts a giant gold star on a framed board in her den.

Steinbeck's milieu overflows with eccentricity, common sense, poetry, and street knowledge, not unlike that found in the stories of Damon Runyon (which Frank Loesser, Jo Swerling, and Abe Burrows translated into the hit musical of 1950, *Guys and Dolls*). As in Runyon, the characters go by colorful names like Old Jingleballicks, Elegant Joe, Wide Ida, and The Patrón. They also demonstrate a comical way of combining formal and informal speech: announcing the plan to help Doc out of his malaise, one of them raps on a stovepipe and says, "Gentleman, let us here highly resolve to get Doc's ass out of the sling of despond."

As it turned out, Rodgers and Hammerstein were good at capturing the characters' decency but unable to convey the reality of the rougher aspects of their lives. Rodgers immediately worried about how they would depict Suzy's profession. Though she is a prostitute for only a short time, and a halfhearted one at that, Rodgers and Hammerstein could not bring themselves to represent that life. They settled on calling her a "girl of the road," which seems to mean that, before arriving in Cannery Row, she rode buses from town to town and gazed moodily into the windows of homes she wishes she could live in one day. She is adrift, a person who might find her way to prostitution but has not thus far.

This change posed an obstacle to the story's flow. In *Sweet Thursday,* Suzie leaves the brothel after she realizes she is in love with Doc. She fixes up a large, abandoned boiler as her abode and finds a job at the local diner. She doesn't do this for Doc specifically; rather, she now realizes she must make a change if she is to attain the kind of life she wants. Doc notices this and admires her, which paves the way to their marriage and the plot's happy ending. But without Suzy's particular need or determination to change her life, the narrative lost its teeth.

Everyone saw the problem but no one could fix it. In a letter, Steinbeck encouraged Hammerstein to let his imagination go to places it had not before (in other words, to loosen up): "But Oscar, time has moved. The form has moved. People love *Oklahoma!* as a classic, but if you brought it in as a new show now people would find it old fashioned and conventional because *S.P.* and *The King and I* carried it further. You're stuck with it. You can't stand still . . . To avoid this fact that Suzy is a hooker is to throw out the only story there is in this particular thing."

Neither Rodgers nor Hammerstein could examine the psychic realities of prostitution outside of Thailand, each for their own reasons. They used Fauna as a stand-in for their own feelings in the musical, now titled *Pipe Dream.* The brothel owner tells Suzy, who is looking for work, "I'd like to help you, but business is off at my place. . . . Ah, it'd be against my better judgment, anyway. There's something about you. I don't know what it is, but you wouldn't be right." Steinbeck understood that this change in Suzy would suck the air out of his story, and he resented what he saw as the cowardice of Rodgers and Hammerstein. Watching Judy Tyler as Suzy sing the woeful "Everybody's Got a Home but Me" in rehearsal, the novelist said that she looked "more like an off-duty nurse" than a prostitute. He pointedly wrote to a friend that the show's new title signaled to the audience "it wasn't true before they started."

When *Pipe Dream* opened in November of 1955, Brooks Atkinson called the show "a pleasant, lazy romance" and advised, "We mustn't expect *Carousel* every season."

■ ■ ■

The published version of *Pipe Dream* is dedicated to the wives of Steinbeck, Rodgers, and Hammerstein: "For Elaine and the Dorothys, for their tireless supervision."

Supervision is an interesting word. During the musical's pre-Broadway run, Dorothy Hammerstein felt it necessary to make an unscheduled trip to New Haven to put a stop to a brewing romance between Oscar and a member of the show's chorus.

When he answered letters from, say, old dance partners from his youth, Oscar could be flirtatious, though usually in an avuncular way. His natural generosity, when directed toward a woman he found attractive, came sometimes with a hint of condescension, as if to knock her down a peg. In a June 1949 letter to Josh Logan, he described being impressed with the actor Helen Hayes when he and Rodgers were being awarded a Medal of Excellence from Columbia University and she a Doctor of Laws: "I think I shall never forget how pretty she looked in her cap and gown as she received her citation—not a bit like Portia, but more like the Barnard seniors. She seemed, however, much more frankly delighted than they were. At the alumni luncheon she made a darling speech. What a girl!"

Rodgers was famously unfaithful to his Dorothy; Meryle Secrest reveals the composer's compulsive womanizing in gory detail in *Somewhere for Me* alongside Rodgers's struggles with alcoholism and depression. However, Secrest sounds as if she's trying to even out the enormous difference in the way Rodgers and Hammerstein lived their lives when she reveals that "Oscar Hammerstein had a secret long-term affair with a beautiful showgirl." She quotes Dorothy Rodgers's niece Judy Crichton as saying, "Dick was very protective of that" (as well he might have been). In her autobiography (written with Jesse Green), Mary Rodgers and Green note, "Whether Hammerstein was a man of better character has been debated; he was at least discreet. He had a longtime affair with a showgirl called Temple Texas, which sounds like a congregation in Dallas but was really named Dora Jane Temple and appeared in *Pipe Dream.*" (More on that in a minute, but I question the adjective "longtime." Compared to Richard Rodgers's innumerable affairs maybe, but there is no evidence the relationship lasted longer than a pipe dream.)

In his Hammerstein biography, Hugh Fordin addressed the issue with a non-denial denial: "In the theatrical world, in which extra marital affairs are the rule, only once were there rumors about Oscar and another woman.

Given the realities of human nature and the gossiping endemic to the theatrical world, where malicious envy thrives, particularly of someone as successful, good and even awesome as Oscar, it is remarkable that there is only one such rumor."

If Oscar did stray, which it seems he did, it must have plagued him. His love notes to Dorothy continued throughout their lives; she collected more than ninety small cards from him, most of which came with gifts of jewelry or flowers (Oscar alone might have kept local florist Max Schling afloat for many years). On the occasion of their twentieth anniversary in 1949 he wrote:

> I love you more deeply than ever. Our lives are two strands that
> have become so tightly braided together as to be one strand,
> stronger and stouter, inseparable and unbreakable. There could
> be no happiness for me except in this sweet bondage—
> Your legal husband and eternal lover—Ockie

For their twenty-fifth anniversary, the couple threw a lavish party in May of 1954 on the rooftop of the Hotel Pierre. One might notice in his note to Dorothy for that occasion just a touch of criticism:

> For
> Dorothy,
> My darling wife
> On our twenty-fifth wedding anniversary
> Three pieces of silver are bestowed
> With my worship for her beauty
> My gratitude for her bounty
> And all the love in my heart.
> They are to be used by her
> For the purchase of real estate,
> Objects of art, clothes, gems,
> Trinkets, fripperies or, indeed,
> Anything but china.

As Fordin noted, in the theater, a long-term, volatile secret is almost impossible to keep. The name Temple Texas was first mentioned publicly in Todd Purdum's 2018 book *Something Wonderful*. I was researching this book at the time, and I had been excited when I found a clue to the then-mystery woman's identity in a self-published volume from 2003 called *Cinderella after the Ball*, a tell-most memoir by Barbara "Basia" Redzisz Hammerstein, who was married to Jimmy Hammerstein from 1954 to 1956.

Born in Warsaw, Basia came with her parents to the United States when she was nine. Bright, pretty, and shapely, she helped finance her degree at Hunter College by working as a chorus member at the Copacabana nightclub, where her boss wedged her up against a wall and accosted her. Broadway being ostensibly more respectful to its dancers—Richard Rodgers at least used a room—Basia happily took a job in the Cole Porter musical *Can-Can*, where Jimmy worked as stage manager. They married six months after meeting.

Cinderella after the Ball has all the earmarks of a book written to settle scores. Basia feels unfairly judged by her in-laws, whom she depicts as haughty and cold. Basia herself is blameless in all encounters. At the same time, many of her observations about the Hammerstein household are vivid and specific. Her assessment of why *Pipe Dream* failed is spot-on; Basia speculates that Oscar's brain froze when he tried to imagine the reality of a prostitute, since his young ladies always "have the hearts of ingénues" and "had to be enchanted with their lives." Of course, she may have been riffing on Billy Rose's widely repeated comment that *Pipe Dream* failed because Hammerstein had "never been to a whorehouse in his life." (Brooks Atkinson took a similar tack: "If it does not constitute a Federal case to say so, Mr. Hammerstein is a more respectable man than Mr. Steinbeck.")

In Basia's view, Oscar is also painfully square, something the younger generation was beginning to feel about Rodgers and Hammerstein in general by this time. She relates that her father-in-law was shocked when Jimmy told him that many in the theater world's gay community had adopted, as their anthem, a song from *Me and Juliet* called "Keep It Gay." (Later, Mel Brooks borrowed the title for a number in *The Producers* that comments on the obliviousness of Hammerstein, who had an unironic fondness for the word.)

As she is watching carefully to learn the habits and the tastes of the rich, Basia offers some useful details about the way the Hammersteins lived. One entered their five-story Manhattan townhouse on Sixty-Third Street just east of Central Park through a vestibule featuring a black-and-white-checkered floor, marked by the crest of a lion at center, plants all around, and gilded mirrors on the walls. A circular marble staircase covered in moss green carpet climbed up four floors. The upstairs walls were covered in beige brocade and lit by crystal chandeliers. Cascading flower arrangements abounded, as did framed family pictures. In the master bedroom hung large painted portraits of Dorothy and Oscar. Dorothy's famous collection of Lowestoft china, decorated with pink and white lotus flowers, was displayed in a lighted glass case on the second floor. Nearby was the dining room, where early American portrait paintings hung above a highly polished mahogany table.

According to the author, Jimmy and Basia meet in a restaurant when he crashes his six-foot-five-inch frame into a lighting fixture, sending dead moths raining down on her. She represents her husband-to-be as a boorish and unattractive klutz; he had skinny legs and a flat behind, his ears stuck out, and his teeth were in horrible condition (which she ascribes, as so much else, to his parents' cheapness). He had a habit of cracking all his knuckles one by one and then his neck, and he'd constantly say twitty things like "Mumsy and Dad are at The Farm" and "How'd you like to have din-din?" (Nor does Basia spare Jimmy the ultimate emasculation—she reveals he was impotent on their wedding night.)

But Basia nonetheless marries him and so gains intimate access to the family. Oscar is stingy, sexist, and uneducated about such basic concepts as the nature of evolution. Dorothy is icy, passive-aggressive, and fond of the joke "God loves poor people. How do you know? Because he made so many of them."

Going through family papers, I saw no sign of this sort of sneering classism in the Hammerstein household, except one joke of Oscar's from around this time. He was writing in the summer of 1952 from Doylestown to Richard Halliday, whose imperiousness apparently brought out the worst in the lyricist. "We have put in a swimming pool, and I now do so much floating about in it that I wonder how I got along for so long," reported Hammerstein. "Dear me, how do the poor people live?"

Since Basia's parents were struggling immigrants, she would naturally be sensitive to comments disparaging the lower classes. When Dorothy learns Basia is Polish, the older woman says, "How wonderful. Our maids at the farm are Polish." Basia may have exaggerated her mother-in-law's haughtiness, but she picks up on behavior she would be in a unique position to see; moreover, it's possible that her own youth might have inspired the worst in Dorothy at a particularly vulnerable time in her own marriage.

Still, it is a bit dispiriting to be handed this version of Dorothy when all we really had of her was a lovely-looking woman who inspired some of the world's most romantic songs, helped raise Stephen Sondheim, and was known for one great witticism delivered when a stranger identified Eva Kern as the woman whose husband had written "Ol' Man River." ("No, my husband wrote 'Ol' Man River,'" corrected Dorothy. "Her husband wrote, Da-da-da-dum.")

With the smoldering hatred of a peasant (to use F. Scott Fitzgerald's phrase), Basia notices the aforementioned foot pedal that Dorothy presses at the dinner table to signal the kitchen when it is time to clear plates. The eagle-eyed daughter-in-law also reports that the plants in the foyer are plastic and the books in the library have uncut pages. Nearly every time Basia looks at Dorothy she sees anxiety in her blue eyes, which she many times describes as "watery." And Basia herself soon feels the hardness of the family's gender expectations. Oscar asks her if Jimmy will "let her" have a career. He believes, he informs her in a suspiciously grand sentence, that "a wife's place is beside her husband to help him fulfill his destiny." Basia is disappointed to find, in this bastion of American sophistication, that wives and mothers act like servants. While they have cleaners to do menial tasks, the women's true function is to keep the house pretty and running smoothly so the men can do their work.

Just as *Pipe Dream* was going into rehearsals, Oscar's eighty-two-year-old Uncle Arthur died in Palm Beach, where he had retired. Then Richard Rodgers got the news that he had cancer of the gums. He was operated on at once, and doctors removed the lower left side of his mouth. He was back at rehearsal in ten days, but this disfigurement was an enormous blow. And of course it rattled Hammerstein—mortality was in the air.

At the opening-night party for *Pipe Dream,* Basia describes the despair on Dorothy's face as she watches Oscar dance with an actor playing one of the play's prostitutes. Basia goes on to report that her father-in-law had "a dalliance" with this woman. Going over the cast list with Basia's physical description of the woman in question, it was easy to ID her as Temple Texas.

Dora Jane Temple.
Courtesy of C. Robert Potter

■ ■ ■

Born in Arkansas as Dora Jane Temple, she would have been around thirty at the time and Oscar sixty. I asked Sondheim if he had ever heard any rumors about Temple Texas. He said that Mary McCarty, who played Stella in his 1971 musical *Follies,* had mentioned it, but he added that he did not know if it was true. (McCarty died in 1980.)

Dora Jane's career as an actor was brief and undistinguished, but she achieved some notoriety as a "glamour girl" throughout the 1940s and 1950s. She often appeared in gossip columns, which guessed at what beaux might have given her a diamond bracelet, a blue fur, or a tiny poodle named

Floosy. In 1945 she entered a brief marriage with nightclub comedian Jackie Miles. In 1959 she shows up in Walter Winchell's column as a "show girl turned publicist" and one of two women dating Billy Rose. In 1962 Dora Jane married Joseph Shribman, a manager whose clients included Rosemary Clooney. She left showbiz, raised two children, and died in 1987. I was able to find her son, Owen, a software engineer who lives in Southern California. He said that his mother kept in touch with many people from her years in the business (Ethel Merman had been like an aunt to him). Dora Jane spoke of *Pipe Dream* with enthusiasm, he remembered, but never said much about Oscar specifically. However, when she got sick in the 1980s, she gave Owen a gold pinkie ring engraved with the initials OH and told him Oscar had given it to her. (Hammerstein can be seen wearing such a ring in the photo in chapter 2 in which he is standing next to his first wife.) Owen regrets he didn't ask his mother more.

In Hammerstein's *Pipe Dream* papers I found this lone sentence, plucked from *Sweet Thursday*, written on a white sheet of paper: "Together they threatened to be a celebration close to a catastrophe."

In adapting *Sweet Thursday*, I believe Hammerstein began to identify with the existential dilemma that haunts Doc, a condition that "nibbled at him," Steinbeck wrote, after he returned from the war: "Where does discontent start? You are warm enough, but you shiver. You are fed, yet hunger gnaws you. You have been loved, but your yearning wanders in new fields. And to prod all these there's time, the bastard Time. The end of life is now not so terribly far away—you can see it the way you see the finish line when you come into the stretch—and your mind says, 'Have I worked enough? Have I eaten enough? Have I loved enough?'"

In 1953, before Rodgers received news of his illness, he and Dorothy were interviewed by Edward R. Murrow for the TV show *Person to Person*. The journalist visited them at their grand Manhattan apartment on the Upper East Side, its walls decorated with paintings by Renoir, Picasso, Matisse, and Bonnard. The Rodgers sit on low chairs covered in chintz before their fireplace. Dorothy is a model of 1950s wifely propriety, wearing a modest pearl choker at her clavicle with matching stud earrings, her black hair pulled back smoothly. Her black silk dress hangs just below the knee, above black patent pumps. When Murrow asks Dorothy her favorite of all her husband's songs, she looks down demurely and says, "Well, I'm just a layman of course, but my favorite song is from *Carousel.* It's called 'You'll Never Walk Alone.' It strikes me as a very good song." This happens to be her husband's opinion as well. They always presented a unified front.

Murrow also asks Rodgers about where he finds inspiration. Rodgers responds, with a little laugh, "People think you have to be out with a blonde in a canoe before you can write a love song," he says, suggesting that isn't true, although he doesn't exactly offer an alternative scenario. His wife smiles stiffly and looks away.

Mary would later say that her mother's role of perfect wife was grounded in hypocrisy, which contributed to Dorothy's anorexia and long addiction to Demerol. Dick and Dorothy, though, were a team, and Rodgers was as protective of his wife's reputation as he was careless about his marriage vows. In 1950 he wrote to *Life* magazine editor Lincoln Barnett about including Dorothy in a profile that Barnett had apparently submitted to the composer before publication:

> Not only for the sake of her feelings, but for the sake of the record, I think something should be said about Dorothy. I know that she doesn't appear in any extraordinarily active light but her influence on my work and my life are very great indeed. It's all quiet, to be sure, but then everything she does is quiet and while her criticisms of my work are never negative, I can judge her opinion by the degree and emphasis with which she expresses it. If her eyes fill with tears and she puts her arms around me, I know she thinks it's wonderful. If she says it's very good, I know she hates it. This way we never get into trouble and it may be one reason we've been together for twenty years.

Murrow also interviewed Oscar and Dorothy Hammerstein at their townhouse in May of 1955, though for this encounter he sent a camera operator and sound technician as his proxies and himself remained twenty blocks away in the studio. Murrow and Hammerstein had both come up against Joseph McCarthy, with Murrow playing a significant role in exposing the senator's reckless accusations. It is widely accepted that Murrow's interview of McCarthy on his show *See It Now* just two months before helped turn public opinion against the senator. (In December the Senate would adopt a resolution reprimanding McCarthy.) CBS chief Bill Paley held it against Murrow that his reporting alienated several sponsors, and he pulled the plug on the journalist's weekly show in 1955 (though it continued, irregularly, into 1956). Murrow producer Fred Friendly explained that Paley was tired of the "constant stomachache every time Murrow covered a controversial subject."

For the *Person to Person* broadcast the sixty-year-old Hammerstein sits in his office on a chintz-covered, high-backed chair, looking elegant in a double-breasted suit and tie with a hankie in his pocket. Shot head-on, his face looks plump, scarred at the sides, chin doubled, ears large, eyes alight. Murrow describes him as a "gentleman farmer," but Hammerstein laughingly protests he's really neither of those things though he is raising a herd of Angus cattle in Doylestown. Three photos sit on a bookcase, which he points out to the camera: Otto Harbach, who taught him "ninety percent" of what he knows about writing libretti; his Uncle Arthur, who did so much to help launch his career; and his grandfather Oscar I, about whom Hammerstein says, "I don't think he cared one way or the other."

Regarding the in-progress filming of *Oklahoma!,* Hammerstein mentions the "new process called Todd-AO," which is "quite a wonderful thing which makes you feel you're involved in the scene and in the numbers." He was self-deprecating about his own work, laughing genially about a state trooper who approached him during filming and said that looked like a real good picture but why are they using all that old music?

The camera then follows Oscar down a spiral staircase to the sitting room where he is met by Dorothy, who has retired (for the third or fourth time) from interior decorating but is happy to share with the American public the work she's done in her own home. She points out a ceramic monkey, saying it reminds them of someone, she won't say whom, and Murrow laughs knowingly (it looks a lot like Richard Rodgers). With no trace of her native Australian accent, she introduces the viewer to an eight-paneled Chinese screen with large painted flowers hung on a living-room wall, as well as the fine china with tiny pink flowers she collects in a lighted glass case (exactly as described by Basia). She is elegantly informal in a shirtdress with a full skirt, an elaborate broach in the shape of a bouquet pinned near her left breast, and high heels. Her hair is swept back, with one curl cascading gently down the right side of her handsome face.

After viewing the china, Hammerstein and Murrow get down to business. The journalist asks Hammerstein about one of his most famous lyrics, "You've got to be taught to hate and fear." Hammerstein replies that teaching children to hate is equivalent to poisoning them, adding that he does not believe that hating comes naturally. Donning his World Federalist mantle he remarks that many people see the United Nations as weak and think it should be abolished, whereas he thinks it's weak and should be made much stronger. "I think it's our only hope for peace and law," he says with calm surety.

The following year Murrow asked Hammerstein to contribute to his radio series called *This I Believe,* in which "thoughtful men and women talk out loud about the rules they live by, the things they have found to be the basic values in their lives." Hammerstein's contribution was prosaic but straightforward in describing the value of optimism. He begins by saying he would call himself as a happy man. Then:

> I believe, therefore, that it is important for a man to announce that he is happy even though such an announcement is less dramatic and less entertaining than the cries of his pessimistic opposite. Why do I believe I am happy? Death has deprived me of many whom I loved. Dismal failure has followed many of my most earnest efforts. People have disappointed me. I have disappointed them. I have disappointed myself.
>
> Further than this, I am aware that I live under a cloud of international hysteria. The cloud could burst, and a rain of atom bombs could destroy millions of lives, including my own. From all this evidence, could I not build up a strong case to prove why I am not happy at all? I could, but it would be a false picture, as false as if I were to describe a tree only as it looks in winter. I would be leaving out a list of people I love, who have not died. I would be leaving out an acknowledgment of the many successes that have sprouted among my many failures. I would be leaving out the blessing of good health, the joy of walking in the sunshine. I would be leaving out my faith that the goodness in man will triumph eventually over the evil that causes war.

In conclusion he said, "I don't believe anyone can enjoy living in this world unless he can accept its imperfection," adding that to insist otherwise would be "childish."

■ ■ ■

Pipe Dream generated huge advance ticket sales—$1.2 million—and ran for 243 performances. This would have been a decent showing for anyone else, but it was a clear failure for Rodgers and Hammerstein. By way of comparison, *The King and I* ran five times as long.

That is why, when CBS's Hubbell Robinson offered the duo a new medium to conquer, they said yes at once. As director of programming, Robinson was the force behind *Playhouse 90*, and his commitment to serious drama helped situate CBS as "the Tiffany network." He suggested that Rodgers and Hammerstein write an original musical version of *Cinderella* for Julie Andrews, the twenty-year-old Broadway star who was bewitching multitudes as Eliza in *My Fair Lady*. Robinson reasoned that this project would help extend CBS into the family market that NBC had cornered with its two live broadcasts of *Peter Pan*, which featured Mary Martin reprising her Broadway role. *Peter Pan*'s first airing in 1955 drew sixty-five million viewers, a record for a standalone program. Rodgers and Hammerstein's *Cinderella* smashed that record when it aired on CBS on March 31, 1957, attracting an audience of more than one hundred million (about 60 percent of the country's population at the time). In his memoir Rodgers notes that the broadcast occurred on the fourteenth anniversary of the opening of *Oklahoma!*, which in its original, five-year Broadway run was seen by only four million people (ten years on the road garnered it eight million more).

After the disappointments of *Pipe Dream*, Rodgers and Hammerstein may have been relieved to embrace the inherent wholesomeness of the Cinderella story. The pair supplied a score of exceptional charm and longevity. Rodgers's music, which has the shimmer of a Prokofiev ballet, envelopes this tale of a despised child rescued by a fairy godmother, a prince, and her own lovely modesty. Cinderella is fairly blank for a Rodgers and Hammerstein protagonist, but she's young, pretty, and behaves well under pressure. For the lovers' duet, Hammerstein supplied some of his most dazzling and effortless internal rhymes, inspired by his favorite occasion—the brain overload that occurs the instant one falls in love. Hammerstein's Prince happens to look up just as his dream girl enters the ball; his abundance of feeling is communicated by an internal rhyme that mimics the headiest of sensations:

Ten minutes ago I saw you
I looked up when you came through the door.
My head started reeling, you gave me the feeling
The room had no ceiling or floor.

In real life, sitting in suits and ties on the set in their directors' chairs (marked "Mr. Rodgers" and "Mr. Hammerstein"), the two were now éminences grises, establishment worthies about to be shunted aside in the generation gap to end all such gaps. Though they would be rejected by teenagers and young adults in a matter of years, the children—the ones who didn't yet care what was cool—embraced both *Cinderella* and its follow-up, *The Sound of Music,* with all their hearts. Moreover, *their* children followed suit, which elevated that show still to come into a touchstone of American culture.

It was at this moment that Vincent Donehue, director of NBC's *Peter Pan,* suggested that Mary Martin and Richard Halliday buy the newly available rights to *The Trapp Family,* a new German film based on the 1949 autobiography of matriarch Maria, a former postulant who transformed her seven stepchildren into a successful singing group. The rights were secured, and Halliday and Leland Hayward were set to produce it as a musical starring Martin as Maria. The score, they thought, would come from the music that the von Trapp family sang in their concerts (mostly folk and liturgical songs). For the book, the producers engaged playwrights Howard Lindsay and Russel Crouse. Halliday then asked Rodgers if he and Hammerstein would consider writing a song for the project. After watching the film, the composer gave them fantastic news: he and Hammerstein wanted to write a full-blown original score.

In late summer 1957, while eating in the Fox commissary during the filming of *South Pacific,* Hammerstein ran into Joe Fields, a writer he'd known all his life. Joe's father, Lew, had been one half of the vaudevillian team Weber and Fields, friends of Hammerstein's father and grandfather. And Lew held a forever place in Rodgers's heart as well, for he was the first person to buy a Rodgers and Hart song, "Any Old Place with You," using it in his 1919 show *A Lonely Romeo.* Joe's sister Dorothy and brother Herbert had written the book for *Annie Get Your Gun.* (Dorothy Fields was the second-most famous lyricist to work with Jerome Kern, penning some of the great

On the set of their 1957 TV musical *Cinderella* with Julie Andrews, Hammerstein and Rodgers were now establishment worthies against which the next generation of songwriters would have to rebel.
Courtesy of Photofest

popular songs of the century like "The Way You Look Tonight" and "Pick Yourself Up.")

Joe Fields told Hammerstein about a new novel he had optioned by Chinese American author C. Y. Lee called *The Flower Drum Song*. It centers on Wang Chi-yang, a sixty-three-year-old immigrant who shows no interest in assimilation, though his two sons of course are sopping up American culture. Wang orders a bride from China for his older son, Wang Ta; however, by the time the woman arrives, Ta has already fallen for another young woman. In the end, the father realizes he must let go of the old ways in order not to lose his sons. Hammerstein was intrigued by the story's clash of cultures as played out in present-day San Francisco and agreed to work with Fields on an adaptation.

Hammerstein and Fields took the focus off Wang and put it on the romantic lives of two young men: Ta and a nightclub comedian named Sammy Fong. The latter is in love with a sassy singer named Linda and so fobs off *his* mail-order or "picture bride," Mei Li, on the Wang family. Ta's father likes Mei Li; Mei Li likes Ta, but Ta is taken with Linda, who is sick of waiting for Sammy to marry her and so has decided to marry Ta. A few mix-ups and songs later, Ta marries Mei Li and Sammy marries Linda. The show depicts both sides of the generation gap—the loath-to-assimilate parents and their with-it offspring—as reasonable, recognizable human beings making choices common to American families. While that hardly sounds groundbreaking, in 1958 it was.

Rodgers and Hammerstein were determined to do better with casting Asian actors than they had done six years earlier for *The King and I*. They advertised for performers in a local Chinese newspaper, attended Chinese beauty pageants and dance schools, and even stopped candidates on the street, though none of these activities yielded an actor. They hired Gene Kelly to direct; he, along with author Lee, scoured San Francisco nightclubs, where they discovered Jack Suzuki, a Japanese entertainer who had changed his name to Soo after spending most of the Second World War in a Utah internment camp. Soo took the part of a nightclub MC called Frankie Wing. He later replaced the white actor Larry Blyden in the role of Sammy Fong, which he also played in the 1961 film version.

The rest of the cast was an ethnic mishmash—Japanese actor Miyoshi Umeki played the shy heroine Mei Li. Juanita Hall, an African American who had played the Tonkinese Bloody Mary in *South Pacific*, was cast as Auntie Liang. Ed Kenney, born in Hawaii, played the patriarch Wang Ta; Pat Suzuki, of Japanese ancestry, took the role of Linda Low and introduced the song "I Enjoy Being a Girl," which was striking at the time for its assumption that the singer was no different from any other young American. Keye Luke, who had played "number-one son" in the Charlie Chan films of the late 1920s and 1930s, took the role of Ta and was the only Chinese actor in the original cast (though born in Guangzhou, he had been raised in Seattle).

Christina Klein writes that the show "created a cultural space in which Asian Americans could be culturally embraced as 'real' Americans." This meant a lot to Asian American baby boomers like playwright David Henry

Hwang; he saw the 1961 film version as a child and remembered it well because it featured "romances between Asian men and women who spoke without accents," which was "nothing short of revolutionary." Hwang found his attitude changed when he started writing plays as a college student in the 1970s: "Along with other writers of color, we Asian Americans sought to define our own identities, rather than permitting those images to be drawn by mainstream society, which had done such a poor job of portraying us in my youth. As part of this movement, we rather simplistically condemned virtually all portrayals of Asian Americans created by non-Asians. So I ended up protesting *Flower Drum Song* as 'inauthentic,' though the show remained a guilty pleasure for many of us."

Writing in the *Los Angeles Review of Books*, Heidi Kim, an associate professor of English and comparative literature at UNC Chapel Hill, also recalled the film as a seminal cultural experience, a "veiled critique of racist immigration policies" and "a dream at a time when mainstream filmmakers regularly cast Caucasian actors to play Asian characters." Kim recounts the high interest in Asian culture in the late 1950s; also on Broadway at the time were *Rashomon, The World of Suzie Wong, A Majority of One,* and *Kataki*. She concludes that though *Flower Drum Song* "is often written off as corny, stereotyped, or patronizing," she admires its "quiet struggle to portray minority issues for a mainstream audience." Furthermore, she claims that in today's racial climate, it "offers us a model from an equally fraught past for resistance and compassion."

Many critics of the time, though, saw condescension in such numbers as "Chop Suey," a celebration of cultural comingling in which the residents of Chinatown perform a square dance, the Charleston, and rock and roll. Wrote *Variety* of the 1961 film, "It is as if we are being asked to note 'how darling' or 'how precocious' it is of them to undertake the execution of American dances . . . to comprehend the science of baseball or to grapple with U.S. idioms." On the stage version, Kenneth Tynan was particularly hard:

> The authors' attitudes toward exotic peoples in general seems to have changed hardly at all since they wrote *South Pacific* and *The King and I*. . . . It seems to have worried neither Mr. Rodgers nor Mr. Hammerstein very much that the behavior of war-torn Pacific Islanders and 19th-century Siamese might be slightly different from that of Chinese residents of present-day California . . . so

> little has it worried them that they entrusted the principal female roles to Japanese actresses. The assumption, which may be justified, is that the audience will not notice the difference.

Rodgers and Hammerstein could not have been happy with this criticism: the team had worked hard and was rightfully proud that of the original cast of fifty-nine actors, only two were non-Asians (one was white and the other Black).

Five decades after the film debut of *Flower Drum Song*, when Kevin Kwan's novel *Crazy Rich Asians* was brought to the screen by director Jon M. Chu, it was still unusual for a big-budget Hollywood film to feature a majority-Asian cast. Cultural journalists remembered that the movie's two cinematic antecedents were *The Joy Luck Club* (1993) and *Flower Drum Song*, which also remained the only Broadway musical with a majority-Asian cast until Sondheim's *Pacific Overtures* (1976) and, after that, the short-lived *Allegiance* in 2015. Even as *Crazy Rich Asians* was heralded as (another) breakthrough for Asian actors, the film took some heat (shades of Tynan) for casting actors with Filipino and Malaysian backgrounds as Singaporean Chinese; it was also criticized for not including other ethnic minorities like Malays and Indians.

Today Rodgers and Hammerstein are frequently mentioned in pieces examining "yellow face" (the casting of white actors in Asian roles). Rodgers waded into this controversy when he commented on the problem of authenticity as it existed in 1958. "This demonstrates one of the wonderful things about theatre audiences," he wrote in his autobiography. "People want to believe what they see on a stage, and they will gladly go along with whatever is done to achieve the desired effect. Ask them to accept Ezio Pinza as a Frenchman, Yul Brynner as a Siamese, or a heterogeneous group of actors as Chinese, and they are prepared to meet you nine tenths of the way even before the curtain goes up."

The debate on authenticity in casting will go on, pitting two salient points against each other: (1) artists should write and represent their own stories; and (2) the very nature of art is nonliteral, and the practice of making imaginative leaps is vital to our understanding of the world. In their commitment to representing other cultures, Rodgers and Hammerstein put themselves on a future generation's firing line, even as they worked to expand their country's view of who is an American.

Born in Los Angeles one year before the musical debuted on Broadway, Hwang thought about revisiting *Flower Drum Song* after seeing Christopher Renshaw's 1996 production of *The King and I.* He received permission from the Rodgers and Hammerstein estates to revamp the book, and he imbued it with a deeper knowledge of Chinese history and culture. Mei Li is no longer a mail-order bride but a refugee from Mao's Cultural Revolution. Since several of the characters are in show business, Hwang has them address the absurdly limited roles available to them in Hollywood. Madam Liang talks of her days as a movie actor when she was nicknamed "Queen of the Oriental Crowd Scenes": "Whenever a Japanese village got bombed, that was me, screaming." When Linda lands her first movie role, it is as "this peasant girl in the Korean War, and when my village gets bombed, I scream." He also transformed the song "Chop Suey" from a celebration of assimilation to a critique of what white visitors to Chinatown expect to see.

Hwang's version opened on Broadway in October 2002 and ran only six months. The show that Rodgers called an "accidental hit" and Hammerstein a "lucky hit" is in truth a lackluster though well-intentioned musical. The show's most impressive aspect is that it attempted to tell a story that many today would say it had no business telling in the first place. But Hwang's impulse to revisit *Flower Drum Song* reveals the debt felt by some artists to those who worked to change the status quo.

CHAPTER TWELVE

No Good Deed

SONDHEIM'S RESPONSES to Hammerstein's work constitute the most productive Oedipal impulse in the history of musical theater. Hammerstein said he'd rather contemplate a tree in summer that is full of green leaves and swaying in the breeze than a bare tree in winter. Sondheim set the tree on fire and danced ecstatically as it burned, and never as much as in 1991's *Assassins*. In this show about the inner lives of presidential killers from John Wilkes Booth to Lee Harvey Oswald, Sondheim offers an antipodal yet somehow equally stirring answer to *Oklahoma!*: as a country we are defined as much by the people left out of the dream promised by the American Songbook. Sondheim's ability to bring a majestic poetry to the racist bile of John Wilkes Booth is, in his hands, not a tribute to an assassin but a eulogy for our own greatness—as a nation, as human beings, whenever and however it is diminished.

Hammerstein lived only to see the start of Sondheim's career. Though he disapproved of his protégé's instinct for biting satire, Hammerstein encouraged him and gave him good advice (e.g., that Sondheim should write the lyrics for *West Side Story* and *Gypsy* even though he wanted to be writing complete scores). The young Sondheim indeed had a strong impulse to critique, and his ire at the pretension and emptiness of certain upper-class households was particularly enflamed by the man who lost as much as he himself did when Hammerstein died—Richard Rodgers.

The one collaboration of Sondheim and Rodgers, in 1965, exposed just how much each man suffered without Hammerstein's spirit of congeniality and collaboration. The rehearsal period for that show, *Do I Hear a Waltz?*, is remembered as one of the most contentious in Broadway history.

By the summer of 1957, Rodgers's drinking was out of control. One night at dinner, playwright Moss Hart kept count as the composer imbibed sixteen scotch and sodas.

As he wrote in his autobiography, Rodgers first noticed signs of a "mystifying illness" around the time *Cinderella* was completed. He had lost interest in work and "barely spoke either to Dorothy or to my children. I simply didn't give a damn about doing anything or seeing anyone." "Because of this, I began to drink," he noted, obscuring the timeline quite significantly. "This never grew to the point of my becoming an alcoholic, but it was a symptom of my emotional condition." The illness originated, he was sure, when he returned to *Pipe Dream* so soon after his cancer diagnosis; maybe he had not fully accepted the loss of part of his jaw. He allowed that this was "an extremely baffling and frightening period of my life." His daughter Mary wrote that he had become "a zombie. Seldom talking, hardly moving, never writing, he was wholly emptied out." Her mother told her, "We're going to have to put him in Payne Whitney." After consulting with a psychiatrist at his Connecticut home, wrote Dick, "we all agreed calmly and rationally" that he would admit himself to the psychiatric clinic for treatment.

According to the composer, he was quickly cured: "Once I was in the clinic, untroubled by problems and pressures, I felt fine. My spirits soon picked up, and before long I was so well adjusted that I became something of a doctor's helper. Dorothy visited me, as did Oscar and a few close friends, but most of the time I read, played cards or chatted with the other patients, some of whom were confined for the same reason. The time passed quickly."

One assumes the clinic administered some form of treatment during Rodgers's twelve-week stay, though the composer gives no details. His experience certainly differed from, say, Marilyn Monroe's, whose psychoanalyst committed her there four years later, when she was thrown into a padded room with barred windows. She wrote plaintively to her teachers Paula and Lee Strasberg, "I'm sure to end up a nut too if I stay in this nightmare. Please help me."

Rodgers was never forthcoming about his inner life. After a fractious upbringing, he longed for a peaceful household; he settled for barring his family access to his intimate emotions. Mary recalled, "Basically he didn't want any kind of unpleasantness with anybody, and he would buy peace at any cost."

Like successful songwriters from George Gershwin to Jim Morrison to Leonard Cohen to Bob Dylan, Rodgers did whatever he decided he needed to in order to produce the music that brought him great wealth and the acclaim of the world. And one of those necessary freedoms, not surprisingly, was to be constantly falling in love (if even for only a day or a week). In a way, it was research. With genius came certain perks, a kind of droit du seigneur, that Rodgers apparently never considered giving up.

In 1990, eleven years after Rodgers's death, Agnes de Mille felt free to speak frankly with Max Wilk: "Dick was an enigma in many ways. I don't think he liked women, you see. Well, he used every woman he could get. . . . I don't think Dick was a homosexual, but he used women in a way that no real man would. Like a piece of toilet paper."

A lot of self-license tends to generate self-disgust, which in Rodgers's case fed depression. The irony must have struck him: here he was playing the delinquent Lorenz Hart role in a collaboration with the universally admired Hammerstein.

It's understandable that Mary Rodgers would try to even the score. In her autobiography, she wrote, "Ockie was no saint, even aside from that long-term affair with Temple Texas. And he was more than kind to me. . . . But a saint? I don't think he was even much of a father." She adds in a footnote, "Maybe you have to be at least a partial monster to clear the path to do great work."

At the time, only his closest friends learned of Rodgers's stay at Payne Whitney. One of them was Clifton Fadiman, a book editor at Simon & Schuster and leading "public intellectual" of his time. He, too, had weathered a depression and wanted to assure Rodgers that such suffering was not at all unusual among the cultured classes. In fact, they kind of owned it. "You must have noticed that longshoremen don't suffer from depression; they suffer from discouragement or frustration or bafflement; but not from the vague constellation of downbeat feelings sometimes oddly known as a 'nervous breakdown,'" he wrote.

Fadiman told Rodgers that he would get over it when he was ready to get over it. His account of his own recovery reveals a white-knuckle approach much like Hammerstein's belief in mind over matter:

> I fell into a profound depression, during which I was good for nothing except the routine work of earning a living. I talked to several analysts, but they did not help me. I tried girls, but that didn't work. I got divorced, which was a good thing for me, but was not the basic solution to my problem. I thought of suicide; I forsook my friends; and (the body always acts in sympathy) I was by a near miracle saved from death from a suppurating appendix. . . .
>
> I re-married—happily—but that marriage, good as it is (just as yours is good) could not cure me, as yours cannot cure you. You may ask what did cure me; and the answer is at once so hard to put into words, and so hard to grasp until you've been through this experience yourself, that it won't make the slightest sense to you.
>
> To put it simply, *I thought myself well*—or well enough to go on with life normally. This thinking involved essentially a revision of the milestone theory of life. I had to stop thinking of myself as a marathon runner, and to think of myself more as a tree or a plant. I had to discover that success, applause, friends, activity—while all good things—somehow failed to live up to their advance notices; and that the only thing that did live up to its advance notices was living inside my own mind and growing without regard to the external signs of progress. In other words, I turned myself, almost by an effort of will, into a half-assed (or maybe a sixteenth-assed) philosopher.

Rodgers responded to this helping hand by concluding he'd been cured and ending the conversation:

> You were pretty accurate in your realization of what had been going on with me for the past few years, but I didn't realize myself what a merry-go-round I'd been on until this summer. I am awfully happy that I realized it when I did and even more pleased that I had the sense and determination to take the steps that led

> me to Payne Whitney. The hospital has done amazing things for me and I am now ready for work and to pick up the threads of a very happy life. Things are clear to me now that I never quite understood with the result that I'll fare better and avoid the possibility of future trouble. Your words to me were deeply encouraging and I can't thank you enough for your kindness and for your friendship.

Growing up in a house of secrets, Mary Rodgers believed in transparency and loved to gossip even with strangers, as she did with me in a 1997 interview for the *Los Angeles Times* in which she merrily announced almost upon arrival that her parents were terrible at parenting. As she related in her oral history, "We were brought up on a myth that this was a tremendously happy marriage, that my father never strayed. It wasn't until I was 25 years old that my mother told me he was an alcoholic. When he had nervous breakdowns, Mommy would say he's had a physical breakdown. It's important for people to know that mental illness is not an irresponsibly acquired social disease. People deserve help. It should not be kept as a deep, dark embarrassing secret."

Agnes de Mille did not see any redemption for Rodgers. "Later when he was sick, he was very gentle," she said. "But don't be fooled—he was never sweet."

And he remained opaque even to those who saw him every day. Lillian Leff, Rodgers's secretary for many years, said she had been around him in every kind of crisis yet still felt she didn't know him. "I've seen him cry," she said. "I've seen him happy, worried, angry, thrilled, even. But never once did I know what was going on inside. With the other man [Hammerstein] I always felt I could help him think, if he needed me, but not with Rodgers."

In his last ten years Rodgers developed a fear of elevators, tunnels, and bridges—the things that connect people to each other.

I don't think that he ever expressed his deepest despair to Hammerstein or to anyone. But I'm sure Hammerstein could see it. In his last months, he told Sondheim he worried about Rodgers; he urged the younger man to consider working with him, although that would mean writing lyrics only. Mary Rodgers expressed a similar concern to her friend Steve. As Sondheim remembered it, after Hammerstein's death Rodgers sent him three or four ideas for musicals to work on together.

Rodgers recalled that after Hammerstein was diagnosed with stomach cancer in 1960, the two men discussed "at great length" what would happen to Rodgers. "He was wonderful about this, the way he was about everything," Rodgers said. "And he felt that I ought to work with someone young. He said, 'Somebody young will give you energy, new ideas, direction. You will give somebody young experience.'"

While this does sound like classic Hammerstein generosity, I can't help but wonder, given what happened, if his suggestion could also have sprung subconsciously from a malevolent impulse (such as the lyricist sometimes displayed in his practical jokes).

It was Sondheim's friend Arthur Laurents, playwright and librettist for *West Side Story* and *Gypsy*, who brought the men together. His idea was to musicalize his 1952 play *The Time of the Cuckoo*, a project he had offered to Rodgers and Hammerstein without success in 1958. Sondheim recalled that Laurents convinced him to do the show by saying "it would be easy to write" and that, with Rodgers's name attached, they would make "a ton of money." Sondheim thought, "Great, I can pay off my promise to Oscar and have the pleasure of working with Arthur again. It made me feel noble to sublimate my need to write music in order to support [Hammerstein's] forlornly abandoned partner." Later the composer saw that "those are all reasons never to write a musical. It had no reason to be. The only reason to write is for love."

Laurents's original play is similar in plot to Tennessee Williams's first novel, *The Roman Spring of Mrs. Stone* (1950), in which an American woman in her fifties goes to Italy, finds romance (with, in Williams, a young hustler or, in Laurents, an age-appropriate married man with a large family), and ultimately must confront both the American-European culture gap as well as her own demons. Laurents has more sympathy for his protagonist, Leona, than Williams had for his, a woman he subjects to life-threatening degradation, but both works share a vicarious pleasure in the vulnerability of a female who feels she is losing her beauty and youth. While in Williams there is nothing in store for her other than humiliation and death, Laurents at least allows Leona the recognition that even fleeting happiness is worth pursuing.

The original production of Laurent's *Cuckoo,* directed by Harold Clurman and starring Shirley Booth, got good reviews and ran a respectable 263 performances. It would be remembered as one of Booth's finest stage roles. Laurents later rewrote the scenario for a 1958 production at the Sheridan Square Playhouse featuring a significantly younger Leona (played by the thirty-three-year-old Kathleen Maguire) who was not as scandalized by her European lover's idea of romantic attachment (which includes guilt-free sex outside of marriage). In the Laurents-Sondheim-Rodgers musical version, *Do I Hear a Waltz?*, Leona remained younger. They cast Elizabeth Allen, an attractive woman in her thirties, and the story morphed once more into a musical about taking chances. It depicts American marriage as a rather gauche affair.

In his autobiography Rodgers recounts that he thought it would be "especially challenging" to work with someone as "thoroughly trained in music" as Sondheim. Indeed, it was. At a vulnerable time, Rodgers joined forces with two collaborators who were not well intentioned toward him and who mercilessly recounted his decline to others.

Recalling his agreement to work with Rodgers, Sondheim said, "I hadn't taken into account the corrosive conviction that his creative powers were failing, that the well had run dry. This manifested itself in his refusal to rewrite, a stubborn ploy to cover his imagined infertility." In fact, Sondheim didn't find the infertility at all imagined. His assessment was that "the adventurous grace of the music [Rodgers] has written for *Oklahoma!* and *Carousel* was now rarely available to him."

The men entered the conception phase of the project already at loggerheads. Sondheim came up with a music-related theory about Leona in an effort to spur new song ideas. He suggested that she was essentially "a girl who can't sing." This was "greeted with a dull thud, and I know why," Sondheim said. "You can't do that kind of story with just song. You've to got to do it as a semi-opera." Regardless of whether this is true (or what it means), the suggestion was not one that helped Rodgers: "Dick thought in terms of song. And to him it was impossible to have a leading lady who didn't sing. He didn't have that kind of imagination."

We can't know exactly how Rodgers related the story. But after spending a long evening with Richard and Dorothy, Josh Logan wrote that Steve's behavior was "appalling at best." He referred to the subject in a 1979 letter to Dorothy Rodgers: "When I think of the adversities he has faced in his personal and professional life—the loss of Larry, then Oscar, the stupidity of some of his collaborators who did not draw on his great wisdom, humor, strength and knowledge, is something that I can scarcely believe when I think back on it. The way Stephen Sondheim treated him and almost ignored Dick's opinion, is one of the ghastliest stories I have ever heard in my life."

Interestingly, Laurents, in his 2011 book *The Rest of the Story,* used identical phrasing to describe Rodgers's treatment of Sondheim—"appalling at best."

In the 2013 HBO documentary *Six by Sondheim,* the composer offered another harsh assessment. It contains some truth but fails to give Rodgers credit for the emotional power of his work with Hammerstein: "I finally came to understand that the Rodgers and Hammerstein revolution was essentially Hammerstein's. Rodgers was an archconservative; his idea of innovation consisted of gimmick, such as having all the action take place within the confines of a theater [*Me and Juliet*], or eliminating strings and having the orchestra wander through the show [*No Strings*], both notions of his and both cosmetic experiments dictated not by content but by whim."

Sondheim's assessment of Hammerstein was correspondingly positive. "People do not understand that Oscar was an experimental playwright, that his major contribution is not the songs but the playwriting," he said. "My entire generation of songwriters, [Jerry] Bock and [Sheldon] Harnick and [John] Kander and [Fred] Ebb, is based on what he encouraged us to do."

As was his way, Laurents offered the most brutal version of the story. He understood that Rodgers took it "as a great insult" that Sondheim had to be convinced to work with him. When the three collaborators met in Rodgers's private office in his New York townhouse, Laurents reported, Rodgers "went to the bathroom, locked the door and, as silently as he could, lifted the top off of the water tank. . . . There was a vodka bottle in there." This means, one assumes, that Laurents himself listened at the door, or checked for the evidence, or both. Laurents also said that when they were trying out the show in Boston at the Colonial Theater, "Jerry Whyte, Dick's man Friday, would guard the bathroom door so Dick could drink."

Then there was the day the whole company gathered to hear a new song the men had written for the shopkeeper's "stupid wife," said Laurents: "Dick had already played the melody for the company to applause. Steve came in and handed Dick the lyric. Dick read it. His face reddened and he flipped the lyric to the floor. 'I'm not going to let my singers sing shit like this!' Everybody froze."

Sondheim descended the steps from the stage, shouting, "I've had it. I'm not taking any more notes from him. I'm leaving." Later Rodgers issued an edict that Laurents was not allowed backstage, not even to rehearse the actors. Why ban Laurents? We don't know; his account of course edits out whatever he did to inflame the situation. (According to Mary Rodgers, "talent excuses almost anything except Arthur Laurents.")

Adding to the pileup of disasters, the cocaine-using British director John Dexter had eyes only for the men in the cast; whenever he had to direct a female chorus member he could never remember her name, saying, "Miss, you go over there" (according to Craig Zadan's dishy 1974 book *Sondheim & Co.*).

Rodgers saw his collaborators ganging up against him: "The more we worked on the show, the more estranged I became from both writers. Any suggestions I made were promptly rejected, as if by prearrangement."

Sondheim could not help poking at the conflict. He wrote "We're Gonna Be Alright," sung by a gossipy couple about another couple whose marriage is a sham, even though it may look perfect from the outside. (Sondheim did not allow me to reprint the lyrics, but they are easily looked up.)

In his book *Finishing the Hat,* Sondheim relates that Rodgers at first loved the lyric's acidity, which reminded him of Hart, and he gave Sondheim a smile and a hug—"both gestures unusual for him, especially if you were a man." Rodgers took home the lyric and showed it to Dorothy, who immediately recognized that it was aimed at them. "I could picture Dick enthusiastically showing her the lyric and her response, which must have dwarfed Krakatoa for explosiveness," recalled Sondheim. (The composer obviously enjoyed tormenting the couple; I have a pet theory that the reason Joanne, the character in *Company* who sings "The Ladies Who Lunch," is so angry is because [a] she's afraid she's one of them and [b] it's a portrait of Dorothy Rodgers.)

The hostility was such that it could not be kept from a *New York Times* reporter who came to the Rodgers apartment to interview him and Sondheim about their collaboration. The charitable headline on the November 1964 piece read "Long Time Friends Aim for Broadway Early Next Year." In the story's second paragraph, Rodgers's knife was already out: "'The first

The creators at a rehearsal for *Do I Hear a Waltz?*—Richard Rodgers (*left*), Stephen Sondheim (*middle*), and Arthur Laurents (*right*).
Courtesy of Photofest

time I saw him,' [Rodgers] said with a mischievous gleam, 'was when I was working on "Oklahoma!" in 1942. I watched him grow from an attractive little boy to a monster.'"

Rodgers and Sondheim learned many things from Hammerstein, but getting along with others was not one of them. The younger composer's friendship with Arthur Laurents later collapsed as well. The famously vitriolic Laurents put forth a variety of reasons for its demise over the years. Reading between the lines, one can speculate that Laurents resented that his most famous work would always be associated with his old friend while the same could not be said of Sondheim.

Sondheim's relationship with Oscar and Dorothy Hammerstein was one of the most loving in his life. In a famous story from the time shortly before Hammerstein's death, the family and some close friends gathered for a lunch at the townhouse on Sixty-Third Street. As Sondheim recalled it for biographer Meryle Secrest, Hammerstein had made two piles of formally posed photographs of himself, and "he invited us to choose one. And I felt very peculiar, because he was a surrogate father to me, but I wanted to have one. And I asked him to sign it. And of course, because our relationship had been so close, he looked baffled as to how to sign it. And everybody else went into the dining room and he stood there trying to think and suddenly he got a smile on his face like the cat that ate the canary. And he scribbled something on the corner of the picture, and then looked at me rather smugly and went into the dining room. And I read it, and it said—and here Sondheim's voice breaks, and there is a pause—'for Stevie, my Friend and Teacher.'"

Hammerstein had given the youthful composer notes on his work throughout his life. *Climb High* was the fourth and the last of the "assignments" he had suggested to Sondheim to hone his skills. The task here was to write an original musical. (The previous ones had been to adapt a play he liked [*Beggar on Horseback*], a play he liked but thought flawed [*High Tor*], and a work of literature [*Mary Poppins*].) *Climb High,* which Sondheim began during his senior year of college, tells the story of Norman, an unproduced playwright who keeps "body and soul together by turning out jingles for TV commercials," and his best friend David, an aspiring actor who also has big ambitions: "I'll be famous and successful and admired and all the other things people try so hard not to care about. I want people to know who I am. I want the whole world to know." To help raise money for Norman's play, David throws a party for some socialites he knows through his parents who have made a fortune in insurance (probably a stand-in for haberdashery, the business of Sondheim's mother, Foxy, and father, Herbert). Norman describes the guests as "this collection of large wallets and tiny minds."

Hammerstein edited a draft of the musical and wrote detailed margin notes. As you might imagine, he was not a fan of the spiteful edge and recommended in a letter that Sondheim tone it down:

> Dear Stevie:
>
> Regarding "Climb High," not only did we like the original conception, but only a couple of months ago when you re-stated your theme it sounded good then. At the time I suggested that it was perhaps your prologue that started us off not liking the boy, whereas if you told the story in its proper chronology, without flashbacks, you could get the audience to like him and go with

> him, as with a son, and be anxious when he went off track and wish that he would go back on the track all throughout the play. Then it would be taking the form of a conventional "race." I think as I look back on it that you have fallen down badly with your other characters. There is nothing wrong with telling the story that you set out to tell, but it is wrong if you don't like or care about the character, or about any other characters with whom he comes in contact. They all seem shallow wisecracking young people. I don't think a play should be filled only with nice people, but it is good to have a variety, and some characters who are foils for others.

This debate went on. Sondheim must have called Hammerstein on his objections. A later Hammerstein letter, quoted by Steve Swayne in *How Sondheim Found His Sound,* went further: "My basic irritation lies in my deep faith in you and in your future. This faith is endorsed and substantiated by so much of the good writing that has been put into this play. What I resent is the story itself and characters. They are getting far better treatment than they deserve, and so whatever irritation I have against the play is felt on behalf of the author, not on my own behalf."

The letter hints at the kind of irritation a father might feel for a son. And just as a child will carve out his own path, Sondheim was greatly interested in unlikeable characters and outsiders, as would befit an artist of his generation. In a sense he was fascinated not by how the American dream could flourish but how it would diminish.

I spoke with Sondheim about Hammerstein; like his mentor, he was generous that way. On the evening I visited his townhouse on East Forty-Ninth Street, PBS was rebroadcasting *Sweeney Todd*—not the Tim Burton movie but the filmed stage version starring Angela Lansbury and George Hearn, the actor who replaced Len Cariou in the title role on Broadway (I had seen the original production twenty-two times; I was young and obsessed). On Sondheim's lap was his large poodle Willie, ecstatic to be let out of whatever room he had formerly been confined in. The dog was now canoodling with his human, rolling on his back and staring adoringly up from Sondheim's lap. "For me, Len Cariou will always be Sweeney Todd," I told Sondheim. His answer was quick: "That's because Len Cariou could actually kill someone." His narrow eyes gleamed. "George Hearn is like this dog." He looked down, saying, "KILL, WILLIE! KILL!" The dog gazed sweetly back, tongue hanging out.

Sondheim was an entertainer and tremendously fun to talk to. He was obviously brilliant and wickedly witty. Once, when he was still in his enfant terrible stage—around the time of *Company* (1970), *Follies* (1971), and *A Little Night Music* (1973)—he seemed to wear a perpetual sneer in public, almost like a teenager. In recordings you can hear his interlocutors laugh eagerly at his usually barbed jokes; they know they are always one misstep away from being called an idiot or shot a glance that said the same thing. Sondheim did not hide his disdain, especially for anyone who considered him primarily a lyricist or used the word "hummable" to describe his melodies. (When I told him that my husband was not a fan of musicals, he said, with a little too much enthusiasm, "How does he *stand* you?")

In one 1973 interview with *CBS Evening News,* a sullen, forty-three-year-old Sondheim draws deeply on a cigarette and looks as if he owns no shampoo. Everything about his aura suggests nicotine was not the only drug he was consuming at this time. He's talking about his father, Herbert, saying, "He was the most liked man in the dress industry but not the most successful, and they go together, I think," sneaking a sideways glance at the journalist to see if he gets it (the point being that while he, Sondheim, may not be the most likeable or popular composer in the world, he might be the best).

He was revered by those "in the know," but his shows were not moneymakers, a sore point for him as he watched other composer-lyricists such as Jerry Herman and Stephen Schwartz score lifelong paydays for *Hello, Dolly!* and *Godspell,* respectively. In financial terms, it looked as if he would never enter the rarified realm of his surrogate father. At this time Sondheim was younger than most of his critics and aesthetically ahead of them. They tended to meet his innovations with stony disapproval. When Sondheim debuted *Follies* (with a book by James Goldman), his most ambitious and innovative work thus far, establishment reviewers were not amused, moved, or even entertained by its depiction of middle-aged emptiness. The *New York Times* had two critics on the job. Clive Barnes called Sondheim "a Hart in search of a Rodgers. . . . His words are a joy to listen to, even when his music sends shivers of indifference up your spine." Walter Kerr said the show was "intermissionless and exhausting, an extravaganza that becomes tedious. . . . Ingenuity without inspiration." The only critic who seemed to comprehend the show's complexities was a Harvard senior named Frank Rich. Writing in the *Crimson,* Rich said that "it is a measure of the show's brilliance (and its brilliance is often mind boggling) that it uses a modern musical form, rather than the old fashioned one that the Follies helped create, to get at its concerns." When Rich became chief drama critic at the *Times* in 1981, Sondheim at last had an Atkinson to his Hammerstein—a powerful voice who understood what he was doing and wanted him to succeed.

Sometime after his heart attack in 1979, a healthier and sunnier Sondheim emerged, characterized by a trimmed beard, silver hair hanging jauntily over his forehead, and a gleaming smile. By this point he had written *Sweeney Todd,* an angry masterwork that seemed to release some of his pent-up fury. At the same time, mainstream critics were finally acknowledging his genius.

In her book Meryle Secrest relates a revealing incident from this time. Sondheim was pleased by the ease with which he wrote the first seven songs in *Sweeney Todd.* He was wondering why Judy Prince (married to Hal), who was usually the first audience for his songs, had not asked how his new score was going. "Oh, you know me and murder mysteries," she explained. He assured her that *Sweeney* was not a murder mystery, and she came over to his place to hear the music. "I played two bars," Sondheim told Secrest, "and she fell off the chair and she said, 'Oh God, I didn't know this is what it was about.' I said, 'Yeah, it's Grand Guignol.' She said, 'It has nothing to do with Grand Guignol. It's the story of your life.'"

Once the terribly wronged Sweeney figures out his life philosophy—that in a corrupt universe he is free to act as he likes—he flings off years of depression and victimhood. In fact, he elevates his lust for revenge into a form of justice and something of an art. He is no longer crushed by life; he crushes life. In this show Sondheim transforms what used to be a sneer at authority and mediocrity into a howl of pain and passion that approaches Greek tragedy. Only funny.

Judy Prince's insight helped me understand why I was so obsessed by the original production. *Sweeney Todd* is Sondheim at his highest pitch, emotionally speaking. It's a personal triumph because Prince was right: it is his life, the great injustice in his case being a malignant mother, who once wrote to him, "The only regret I have in life is giving you birth." When I venture this opinion, Sondheim merely smiles and says, "The difference between Sweeney and me is that I turned it into art."

In 1983 Sondheim joined up with a writing partner and director nineteen years his junior, James Lapine, who took him into his mature phase. Their first musical, *Sunday in the Park with George,* was literally about making art: the first act focused on the painter Georges Seurat (referred to in the play as George) and the second on his great-grandson (also named George and also an artist). For Frank Rich, this was the show in which Sondheim was "at last" able to "channel his own passion into a musical that is not about marriage, class inequities or other things he doesn't seem sincerely to care about, but is instead about what does matter to him—art itself, and his own predicament as a driven artist whose austere vision, like Seurat's, is often incorrectly judged as heartless."

The two artists depicted in *Sunday* were men characterized by "straightforward, unembarrassed goodness," Sondheim told Rich, though probably no one else on earth would describe the two brooding, uncommunicative Georges in such terms. Still, while writing them, Sondheim said, "I discovered the Hammerstein in myself—and I was the better for it."

Hammerstein himself confessed he was not interested in writing about sophisticates living in high-rise apartments. (When he does, as in *Allegro,* they are hypochondriacs, or as in *Me and Juliet,* they have little on their minds but petty inconveniences.) He believed that sophistication was both a pose and a way of cutting oneself off from life. Pushing back against the Kenneth Tynans of the world, he said, "In my book, there's nothing wrong with sentiment because the things we're sentimental about are the fundamental things in life, the birth of a child, the death of a child or of anybody, falling in love. I couldn't be anything but sentimental about these basic things. I think to be anything but sentimental is being a poseur."

In a letter to Dorothy written while they were waiting for her divorce to come through in the early months of 1929, Hammerstein shared a more personal and visceral plea for the "primitive": "For God's sake, as we lead our cosmopolitan lives among the sophisticates of all nations don't forget what I really love about you. Let us stay low and primitive, even if I have to buy a sailor suit and every once in a while take you to a two shilling room in a waterfront pub."

As Sondheim matured, Hammerstein was not at all embarrassed to seek guidance from his brilliant young friend. He admitted to being baffled by "modern" music. Sondheim gave him a recording of a Maurice Ravel trio and followed it throughout the years with increasingly contemporary-sounding pieces. "I never got him quite as far as *Wozzeck,* but by the time he died seventeen years later, I'd led him through Prokofiev and into the thickets of Stravinsky," he said.

Hammerstein was particularly interested when the twenty-eight-year-old Sondheim went into analysis. As a person who believed he could handle grief without outside help, Hammerstein was curious about other modes of coping. Sondheim recalled:

> Each time we'd meet he'd ask pointed, if considerately impersonal, questions. Was it painful? Did childhood experience really leave scars? Did I feel any change? I don't think he was considering therapy for himself, but I think he was looking for insights through osmosis; he hoped that my fumbling attempts at self-exploration would help to explain things about himself that he had never understood. Among them were his conflicted feeling about his collaborator and the relationship between work and sex—he had never been so intimate with me, and it wasn't merely the result of my having grown to personal and professional manhood that made it possible; the analysis was a bond between us, almost a secret.

Sondheim's career was in a sense a continuing conversation with Hammerstein. He took notes and career advice from his mentor, and he certainly followed Hammerstein's rule of not repeating himself as an artist. In fact, Sondheim wrote one of his great songs on the importance of this—"Move On" (again, you will have to look up the lyric).

He also scatters throughout his work references to, or echoes of, Hammerstein that fans have fun spotting. For instance, in *Follies,* a young couple teases each other. The man sings, "I may play cards all night / And come home at three," to which the woman answers with Ado Annie's joke from *Oklahoma!:* "Just leave a light / On the porch for me." Then they both sing, "Well, nobody's perfect," a wink at Sondheim's tiny theft.

Like Hammerstein in *Me and Juliet,* Sondheim skewered the talk of first-nighters and showbiz folk in his 1981 musical *Merrily We Roll Along.* Whereas Sondheim's characters are bitchy, shallow, and insincere, Hammerstein's are less snide and perhaps less bright, as in this bit from "Intermission Talk" where they simply long for the good old days:

> They don't write music any more
> Like the old Vienna valses!
> The guy today who writes a score
> Doesn't know what schmaltz is.

That Hammerstein wrote a lot of that schmaltz with Sigmund Romberg and Rudolf Friml was a gentle jibe at both the chatterers as well as himself. Sondheim wrote an addendum to the joke in *Merrily*. Producer Joe Josephson instructs a young composer to write something "hummable," advice that Sondheim himself detested. To demonstrate the kind of music he wants to hear, Joe hums the melody of *South Pacific*'s "Some Enchanted Evening." Critics and producers, it seems, are always stuck in the past.

Follies, about a reunion of actors who worked in a Ziegfeld Follies–type show in the 1920s and '30s, offered Sondheim a chance to show off his virtuosity and write songs in the style of Hammerstein's early career. *Follies,* according to Frank Rich, was

> at once the seminal Sondheim-Prince musical and a dead end. The show's climactic phantasmagoric flashback sequence was a rite of exorcism. Sondheim filled it with songs in the style of old-time musical comedy numbers by Kern and Hammerstein, and others; then, at the sequence's conclusion, he blended them all together in a nightmarish aural-visual spectacle of dissonance and chaos. Both in form and substance, "Follies" seemed to be saying that the musical theater's old traditions were as unsalvageable as the gutted, ghostly theater in which "Follies" was set. But, having made this statement, neither Sondheim, Bennett nor Prince seemed to know how to move beyond those traditions.

Follies also showed a Sondheim still aching to reveal the inner rot of outwardly successful lives. Foxy and her society friends may have been the original models for these worthies, but the ultimate targets had since become Richard and Dorothy Rodgers, whom Sondheim described as "dedicated homophobes."

Following again in the footsteps of Hammerstein and *The King and I,* in 1976 Sondheim wrote (with John Weidman) a musical about the Westernization of an Asian nation, specifically Matthew Perry's use of gunboat diplomacy to open Japan to trade with the West in 1853. This, again, is a concept musical—as if written by a Japanese playwright familiar with American musicals. Sondheim was more adept than his mentor at translating Asian culture with real sensitivity. A good example is the song "Poems," in which two Japanese men on a walking journey pass the time tossing verses back and forth. But the score's real gem, "Someone in a Tree," is a unique song ostensibly about what happened in the treaty house between Commodore Perry and the Japanese leaders. But more than that, it's about the pure joy of boyhood and being a small part of history (one thinks of the twelve-year-old Sondheim being at the house in Doylestown at the time of *Oklahoma!*'s creation). In the end, the thesis of *Pacific Overtures* was opposite to that of *The King and I*—Sondheim asks the audience to consider what was lost when Japan abandoned its ancient, more contemplative culture, whereas Hammerstein saw modernization only as a healthy evolution toward democracy and fairness.

Finally, there is an actual, literal psychic connection between Sondheim and his mentor. In Hammerstein's notes at the Library of Congress I found a scribbled thank-you speech for an award from the Father's Day Council (apparently a thing in 1959). In the late spring, only four months before his death, he wrote:

All I know could be
Written on one page. . . .

Instead of concentrating
on guiding your children's
Lives, concentrate on
Guiding your own life

They watch you. They
Don't listen very hard
When you give them advice.

But they listen
When you are talking
To other people.

This passage is closely mirrored in "Children Will Listen" from *Into the Woods*—though, as Sondheim told me, he was unaware of the connection.

Two months before he died in November 2021, Sondheim read through some of the correspondence that Mark Horowitz collected for his then-upcoming book *The Letters of Oscar Hammerstein II*. In an email to Horowitz he wrote, "Thanks so much, Mark. What a generous man he was. To write so many letters that actually went into detail about the art and the craft (and life itself) was a time-consuming job. Reading these makes me feel proud and privileged to have known him. And sad that he isn't around. How I wish he were alive so that he could see how I've followed his principles (or not). —Steve."

CHAPTER THIRTEEN

A Kind of Profundity

IN THE HAMMERSTEIN PAPERS at the Library of Congress there are many drafts of well-known lyrics that can teach any writer about the importance of revision, but this one is my favorite. On a slip of paper, in pencil, is written:

Doe is a ~~very~~ word
For feminine ~~female~~ deer
Ray is a very bright light
Me is what I call myself
Fa with an R very long way

It's always good to remember that someone sweated over lines that now seem effortless and inevitable.

Here's another draft:

Raindrops on roses and whiskers on kittens,
Curling my finger in warm woolen mittens,
Riding down hill on my big brother's bike—
These are a few of the things that I like.

Hammerstein also labored over a number that was misguidedly cut from the 1965 *Sound of Music* film, which he did not live to see. Captain von Trapp returns from his honeymoon to find he's been called to report for duty to the new Austrian government, now run by the Nazis, to whom he is adamantly opposed. "No Way to Stop It" is an attempt by the Captain's fiancée, Elsa, and their friend Max to convince him of the futility of his opposition. It raises the most urgent moral question posed by the show: how do people decide that they will do nothing in the face of sudden and terrifying violence such as the Nazis unleashed in the Anschluss?

Perhaps to bring the dilemma home to Americans, Hammerstein's first titles for the song were "City Hall" and "Play Safe!" In early drafts, he employed Reich-related imagery, such as "brown shirt" and "barbed wire" but decided in the end to drop these specific details, thereby broadening the song's relevance. Elsa's opening salvo to the Captain—"You dear attractive dewy-eyed idealist / Today you have to learn to be a realist"—recalls Hammerstein's annoyance at being labeled a dreamer during his World Federalist period. Often, he would turn the argument around and say it was those who refused to see the nuclear threat that lived in a kind of a fantasy. He rejected the definition of a "realist" as someone who sides with whatever is the most likely outcome; he believed that human society is shaped by what the greatest number of people decide it will be. "I have no patience, for instance, with people who say, 'There will always be wars,'" Hammerstein said in a 1949 speech at Missouri's Drury College, which bestowed on him an Honorary Doctorate of Law. "I don't believe there will always be wars. I do admit, however, that if enough people believe that there will always be wars, then, of course, there will be. The reiteration of such a tragic fallacy is of no use to us."

His argument on nuclear disarmament is relevant to today's equally urgent arguments about climate survival, as well as the alarming rise of new authoritarian leaders across the globe. In a 1950 speech for the Federalists Hammerstein said that "as a citizen living in this world today, you have no right not to do anything at all." He continued:

> I am convinced that if this world is to be saved from the destruction that modern warfare promises, it will be saved by the people whom hard-headed men call dreamers. . . . As you may have gathered, I am tired of this practical man, with the hard head—and a soft brain. I am tired of his patronizing smile when he calls me an idealist. He has a good-natured and tolerant way of disposing of you, by merely calling you an idealist, and in his kindly

eyes there is an implication that he will forgive you, but that he has some secret that you don't know, because he is a practical man and you are not. All right, I am willing to believe this. Only, let him roll around with one practical idea—one plan for meeting the crisis that faces mankind today. And while I am waiting for him, I am going to follow the only course that I can see—the common sense dream of establishing world law to create world order.

In the last years of his life Hammerstein devoted himself to an organization with a more achievable goal than the Federalists, the National Committee against Discrimination in Housing (he joined its board in 1955). He was moved to back the Committee after he discovered that some homeowners in Bucks County were asking their neighbors not to sell their homes to "Negros" and thereby lower the area's real-estate values. In his notes, possibly for a speech he made at a 1954 neighborhood meeting, he wrote of the "traditional panic of the adjoining white property owners" and how "they CREATE the problem because of what they see." Around this time he undertook a letter-writing campaign, asking his long list of contacts to present their thoughts on the racist housing practices that were common in Doylestown and throughout the country. His intent was to start a wide-ranging discussion and to gain access to the private thoughts of his fellow high earners on the issue. He tried several similar approaches; here is one such letter:

Dear Mr. Doe:

Do you believe that the simple fact of a negro family moving into a neighborhood reduces realty values there?

Or do you believe this is an outdated theory that should be and can be exploded now?

Within the past three years, twenty odd miles from my home in Bucks County, Pennsylvania, the United States Steel Corporation has built the largest integrated steel mill in the country. Other plants involving products that use steel are rapidly rising near the mill. Since March 1952, the number of factory jobs in that part of the country has more than doubled. Some twenty thousand new homes have been or are being built to house prospective employ-

> ees. The sale of these homes, however, has been restricted to white residents.

> He summed up the matter further and closed with the following:

> What are your thoughts on this subject? Will you please write and tell me? I know you are busy, but I think we are all obligated to give some time to this question. It must be faced. No thoughtful American in any part of the country can afford not to face it. We cannot stand by and let the matter of segregated housing drift on as it has in the new and important industrial area recently established in Bucks County, Pennsylvania, U.S.A. Something must be done to avert a repetition of a mistake so tragically unjust as this one.

In "No Way to Stop It," Hammerstein gives us his best guess about the thinking of people who decide to do nothing in the face of racism, fascism, or any obvious injustice. Elsa and Max believe that the Nazis will prevail no matter what they or the Captain chose to do; Hitler's rise is as inevitable as the pull of the sun and the moon:

> A crazy planet full of crazy people,
> Is somersaulting all around the sky.
> And every time it turns another somersault,
> Another day goes by.
> And there's no way to stop it,
> No, there's no way to stop it.
> No, you can't stop it even if you tried.
> So, I'm not going to worry,
> No, I'm not going to worry,
> Every time I see another day go by.

In this song Hammerstein depicts the liberating force of selfishness, an idea that gives this song its special flavor. Its mood is jaunty—not joyful exactly, but certainly high-spirited. It picks up speed and builds to a mad exuberance:

> And there's no way to stop it.
> No, there's no way to stop it,
> And I know, though I cannot tell you why.

Just as long as I'm living,
Just as long as I'm living,
There'll be nothing else as wonderful as I.
I! I! I!
Nothing else as wonderful as I!

One thinks back to how Hammerstein the cosseted child was made to feel about himself: "The little atom swirling around among millions of atoms very much like himself [who] must be given the illusion that they are not so like himself, that he is something very special, worth promoting, worth perfecting, worth building up to that position of prominence and achievement." But whereas this perspective allowed the child to feel safe and confident, it allows Max and Elsa to believe that the Anschluss "has nothing to do with me."

Finally, one also wonders if Hammerstein thought back to (or even subconsciously made use of) his HUAC experience. Did he allow himself to feel a pang of guilt over his refusal to help the twenty-four-year-old student Alan McGowan, who asked him to stand up and say publicly, "This committee violates the rights of all people called before it"? At that moral crossroads, he hid behind some very proper-sounding words: "I have many times disapproved of some of the procedures of the House Un-American Activities Committee. I believe, however, that for a group of citizens to attempt to stop its hearings is not only hopeless, but highly improper, and I will not lend my name to any such project."

Perhaps he thought of his own failings when the Captain proudly sings, "I will not bow my head to the men I despise!" and his friend Max answers, "You don't have to bow your head—just stoop a little."

The Sound of Music was the first Rodgers and Hammerstein musical for which Hammerstein had no hand in the book. Recovering from gall bladder surgery in the summer of 1958, he was happy to have someone else lay the story's pipes. Howard Lindsay and Russel Crouse created a draft in which they shrewdly altered key points in Maria von Trapp's story to fashion the tale we all know. They turned the Captain from a warm father into a cold one, thereby making Maria's job as caretaker more daunting. They also redated the couple's marriage to the brink of the Anschluss (in fact it had occurred in 1927, eleven years earlier). Lastly, they fabricated a dramatic family escape by having the von Trapps slip out at night after a concert and cross the Alps into Switzerland (in real life they boarded a daytime train to Italy).

In March 1959, Rodgers and Hammerstein started working from the writers' sixty-page treatment. The first songs Hammerstein penned were "The Sound of Music" and "Climb Ev'ry Mountain." Rehearsals began in late August. In September, suspecting an ulcer, Hammerstein's doctor sent his patient for tests. This was how Hammerstein learned he had cancer. The malignant tumor was removed on September 21 at New York Hospital.

According to Mary Martin, Hammerstein showed up at the stage door of the Lunt-Fontanne Theater on September 18, about a month before the show's opening. "I wrote a little couplet and I really don't know where it's going to go in the show because I haven't thought past this, but I'd like you to have it," he said, handing her a slip of paper. "Don't look at it now. Look at it later." And with that, he left.

Written on the paper were the following lines:

A song is no song
Till you sing it
A bell is no bell
Till you ring it
And love in your heart
Isn't put there to stay
Love isn't love
Till you give it away.

Though the lyric arrived a few days short of Hammerstein's diagnosis, Martin believed it was inspired by a closeness to death. It has the force of an epiphany.

In a 1950 letter to Billy, Oscar imagined himself as an old man, free of responsibility and able to enjoy himself like a child again. He saw himself as "lean and slippered pantaloon with white hair, wearing tweeds whose cut has become out of date, sitting on the porch watching the younger people playing tennis and receiving my sons and daughters when they come to visit me, and listening to them tell me of their doings in the great world outside." That old age was not to be.

Hammerstein was operated on by Dr. Frank Glenn, chief surgeon at New York Hospital. Dorothy and the children gathered to await the outcome. Alice recalled that Dorothy wore a bright red coat, as if to ward off bad news. The Hammerstein children watched as the doctors spoke to Dorothy at the end of a corridor, and they saw her body slump when she got the diagnosis. Oscar had stage 4 carcinoma; they had removed more than half of his stomach.

Hammerstein stayed in the hospital until October 4 and was too ill to attend the show's pre-Broadway performance in New Haven. He joined the company in Boston, where the creators agreed they needed a song to soften the Captain's character and show his love for his homeland. Hammerstein wrote the lyric to "Edelweiss" in six days. It is both the Captain's and Oscar's farewell, perfect in its simplicity, characteristic in its generosity. Just as in the first song he wrote with Rodgers, Hammerstein gives us a protagonist who appreciates the world and feels welcomed by it:

> Edelweiss, edelweiss,
> Every morning you greet me.
> Small and white,
> Clean and bright,
> You look happy to meet me.

It seems fitting that Hammerstein's final lyric was a prayer for his country:

> Blossom of snow
> May you bloom and grow,
> Bloom and grow forever—
> Edelweiss, edelweiss,
> Bless my homeland forever.

Hammerstein saw before he died the first serious eroding of his reputation. For *The Sound of Music,* certain critics wrote the kind of reviews Rodgers and Hammerstein would have been looking for—"the full ripening of these two extraordinary talents" (*New York Journal-American*), "the loveliest musical imaginable" (*New York World-Telegram & Sun*), "there's no doubt that it is a titanic hit" (*New York Mirror*). But most reviewers at least touched on the idea that the team's pioneering spirit was no longer evident; what had been unbearably moving and truthful in their collaboration now left a saccharin residue. "The revolution of the Forties and Fifties has lost its fire," said Brooks Atkinson. "Too sweet for words and almost too sweet for music" wrote the *New York Herald Tribune*'s Walter Kerr.

It is common for friends of an artist who has received a negative review to psychoanalyze the critic, searching for the mental flaw that renders him or her unable to appreciate the brilliance of the work in question. This was the path taken by Sister Gregory Duffy, a Dominican nun and friend of Mary Martin who had advised the creative team through the process of writing *The Sound of Music*. In a kind of condolence letter, Sister Gregory offered this insight into Walter Kerr's resistance to the musical: "No critic comes to a production a disembodied intellect but brings all the elements that compose his personality with him," she wrote. "As you know Walter is a short man and in his college days his features were rather delicate and lacked the rugged masculinity they now reflect. He was a brilliant lad, a born romantic, intensively sensitive to beauty and much more interested in intellectual things than in football teams and such. All this put him a bit on the defensive and on occasion he felt compelled to prove his toughness to his peers—he still does."

Kenneth Tynan, whose resistance to the pair grew ever more disdainful, weighed in for the *New Yorker*: "I confess I never thought I would see the day when the two brave innovators who wrote 'Oklahoma!' would turn out the very kind of musical they had labored so hard, and so successfully, to abolish. But this is what has happened. . . . Listening to 'The Sound of Music' one begins to suspect that the collaborators have succumbed to a sort of joint amnesia and forgotten everything that Broadway learned, partly under their tutelage, in the forties and fifties."

In May of 1961, *The Sound of Music* had its London premiere at the Palace Theatre. *Financial Times* reviewer T. C. Worsley was offended by the show's abundance of children and nuns. He was not one for throat clearing; his review began, "If the public taste is really as debased as the pessimists (and some television producers) suppose, this new Rodgers and Hammerstein musical, at the Palace, will run forever." Scan the rest of the review and out pop such words and phrases as "vulgar," "shameless," "shallow," "ghastly," "disgusting," "torture," and "exploits the Nazi Anschluss as shallowly and nauseatingly as it has treated love, nuns and kiddies." Worsley included a gratuitous appeal at the end: "As a patriotic Englishman, I devoutly hope my countrymen will reject this American show emphatically. It is low, common and vulgar. But I doubt if they will. The combination of sex and nuns is as old as pornography, and as popular; and cute children are known in the profession as certain winners. Mix these two elements together, and you can't go wrong, I'm afraid."

Worsley's compatriots did in fact embrace the show—London's *The Sound of Music* was a bigger hit than its Broadway counterpart and ran for an unprecedented 2,385 performances.

Somehow this review found its way to Rodgers (no doubt despite the best efforts of his wife and his aide-de-camp Jerry Whyte, who usually shielded him from the Worsleys of the world). Unused to contempt, Rodgers went into a tailspin. He penned a letter to Orvil E. Dryfoos, the newly installed publisher of the *New York Times.* Rodgers reminds Dryfoos that they had lunched together along with Hammerstein and some other editors at the paper to discuss the American theater. He then says he is now writing "to express my shock at discovering a dispatch under the name of T. C Worsley from London," seeming to doubt even the veracity of the critic's name. "I automatically assume that you are not aware of the stuff of which Mr. Worsley is made, and I enclose his review of THE SOUND OF MUSIC so that you will know the kind of distortion and viciousness to which he is capable of resorting." Rodgers was not above searching for non-germane reasons for a critic's ire: "The London press, as you must know, is notoriously anti-American, but this review is the nastiest example of it I have ever seen."

Rodgers expected Dryfoos to share his belief that a man who hates *The Sound of Music* should be run out of the industry. Rather like Worsley, Rodgers concludes with an unnecessary fillip: "Perhaps you will return the piece from *The Financial Times* to me after you have seen it as I want to have it in my book for my grandchildren to examine as an example of the dishonesty of the British press. I pray that *The New York Times* will not be a party to it."

As a stringer reporting from London, Worsley had written four pieces about theater for the *Times,* a relationship Rodgers clearly wanted to end. How else are we to interpret "I pray that *The New York Times* will not be a party to it"? In fact, Worsley went on writing for the paper until shortly after Dryfoos's death in May of 1963.

The 1965 film version of *The Sound of Music* underlined all the qualities that inflamed its naysayers. The two numbers that brought a wider perspec-

For the original young audience, *The Sound of Music* film became a shrine to childhood itself.
Courtesy of Photofest and 20th Century Fox

tive to the story—"No Way to Stop It" and "How Can Love Survive?"—were scrapped. Hammerstein fans might mourn this decision; both songs displayed his most sophisticated understanding of the tragicomedy of great wealth. Screenwriter Ernest Lehman and director Robert Wise saw no reason for these piquant songs, as they did not want to shift focus from Julie Andrews and the children.

The tone of the show and that of the film are quite different. On the original cast album, the most moving moments are children singing to a simple guitar accompaniment, or a man offering an aching farewell to his country. The movie, on the other hand, is a string-filled fantasia that underlines every glance, every feeling, and encases it all in a suffocating sureness. You might say it has the subtlety of the Anschluss. But children loved it, and the movie broke box-office records in more than twenty countries. For its original young audience, the baby boomers, *The Sound of Music* became a shrine to childhood itself.

■ ■ ■

Also cut from the film was "An Ordinary Couple," a song in which Maria and the Captain embrace the unexceptional miracle of their love; Wise asked Rodgers to pen a substitute ballad. Rodgers wrote music *and* lyrics for "Something Good," which displays slightly more personality than the song it replaced. Rodgers was also asked to supply another number, for Maria to sing as she journeys from the Abbey to the von Trapp homestead. For this song, the director wanted to film an exuberant travelogue to showcase Salzburg's fountains and public squares. Rodgers turned in "I Have Confidence in Me," a tribute to "I Whistle a Happy Tune" that is twice as long and half as interesting. While "Whistle" is not complex, it allows the listener to see a progression, a space, between laying claim to a belief and taking on that belief as reality:

For when I fool
The people I fear
I fool myself as well.

In Rodgers's hand this becomes:

I must dream of the things I am seeking.
I am seeking the courage I lack.
The courage to serve them with reliance,
Face my mistakes without defiance.
Show them I'm worthy
And while I show them
I'll show me!

These overstated lyrics became the lodestar for one of the most successful musical comedies of the next century, when the parodists Trey Parker, Matt Stone, and Robert Lopez made them mincemeat in *The Book of Mormon.* This musical about musicals essentially tests Hammerstein's belief that the form is elastic enough to handle any horror we might encounter in the world. Scamps that they are, Parker, Stone, and Lopez send their protagonists to Uganda, a country ravaged by poverty and disease, and arm them with nothing but a Hammersteinian can-do attitude. Compared to nuns trying to solve a problem like Maria, these Mormon missionaries are faced with AIDS, female genital mutilation, and warlords. The lyrics of one song, "I Believe," closely imitate Rodgers's imitation of Hammerstein in "I Have Confidence in Me," swapping the phrases "a captain with seven children / what's so fearsome about that?" with "a warlord who shoots people in the face / what's so scary about that?" While it may seem that *Mormon* seeks only to mock the application of platitudes in the face of terrible suffering, in fact it poses a complex question: can faith, goodwill, and perseverance get us through anything the world throws at us? Surprisingly (and despite a comic feint toward "no" in the song "Turn It Off") their answer is yes, the power of belief works even here.

For some critics, it was simply not OK for white men in America to write a comedy set in Africa. In the *New York Review of Books,* the British critic James Fenton took vigorous exception to the raves the musical received in the national press, seeing only the show's "smut and glee": "Most of the [African] inhabitants are suffering from AIDS, which is treated, casually and abruptly, as a big joke." He also listed the moral crimes of the Church of Jesus Christ of Latter-Day Saints, including its long and vivid history of racism (which the musical addresses), as more reasons why *The Book of Mormon* cannot be amusing. The *South Park* creators' comic stylings notwithstanding, this debate abuts critical discussions of whether Hammerstein's persistent optimism about human beings excludes him from the canon of serious artists. For Hammerstein and other writers of musicals, hope and laughter are not only appropriate in this vale of tears, they are the only viable choice.

Parker and Stone were born after *The Sound of Music* movie's theatrical run; however, like all middle-class Americans growing up in the 1970s, 1980s, or 1990s, they had no choice but to know much of it by heart. While critics were busy detesting the film, it always held its child audience rapt, followed by their offspring, and then theirs. To critics, questions like "How do you keep a wave upon the sand?" and "How do you hold a moonbeam in your hand?" seemed treacly metaphors that revealed more about the author's sentimentality than they did about the uncontainable curiosity of youth. But to actual children, these are delightful questions, delightfully posed. Kenneth Tynan was not wrong when he wrote in the *New Yorker* that the show was "for children of all ages, from six to about 11½." He could not foresee the cultural veneration those children would bestow on the musical.

Starting in the late 1960s, *The Sound of Music* fulfilled a purpose unforeseen by Rodgers or Hammerstein: as a balm to the children of what we now call "blended families" (or those about to go in the blender). Partly because of the no-fault divorce laws of the 1970s, divorce rates more than doubled from 1960 to 1980. Approximately half of the children born to married parents in the 1970s were eventually told it was "not their fault."

For any lonely child whose family has been torn asunder by divorce, substance abuse, or worse, *The Sound of Music* offers an irresistible fantasy—lots of siblings and the appearance of a kind stranger with a cute haircut and a guitar who makes everything okay by teaching everyone to sing in harmony. There's a scene in the 2013 musical *Fun Home* in which a child escapes into a fantasy musical number based on her favorite TV show, *The Partridge Family*. In the imagined version of her life, her father stops calling her mother "a stupid cow," and she and her parents and siblings perform an up-tempo number titled "Raincoat of Love." All the child's fears disappear for the duration of that number. That's what *The Sound of Music* did (and maybe still does) for any young person trapped in an untenable situation.

Piling fantasia on top of fantasy, *The Sound of Music*'s healed family works as a team, become singing stars, and outwit the Nazis while an adoring audience clamors for more of them at a music festival.

The Sound of Music was so successful that it saved 20th Century Fox from being brought down by the budgetary fiasco of *Cleopatra*, a $44 million film spectacular that even its star, Elizabeth Taylor, found vulgar. Was there nothing that Rodgers and Hammerstein could not do? Today, adjusted for inflation, *The Sound of Music* is the third-highest-grossing film of all time. It's considered the most successful musical ever filmed.

The "sing-alongs" started in 1999 at the London Gay and Lesbian Film Festival. With audience members dressing up as golden rays of sun or brown paper packages tied up with string, they participated in coordinated sing-alongs in front of movie screens all over the world, including Australia, Holland, Sweden, Norway, Belgium, Switzerland, Malaysia, and, of course, the United States. As the lyrics scroll across the screen, raucous crowds sing, talk back, hiss, and offer all manner of witty comment. To mark the movie's fiftieth anniversary in 2015, the Hollywood Bowl produced its fifteenth sing-along, prompting the *Los Angeles Times* to write, "It was a sell-out. Let me underline that remarkable point. More than 17,000 seats were filled for a half-century-old film that probably 95 percent of the audience had seen multiple times."

For that same anniversary, Lady Gaga performed a medley of the show's songs ("The Sound of Music," "My Favorite Things," "Edelweiss," and "Climb Ev'ry Mountain") at the Academy Awards. With her flaxen tresses flowing down the front of a diaphanous white halter gown, Gaga raised two tattooed arms at the triumphant finish. She cut a twenty-first-century path between parody and veneration, showing that the two can coexist in perfect harmony.

Rodgers and Hammerstein might have been remembered for *The Sound of Music,* the best musical for children ever, if not for André Bishop and Lincoln Center Theater. Over the last two and a half decades, their productions returned the duo to the fore as essential American artists. While in his thirties, the gentlemanly Bishop presided over Playwrights Horizons, a 147-seat off-Broadway theater that was the white-hot center for new American work in the 1980s. He helped launch the careers of James Lapine, William Finn, Wendy Wasserstein, Christopher Durang, A. R. Gurney, and Jon Robin Baitz, developed lifelong artistic relationships, and accumulated a steady stream of prizes (including three Pulitzers). Bishop gave artists space and time to figure themselves out while exerting the right amount of pressure to help them finish. Sondheim and Lapine's *Sunday in the Park with George* had its first home at Playwrights, as did Lapine and Finn's *March of the Falsettos* and *Falsettoland* (which together became *Falsettos*). In 1991 Bishop was named artistic director at Lincoln Center Theater, where he continued producing new plays while at the same time targeting older works for reappraisal. His trio of Rodgers and Hammerstein revivals, all of which I have mentioned in prior chapters—*Carousel* (1994, which began life two years before at London's National Theatre), *South Pacific* (2008), and *The King and I* (2015)—revived three heirlooms in vibrant new settings. The Vivian Beaumont Theater's thrust stage revealed works first viewed in proscenium theaters from never-before-seen angles, literally and figuratively.

As a child, Bishop closely followed theater news after seeing his first show, *Peter Pan* starring Mary Martin. He remembers his mother sitting on their porch in Martha's Vineyard and opening the *New York Times* to a full-page ad announcing the new Rodgers and Hammerstein show, *The Sound of Music*. "They're over," she said as she perused the ad. "They're shot, they're finished."

"My mother could be a negative person," Bishop said in a calm bass voice that tilts always toward understatement. But she took him to the show just a week after it had opened (he recalled the exact date: November 23, 1959). He enjoyed that his mother was wrong about Rodgers and Hammerstein. Additionally, from his producer's brain he recalls that the scene changes took much longer than they do today. (Dorothy Hammerstein remembered that these delays greatly annoyed Oscar.)

The following summer, on that same porch, Bishop read about Hammerstein's death. The boy was struck by a phrase that Rodgers used to describe his loss: "permanently grieved."

"I thought of Oscar as a father figure, tall, ungainly, upper-middle-class-accent, a kind of elegance, a serious person," said Bishop. "Later I came to think of him as a genius." He describes Hammerstein as "the motor" of his collaboration with Rodgers, which reminded me of a comment Hal Prince made to Max Wilk. "Oscar was revolutionary," he said, "and Dick was willing."

By the late 1950s Hammerstein was aware that his aesthetic was becoming passé. In a March 1958 television interview, Mike Wallace confronted the lyricist on two "controversial" aspects of his career: his progressive politics; and the idea that his work was sentimental, irrelevant, and would pass gently into forgotten history like Perry Como or strawberry Jell-O.

The tone of the interview is strikingly different from the friendly chat between Hammerstein and Edward R. Murrow two years earlier. In the black-and-white telecast (available online) Hammerstein looks regal and patient, watching as Wallace pivots from his serious newsman demeanor to hawk his sponsor's product, Parliament cigarettes with the "high-filtration filter"—"Unless the filter on your cigarette is recessed, it's only doing part of the job." Getting back to serious journalism business, Wallace reads aloud Kenneth Tynan's comment "that you and Richard Rodgers are so infatuated with your, quote, love for the trees and earth and the simple life, that you forfeited the civilized virtue of mature wit and urban irony."

"Well, maybe I have," says an unfazed Hammerstein. He is steadfast, looking as if he is posing to have his head etched onto a coin. He continues: "I'm not very interested in urban irony. I'm not that kind of man, I'm not ironic, I'm not very urban. I love trees. I hope I'll never stop loving them. Trees, green meadows, who cannot love them? Doesn't Kenneth Tynan like them? I imagine he does. I know Kenneth Tynan. I think he's a very witty and sound critic himself." It's always a smart policy to praise your attacker.

(I recently spoke to Tynan's daughter Tracy, who said that in fact her father was, at best, only fitfully fond of nature.) Wallace goes on to quote bits of "You'll Never Walk Alone" and "Whistle a Happy Tune" in a singsong rhythm intended to help make his point. He recites:

> Make believe you're brave
> And the trick will take you far
> You may be as brave
> As you make believe you are.

"In a sense, Oscar," asks Wallace, "is this not the same philosophy as that of Dr. Norman Vincent Peale?" referring to the best-selling author of *The Power of Positive Thinking*. On the profundity scale of positive philosophy, from Hallmark to William James, Wallace is suggesting Oscar may be on the lower end. Hammerstein seems pinned to his seat but is not defensive. He answers with quiet conviction: "Maybe it is. I don't care. It's a philosophy I believe in. Both those songs I heartily endorse and wouldn't change of word of either one. I think it's quite a thought that if you whistle to keep up your courage, you'll find that actually you have courage. I think this is important. I think it's got a kind of profundity about it, even."

Hammerstein also offers an eloquent defense of Paul Robeson, with whom he had tussled over the lyrics to "Ol' Man River." Wallace asks for his thoughts on the singer, who had been targeted by federal authorities for supporting "subversive organizations" like the Council on African Affairs:

> I don't accuse Paul Robeson of being a Communist. I don't know whether he is or not, but many people think he is and let's assume that he is. It troubles me to sit as a judge upon Paul, because I think of myself and try to wonder how I would feel if I were the son of a minister, a Phi Beta Kappa student at Rutgers, an All-American tackle, a tall, handsome man, a singer, an actor, an athlete and could not live in the same hotel with the other members of my theatrical troupe. I would be good and sore and I don't know what I might do.

In a letter to Billy, Oscar imagined himself as an old man, free of responsibility and able to enjoy himself like a child again. That old age was not to be.
Courtesy of Photofest

Robeson might have appreciated the support more in the early 1950s when the State Department revoked his passport. (At that time, to be fair, Hammerstein might have taken issue with Robeson's belief that Joseph Stalin had a "deep humanity" and was a force for peace.) Though Hammerstein's backing may have been late in coming, it was exquisitely articulated.

As the critics weighed in after the opening of *The Sound of Music,* the creative team was anxious about the show's fate. They all felt easier on the second night when, watching from the back of the theater, Hammerstein declared, "Make no mistake, this is a smash hit."

And so it was. Hammerstein believed he was completely recovered at the end of 1959, and wrote as much to his friends Walter and Marian Knapp:

> The show has opened in New York and I believe it will be a very big hit. Of course there is no doubt about the next eight months because we are all sold out and there is therefore no doubt about getting our money back. . . . Most of the notices were fine with two exceptions, and at least one, The New Yorker, was really bad, but I've been getting bad treatment from this young man [Kenneth Tynan] for a long time. I don't think that he and I have the same ideas of what a good show is, especially musicals.
>
> Dorothy and I are off to Jamaica next week and never have I looked forward to anything with more relief. . . . I don't expect to do anything except lie on the beach in the morning and play tennis in the afternoon. I am all well again but need some exercise to harden me up. We have grass courts down at Round Hill and they are much more fun to play on and not so hard on these old feet.

After Jamaica, the Hammersteins met the Rodgers in London to oversee a production of *Flower Drum Song* that opened in March of 1960. Hammerstein returned to New York; he took B12 shots for his low energy and kept close to his family. In May his appetite abated. In July, an X-ray showed a recurrence of cancer. After a brief discussion with his wife, he chose not to pursue chemotherapy treatment. He told his doctor, Ben Kean, that between the choice of living longer or "dying on Dorothy's pillow," he wanted the pillow. On July 12, his sixty-fifth birthday, he started an autobiography but did not get far. He scheduled individual lunches with each of his close friends. Though he never expressly laid out the situation, many sensed what was happening. Sondheim recalled their lunch together:

> He took me to his club—I didn't even know he had one. I figured he must have something of particular importance to tell me and kept waiting for him to reveal it. Among other things, we talked about analysis, *The Sound of Music,* my parents, his children, the show I was writing. On the walk home, I tried to figure out the reason for the lunch. To this day I don't know why I was so slow, but I finally got it. It was the elegant and moderate thing to do,

and he'd done it. He'd never come close to saying goodbye, but
he'd been saying goodbye.

Hammerstein had discussions with each of his children. He told Jimmy that he'd had "a very happy childhood," "a terrific middle age," and that "the only thing I'm disappointed in is that I was looking forward to having a really good old age." He also wrote letters to his children to inform them that he would leave 3 percent of his estate (valued at $6.6 million) to Howard Reinheimer, the lawyer who introduced him to Dorothy and who had played the heavy in Hammerstein's toughest negotiations. Forty-nine percent would go to Dorothy and the bulk of the rest of it to his children and stepchildren.

He implored Dorothy not to fall apart when he died; to do so, he said, would be "like having everything in the world and then crying for more."

Days before his death he told Jimmy he was contemplating whether—if he could live life over—he would prefer to be Albert Einstein or Babe Ruth, but he could not decide. Physician Harold Hyman said that Hammerstein had been reciting the names of baseball players just before he died in the early hours of August 23.

While Dorothy waited by herself in a dark room as the undertaker arrived, she says she felt Oscar put his arms around her and say, "Everything is alright."

An outpouring of grief arrived in hundreds of letters and telegrams. Playwright Sidney Kingsley telegrammed Rodgers:

DEAR DICK
WE MOURN THE WHOLE HUMAN RACE
MADGE AND I SEND LOVE MINGLED WITH OUR TEARS

And Edwin Knopf wrote Dorothy, "I am no longer afraid of death. If it is good enough for Oscar, it is good enough for me."

Brooks Atkinson, who had written about Hammerstein's work since the 1920s, added that the theater had "lost a man of character who stood for all that is decent in life."

In his autobiography Rodgers compared the two great losses of his life, the first being Larry Hart: "Oscar's death was the greater blow simply because almost to the day he died everything about him was an affirmation of life."

It seems right to give the last word on the subject to Sondheim. In the early days of September, he wrote a thank-you to his friend Hal Prince, who had sent condolences:

> Thanks for your nice note about Ockie. Everybody else is taking it so well, who am I to wail? It's only self pity that brings on the tears—I've lost something, that's all. When Ockie found out (a month ago) that he was going to die, he said to Dorothy, "If we were to complain now, we'd be poor sports." He had a marvelous life, mostly due to himself, and he shows the way to live if we look—*and* the way to die.

SOURCES

ABBREVIATIONS

LOC	Library of Congress, James Madison Memorial Building, Washington, DC
NYPL	New York Public Library at Lincoln Center, New York
OHII	Oscar Hammerstein II
RR	Richard Rodgers

INTRODUCTION: AN UNFASHIONABLE TAKE ON AN UNFASHIONABLE MAN

Works

Banfield, Stephen. *Jerome Kern*. New Haven, CT: Yale University Press, 2006.

The Bulletin (Sydney), 1930 (exact date unreadable), Hammerstein Collection, LOC.

Carter, Tim. *"Oklahoma!" The Making of an American Musical.* New Haven, CT: Yale University Press, 2007.

Emerson, Ken. *Doo-dah! Stephen Foster and the Rise of American Popular Culture.* New York: Simon & Schuster, 1997.

Esterow, Milton. "Blackout Staged for Hammerstein," *New York Times,* September 2, 1960.

Fordin, Hugh. *Getting to Know Him: A Biography of Oscar Hammerstein II*. New York: Random House, 1977.

Halberstam, David. *The Fifties*. New York: Villard, 1993.

Hammerstein, Oscar, II. Columbia College speech, 1956, Hammerstein Collection, LOC.

Hammerstein, Oscar, II. Notes on a speech, undated, Hammerstein Collection, LOC.

Hughes, Spike, and Barbara McFadyean. *Nights at the Opera*. London: Pilot Press, 1948.

James, William. *Writings, 1902–1910*. New York: Library of America, 1988.

Kaufman, David. *Some Enchanted Evenings: The Glittering Life and Times of Mary Martin*. New York: St. Martin's Press, 2016.

Lindsay, Howard. Eulogy for OHII, August 24, 1960, NYPL.

Lindsay, Howard. "Oscar Hammerstein," *Saturday Review*, September 10, 1960.

McConachie, Bruce A. "The 'Oriental' Musicals of Rodgers and Hammerstein and the U.S. War in Southeast Asia," *Theatre Journal*, 1994.

Michaelis, Arnold. Interview with OHII, Hammerstein Collection, 1958, LOC.

Michaelis, Arnold. Interview with RR, 1961, University of Georgia Special Collections, Athens.

Nietzsche, Friedrich. *The Portable Nietzsche*, edited and translated by Walter Kaufmann. New York: Viking Press, 1954.

Nolan, Frederick. *Lorenz Hart: A Poet on Broadway*. New York: Oxford University Press, 1994.

Oliver, Phil. *William James's "Springs of Delight": The Return to Life*. Nashville: Vanderbilt University Press, 2000.

Proust, Marcel. *Swann's Way*, translated by Scott Moncrieff and Terence Kilmartin. New York: Vintage Classics, 1989.

Ross, Alex. *Wagnerism: Art and Politics in the Shadow of Music*. New York: Farrar, Straus and Giroux, 2020.

Shakespeare, William. *The Riverside Shakespeare*, edited by G. Blakemore Evans. Boston: Houghton Mifflin, 1973.

Sheean, Vincent. *Oscar Hammerstein I: The Life and Exploits of an Impresario*. New York: Simon & Schuster, 1956.

Sheed, Wilfred. *The House That George Built: With a Little Help from Irving, Cole, and a Crew of About Fifty*. New York: Random House, 2007.

Wagner, Richard. *Opera and Drama*, translated by W. Ashton Ellis. Lincoln: University of Nebraska Press, 1995.

Wilder, Alec. *American Popular Song: The Great Innovators, 1900–1950*. New York: Oxford University Press, 1972.

Wilk, Max. Interview with Agnes de Mille, 1990, NYPL.

Winer, Laurie. Interview with Stephen Sondheim, 2018.

Young, Jo Ann, dir. *Out of My Dreams: Oscar Hammerstein II*, Creative Retrospectives, 2012.

Correspondence

OHII to Josh Logan, June 3, 1949, Hammerstein Collection, LOC.

OHII to Martin Luther King Jr., May 31, 1960, Howard Gotlieb Archival Research Center, Boston University.

RR to "Florence," March 21, 1948, NYPL.

CHAPTER 1: A GOOD BOY

Works

Barnes, Clive. "Theater: Shubert Theater Gets 'Golden Rainbow,'" *New York Times*, February 5, 1968.
Citron, Stephen. *The Wordsmiths: Oscar Hammerstein II and Alan Jay Lerner*. New York: Oxford University Press, 1995.
Fordin, Hugh. *Getting to Know Him: A Biography of Oscar Hammerstein II*. New York: Random House, 1977.
Gordon, Max, and Lewis Funke. *Max Gordon Presents: The Star-Studded Story of His Life on Broadway*. New York: Bernard Geis Associates, 1963.
Hamilton, Marybeth. *When I'm Bad, I'm Better: Mae West, Sex, and American Entertainment*. New York: HarperCollins, 1996.
Hammerstein, Oscar, II. Columbia Center for Oral History Archives, June 1959, Columbia University, New York.
Hammerstein, Oscar, II. Eulogy for Gertrude Lawrence, 1952, Hammerstein Collection, LOC.
Michaelis, Arnold. Interview with OHII, Hammerstein Collection, 1958, LOC.
Rodgers, Richard. *Musical Stages*. New York: Random House, 1975.
Secrest, Meryle. *Stephen Sondheim: A Life*. New York: Alfred A. Knopf, 1998.
Sheean, Vincent. *Oscar Hammerstein I: The Life and Exploits of an Impresario*. New York: Simon & Schuster, 1956.
Sondheim, Stephen. *Finishing the Hat: Collected Lyrics (1954–1981) with Attendant Comments, Principles, Heresies, Grudges, Whines, and Anecdotes*. New York: Alfred A. Knopf, 2010.
Wilk, Max. Interview with Agnes de Mille, 1990, NYPL.
Wood, Ean. *George Gershwin: His Life and Music*. London: Sanctuary Publishing, 1999.
Young, Jo Ann, dir. *Out of My Dreams: Oscar Hammerstein II*, Creative Retrospectives, 2012.

Correspondence

OHII to Dr. J. N. Ferryman, March 19, 1952, Hammerstein Collection, LOC.
Arthur Hammerstein to OHII, July 4, 1945, Hammerstein Collection, LOC.
OHII to William Hammerstein, late 1952, Hammerstein Collection, LOC.
OHII to William Hammerstein, January 4, 11, 18, 25, February 2, 8, 1953, Hammerstein Collection, LOC.
OHII to Otto Harbach, August 18, 1956, Hammerstein Collection, LOC.
OHII to Harry Kurnitz, July 31, 1952, Hammerstein Collection, LOC.

CHAPTER 2: FREE FOR ALL

Works

Asch, Amy, ed. *The Complete Lyrics of Oscar Hammerstein II*. New York: Alfred A. Knopf, 2008.

Atkinson, Brooks. "Abe and Mawruss (God Forbid!)," *New York Times*, September 1, 1926.
Atkinson, Brooks. "Native Opera of the South," *New York Times*, October 5, 1926.
Baker, Belle. Clippings file, NYPL.
Banfield, Stephen. *Jerome Kern*. New Haven, CT: Yale University Press, 2006.
Bennett, Robert Russell. *The Broadway Sound*. Rochester, NY: University of Rochester Press, 1999.
Bordman, Gerald. *Jerome Kern: His Life and Music*. New York: Oxford University Press, 1980.
Broun, Heywood. "Chorus Gets Its Rights at Last," *New York Herald Tribune*, December 24, 1915.
Cullen, Frank. *Vaudeville Old and New: An Encyclopedia of Variety Performances in America*. London: Routledge, 2006.
Davis, Hartley. "In Vaudeville," *Everybody's Magazine*, August 1905, NYPL.
Duberman, Martin. *Paul Robeson*. New York: Alfred A. Knopf, 1989.
Everett, William A. *Sigmund Romberg*. New Haven, CT: Yale University Press, 2007.
Forbes, Camille F. *Introducing Bert Williams: Burnt Cork, Broadway, and the Story of America's First Black Star*. New York: Basic Books, 2008.
Fordin, Hugh. *Getting to Know Him: A Biography of Oscar Hammerstein II*. New York: Random House, 1977.
Fountain, Nigel. *When the Lights Went Out: Reporting on the Great War*. London: Guardian Faber, 2014.
Freedland, Michael. *Jerome Kern: A Biography*. New York: Stein & Day Publishers, 1981.
Garner, Rosemary, and Greg Palmer, dir. *Vaudeville*, American Masters Pictures, 1997.
Gelb, Arthur, and Barbara Gelb. *By Women Possessed: A Life of Eugene O'Neill*. New York: Marian Wood Books / Putnam, 2016.
Gershwin, George. "The Voice of the American Soul Is Jazz," *Theater Arts*, June 1926.
Giordana, Ralph G. *Satan in the Dance Hall: Rev. John Roach Straton, Social Dancing, and Morality in 1920s New York City*. Lanham, MD: Scarecrow Press, 2008.
Gordon, Max, and Lewis Funke. *Max Gordon Presents: The Star-Studded Story of His Life on Broadway*. New York: Bernard Geis Associates, 1963.
Green, Benny. *P. G. Wodehouse: A Literary Biography*. New York: Oxford University Press, 1983.
Hamilton, Marybeth. *When I'm Bad, I'm Better: Mae West, Sex, and American Entertainment*. New York: HarperCollins, 1996.
Hammerstein, Oscar Andrew. *The Hammersteins: A Musical Theatre Family*. New York: Black Dog & Leventhal, 2010.
Hammerstein, Oscar, II. Columbia Center for Oral History Archives, June 1959, Columbia University, New York.
Hammerstein, Oscar, II. "Through the Years with the Song and Dance Shows," *New York Herald Tribune*, January 28, 1951.

Hammerstein, Oscar, II. "Voices versus Feet," *Theatre Magazine,* May 1925, NYPL.
Harbach, Otto. Columbia Center for Oral History Archives, 1958, Columbia University, New York.
Harling, Franke. "Harling's 'Deep River,'" *New York Times,* September 5, 1926.
Henehan, Donal. "City Opera: 'The Desert Song,'" *New York Times,* August 27, 1987.
Holusha, John. "A Theater's Muses, Rescued," *New York Times,* March 24, 2000.
Johnson, James Weldon. *The Book of American Negro Spirituals.* New York: Viking Press, 1925.
Kantor, Louis. "O'Neill Defends His Play of Negro," *New York Times,* May 11, 1924.
Kenrick, John. "1860s: *The Black Crook,*" *Musicals 101,* 1996, https://www.musicals101.com/1860to79.htm.
Laurie, Joe, Jr. *Vaudeville from the Honky Tonks to the Palace.* New York: Henry Holt, 1953.
Library of Congress. "Immigrants in the Progressive Era," n.d., https://www.loc.gov/classroom-materials/united-states-history-primary-source-timeline/progressive-era-to-new-era-1900-1929/immigrants-in-progressive-era/.
Marx, Groucho, and Richard J. Anobile. *The Marx Bros. Scrapbook.* New York: Darien House, 1973.
Michaelis, Arnold. Interview with OHII, 1958, Hammerstein Collection, LOC.
Morris, Wesley, and Hannah-Jones, Nikole. "The Birth of American Music," *1619,* podcast, September 6, 2019, https://www.nytimes.com/2019/09/06/podcasts/1619-black-american-music-appropriation.html.
Most, Andrea. *Making Americans: Jews and the Broadway Musical.* Cambridge, MA: Harvard University Press, 2004.
New York Times. "'Always You' Is Amusing," January 5, 1920.
New York Times. "New Musical Play, 'Rose-Marie,' Dazzles," September 3, 1924.
New York Times. "The Rise of Romberg," March 26, 1922.
New York Times. "A Trio of Stars Are All the Light," August 25, 1914.
New York Times. "'Wildflower' Is Melodious," February 7, 1923.
Nolan, Frederick. *Lorenz Hart: A Poet on Broadway.* New York: Oxford University Press, 1994.
Page, Brett. *Writing for Vaudeville.* Springfield, MA: Home Correspondence School, 1915.
Pollock, Channing. *The Footlights Fore and Aft.* Boston: Gorham Press, 1911.
Rich, Frank. "Conversations with Sondheim," *New York Times,* March 12, 2000.
Rodgers, Richard. *Musical Stages.* New York: Random House, 1975.
Sanborn, Frederic R. "'Jump Jim Crow!': The Opening of an Era," *New York Times,* November 13, 1932.
Sculthorpe, Derek. *The Lost World of Music Hall: A Celebration of Ten Greats.* Albany, GA: BearManor Media, 2021.
Smith, Cecil. *Musical Comedy in America.* New York: Theatre Arts Books, 1950.
Smith, Eric Ledell. *Bert Williams: A Biography of the Pioneer Black Comedian.* Jefferson, NC: McFarland, 1992.

Statue of Liberty–Ellis Island Foundation, "Overview and History," n.d., https://www.statueofliberty.org/ellis-island/overview-history/.
Unrau, Harlan D. *Ellis Island, Statue of Liberty National Monument, New York–New Jersey.* Denver: U.S. Department of the Interior, National Park Service, 1984.
Wilder, Alec. *American Popular Song: The Great Innovators, 1900–1950.* New York: Oxford University Press, 1972.
White, Matthew, Jr. "The Stage," *Munsey's Magazine,* November 1920.

Correspondence

Arthur Hammerstein to Harold Thomas Hyman, MD, undated 1949, Hammerstein Collection, LOC.
OHII to Anna "Mousie" Hammerstein, August 21, 1917, Hammerstein Collection, LOC.
OHII to Marc Holstein, February 13, 1945, Hammerstein Collection, LOC.
OHII to Jerome Kern, March 26, 1931, Hammerstein Collection, LOC.
OHII to Elizabeth Rider Montgomery, June 12, 1956, Hammerstein Collection, LOC.
Jerome Kern to OHII, April 10, 1942, Hammerstein Collection, LOC.

CHAPTER 3: THE INVENTION OF THE MUSICAL

Works

Armour, Jody. *N*gga Theory: Race, Language, Unequal Justice, and the Law.* Los Angeles: LARB Books, 2020.
Asch, Amy, ed. *The Complete Lyrics of Oscar Hammerstein II.* New York: Alfred A. Knopf, 2008.
Atkinson, Brooks. "Spilt Milk," *New York Times,* December 16, 1928.
Bennett, Robert Russell. *The Broadway Sound.* Rochester, NY: University of Rochester Press, 1999.
Cantwell, David. "The Unlikely Story of 'A Change Is Gonna Come,'" *New Yorker,* March 17, 2015.
Carter, Randolph. *Ziegfeld: The Time of His Life,* rev. ed. London: Bernard Press, 1988.
Decker, Todd. *"Show Boat": Performing Race in an American Musical.* New York: Oxford University Press, 2012.
Decker, Todd. *Who Should Sing "Ol' Man River"?: The Lives of an American Song.* New York: Oxford University Press, 2014.
Duberman, Martin. *Paul Robeson.* New York: Alfred A. Knopf, 1989.
Edney, Kate. "Musical of the Month: Golden Dawn," New York Public Library, September 4, 2015, https://www.nypl.org/blog/2015/09/04/musical-month-golden-dawn.
Encyclopedia Virginia, "Opinion of Judge M. Bazile, January 22, 1965," n.d., https://encyclopediavirginia.org/entries/judgment-against-richard-and-mildred-loving-january-6-1959/.

Ewen, David. *The Story of Jerome Kern.* New York: Henry Holt, 1953.
Ferber, Edith. *Show Boat.* New York: Grosset and Dunlap, 1926.
Foner, Philip S., ed. *Paul Robeson Speaks: Writings, Speeches, and Interviews, 1918–74.* Secaucus, NJ: Citadel Press, 1978.
Fordin, Hugh. *Getting to Know Him: A Biography of Oscar Hammerstein II.* New York: Random House, 1977.
Hammerstein, Oscar, II. Liner notes for *South Pacific* cast album, Hammerstein Collection, LOC.
Hammerstein, Oscar, II. Notes on "Writing the Book for a Musical Play," 1953, Hammerstein Collection, LOC.
Hammerstein, Oscar, II. *Show Boat,* libretto published along with producer John McGlinn's recording. London: EMI Records, 1988.
Hammerstein, Oscar, II. Swarthmore College speech, 1957, Hammerstein Collection, LOC.
Holden, Stephen. "'Show Boat' Makes New Waves," *New York Times,* September 24, 1988.
Kreuger, Miles. *"Show Boat": The Story of an American Musical.* New York: Oxford University Press, 1977.
Michaelis, Arnold. Interview with OHII, 1958, Hammerstein Collection, LOC.
Mordden, Ethan. *Ziegfeld: The Man Who Invented Show Business.* New York: St. Martin's Press, 2008.
New York Times. "Ovation to Paul Robeson," October 30, 1927.
New York Times. "The Theatres," October 1, 1889.
Rodgers, Richard, and Oscar Hammerstein II. *South Pacific: An Original Soundtrack Recording.* New York: RCA, 1958.
Rogers, J. A. "Rogers Gives New View," *Pittsburgh Courier,* reprint from the *Amsterdam News,* October 6, 1928.
Schwab, Laurence. "How to Write a Successful Musical Comedy," *Theatre Magazine,* February 1929.
Time. "The Careful Dreamer," October 20, 1947.
Van Gelder, Robert. "An Interview with Edna Ferber," *New York Times,* February 4, 1945.
Woollcott, Alexander. *While Rome Burns.* New York: Grosset & Dunlap, 1934.

Correspondence

OHII to Mrs. Herman Fox, August 6, 1949, Hammerstein Collection, LOC.
OHII to Dorothy Hammerstein, undated letters, December 18, 1928, January 22, 28, February 6, April 6, 9, 1929, June 4, 1939, Hammerstein Collection, LOC.
OHII to Jerome Kern, February 14, 1942, Hammerstein Collection, LOC.
OHII to Elizabeth Rider Montgomery, June 12, 1956, Hammerstein Collection, LOC.
Jerome Kern to OHII, April 10, 1942, Hammerstein Collection, LOC.

CHAPTER 4: DARK DECADE

Works

Atkinson, Brooks. "Indo-Chinese Serenade," *New York Times,* October 28, 1931.

Atkinson, Brooks. "'May Wine,' a Musical Drama with Book and Tunes but No Chorus," *New York Times,* December 6, 1935.

Atkinson, Brooks. "Music Being in the Air," *New York Times,* November 20, 1932.

Atkinson, Brooks. "'Very Warm for May,'" *New York Times,* November 18, 1939.

Bennett, Robert Russell. *The Broadway Sound.* Rochester, NY: University of Rochester Press, 1999.

Citron, Stephen. *The Wordsmiths: Oscar Hammerstein II and Alan Jay Lerner.* New York: Oxford University Press, 1995.

Divall, Colin. *Cultural Histories of Sociabilities, Spaces and Mobilities.* London: Routledge, 2015.

Fordin, Hugh. *Getting to Know Him: A Biography of Oscar Hammerstein II.* New York: Random House, 1977.

Franceschina, John. *Hermes Pan: The Man Who Danced with Fred Astaire.* New York: Oxford University Press, 2012.

Gordon, Max, and Lewis Funke. *Max Gordon Presents: The Star-Studded Story of His Life on Broadway.* New York: Bernard Geis Associates, 1963.

Hammerstein, Oscar, II. Notes on *Music in the Air,* 1932, Hammerstein Collection, LOC.

Hammerstein, Oscar II. *Very Warm for May,* 1939, Hammerstein Collection, LOC.

Hammerstein, Oscar II. *Very Warm for May,* 1940, Hammerstein Collection, LOC.

Harbach, Otto. Columbia Center for Oral History Archives, 1958, Columbia University, New York.

Helburn, Theresa. *A Wayward Quest: The Autobiography of Theresa Helburn.* New York: Little, Brown, 1960.

Hyland, William G. *Richard Rodgers.* New Haven, CT: Yale University Press, 1998.

Los Angeles Times. "Dorothy Hammerstein, Interior Designer," September 15, 1957.

Michaelis, Arnold. Interview with OHII, 1958, Hammerstein Collection, LOC.

Michaelis, Arnold. Interview with RR, 1961, University of Georgia Special Collections, Athens.

New Statesman and Nation. "Operetta at Drury Lane," September 16, 1933.

Nolan, Frederick. *The Sound of Their Music: The Story of Rodgers and Hammerstein.* New York: Applause Theatre & Cinema Books, 2002.

Piker, Steven, ed. *The Psychological Study of Theravada Societies.* Boston: Brill Academic Publishers, 1975.

Rodgers, Dorothy. *My Favorite Things: A Personal Guide to Decorating and Entertaining.* New York: Atheneum, 1964.

Rodgers, Mary, and Jesse Green. *Shy: The Alarmingly Outspoken Memoirs of Mary Rodgers.* New York: Farrar, Straus and Giroux, 2022.

Rodgers, Richard. *Musical Stages.* New York: Random House, 1975.

Secrest, Meryle. *Somewhere for Me: A Biography of Richard Rodger.* New York: Alfred A. Knopf, 2001.
Smith, Wallace. *The Happy Alienist.* New York: Harrison Smith and Robert Haas, 1936.
Strauss, Theodore. "Something about Seven Lean Years," *New York Times,* November 19, 1939.
Time. "The Boys from Columbia," September 26, 1938.
Trask, C. Hooper. "Berlin Bursts into Song," *New York Times,* February 19, 1933.
von Mises, Margit. *My Years with Ludwig von Mises.* New Rochelle, NY: Arlington House Publishers, 1976.
Waller, Klaus. *Paul Abraham: Der Tragische König Der Operette.* Norderstedt, Germany: Books on Demand, 2017.
Woolf, S. J. "Hammerstein the Second," *New York Times,* March 31, 1946.
Wyatt, Robert, and John Andrew Johnson, eds. *The George Gershwin Reader.* New York: Oxford University Press, 2004.
Young, Jo Ann, dir. *Out of My Dreams: Oscar Hammerstein II,* Creative Retrospectives, 2012.

Correspondence

Arthur Hammerstein to OHII, undated, 1930, Hammerstein Collection, LOC.
Arthur Hammerstein to Otto Harbach, January 15, 1930, NYPL.
OHII to Leighton Brill, October 31, 1934, December 2, 1935, Hammerstein Collection, LOC.
OHII to Buddy Ebsen, March 18, 1938, Hammerstein Collection, LOC.
OHII to Myra Finn, November 9, 1931; March 22, April 14, June 12, July 2, 21, 1932; April 5, 1933; May 18, June 11, July 8, December 6, 1934; August 16, 1938, Hammerstein Collection, LOC.
OHII to Lloyd Foster, April 9, 1957, Hammerstein Collection, LOC.
OHII to Reginald Hammerstein, June 21, 1938, Hammerstein Collection, LOC.
OHII to Hy Kraft, February 7, 1938, Hammerstein Collection, LOC.
OHII to Miss Liveright, January 9, 1936, Hammerstein Collection, LOC.
OHII to Rouben Mamoulian, February 19, 1937, November 4, 1943, Hammerstein Collection, LOC.
OHII to Harry Rapf, May 5, 1938, Hammerstein Collection, LOC.
OHII to Howard Reinheimer, March 14, May 6, 1935, January 8, 1936, Hammerstein Collection, LOC.
OHII to Sigmund Romberg, December 12, 1938, Hammerstein Collection, LOC.
OHII to Jack Warner, January 13, 1931, Hammerstein Collection, LOC.
OHII to Florenz Ziegfeld, February 16, 1931, Hammerstein Collection, LOC.
Reginald Hammerstein to OHII, June 28, 1938, Hammerstein Collection, LOC.
Lorenz Hart to Ira Gershwin, March 31, 1926, LOC.
Jerome Kern to OHII, November 29, 1938, Hammerstein Collection, LOC.
David Loew to OHII, July 7, 1938, Hammerstein Collection, LOC.

John Mosher to OHII, June 5, July 1, 1936, Hammerstein Collection, LOC.
RR to OHII, July 6, 1941, Hammerstein Collection, LOC.
RR to Dorothy Rodgers, August, September 14, 1930; August 1, 3, 1934; February, March 1936; March, May, July, 10, 1937, NYPL.
Sigmund Romberg to OHII, undated, 1930s, Hammerstein Collection, LOC.
Florenz Ziegfeld to OHII, January 22, 1931, Hammerstein Collection, LOC.

CHAPTER 5: THUS THE WORLD BROKE OPEN

Works

Barron, James. “Did ‘Hamilton’ Get the Story Wrong?,” *New York Times*, January 13, 2019.
Bennett, Robert Russell. *The Broadway Sound*. Rochester, NY: University of Rochester Press, 1999.
Bordman, Gerald. *Jerome Kern: His Life and Music*. New York: Oxford University Press, 1980.
Carter, Tim. *“Oklahoma!”: The Making of an American Musical*. New Haven, CT: Yale University Press, 2007.
Crowther, Bosley. “Negros in a Film,” *New York Times*, October 30, 1954.
de Mille, Agnes. *Dance to the Piper*. New York: Little, Brown, 1952.
Downes, Olin. “Carmen Jones,” *New York Times*, December 19, 1943.
Fordin, Hugh. *Getting to Know Him: A Biography of Oscar Hammerstein II*. New York: Random House, 1977.
Funke, Lewis. “The Play,” *New York Times*, January 8, 1943.
Haines, Michael R., and Richard H. Steckel. *A Population History of North America*. Cambridge: Cambridge University Press, 2000.
Jones, John Bush. *Our Musicals, Ourselves: A Social History of the American Musical Theater*. Lebanon, NH: Brandeis University Press, 2004.
Michaelis, Arnold. Interview with OHII, 1958, Hammerstein Collection, LOC.
Michaelis, Arnold. Interview with RR, 1961, University of Georgia Special Collections, Athens.
Nichols, Lewis. “‘Oklahoma!’ a Musical Hailed as Delightful,” *New York Times*, April 1, 1943.
Nolan, Frederick. *Lorenz Hart: A Poet on Broadway*. New York: Oxford University Press, 1994.
Reed, Rex. “Broadway’s Latest ‘Oklahoma!’ Revival Is a Gimmicky Travesty,” *The Observer*, July 7, 2019.
Rich, Frank. “Oklahoma Was Never Really OK,” *New York*, April 2, 2019.
Riggs, Lynn. *Green Grow the Lilacs*. New York: Samuel French, 2010.
Rodgers, Mary, and Jesse Green. *Shy: The Alarmingly Outspoken Memoirs of Mary Rodgers*. New York: Farrar, Straus and Giroux, 2022.
Rodgers, Richard. *Musical Stages*. New York: Random House, 1975.
Rodgers, Richard, and Oscar Hammerstein II. *Six Plays by Rodgers and Hammerstein*. New York: Modern Library, 1959.

Teachout, Terry. "'Oklahoma!' and 'The Cradle Will Rock' Review," *Wall Street Journal*, April 11, 2019.
Thompson, Cheryl W., prod. "Fatal Police Shootings of Unarmed Black People Reveal Troubling Patterns," *Morning Edition* (NPR), January 25, 2021.
Wilk, Max. Interview with Agnes de Mille, 1990, NYPL.
Wilk, Max. Interview with William Hammerstein, 1990, NYPL.
Wilk, Max. *OK! The Story of "Oklahoma!": A Celebration of America's Most Beloved Musical*. New York: Grove Press, 1993.
Winer, Laurie. Interview with Miles Kreuger, 2018.
Young, Jo Ann, dir. *Out of My Dreams: Oscar Hammerstein II*, Creative Retrospectives, 2012.

Correspondence

Ralph Blum to OHII, November 19, 1941, Hammerstein Collection, LOC.
Agnes de Mille to RR, December 13, 1979, NYPL.
Edna Ferber to OHII, July 19, 1941, Hammerstein Collection, LOC.
Ira Gershwin to OHII, February 12, 1942, Hammerstein Collection, LOC.
Tim Girton to OHII, October 14, 1941, Hammerstein Collection, LOC.
OHII to Ralph Blum, November 10, 1941, Hammerstein Collection, LOC.
OHII to Jack Chertok, MGM Studios, January 1935, Hammerstein Collection, LOC.
OHII to Charles Einach, March 19, 1953, Hammerstein Collection, LOC.
OHII to Lloyd Foster, April 9, 1957, Hammerstein Collection, LOC.
OHII to Ira Gershwin, February 2, 1942, Hammerstein Collection, LOC.
OHII to Tim Girton, October 4, 1941, Hammerstein Collection, LOC.
OHII to Arthur Hammerstein, March 23, 1943, Hammerstein Collection, LOC.
OHII to William Hammerstein, October 25, 1943; January 18, 1953, Hammerstein Collection, LOC.
OHII to Alfred A. Knopf, 1943, Hammerstein Collection, LOC.
OHII to Josh Logan, May 31, 1950, Hammerstein Collection, LOC.
OHII to Louis B. Mayer, August 4, 14, 1950, Hammerstein Collection, LOC.
OHII to Elizabeth Rider Montgomery, June 12, 1956, Hammerstein Collection, LOC.
OHII to Lynn Riggs, March 23, 1943, Hammerstein Collection, LOC.
Jerome Kern to OHII, January 19, 1942, Hammerstein Collection, LOC.
RR to OHII, June 29, July 6, 29, 1941, NYPL.

CHAPTER 6: THE NAMESAKE

Works

Aldrich, Richard. "Mme. Bressler-Gianoli," *Century Magazine*, November 1907.
Als, Hilton. "Anika Noni Rose's Star-Making Self-Possession in 'Carmen Jones,'" *New Yorker*, July 9, 2018.
Baldwin, James. "*Carmen Jones:* The Dark Is Light Enough," *Collected Essays*. New York: Library of America, 1998.
Barnes, Howard. "Bravo Muriel Smith," *New York Herald Tribune*, December 4, 1943.

Barone, Joshua. "'Carmen Jones' Is Back, and Its Director Knows What You're Thinking," *New York Times,* June 1, 2018.
Blumenthal, George, as told to Arthur H. Menkin. *My 60 Years in Show Business.* New York: Frederick C. Osberg, 1936.
Boyd, Melinda. "The Politics of Color in Oscar Hammerstein's *Carmen Jones,*" *Blackness in Opera.* Urbana: University of Illinois Press, 2012.
Brantley, Ben. "Bad Girl Makes Good in a Glorious 'Carmen Jones,'" *New York Times,* June 27, 2018
Burley, Dan. "All-Negro Opera, 'Carmen Jones,' Scores in Philly Premiere," *New York Amsterdam News,* October 30, 1943.
Carter, Tim. *"Oklahoma!": The Making of an American Musical.* New Haven, CT: Yale University Press, 2007.
Collins, Theresa M. *Otto Kahn: Art, Money, and Modern Time.* Chapel Hill: University of North Carolina Press, 2002.
Crowther, Bosley. "Negroes in a Film," *New York Times,* October 30, 1954.
Downes, Olin. "'Carmen Jones,'" *New York Times,* December 19, 1943.
Fauser, Annegret. "'Dixie Carmen': War, Race, and Identity in Oscar Hammerstein's Carmen Jones," *Journal of the Society for American Music,* April 2010.
Fordin, Hugh. *Getting to Know Him: A Biography of Oscar Hammerstein II.* New York: Random House, 1977.
Galer, Sophia Smith. "How Carmen Went from Tragic Heroine to Feminist Icon," *BBC Culture,* February 7, 2018, http://www.bbc.com/culture/story/20180207-how-carmen-went-from-tragic-heroine-to-feminist-icon.
Hamilton, Marybeth. *When I'm Bad, I'm Better: Mae West, Sex, and American Entertainment.* New York: HarperCollins, 1996.
Hammerstein, Oscar, II. *Carmen Jones.* New York: Alfred A. Knopf, 1945.
Hammerstein, Oscar Andrew. *The Hammersteins: A Musical Theatre Family.* New York: Black Dog & Leventhal, 2010.
Henderson, Mary C., and Alexis Greene. *The Story of 42nd Street: The Theatres, Shows, Characters, and Scandals of the World's Most Notorious Street.* New York: Back Stage Books, 2008.
Holt, Nora. "'Carmen Jones' Magnificent with Quips," *New York Amsterdam News,* January 8, 1944.
Huizenga, Tom, prod. "Carmen on the Couch: Analyzing Bizet's Bold Heroine," *Weekend Edition Saturday* (NPR), September 22, 2007.
Hume, Ruth. "Oscar and the Opera: An Impresario Named Hammerstein Set His Sights on Tumbling an Institution Called the Met," *Heritage,* February 1973.
Jeal, Erica. "Carmen Jones," *The Guardian,* August 1, 2007.
Jefferson, Miles. "The Negro on Broadway," *Phylon,* vol. 17, no. 3, 1956.
Keating v. Hammerstein, Supreme Court New York County, April 21, 1921.
Lovell, John, Jr. "Roundup: The Negro in the American Theatre," *The Crisis,* July 1947.
Maslon, Laurence, and Michael Kantor. *Broadway: The American Musical.* New York: Bulfinch, 2004.

Mérimée, Prosper. *"Carmen" and Other Stories,* translated by Nicholas Jotcham. New York: Oxford University Press, 1989.
Nathan, George Jean. *Theater Book of the Year 1933–34.* Madison, NJ: Fairleigh Dickinson University Press, 1972.
New York Times. "About a Theatre License; Oscar Hammerstein Does Not Intend to Be Bulldozed," May 3, 1890.
New York Times. "Aids Mrs. Hammerstein," November 18, 1930.
New York Times. "A Bit of Police Spite," May 1, 1890.
New York Times. "More Blows Pass in Hammerstein Row," January 25, 1909.
New York Times. "Hammerstein Won't Support Daughters," October 9, 1912.
New York Times. "Harry Hammerstein Dead," July 29, 1914.
New York Times. "Mrs. Hammerstein Again Is Missing," November 7, 1922.
New York Times. "O. Hammerstein, Long in Coma, Dies," August 2, 1919.
New York Times. "William Hammerstein, 82, Director with a Famous Father," March 12, 2001.
Nichols, Lewis. "About 'Carmen Jones,'" *New York Times,* December 12, 1943.
Schriftgiesser, Karl. "Hassard Short: The Palette Mixer," *New York Times,* June 18, 1944.
Sheean, Vincent. *Oscar Hammerstein I: The Life and Exploits of an Impresario.* New York: Simon & Schuster, 1956.
Solis, Jose. "Anika Noni Rose Was Waiting for This Moment," *New York Times,* August 1, 2008.
Spiegel, Irving. "Negro Cast Will Sing 'Carmen,'" *New York Times,* August 23, 1942.
Tanner, Michael. "Could Do Better," *The Spectator,* August 15, 2007.
Wong, Edward. "Cultures Clash Where Divas Once Held Stage," *New York Times,* May 16, 2000.

Correspondence

Leo Brady to Walter Kerr, October 19, 1943, Walter Kerr Collection, University of Wisconsin, Madison.
Arthur Hammerstein to OHII, December 22, 1954, Hammerstein Collection, LOC.
OHII to William Hammerstein, December 6, 1943, Hammerstein Collection, LOC.
OHII to Alfred Knopf, 1945, Hammerstein Collection, LOC.
OHII to Howard Reinheimer, November 5, 1957, Hammerstein Collection, LOC.
OHII letter to Vincent Sheean, November 30, 1953, Hammerstein Collection, LOC.

CHAPTER 7: DON'T BE AFRAID OF THE DARK

Works

Citron, Stephen. *The Wordsmiths: Oscar Hammerstein II and Alan Jay Lerner.* New York: Oxford University Press, 1995.
Fordin, Hugh. *Getting to Know Him: A Biography of Oscar Hammerstein II.* New York: Random House, 1977.

Hammerstein, Oscar II. Drafts of *Carousel,* Hammerstein Collection, LOC.
Holden, Stephen. "Cabaret: Love Songs of the '40s," *New York Times,* October 25, 1990.
Kazan, Elia. *A Life.* New York: Alfred A. Knopf, 1988.
Kronenberger, Louis. "The Brighter Side of Farm Life," *New York Times,* May 8, 1932.
Michaelis, Arnold. Interview with OHII, 1958, Hammerstein Collection, LOC.
Michaelis, Arnold. Interview with RR, 1961, University of Georgia Special Collections, Athens.
Rich, Frank. "You'll Always Walk Alone," *New York Times,* March 31, 1994.
Rodgers, Richard, and Oscar Hammerstein II. *Six Plays by Rodgers and Hammerstein.* New York: Modern Library, 1959.
Smith, Cecil A. *Musical Comedy in America.* New York: Theatre Arts Books, 1950.
Weber, Bruce. "Placing Heaven on Earth for the World of 'Carousel,'" *New York Times,* March 31, 1994.
Wilk, Max. Interview with William Hammerstein, 1990, NYPL.

Correspondence
OHII to Otto Harbach, August 18, 1956, Hammerstein Collection, LOC.
OHII to William Perlberg, June 4, 1945, Hammerstein Collection, LOC.
RR to Josh Logan, September 28, 1945, LOC.

CHAPTER 8: THEY TOIL NOT

Works
Amory, Cleveland. "The Nicest Guys in Show Business," *Holiday,* February 1959.
Bordman, Gerald. *Jerome Kern: His Life and Music.* New York: Oxford University Press, 1980.
Fordin, Hugh. *Getting to Know Him: A Biography of Oscar Hammerstein II.* New York: Random House, 1977.
Gray, Simon. "Obituary: James Hammerstein," *Independent,* January 11, 1999.
Hammerstein, Oscar, II. "Happy Birthday, Dear Dick," *Town and Country,* June 1952.
Hemingway, Ernest. *Death in the Afternoon.* New York: Charles Scribner's Sons, 1932.
Jablonski, Edward. *Irving Berlin: American Troubadour.* New York: Henry Holt, 1999.
Ladies' Home Journal. "Femininity," March 23, 1962.
Lahr, John. "O.K. Chorale: An English Take on Rodgers and Hammerstein," *New Yorker,* April 1, 2002.
Lapine, James, and Frank Rich, prods. *Six by Sondheim,* Sabella Entertainment, 2013.
Mercer, Marilyn. "Orphans to Benefit from a New Musical," *New York Herald Tribune,* November 11, 1959.
Michaelis, Arnold. Interview with OHII, 1958, Hammerstein Collection, LOC.
Michaelis, Arnold. Interview with RR, 1961, University of Georgia Special Collections, Athens.

Purdum, Todd. *Something Wonderful: Rodgers and Hammerstein's Broadway Revolution*. New York: Henry Holt, 2018.
Reif, Rita. "Mrs. Rodgers Takes Decor as a Theme," *New York Times*, March 27, 1964.
Rich, Frank. "Conversations with Sondheim," *New York Times Magazine*, March 11, 2000.
Rodgers, Dorothy. *The House in My Head*. New York: Random House, 1967.
Rodgers, Dorothy. *My Favorite Things: A Personal Guide to Decorating and Entertaining*. New York: Atheneum, 1964.
Rodgers, Mary. Columbia Center for Oral History Archives, 1982, Columbia University, New York.
Rodgers, Mary, and Jesse Green. *Shy: The Alarmingly Outspoken Memoirs of Mary Rodgers*. New York: Farrar, Straus and Giroux, 2022.
Rodgers, Richard. *Musical Stages*. New York: Random House, 1975.
Rodgers, Richard, and Oscar Hammerstein II. *Six Plays by Rodgers and Hammerstein*. New York: Modern Library, 1959.
Secrest, Meryle. *Stephen Sondheim: A Life*. New York: Alfred A. Knopf, 1998.
Time. "The Careful Dreamer," October 20, 1947.
Wilk, Max. Interview with Agnes de Mille, 1990, NYPL.
Wilk, Max. Interview with William Hammerstein, 1990, NYPL.
Winer, Laurie. Interview with Nicholas Hytner, 2018.
Winer, Laurie. Interview with Stephen Sondheim, 2018.
Wittels, David G. "How to Make $4,000,000 on Broadway," *Saturday Evening Post*, October 4 and 11, 1947.
Young, Jo Ann, dir. *Out of My Dreams: Oscar Hammerstein II*, Creative Retrospectives, 2012.

Correspondence
OHII to Jack Goodman, August 8, 1951, Hammerstein Collection, LOC.
OHII to Alice Hammerstein, November 17, 1945, Hammerstein Collection, LOC.
OHII to William Hammerstein, December 6, 1943, Hammerstein Collection, LOC.
OHII to Lars Schmidt, July 20, 1948, Hammerstein Collection, LOC.
OHII to John Steinbeck, August 24, 1955, Hammerstein Collection, LOC.
William Hammerstein to Josh Logan, August 29, 1960, Hammerstein Collection, LOC.

CHAPTER 9: YOU'VE GOT TO BE TAUGHT

Works
Atkinson, Brooks. "At the Theatre," *New York Times*, September 8, 1948.
Atkinson, Brooks. "War Idyll to Music," *New York Times*, June 4, 1949.
Bennett, Robert Russell. *The Broadway Sound*. Rochester, NY: University of Rochester Press, 1999.
Committee on Un-American Activities, U.S. House of Representatives. *Annual Report for the Year 1960*. Washington, DC: Government Printing Office.

de Mille, Agnes. *Dance to the Piper.* New York: Little, Brown, 1952.
Duberman, Martin. *Paul Robeson.* New York: Alfred A. Knopf, 1989.
Fadiman, Clifton, Oscar Hammerstein II, and Rex Stout. *The Myth That Threatens the World,* 1947, LOC.
Federal Bureau of Investigation, Records Branch, file on OHII, October 26, 1951–December 21, 1959, National Archives, Washington, DC.
Fordin, Hugh. *Getting to Know Him: A Biography of Oscar Hammerstein II.* New York: Random House, 1977.
Hammerstein, Oscar, II. Affidavit to FBI, November 1953, Hammerstein Collection, LOC.
Hammerstein, Oscar, II. "Policy of the United World Federalists," 1950, NYPL.
Hammerstein, Oscar, II. Speech to the World Federalists, 1950 and 1951, Hammerstein Collection, LOC.
Kaufman, David. *Some Enchanted Evenings: The Glittering Life and Times of Mary Martin.* New York: St. Martin's Press, 2016.
Kazin, Alfred. "We Who Sit in Darkness," *Commentary,* June 1, 1950.
Klein, Christina. *Cold War Orientalism: Asia in the Middlebrow Imagination.* Berkeley: University of California Press, 2003.
Logan, Josh. *Josh: My Up and Down, In and Out Life.* New York: Delacorte Press, 1976.
Logan, Josh. *Movie Stars, Real People, and Me.* New York: Bantam Doubleday Dell, 1978.
Logan, Josh. "New Tales of 'South Pacific,'" *New York Times,* April 3, 1949.
Lovensheimer, Jim. *"South Pacific": Paradise Rewritten.* New York: Oxford University Press, 2010.
Michaelis, Arnold. Interview with RR, 1961, University of Georgia Special Collections, Athens.
Michener, James A. *Tales of the South Pacific.* Robbinsdale, MN: Fawcett Crest, 1947.
Newton, Lee. "An Open Letter to Rodgers and Hammerstein," *Daily Worker,* September 16, 1948.
Rice, Charles D., and Ben Feiner Jr. "A Couple of Stage-Struck Guys," *Cincinnati Enquirer,* November 9, 1947.
Rockwell, John. "A New 'South Pacific' by the City Opera," *New York Times,* March 2, 1987.
Rodgers, Mary. Columbia Center for Oral History Archives, 1982, Columbia University, New York.
Rodgers, Richard. *Musical Stages.* New York: Random House, 1975.
Rodgers, Richard. "Two Modes in Musicals," *New York Times,* June 21, 1964.
Rodgers, Richard, and Oscar Hammerstein II. "Rodgers, Hammerstein Reply to Lee Newton on 'Show Boat,'" *Daily Worker,* October 25, 1948.
Rodgers, Richard, and Oscar Hammerstein II. *Six Plays by Rodgers and Hammerstein.* New York: Modern Library, 1959.
Smith, P. D. *Doomsday Men: The Real Dr. Strangelove and the Dream of the Super Weapon.* New York: St. Martin's Press, 2007.

Thomas, Tony. Interview with RR, 1960, *CBC Radio.*
Wilk, Max. Interview with Agnes de Mille, 1990, NYPL.

Correspondence

Agnes de Mille to OHII, March 12, 1949, Hammerstein Collection, LOC.
Myra Finn to OHII, 1949, Hammerstein Collection, LOC.
Dorothy Hammerstein to Nedda Harrington, June 5, 1949, Hammerstein Collection, LOC.
OHII to Frank Adams, June 7, 1949, Hammerstein Collection, LOC.
OHII to Richard Halliday, March 18, May 15, 1952, Hammerstein Collection, LOC.
OHII to Josh Logan, July 11, 1949, November 28, 1953, Hammerstein Collection, LOC.
OHII to Gordon Manning, January 3, 1952, Hammerstein Collection, LOC.
OHII to Alec [*sic*] McGowan, February 1, 1960, Hammerstein Collection, LOC.
OHII to Thomas McWhorter, April 11, 1949, Hammerstein Collection, LOC.
OHII to Rex Stout, December 28, 1943, Hammerstein Collection, LOC.
William Hammerstein to Josh Logan, August 2, 1983, Hammerstein Collection, LOC.
Yip Harburg to OHII, April 8, 1949, Hammerstein Collection, LOC.
Nunnally Johnson to OHII, June 6, 1949, Hammerstein Collection, LOC.
Josh Logan to H. William Fitelson, July 28, 1967, LOC.
Josh Logan to Dorothy Hammerstein, June 23, 1986, Hammerstein Collection, LOC.
Josh Logan to OHII, September 4, 6, 1947, Hammerstein Collection, LOC.
Josh Logan to William Hammerstein, July 28, 1967, Hammerstein Collection, LOC.
Josh Logan to RR, July 11, September 19, 1967, LOC.
Josh Logan to RR and Dorothy Rodgers, January 1979, LOC.
Alan McGowan to OHII, January 1960, Hammerstein Collection, LOC.
Thomas McWhorter to OHII, April 2, 1949, Hammerstein Collection, LOC.
Thomas McWhorter to OHII, April 11, 1949, Hammerstein Collection, LOC.
John O'Hara to RR, June 1947, private collection.
RR to OHII, January 17, 1958, NYPL.
RR to Neda Harrington, June 15, 1967, LOC.
RR to Theresa Helburn and Lawrence Langner, June 15, 1943, LOC.
RR to Josh Logan, September 28, 1945, July 11, 1967, LOC.
RR to John O'Hara, June 14, 1951, NYPL.
Stephen Sondheim to Dorothy Hammerstein, June 1948, Hammerstein Collection, LOC.

CHAPTER 10: WOMEN'S WORK

Works

Atkinson, Brooks. "The King and I," *New York Times,* April 8, 1951.
Baldwin, James. "The Devil Finds Work," *Collected Essays.* New York: Library of America, 1998.

Baldwin, James. "Everybody's Protest Novel," *Collected Essays*. New York: Library of America, 1998.
Bristowe, W. S. *Louis and the King of Siam*. London: Chatto and Windus, 1976.
Buruma, Ian. "Thailand's Banned 'King,'" *New York Review of Books,* May 19, 2015.
Craven, Lady Elizabeth. *A Journey through the Crimea to Constantinople,* reprint. N.p.: Sagwan Press, 2018.
Crowther, Bosley. "Musical Memories," *New York Times,* July 1, 1956.
Dickens, Charles. "North American Slavery," *Household Words,* September 18, 1852.
Douglass, Frederick. *The Life and Times of Frederick Douglass, Written by Himself. His Early Life as a Slave, His Escape from Bondage, and His Complete History to the Present Time*. Hartford, CT: Park Publishing Co., 1881.
Erlanger, Steven. "A Confection Built on a Novel Built on a Fabrication," *New York Times,* April 7, 1996.
Fields, Annie. *Life and Letters of Harriet Beecher Stowe*. Boston: Houghton Mifflin, 1898.
Fordin, Hugh. *Getting to Know Him: A Biography of Oscar Hammerstein II*. New York: Random House, 1977.
Gates, Henry Louis, Jr. "Slavery, by the Numbers," *The Root,* February 10, 2014, https://www.theroot.com/slavery-by-the-numbers-1790874492.
The Guardian. "Turkish First Lady Praises Harem as 'School for Women,'" March 9, 2016.
Habegger, Alfred. *Masked: The Life of Anna Leonowens: Schoolmistress at the Court of Siam*. Madison: University of Wisconsin Press, 2014.
Hammerstein, Oscar, II. *The Night Is Young,* script, Margaret Herrick Library, Beverly Hills, CA.
Hammerstein, Oscar, II. "Policy of the United World Federalists," 1950, NYPL.
James, William. "Confidences of a Psychical Researcher," *American Magazine,* October 1909.
Jefferson, Margo. "Culture Clashes Still Intrigue in 'King and I,'" *New York Times,* April 28, 1996.
Kazin, Alfred. *God and the American Writer*. New York: Alfred A. Knopf, 1997.
Klein, Christina. *Cold War Orientalism: Asia in the Middlebrow Imagination*. Berkeley: University of California Press, 2003.
Leonowens, Anna Harriette. *The English Governess at the Siamese Court: Being Recollections of Six Years in the Royal Palace at Bangkok,* reprint. Wolcott, NY: Scholar's Choice, 2015.
Leonowens, Anna Harriette. *The Romance of the Harem,* reprint. New York: Andesite Press, 2015.
Live from the NYPL. "Uncle Tom's Cabin Reconsidered: A Conversation with Henry Louis Gates and Margo Jefferson," November 29, 2006.
Logan, Josh. *Josh: My Up and Down, In and Out Life*. New York: Delacorte Press, 1976.
Lott, Eric. *Love and Theft: Blackface Minstrelsy and the American Working Class*. New York: Oxford University Press, 1993.

Morgan, Susan. *Bombay Anna: The Real Story and Remarkable Adventures of "The King and I" Governess.* Berkeley: University of California Press, 2008.
New York Times. "Lecture in Brooklyn," October 31, 1871.
Price, Leah. "'Bombay Anna': A Governess Continues to Charm," *New York Times,* October 10, 2008.
Rodgers, Richard, and Oscar Hammerstein II. *Six Plays by Rodgers and Hammerstein.* New York: Modern Library, 1959.
Stowe, Harriet Beecher. *The Annotated Uncle Tom's Cabin.* New York: W. W. Norton, 2006.
Tadepalli, Sravya. "Can 'The King and I' Be Decolonized?," *American Theatre,* April 26, 2021.
Tompkins, Jane. *Sensational Designs: Cultural Work of American Fiction, 1790–1860.* New York: Oxford University Press, 1985.
Weinraub, Bernard. "Briton Says Anna Was Awful in Siam," *New York Times,* August 8, 1970.
Winer, Laurie. Interview with Bartlett Sher, 2018.

Correspondence
OHII to RR, November 28, 1956, NYPL.
Josh Logan to RR and OHII, January 18, 1951, Hammerstein Collection, LOC.
RR to OHII, October 15, 1951, January 17, 1958, NYPL.
John Steinbeck to OHII and RR, July 4, 1952, Hammerstein Collection, LOC.
Harriet Beecher Stowe to the Glasgow Female New Association for the Abolition of Slavery, December 4, 1852. Reprinted in *Frederick Douglass' Paper,* March 4, 1853, http://utc.iath.virginia.edu/africam/afar03vt.html.

CHAPTER 11: CINDERELLA AND OTHER MYTHS

Works
Atkinson, Brooks. "'Me and Juliet,'" *New York Times,* June 7, 1953.
Atkinson, Brooks. "'Pipe Dream,'" *New York Times,* December 1, 1955.
Atkinson, Brooks. "'Pipe Dream' Is Based on a Steinbeck Novel," *New York Times,* December 1, 1955.
Bennett, Robert Russell. *The Broadway Sound.* Rochester, NY: University of Rochester Press, 1999.
Ewen, David. *With a Song in His Heart: The Story of Richard Rodgers.* New York: Holt, Rinehart and Winston, 1965.
Faber, Nancy. "Mary Martin," *People,* November 23, 1981.
Fordin, Hugh. *Getting to Know Him: A Biography of Oscar Hammerstein II.* New York: Random House, 1977.
Hammerstein, Barbara Redzisz. *Cinderella after the Ball: Or, Just Keep Going.* Sarasota, FL: Peppertree Press, 2009.
Hammerstein, Oscar, II. "Acting and Singing on the Screen," notes on a speech, 1957, Hammerstein Collection, LOC.

Hammerstein, Oscar, II. *Pipe Dream*. New York: Viking Press, 1956.
Hammerstein, Oscar, II. *This I Believe*, 1955, Hammerstein Collection, LOC.
Hwang, David Henry. "A New Musical by Rodgers and Hwang," *New York Times*, October 13, 2002.
Isherwood, Christopher. *Diaries, 1939–1960*. London: Methuen, 1996.
Ives, Mike. "For Some Viewers, 'Asians' Is Not Asian Enough," *New York Times*, August 16, 2018.
Kaufman, David. *Some Enchanted Evenings: The Glittering Life and Times of Mary Martin*. New York: St. Martin's Press, 2016.
Kim, Heidi. "'Flower Drum Song,' Whitewashing, and Operation Wetback: A Message from 1961," *Los Angeles Review of Books*, September 22, 2016.
Klein, Christina. *Cold War Orientalism: Asia in the Middlebrow Imagination*. Berkeley: University of California Press, 2003.
Lee, C. Y. *The Flower Drum Song*, introduction by Henry David Hwang. New York: Penguin, 2002.
Murrow, Edward R. *Person to Person*, guests Oscar II and Dorothy Hammerstein, CBS, 1955.
Murrow, Edward R. *Person to Person*, guests Richard and Dorothy Rodgers, CBS, 1953.
Peck, Seymour. "About 'Me and Juliet,'" *New York Times*, May 24, 1953.
Rodgers, Mary. Columbia Center for Oral History Archives, 1982, Columbia University, New York.
Rodgers, Mary, and Jesse Green. *Shy: The Alarmingly Outspoken Memoirs of Mary Rodgers*. New York: Farrar, Straus and Giroux, 2022.
Rodgers, Richard. *Musical Stages*. New York: Random House, 1975.
Rodgers, Richard, and Oscar Hammerstein II. *Six Plays by Rodgers and Hammerstein*. New York: Modern Library, 1959.
Secrest, Meryle. *Somewhere for Me: A Biography of Richard Rodgers*. New York: Knopf, 2001.
Shelley, Dan. "It's No Secret: Truth and Integrity Made Murrow a Model," *RTDNA*, April 24, 2018.
Shin, Andrew. "Forty Percent Is Luck: An Interview with C. Y. (Chin Yang) Lee," *Melus*, vol. 29, no. 2, 2004.
Smith, Sally Bedell. *In All His Glory: The Life of William S. Paley*. New York: Simon & Schuster, 1990.
Steinbeck, John. *Sweet Thursday*. New York: Viking Press, 1954.
Tynan, Kenneth. "Tiny Chinese Minds," *New Yorker*, December 13, 1958.
Wilk, Max. *OK! The Story of "Oklahoma!": A Celebration of America's Most Beloved Musical*. New York: Grove Press, 1993.

Correspondence

Richard Halliday to OHII and RR, February 1, 1952, Hammerstein Collection, LOC.
Dorothy Hammerstein to Betty Kern, September 18, 1960, Hammerstein Collection, LOC.

OHII to Richard Halliday, March 18, May 15, June 9, July 10, 1952, Hammerstein Collection, LOC.
OHII to Arthur Hammerstein, February 12, 1954, Hammerstein Collection, LOC.
OHII to Dorothy Hammerstein, May 14, 1954, Hammerstein Collection, LOC.
OHII to Dorothy Hammerstein, handwritten notes, many undated, Hammerstein Collection, LOC.
OHII to Felicia Lamport, October 24, 1952, Hammerstein Collection, LOC.
OHII to Josh Logan, June 3, 1949, Hammerstein Collection, LOC.
OHII to John Steinbeck, August 5, 1952, Hammerstein Collection, LOC.
Josh Logan to OHII, September 12, 1957, Hammerstein Collection, LOC.
RR to Lincoln Barnett, April 12, 1950, NYPL.
Jerry Whyte to RR, February 22, 1952, LOC.

CHAPTER 12: NO GOOD DEED

Works

Barnes, Clive. "'Follies' Couples, Year Later," *New York Times*, April 5, 1971.
Calta, Louis. "Rodgers and Sondheim Preparing a Musical," *New York Times*, November 6, 1964.
Chapin, Ted. *Everything Was Possible: The Birth of the Musical "Follies."* New York: Alfred A. Knopf, 2003.
Flatley, Guy. "When Stephen Sondheim Writes Words and Music Some Critics Don't Leave the Theater Humming," *People*, April 5, 1976.
Green, Jesse. "When You're a Shark You're a Shark All the Way," *New York*, March 15, 2009.
Hammerstein, Oscar, II. Drafts of lyrics, Hammerstein Collection, LOC.
Hammerstein, Oscar, II. Notes on "Father of the Year," 1959, Hammerstein Collection, LOC.
Kerr, Walter. "Yes, Yes, Alexis! No, No, 'Follies'!," *New York Times*, April 11, 1971.
Lapine, James, and Frank Rich, prods. *Six by Sondheim*, Sabella Entertainment, 2013.
Laurents, Arthur. *The Rest of the Story: A Life Completed*. New York: Applause, 2012.
Michaelis, Arnold. Interview with RR, 1961, University of Georgia Special Collections, Athens.
Rich, Frank. "Conversations with Sondheim," *New York Times Magazine*, March 11, 2000.
Rich, Frank. "A Musical Theater Breakthrough," *New York Times*, October 21, 1984.
Rodgers, Mary. Columbia Center for Oral History Archives, 1982, Columbia University, New York.
Rodgers, Mary, and Jesse Green. *Shy: The Alarmingly Outspoken Memoirs of Mary Rodgers*. New York: Farrar, Straus and Giroux, 2022.
Rodgers, Richard. *Musical Stages*. New York: Random House, 1975.
Secrest, Meryle. *Somewhere for Me: A Biography of Richard Rodgers*. New York: Alfred A. Knopf, 2001.
Secrest, Meryle. *Stephen Sondheim: A Life*. New York: Alfred A. Knopf, 1998.

Sondheim, Stephen. *Finishing the Hat: Collected Lyrics (1954–1981) with Attendant Comments, Principles, Heresies, Grudges, Whines, and Anecdotes*. New York: Alfred A. Knopf, 2010.

Sondheim, Stephen. *Look, I Made a Hat: Collected Lyrics (1981–2011) with Attendant Comments, Amplifications, Dogmas, Harangues, Digressions, Anecdotes, and Miscellany*. New York: Alfred A. Knopf, 2011.

Swayne, Steve. *How Sondheim Found His Sound*. Ann Arbor: University of Michigan Press, 2005.

Symonds, Dominic. *We'll Have Manhattan: The Early Works of Rodgers and Hart*. New York: Oxford University Press, 2015.

Taraborrelli, J. Randy. *The Secret Life of Marilyn Monroe*. New York: Grand Central Publishing, 2009.

Wallace, Mike. *The Mike Wallace Interview*, guest OHII, 1958, Harry Ransom Center, University of Texas, Austin.

Wilk, Max. Interview with Agnes de Mille, 1990, NYPL.

Wilk, Max. Interview with RR, May 26, 1971, NYPL.

Winer, Laurie. Interview with Mary Rodgers, 1997.

Young, Jo Ann. *Out of My Dreams: Oscar Hammerstein II*, distributed by PBS, 2012.

Zadan, Craig. *Sondheim & Co.*, rev. ed. New York: Harper and Row, 1986.

Correspondence

Clifton Fadiman to RR, October 1957, NYPL.

OHII to Dorothy Hammerstein, 1929, Hammerstein Collection, LOC.

OHII to Alec [*sic*] McGowan, February 1, 1960, Hammerstein Collection, LOC.

OHII to Stephen Sondheim, August 6, 1953, University of Wisconsin, Madison.

Josh Logan to Dorothy Rodgers, 1979.

RR to Clifton Fadiman, October 10, 1957, NYPL.

Stephen Sondheim to Mark Horowitz, September 20, 2021.

Stephen Sondheim to Hal Prince, April 26, 1964, Hammerstein Collection, LOC.

CHAPTER 13: A KIND OF PROFUNDITY

Works

Atkinson, Brooks. "'The Sound of Music': Show about a Singing Family Arrives," *New York Times*, November 17, 1959.

Bikel, Theodore. *Theo: An Autobiography*. Madison: University of Wisconsin Press, 2014.

Duberman, Martin. *Paul Robeson*. New York: Alfred A. Knopf, 1989.

Fenton, James. "'The Book of Mormon': No Offense," *New York Review of Books*, June 11, 2011.

Foner, Philip S., ed. *Paul Robeson Speaks: Writings, Speeches, and Interviews, 1918–74*. Charleston, SC: Citadel Press, 1978.

Fordin, Hugh. *Getting to Know Him: A Biography of Oscar Hammerstein II*. New York: Random House, 1977.

Hammerstein, Oscar, II. Notes for a speech at Drury College, 1949, Hammerstein Collection, LOC.
Hammerstein, Oscar, II. Notes for a speech about property values, 1954, Hammerstein Collection, LOC.
Hammerstein, Oscar, II. "Policy of the United World Federalists," 1950, NYPL.
Kaufman, David. *Some Enchanted Evenings: The Glittering Life and Times of Mary Martin*. New York: St. Martin's Press, 2016.
Kerr, Walter. "The Sound of Music," *New York Herald Tribune,* November 17, 1959.
Maslon, Laurence. *"The Sound of Music" Companion*. New York: Fireside, 2007.
Miller, Martin. "The Hills Are Alive with the Sound of a Bowl Sing-Along," *Los Angeles Times,* June 27, 2015.
"Oscar Hammerstein 2D," *New York Times,* August 24, 1960.
Rodgers, Richard. *Musical Stages*. New York: Random House, 1975.
Santopietro, Tom. *"The Sound of Music" Story*. New York: St. Martin's Press, 2015.
Secrest, Meryle. *Stephen Sondheim: A Life*. New York: Alfred A. Knopf, 1998.
Thomas, Tony. Interview with RR, 1960, *CBC Radio.*
Tynan, Kenneth. "The Case for Trappism," *New Yorker,* November 28, 1959.
Wallace, Mike. *The Mike Wallace Interview,* guest OHII, 1958, Harry Ransom Center, University of Texas, Austin.
Wilcox, W. Bradford. "The Evolution of Divorce," *National Affairs,* Fall 2009.
Wilk, Max. Interview with Hal Prince, 1990, NYPL.
Winer, Laurie. Interview with André Bishop, 2018.
Winer, Laurie. Interview with Tracy Tynan, 2018.
Worsley, T. C. "The Sound of Music," *Financial Times,* May 1961, NYPL.
Young, Jo Ann. *Out of My Dreams: Oscar Hammerstein II,* distributed by PBS, 2012.

Correspondence
Sister Gregory Duffy to Mary Martin, undated, LOC.
OHII to "John Doe," December 20, 1954, Hammerstein Collection, LOC.
OHII to William Hammerstein, January 18, 1953, Hammerstein Collection, LOC.
OHII to Martin Luther King Jr., April 21, 1960, Howard Gotlieb Archival Research Center, Boston University.
OHII to Walter and Marian Knapp, December 7, 1959, Hammerstein Collection, LOC.
OHII to Alec [*sic*] McGowan, February 1, 1960, Hammerstein Collection, LOC.
Ben Kean to Dorothy Hammerstein, September 16, 1960, Hammerstein Collection, LOC.
Sidney Kingsley to RR, August 1960, NYPL.
Edwin Knopf to Dorothy Hammerstein, August 1960, Hammerstein Collection, LOC.
Stephen Sondheim to Hal Prince, September 1960, LOC.
RR to Orvil E. Dryfoos, June 27, 1961, NYPL.

CREDITS

"The Farmer and the Cowman" By Richard Rodgers, Oscar Hammerstein II
© 1943, Renewed 1983 by Williamson Music Company (ASCAP), c/o Concord Music Publishing All Rights Reserved. Used by Permission.

"Oh, What A Beautiful Mornin'" By Richard Rodgers, Oscar Hammerstein II
© 1943, Renewed 1983 by Williamson Music Company (ASCAP), c/o Concord Music Publishing All Rights Reserved. Used by Permission.

"The Surrey with the Fringe on Top" By Richard Rodgers, Oscar Hammerstein II
© 1943, Renewed 1983 by Williamson Music Company (ASCAP), c/o Concord Music Publishing All Rights Reserved. Used by Permission.

"It Might As Well Be Spring" By Richard Rodgers, Oscar Hammerstein II
© 1945 (Renewed) by Williamson Music Company (ASCAP), c/o Concord Music Publishing All Rights Reserved. Used by Permission.

"Allegro" By Richard Rodgers, Oscar Hammerstein II
© 1947 (Renewed) by Williamson Music Company, Copyright Renewed All Rights Reserved. Used by Permission.

"Money Isn't Everything" By Richard Rodgers, Oscar Hammerstein II
© 1947 (Renewed) by Williamson Music Company, Copyright Renewed All Rights Reserved. Used by Permission.

"Hello, Young Lovers" By Richard Rodgers, Oscar Hammerstein II
© 1951, Renewed 1979 Williamson Music Company (ASCAP), c/o Concord Music Publishing All Rights Reserved. Used by Permission.

"I Have Dreamed" By Richard Rodgers, Oscar Hammerstein II
© 1951, Renewed 1979 Williamson Music Company (ASCAP), c/o Concord Music Publishing All Rights Reserved. Used by Permission.

"I Whistle a Happy Tune" By Richard Rodgers, Oscar Hammerstein II
© 1951, Renewed 1979 Williamson Music Company (ASCAP), c/o Concord Music Publishing All Rights Reserved. Used by Permission.

"A Puzzlement" By Richard Rodgers, Oscar Hammerstein II
© 1951, Renewed 1979 Williamson Music Company (ASCAP), c/o Concord Music Publishing All Rights Reserved. Used by Permission.

"Song of the King" By Richard Rodgers, Oscar Hammerstein II
© 1951, Renewed 1979 Williamson Music Company (ASCAP), c/o Concord Music Publishing All Rights Reserved. Used by Permission.

"The Big Black Giant" By Richard Rodgers, Oscar Hammerstein II
© 1953 (Renewed) by Williamson Music Company, Copyright Renewed All Rights Reserved. Used by Permission.

"Intermission Talk" By Richard Rodgers, Oscar Hammerstein II
© 1953 (Renewed) by Williamson Music Company, Copyright Renewed All Rights Reserved. Used by Permission.

"It Feels Good" By Richard Rodgers, Oscar Hammerstein II
© 1953, Renewed 1981 Williamson Music Company (ASCAP), c/o Concord Music Publishing All Rights Reserved. Used by Permission.

"Ten Minutes Ago" By Richard Rodgers, Oscar Hammerstein II
© 1957, Renewed 1985 Williamson Music Company (ASCAP), c/o Concord Music Publishing All Rights Reserved. Used by Permission.

"Edelweiss" By Richard Rodgers, Oscar Hammerstein II
© 1959 (Renewed) by Williamson Music Company, Copyright Renewed All Rights Reserved. Used by Permission.

"Sixteen Going On Seventeen" By Richard Rodgers, Oscar Hammerstein II
© 1959 (Renewed) by Williamson Music Company, Copyright Renewed All Rights Reserved. Used by Permission.

"No Way To Stop It" By Richard Rodgers, Oscar Hammerstein II
© 1960 (Renewed) by Williamson Music Company, Copyright Renewed All Rights Reserved. Used by Permission.

"I Have Confidence In Me" By Richard Rodgers
© 1964, 1965 (Renewed) by Williamson Music Company, Copyright Renewed All Rights Reserved. Used by Permission.

All other lyrics by Oscar Hammerstein II reproduced with permission of the Trust and under the Will of Oscar Hammerstein II and Hammerstein Properties LLC.

INDEX